SUSTAINING ARCHITECTURE IN THE ANTI-MACHINE AGE

Ian Abley and James Heartfield

Acknowledgements

For their contributions to this book, we would like to thank Paul Hyett, Austin Williams, Daniel Lloyd, Pamela Charlick, Natasha Nicholson, Helene Guldberg, Peter Sammonds, Phil Macnaghten, Miffa Salter, Alan Hudson, Margaret Casely-Hayford, Miles Glendinning, Stefan Muthesius, Martin Pawley, Shane Slater, Ben Madden, Duncan Price, Sean Stanwick, Deborah Brown and Peter Walker.

We would also like to thank Jonathan Schwinge for his valued support through the writing of this book, the images of his project work and his photography and sketches that appear throughout the book. We thank Viewpoint (www.viewpoint.com) for kindly providing the V22 Osprey tilt-rotor CAD aircraft model, and Roger Townsend (RogerTownsend@zetekpower.com) of ZeTek Power Plc (www.zetekpower.com) for his advice on the fuel cell technology and the wider hydrogen economy. In addition, we thank Katy Harris and Elizabeth Walker of Foster and Partners, as well as Jan Bobrowski & Partners. We are also grateful for the information on ISO 14001 from Marie O'Connor at Nicholas Grimshaw and Partners.

We are particularly grateful to housing market consultant John Stewart who kindly provided permission to reprint research on housing production from Building a Crisis – Long-term Housing Under-supply in England, a draft of an unpublished report researched for the House Builders Federation. Thanks go to Julie Foley of ippr (j.foley@ippr.org.uk, www.ippr.org/sustainability) for an early copy of H2 – Driving the Future on the policy implications of developing hydrogen as a fuel for road behicles. We also thank Paul Moore (paul.moore@echarris.com), Head of the Cost Research Department at EC Harris, for kindly supplying the comparison of GDP and construction output figures for Chapter 18. EC Harris is a leading international Capital Project and Facilities Consultancy committed to delivering better value projects to clients through the continuous development and innovative application of traditional professional skills. In addition, we thank Les Greenacre and Mary Farr (mary.farr@citb.co.uk) of the Construction Industry Training Board for permission to reprint CITB data.

For their advice and support we thank Kate Abley, Len and Pat Abley, Hilary Bailey, Lizzy Barnfield, Justine Brian, the staff at The Building Centre, London, Alec Cameron, Patrick Deigan, Valerie Fogleman of Barlow Lyde & Gilbert, Claire Fox, Rachel Fox, Tony Gilland, Ciaran Guilfoyle, Fraser Haran, David Harland, Caspar Hewett, Stuart Hutchinson of Techniker, Ruth Jindal of the Design Museum, Eve Kay, Rachel Kelly, Geoff Kidder, Debra King, Rose Landthaller, Graham Lee, Penny Lewis, Sonny Masero, Ian McInnes, Lisa Melvin at Ryder, Duncan Mitchell, Bruce Nevison, Mick Owens, Shobie Patel at Ryder, Vicky Richardson, Maisie Rowe, Andrew Scoones of the Building Centre Trust, Rita Singh of the Construction Products Association, Nicholas Spencer of the Construction Industry Council, Mark Tyson, Robin Vaughan at the Architects Registration Board, Brian Waters, Robert Webb, Mark Webster, Paul Welterveden and Ant Wilson of Oscar Faber. Finally we thank Maggie Toy, Abigail Grater and Amie Tibble at John Wiley & Sons and all of the staff at Artmedia Press for all their help and support.

Photo credits:
The author and publishers would like to thank those who have kindly permitted the use of images in the illustration of this book. Attempts have been made to locate all of the sources of illustrations to obtain full reproduction rights, but in the very few instances where this process has failed to find the copyright holder, apologies are offerred. In the case of an error, correction would be welcomed. Please note that sources are listed alphabetically and quote page number and position of image.

Ian Abley, 6; Nic Bailey, Nic Bailey Design (nic.bailey@btinternet.com, www.nic.bailey.btinternet.co.uk), 184-186, 203; Chetwood Associates (www.chetwood.co.uk), 31; Richard Davies, Foster and Partners (richarddavies@easynet.co.uk), 13 second from top, 140-141, 206, 207; Bill Dunster Architects (billdunster@btinternet.com or www.zed-factory.com), 27; Famous Players Canada, 173 bottom; Norman Foster and Nigel Young, Foster and Partners, 13 bottom, 40, 41, 51, 84, 169, 171 bottom left, top centre right; Jude Harris, Jestico + Whiles (j+w@jesticowhiles.co.uk), 28; Guy Hearn (07768 111274), Wilkinson Eyre Architects, 38 bottom; Stuart Hutchinson, Consulting Structural Engineers Techniker (mail@techniker.ltd.uk), 62, 63; Paul Hyett Architects, 22; Susan Kay, Wilkinson Eyre Architects (0208 778 7912), 36; Ben Luxmoore, Wilkinson Eyre Architects (luxmoore@appleonline.net), 209 top; Sean Nelson, 173 top; James Pickard, Cartwright Pickard (cartwrightpickard@dial.pipex.com), 216 upper right; Simon Punter (Simon Punter Photography, 27 Holland Road, Hove, East Sussex, BN3 1JE on 07074 770730), 8, 79, 80, 91, 92, 95, 99, 132-134, 142, 145, 147-152, 165, 168, 229; Jonathan Schwinge (jonathan@schwinge.co.uk), 14, 16, 65, 81, 82, 87 bottom, 121-129, 153 centre, bottom, 156, 158, 160-164, 179-183, 194; Mike Sherwood, Yorkon Ltd (contact@yorkon.com, Huntington, York YO32 9PT), 216 bottom, 217; Sean Stanwick, 171, 172 top, bottom,; 174 top, centre, 175 top; Morley von Sternberg, Wilkinson Eyre Architects, 110; John Tassiopoulos, 172 bottom; Andrew Ward (andward@wards.u-net.com), 13 second from bottom; Chris Wilkinson, Wilkinson Eyre Architects, 36, 38, 39, 111-113, 208, 209.

Cover: Airlander - 'Fly-by-Light' architecture 1999 by Jonathan Schwinge.
Page 2: Simon Punter Photography, 27 Holland Road, Hove, East Sussex, BN3 1JE

To Kate, my love
To Rennie

First published in Great Britain in 2001 by
WILEY-ACADEMY

a division of
JOHN WILEY & SONS LTD
Baffins Lane
Chichester
West Sussex PO19 1UD

ISBN 0-471-48660-4

Other Wiley Editorial Offices
New York • Weinheim • Brisbane • Singapore • Toronto

Design and Prepress: ARTMEDIA PRESS Ltd, London

Printed and bound in Italy

Cartwright Pickard architects

Foster and Partners
architects and designers

 Viewpoint

WilkinsonEyre.Architects

Books are to be returned on or before
the last date below.

RE

GE

LIBREX —

www.audacity.org

CONTENTS

Introduction

Ian Abley, audacity.org

THE BANAL APOCALYPSE

Sustainability is the moral imperative of the age for architects, insists Paul Hyett, President of the Royal Institute of British Architects (RIBA). At the beginning of the twenty-first century architects are expected to be ever more creative, while being mindful of the impact of their building designs on the ecological systems of the planet. In the Brundtland Report, the World Commission on Environment and Development (WCED) described the requirement to reconcile architecture to the environment as follows:

> There are thresholds which cannot be crossed without endangering the basic integrity of the system. Today we are close to many of these thresholds; we must be ever mindful of endangering the survival of life on earth.[1]

Writing for the January 2000 edition of *The Architectural Review*, Catherine Slessor sensibly observed that the Brundtland Report 'serves as a starting point, but it hardly suffices as an analytical guide or policy directive'. Slessor also articulates the hopes of many practitioners when she argues that 'sustainability should not be seen simply as a corrective force, but as a new mandate for architecture'.[2] The starting point of agreement is that no-one wants to endanger life on earth, or to develop in unsustainable ways.

A fundamental contention is whether human life is to be prioritised over all other species. With that privileging rests the legitimacy of architects to build a human environment out of nature, extending the stock of natural resources through the developmental process. Through agriculture and architecture humanity has successively transformed the natural environment to sustain human society. Even to imagine that humanity should make corrections (or apologies) for living on the planet recognises, in its weakest possible expression, that humans are the only species capable of developing science and technology to work out what these 'corrections' might be. If we can do this, then why not accept that humanity can make transformative change for the better? Pamela Charlick and Natasha Nicholson consider the privileged human position in nature in Chapter 4, 'Ecological frequencies and hybrid natures'. It is interesting, as John Gillott and Manjit Kumar explored in *Science and the Retreat from Reason*, that science has sharpened our self-identity despite any cultural reaction against science and technology:

> Science has also changed forever humanity's perception of its place in the cosmos. From being the inhabitants of a body at the centre of the universe, around which the rest of the universe revolved, we now see ourselves as the inhabitants of a tiny planet. We revolve around an ordinary star, on the fringes of a galaxy which is one among countless others.[3]

Sustaining Architecture in the Anti-Machine Age considers this cultural reaction against science and technology among architects in particular. The anti-machine reaction co-exists with an increasing dependence on advancing science and technology. However, standing for the privileging of humanity is not how most architects attempt to formulate an analytical guide or policy directive out of the morality of sustainability. Rather than cut to the core issue of the relativisation of humanity as one species among many, as Charlick and Nicholson are prepared to do, most architects come to a criticism of science and technology through a moral condemnation of consumerism. The argument is usually in the form articulated in *Cities for a Small Planet*, where Richard Rogers imagines that the suburban semi-detached in sprawling aggregate might be the death of us:

> The world-wide growth of urban populations and grossly inefficient patterns of living are accelerating the rate of increase of pollution and erosion. It is ironic that mankind's habitat – our cities – is the major destroyer of the ecosystem and the greatest threat to humankind's survival on the planet.[4]

The accusation is that in their concern for our wellbeing our parents have pursued the unsustainable development of suburbia. The claim is that unless we change patterns of development we will continue to threaten the wellbeing of our children, or their children. This is an unwarranted insult to our parents. Their efforts to make a better life have been recast as a destructive act against the wellbeing of their grandchildren or great-grandchildren. A conventional semi-detached house, a garden and a car or two seems modest enough, and hardly the end of the world. It is difficult to have any sympathy with the proponents of sustainability when they repose the finest of motives, maintained over the working lives of many parents, as a moral lapse of self-restraint in consumption. This sits very uneasily with what we know to be the real familial relationships that have sustained successive generations through the twentieth-century growth of suburbia.

The accusation is that in their concern for our wellbeing our parents have pursued the unsustainable development of suburbia.

It is only when sustainability is depersonalised that the blame can be diffused. However, the imperative to act responsibly remains. In *Modernity and Self-Identity* Anthony Giddens recognised that 'apocalypse has become banal, a set of statistical risk parameters to everyone's existence'.[5] It is at the level of personal behaviour that Paul Hyett wants to apply sustainability, asking in Chapter 1: 'If Sustainable Design isn't a Moral Imperative, What is?'. Hyett agrees that sustainability is a mandate for architecture, adopting the approach that Phil Macnaghten recommends in Chapter 6 to relate sustainable development to everyday life. It is through mundane demand management that architects are encouraged to foster a sense of environmental responsibility, to overcome the remoteness of global issues to local reality.

FROM MORAL IMPERATIVE TO ENVIRONMENTAL DUTY OF CARE

Sustaining Architecture in the Anti-machine Age has been produced following the Building Audacity conference in July 2000 at The Building Centre, London, and as Paul Hyett announced his candidacy for the presidency of the RIBA. (We are very grateful that Hyett kept with this book project over the election. For the transcript of the Building Audacity conference, visit www.audacity.org.)

Hyett predicted that 'sustainability issues will grow in the new warmer millennium', and he is raising the debate:

> What is now needed is a crusade through which British architects and the RIBA address both their obligations to future generations – with respect to the delivery of a truly sustainable environment – and the opportunity to lead the development and construction industries towards that goal. Obligation and opportunity confront British architects and the RIBA as never before.[6]

Professor Brian Edwards, Head of the Huddersfield School of Architecture and author since the conference of *Green Architecture – An International Comparison*[7] and the *Rough Guide to Sustainability*[8] (written with Paul Hyett), was also one of the keynote speakers at Building Audacity.

> The new president will have to continue Marco Goldschmied's work on sustainable design. Without policy continuity the profession may lose credibility with government, clients and the construction industry which the RIBA still aspires to lead.

> When an industry uses 60 per cent of the world's material resources, half of fossil fuel energy and half of global water supplies, you cannot relegate sustainability to a secondary concern. Goldschmied brought the green agenda to the fore...the RIBA needs that message more than ever.[9]

Sustainability is a moral imperative, and one that Austin Williams considers in Chapter 2, 'Zen and the Art of Life-cycle Maintenance'. Here he challenges the idea that a local view of global problems necessarily leads to the clear social agenda that sustainability is supposed to encourage. As Allan Ashworth and Keith Hogg observed:

> The concept of a green building is an elusive one. The definition is broad and being green in a professional sense may merely come down to a change in attitude.[10]

As Rab Bennetts put it in 'The Green Century' edition of *Building* magazine, architects 'don't have to be perfect, but we do all have to try and do something'.[11] However, being a little greener may not be sufficient as a good intention for a new century. In addition, according to Brian Edwards, the reduction of sustainability to 'energy-conscious design by itself will be of little value'.[12] Various assessment initiatives are launched and used without any co-ordination. This is not for the want of discussion. *Constructing the Team*, the Latham report of 1994,[13] led to the formation of the Construction Industry Board (CIB) under Sir Michael Latham. The intervening years saw the publication of the Construction Task Force report *Rethinking Construction* under Sir John Egan.[14] In January 2001 the National Audit Office charged the CIB with sorting out the plethora of initiatives that had arisen since the Latham and Egan reports. Seemingly bored with the interminable debates the Confederation of Construction Clients (CCC) withdrew from the CIB, took away its £50,000, and apparently brought down the institutional edifice.[15] John Gummer, rather than seeing that initiative fatigue might be more of a reason for the collapse of his CIB forum, blamed the CCC:

> I always thought clients would create the circumstances in which the industry could bury its differences. Now the clients are driving it back into division and disunity.[16]

The assumption that there could be unity in a marketplace with irreconcilable economic interests was perhaps the original mistake. Nevertheless, it meant that the confusion of construction initiatives remains, and that sustainability is still to be coherently addressed by the array of construction industry representative bodies. The moral imperative of sustainable design fails to confront the economic and social conflicts of interest in architectural development, which are irresolvable by bureaucratic analytical guides or policy directives regarding the environment. Phil Macnaghten and John Urry warned that 'an emphasis on limits, implemented with a series of don'ts, or do less, can promote the belief that environmental responsi-

The assumption that there could be unity in a marketplace with irreconcilable economic interests was perhaps the original mistake.

Royal Institute of British Architects.

For the transcript of the
Building Audacity conference,
visit www.audacity.org

bility is something that is ultimately restrictive and disciplinary'.[17] Yet formally resolving the standard of service the profession of sustainable design remains a problem for the RIBA.

The RIBA has been trying to incorporate sustainability since 1997, the period when David Rock was president and the Institute had published *Meeting the Challenge – RIBA Strategy for Architecture and Architects 1999–2003*. One of a range of challenges was 'the need for sustainability in buildings and the environment – buildings contribute half the UK's carbon dioxide emissions in their production and use, architects have a responsibility to reduce this figure in the way they design and specify'. Another was 'the need to limit risk – in an increasingly litigious and regulated world, clients need to know they are protected as far as possible from expensive disputes and legal actions and that should the worst happen, the mechanisms are in place and the expertise available to deal with the situation'.[18] Succeeding David Rock in 1999 as President of the RIBA, Marco Goldschmied publicly and repeatedly raised the idea of an environmental duty of care.[19]

Despite Paul Hyett's considerable support as Vice-President for Education at the time, Goldschmied tried and failed to incorporate sustainability into the RIBA Code of Conduct. The importance of the attempt to make sustainability an environmental duty of care for architects is not that this proved harder to institute than Goldschmied's supporters probably imagined, but that it was attempted at all. Even before Goldschmied was elected, Hyett had indicated in the *Architects' Journal* that changes were envisaged to establish codes, accompanied by the implication that these would have attendant disciplinary measures. As Vice-President for Education Hyett could begin to promote sustainable architectural practice through the influence the RIBA enjoys over the professional education:

> No longer can we tolerate the selfish or the irresponsible designer who leaves an environmentally destructive legacy due to ignorance. For them, the game is up.
> As the world's biggest validation service, the RIBA is in a unique position to encourage and assist the schools in repositioning themselves to lead the designing disciplines in this urgent agenda. And lead they must, for only architects combine the breadth of involvement and experience with the creative capacity to envisage alternative, aesthetically pleasing, socially functional and ecologically sustainable urban futures.[20]

Few seem to disagree in principle with the idea of an environmental duty of care. However, we will do well to remember Hyett's advice on being precise about what an architect professes to provide:

> distinctions are very important, particularly at a time when our capacity to deliver the quality professional service that the courts expect of us (if we are unfortunate enough to be sued) is increasingly threatened by those who meddle with our terms of engagement.[21]

For Hyett, 'while such a duty is difficult to enforce, real progress has been made'. This is confusing because at the Building Audacity conference and in Chapter 1 of this book, Hyett claims such a professional duty to be unenforceable, which is obviously not the same as 'difficult to enforce'. One of these positions must be wrong. Or perhaps both. Perhaps a duty of environmental care will prove incredibly easy to enforce. We might look beyond the internal workings of either the RIBA or the Architects Registration Board (ARB) and consider what the law might do to discipline the profession.

At Building Audacity we tried unsuccessfully to press the point that a legal duty will not lie with everyone subscribing to the same morality. The law as it exists may decide to take the word of the pre-eminent architectural institute seriously. The rest of society is going to have something to say about the duty of care in a legal realm that the RIBA does not control. It is a simple fact that the more we claim as our standard of professionalism, the more we will be sued. On the question of whether 'duty' could be established beyond morality in a code of conduct, or in law, Hyett initially answered with an emphatic 'No!'. Later, during question time, he modifies this to 'not yet'.

> Marco cannot, certainly not yet, establish any direct obligation on architects through the RIBA Code of Conduct beyond a moral duty. The reasons are both political, in the sense of the politics of our profession and our members' interests, and practical. By that I mean unenforceable in law.[22]

The presidential task has now been passed from Goldschmied to Hyett, who has been elected to resolve the first part of his objection. The second part is entirely hostage to developments in the law, which is not in our view a remote possibility. The more we claim to be expert in, the more the law will allow claimants to test us in the courts. Architects are asking for an insecure legal future, as Daniel Lloyd convincingly argues in Chapter 3. The prospect of an environmental duty of care is a real one if the law will entertain what he calls a 'popular legal fiction'.

If realised by the RIBA, an environmental duty of care will affect all architects. The RIBA wants to achieve a membership of 25,000 architects in Britain and 8,000 overseas by 2003, as well as 5,000 student members and 2,000 subscribers by the same date. This would mean a membership of 40,000 or a rise of 21 per cent from 1999 levels.[23]

The RIBA is the pre-eminent voluntary institute for British architects, all of whom, since the 1996 Housing Grants Construction and Regeneration Act, are legally required to register with the Architects Registration Board (ARB).[24] Architects were previously subject to the Architects Registration Council of the UK (ARCUK). Legally developed through the Architects Act of 1997, the ARB board comprises a majority of non-architect appointees from the industry, the remaining architects being elected with the aim of 'protecting the consumer and safeguarding the reputation of architects'. Only 23 per cent of the full ARB register of architects voted for their minority of electable representatives.[25] This suggests little enthusiasm for the fact that the ARB protects the use of the title 'architect', while delegating important powers of validation for professional training to the RIBA to 'enhance the quality of architectural education and to encourage experiment, innovation, and contemporary relevance in course delivery and teaching methods'.[26] In 2000, the ARB had 29,905 legally registered architects, 88 per cent of which are male and 12 per cent female, with 27,560 registered in Britain and 2,345 overseas. In 1999 the ARB registration has fallen from the 1989 figure by about 5 per cent, though during the recession remained reasonably stable. Between 1999 and 2000 the number of registrations increased by only 76 members.[27] Basically, the RIBA commands the profession not legally but influentially, and therefore its policy provides the benchmark by which all architects are judged.

In 1995–96, the total value of construction professional services was £6.7 billion, or less than 1 per cent of GDP, including 15 per cent of that figure from overseas work. Of this, about 40 per cent went to engineering, about 22 per cent or just under £1.5 billion to architecture, and 19 per cent to surveying.[28]

THE MAKING OF LEGAL HISTORY AND THE DESCENT INTO BUREAUCRACY

We should remember that the Law Society allows lawyers to further environmental campaigns, and lawyer-led litigation is a fact. Firms of solicitors can identify potential complaints, advertise for clients, advise action groups and mobilise media support before launching a formal action. Morally motivated lawyers see no consequence from attempting social reform through the courts. The judiciary is only too willing to encourage this expansion of influence, and the legal profession has grown accordingly. Of course, most solicitors and barristers are not specialised in construction or the environment. What matters more is that it takes only one case to make case law, which means one highly resourced and brilliant lawyer, or one tired old judge could affect the entire architectural profession. While architects have their 'trophy architects', with an ongoing portfolio of a lifetime of work, the legal profession glorifies itself by making or clarifying law. Not all architects get to be concept designers, and it is both far more lucrative and eminently possible to be a concept lawyer.

This is not to underestimate the legal difficulties ahead for would-be lawmakers, but more to point out that a longstanding legal effort allows for a breakthrough by environmentalists. Since the early 1970s a substantial body of environmental legislation has been produced, mostly in the form of directives designed to reduce pollutants during industrial processes. However, this commercial modernisation did not deal with the social and environmental consequences of abnormal or unintentional pollution, either as major events or unnoticed over time. In such instances the need for a means of remedying damage and reducing the chances of a repetition was recognised. In 1986 the Single European Act consequently incorporated environmental policies into the European Community (EC) Treaty and the 1957 Treaty of Rome, and the EC's objective of securing ever closer market integration between member states was realigned to further sustainable development.

Following consultation with the European Parliament, the 1989 Draft Directive *(COM(89)282fin Commission Proposal for a Council Directive on Civil Liability for Damage Caused by Waste (1989) OJ C251/3)* was superseded by a more powerful proposal – the 1991 Draft Directive *(COM(91)219fin Amended Commission Proposal for a Council Directive on Civil Liability for Damage Caused by Waste (1991) OJ C192)*. This included a proposal to establish remedial funding for environmental damage, suggested increased standing for non-governmental organisations (NGOs), such as environmental lobby groups, and argued for the burden of proof on causation to be on the lower standard of a balance of probabilities. In Germany the 1990 Environmental Liability Act only requires plaintiffs to establish a well-founded assumption of causation for the defendant to have to prove the case false, so things could much be worse in Britain.

The debate widened with the publication of the 1993 Green Paper *(COM(93)47fin Commission Communication to the Council and European Parliament on Remedying Environmental Damage (1993))*. This went further than the two draft directives and was intended to stimulate debate on the possibility of creating a civil liability in respect of damage to the environment by industrial processes in normal and abnormal operation. The paper addressed issues of strict liability, the difficulty of establishing causation in environmental damage cases, whether existing civil remedies were adequate, and the question of adequate insurance for increased civil liabilities. A joint public hearing followed, and in 1994 the European

Morally motivated lawyers see no consequence from attempting social reform through the courts. The judiciary is only too willing to encourage this expansion of influence, and the legal profession has grown accordingly.

Parliament instructed the European Commission to submit a proposal for a directive on civil liability in respect of environmental damage.

Following independent reports the European Commission resolved to produce a White Paper setting out the various issues raised and the options for addressing them. To that end industry, insurance companies and environmental NGOs were consulted through the European Commission's 1997 *Working Paper on Environmental Liability*. Eventually the White Paper draft was published in February 2000, for comment by July 2000. Writing just prior to that event, Martin Hedemann-Robinson and Mark Wilde recognised that the European Commission continues to struggle with legal definitions of sustainability despite all the effort expended since 1986:

> The Commission's 1993 Green Paper recognises the 'fundamental importance' of securing a legal definition of environmental damage without, however, actually favouring any particular model description.[29] It also points out the difficulty of delineating an appropriate cut-off point between significant and insignificant ecological damage. Whilst the 1997 Working Paper is silent on defining ecological harm, it does reveal that the Commission is keen to provide a workable list of 'weighting factors' in order for the courts and parties alike to be able to make sense of understanding when the minimum threshold of damage has been reached in order to trigger liability.[30]

The European Commission is proceeding to draft a framework directive on environmental liability on the basis of the White Paper consultation, but this will not be straightforward. The number of irreconcilable 'tick-box' schemes to check the sustainability rating of projects is already bewildering, requiring that sustainability consultants not only compile and adjust the complex set of statistically weighted indices, but fill out the incomprehensible paperwork. The alternative to any bureaucratically compiled checklist is pragmatism, leaving the court to decide what constitutes environmental harm on a case-by-case basis. Either way, architects will lose control by allowing the courts to judge whether their architecture is sustainable or unsustainable.

Getting sued is bad enough, but the efforts to avoid this will be far more debilitating for architects due to the costs of litigation avoidance. As architects, we may soon have to demonstrate that we have thought about how we could design out the unsustainable aspects of our architecture. At the Building Audacity conference, Brian Edwards promoted the environmental audit, and ISO 14001 is already an environmental management system (EMS) that clients or their lawyers may start to expect. The *ISO 14001 EMS – Implementation Handbook* by Hewitt Roberts and Gary Robinson includes a list of why everyone may need to buy environmental management system software:

- Are your customers expressing interest in the environmental implications of your products or services?
- Are your suppliers or clients becoming more concerned about the environmental implications of your products or services?
- Is it possible that your company or organisation does not comply with all the environmental legislation and regulations that it should?
- Is environmental legislation regulating your industry sector increasing or becoming more stringent?
- Are the costs of energy, waste, waste treatment, water use, water treatment, or air pollution abatement of concern to your organisation?
- Are other companies in your industry developing environmental management systems?
- Do you have international customers or clients?

They advise that in ISO 14001 'environment' is defined as the 'surroundings in which an organization operates, including air, water, land, natural resources, flora, fauna, humans, and their interrelation'.[31] That is everything including social and economic interrelations. The daunting ISO 14000 series are international standards for environmental management with the aim of allowing organisations to assess their activities against 'internationally accepted criteria'. Developed by the International Organization for Standardization, Geneva, ISO 14001 is a voluntary standard that could become a default requirement applicable to 'all types and sizes of organizations and to accommodate diverse geographical, cultural and social conditions'.[32] It requires a cyclical approach to continual improvements which Roberts and Robinson describe as 'plan, do, check, correct', and start again. ISO 14001 is the only international standard for an EMS. Since 1993 there has been an independently assessed but otherwise voluntary scheme for European industrial enterprises, not really suited to architects but possibly demanded by customers of product or material manufacturers, under European Council Regulation 1836/93. This is the Community Eco-Management and Audit Scheme (EMAS).[33] If one really wants to knock oneself out there are ways of bridging between the EMS and the EMAS. The handbook shows the stifling inclusivity of business by audit:

> For any system to function properly, whether it is a quality management system or an environmental management system, each player within that system must clearly understand their position and how their actions affect the system as a whole.[34]

...architects will lose control by allowing the courts to judge whether their architecture is sustainable or unsustainable.

The burden that the possibility of an environmental duty of care being created will place on professionals having to demonstrate they have considered the sustainability of their designs will be as immense and mundane as ISO 14001 threatens. If anyone doubts the relentless character of this irrationality they should read *The Mad Officials* by Christopher Booker and Richard North, who point out that one of these certificates 'does not guarantee in any way the quality of goods or services a business provides to its customers. It merely shows that the company is complying with the paperwork and procedures which it itself has drawn up for its own operations – usually in conjunction with highly expensive management consultants', for no other illogic than 'to avoid losing business from other companies engaged in the same act of suicide'.[35] If something like ISO 14001 becomes expected by clients, perhaps because the courts need a benchmark, or through good practice recommendations by professional institutes like the RIBA, everyone from materials suppliers to architects will comply with this madness. The present plethora of regulations, guidance, indicator schemes and methods of codification being experimented with certainly seem incoherent, while ISO 14001 shows only how the entire discussion can be bureaucratised. At Building Audacity, Paul Hyett seemed less concerned that these measures will be considered useful:

> It is no good standing up in court saying 'this architect did not have "due regard" or did not "conserve" or did not "enhance"'. You have got to be able to define it or we will be there all day and nobody will get anywhere! They are not measurable.[36]

However, the courts will only refer to expert-endorsed standard professional practice, which need not be objective at all. In any event the RIBA already expects sustainability when 'measuring the work of students in the schools. It has got to be a deliverable, and it has got to be evident in the nature of the project work that we see'.[37] So the RIBA should be able to assess a practitioner. Either sustainability is measurable, or it is not.

> Sustainability will be an issue in its own right, not a part of technology, and it will be a central issue in assessing schools. We aim to increase awareness amongst students, persuade them to sign up to the agenda and equip them with the skills to deliver ecologically responsible design.[38]

While seeking to educate architects, the RIBA is seeking to influence allied professions, clients and the public at large to take sustainability seriously. The RIBA should expect the allied professions, clients and the public to take its members seriously when an understanding of sustainability is being professed. Unsustainable architecture has not so far been defined. In the effort to establish sustainability as a popular morality, proponents have avoided narrowly prescribing architectural expression, trying to incorporate all members of the profession in the moral project without excluding methods of building production. The public process of legal interpretation will fragment the vague professional consensus and will reveal the practical inadequacy of sustainability as architectural theory. Sustainability will weaken as it becomes established as orthodoxy, but then it will be too late. However, the present impasse cannot continue indefinitely, because failure to formalise sustainability will be the embarrassment of policy-makers. It is not likely that architects will want to leave the definition of sustainability to the courts, but will neither enjoy confronting each other over ideas that seem superficially reasonable.

Acting in ways considered unsustainable, or ignoring sustainability when everyone else accepts the principle, seems unreasonable. The test of reasonableness is if anything an encouragement to the introduction of an environmental duty of care. The point we were trying to make at Building Audacity was that by talking of an environmental duty of professional care in speeches, conferences, literature, the validation processes and Continuing Professional Development (CPD) the courts will already take these as a measure of professional conduct. Changes to codes of conduct are more than a formality, but the EC already sees potential for an environmental duty in common law:

> Apart from the not inconsiderable lack of political will which has dogged the development of legislation in this field, another significant factor which has created stumbling blocks has been the Commission's choice to attempt to craft law enforcement...in the form of tort as opposed to public law. Conceptualising environmental harm as being part of a bargaining process on the basis of an individualistic private rights discourse between two competing and equal parties in a market, as opposed to constituting an infringement of group rights defended under the public law, necessarily prepares the ground for compromise and relativism built upon competing values of 'right', of which environmental protection is only one amongst many.[39]

As Karen Morrow argues, 'the virtue of the common law – indeed one of the characteristics that give it life and vigour – lies in its ability to adapt to the needs of society'.[40] Architects have found popularity in sustainability, are helping to popularise sustainable architecture, and will find it near impossible to back away from the duty they have volunteered to bear. At the end of the Building Audacity conference, Hyett ended the proceedings by saying:

The RIBA should expect the allied professions, clients and the public to take its members seriously when an understanding of sustainability is being professed.

Architects have found popularity in sustainability, are helping to popularise sustainable architecture, and will find it near impossible to back away from the duty they have volunteered to bear.

I am an optimist, or I wouldn't be an architect, and I think that this issue is coming to the table. We are making progress and we're beginning to understand it better. Lots of good people have entered the debate. We are struggling as a community to get there.[41]

Architects may regret being reduced further to the role of a form-filling functionary that Williams deplores in Chapter 2 and that Daniel Lloyd and Deborah Brown recognise as a prospect in Chapter 16, 'Architecture or Clerkitecture?'. Most architects did not choose to be an architect for the administration. Yet will the courts be satisfied with the imaginative explorations of the relationship between the human species, nature and technology that Charlick and Nicholson posit in Chapter 4? The courts will definitely not be the best place to recover the sense of scientific proportion that Helene Guldberg and Peter Sammonds argue for in Chapter 5, 'Design Tokenism and Global Warming'. In Chapter 6, 'Sustainable Development and Everyday Life', Phil Macnaghten is right when he says that the proper place for the resolution of environmental conflicts of interest is in the world of social contestation. If this is understood as developing a sense of 'dwelling', then so be it, provided the parties take it upon themselves to resolve their differences. Reliance on the courts to decide whether the environmental duty of care has been exercised adequately will render the profession of architecture less imaginative, less scientific, and far more conciliatory when confronted with conflicts of interests.

FROM THE CULTURE OF LOW EXPECTATIONS TO THE PROMISE OF LIVING SPACE

In Chapter 7, 'The Economics of Sustainable Development', James Heartfield asks whether the ideas reworked in sustainability were ever about encouraging imagination, promoting scientific and technological solutions to supply-side problems, or contesting the social limitations of capitalism. As a moral self-discipline, sustainability need not be cynically understood as promoting a culture of low expectations. There is, however, scope for sustainability to be used cynically, as Miffa Salter warns against in Chapter 8, 'Engaging the Stakeholder in the Development Process'. In addition, there is the mistake of advocating public participation and consultation without any clear professional responsibility being taken for either architectural analysis or policy. The impulse to include ever more public opinion in both public and commercial decision-making processes is thought of as democratisation, but may be little more than a diffusion or evasion of responsibility. The promotion of 'stakeholding' and third-party interests is having strange effects on those attempting to realise social sustainability through inclusivity, as Margaret Casely-Hayford considers in Chapter 10, 'Why it is No Longer Appropriate to Underestimate the Opposition'. Strangest of all is the recasting of developers in the role of victim in the planning process. This suggests that developers need confrontational ways of resolving economic and social conflicts of interest, but are reluctant to jettison the initial consensus and compromise that can be realised through the discussion of sustainability.

The attempt to frame analytical guidance or policy directives for sustainable development is torn between the impulse to include a growing constituency of stakeholders, revealing a profound loss of executive confidence, and the frustration this causes to the technocratic planner or manager. Third-party interests are being promoted through the common law, as Daniel Lloyd recognises in Chapter 3, and through statute, as Margaret Casely-Hayford notes in Chapter 10, reiterated in Chapter 16 by Daniel Lloyd and Deborah Brown. Moreover, the Third Way of social inclusion is a government project in pursuit of the wider goal of sustainability. In Chapter 9, 'The Trouble with Planners' (using planners as the broad class of technocrats in the construction industry), Alan Hudson recognises the distance that has developed between policy-making elites brokering a Third Way of public- and private-sector partnerships, and those affected. The perceived need for consultation and the impulse to include more stakeholders in decision-making is simply the recognition of that political distancing. As Salter reminds us, policy-makers assume people want to be involved. The political disengagement is not a problem limited to or determined by suburbia, as architects often imagine. The suburb is not the cause of social alienation but is experienced as the phenomenal form of that disengagement. There is no intrinsic reason why having a back garden should cause alienation.

Equally, there is no reason why proximity will create a sense of citizenship or community. The old deterministic claims that flatter the architect into the conceit that society can be better designed are reposed through the Urban Task Force promotion of sustainable urban density. Yet in Chapter 11, 'Reinvigorating the English Tradition of Architectural Polemic', Miles Glendinning and Stefan Muthesius remind us that while the density prescriptions are contemptuous of popular demand for gardens and mobility, they are far less adventurous than previous urban planning policy. The modest density policies accommodate to the declining productive capacity of British construction and say nothing about what the countryside is for if not farming.

In Chapter 12, 'Town and Country in Perspective', James Heartfield situates the architectural discussion of sustainable development in relation to the fortunes of British agriculture. The development poten-

As a moral self-discipline, sustainability need not be cynically understood as promoting a culture of low expectations. There is, however, scope for sustainability to be used cynically...

The suburb is not the cause of social alienation but is experienced as the phenomenal form of that disengagement.

tial of the countryside has been resisted on the grounds of sustainability since John Gummer was in ministerial office at the Department of the Environment, but confronts Margaret Beckett at the Department of the Environment, Food and Rural Affairs more than ever. It is this insight that informs Chapter 13, 'The Sand-heap Urbanism of the Twenty-first Century', by Martin Pawley. Since Pawley wrote *Theory and Design in the Second Machine Age* in 1990,[42] new sustainability enthusiasts have repeated earlier failures to regard architecture as a problem of technological development through machine-age production.

THEORY AND DESIGN IN THE MACHINE AGES

Born in 1895, American inventor Richard Buckminster Fuller found an audience in the architectural profession for his work and ideas up to his death in 1983. He was not an architect, but the relationship was founded on innovative criticism of architectural practice. It ended in reconciliation through numerous honorary architectural degrees, professional fellowships, awards and design-hero status among generations of architects and students across the world. Norman Foster acknowledges the influence of Fuller's thinking, summarised by Martin Pawley in *Buckminster Fuller – How Much Does the Building Weigh?*:

> It was Richard Buckminster Fuller who originated the concept of cumulative technical advantage that is called synergy, and he too who gave the whole evolutionary process of which it is a part the name of 'Ephemeralization', from the Greek *ephemeros* meaning 'lasting only a day'. For him…the intractable limitations of nature would yield, one by one, to the power of the human mind.[43]

For Fuller, ephemeralisation was the principle of 'doing the most with the least'. At the fascinating two-day symposium 'The Art of Design Science' at the RIBA in June 2000, with an exhibition at the Design Museum, the co-founder of the R. Buckminster Fuller Institute Jaime Snyder argued that Fuller had anticipated sustainability.[44] This is a ridiculous claim based on nothing more than the attribution of current meaning to the idea he did in fact articulate from 1951 onwards – that of 'spaceship earth' as a closed ecological system.

As was pointed out in *Your Private Sky – R. Buckminster Fuller – The Art of Design Science*, Fuller's achievement was that he was thinking this way prior to pictures of the earth being taken from the moon, and before he wrote *Operating Manual for Spaceship Earth* in 1969. Asking 'is it an image of catastrophe?', Claude Lichtenstein and Joachim Krausse answer: 'no, but it plays skilfully on the possibility that it could become one. It is our task to avoid that possibility'.[45] For Fuller the intellectual and practical task at hand was how to make the world work, not a resignation to limitations or imagined disaster. Fuller believed in the 'possibility of a synergy between growth and environment that goes beyond mere compatibility':

> He concluded that human inventive ingenuity could be pitted against the exhaustion of resources and the injustice of poverty to produce more by design than existed in nature. Thus mankind could succeed instead of failing. Adherence to the old economy of scarcity was in fact just another conspiracy in restraint of trade, this time by financiers and businessmen determined to make the new 'more for less' technology maximize profits instead of benefit humanity.[46]

Nevertheless, many architects cite Fuller as an influential environmentalist, which he was not in any contemporary sense. In *Theory and Design in the First Machine Age* of 1960, Peter Reyner Banham made the same mistake of reading Fuller backwards into history.[47] He used a long elided quotation that Pawley identified 30 years later in *Theory and Design in the Second Machine Age* as contemporary with Banham in the 1950s:

> Although Banham nowhere explains this, the definitive criticism of Modern architecture, for which *Theory and Design* is famous, actually comes from a long letter that Buckminster Fuller wrote to John McHale dismissing any suggestion that the teachings of the Bauhaus had had any influence on his work. This letter was dated January 1955…

> He does Fuller no service here. Extracts from a letter written in 1955 that are presented as a statement made 'as early as 1927' are 'after the fact', even if the Dymaxion project was not. The letter, like Banham himself, belongs to the Second Machine Age, not the first.[48]

In *Theory and Design in the First Machine Age* Banham asked 'whether the aims of the International Style were worth entertaining, and whether its estimate of a Machine Age was a viable one'. He contends that: 'something like a flat rebuttal of both aims and estimate can be found in the writings of Buckminster Fuller'. However, Banham did not explain that this rebuttal was only to be found in Fuller's writings of 1955 with the benefit of hindsight:

> It was apparent that the going design-blindness of the lay level…afforded European designers an opportunity…to develop their preview discernment of the more appealing simplicities of the industrial structures that had inadvertently earned their architectural freedom, not by conscious aesthetical innovation, but through profit-inspired discard of economic irrelevancies…This surprise discovery, as the European designer well knew, could soon be made universally appealing

Farnsworth House by Mies van der Rohe.

as a fad, for had they not themselves been so faddishly inspired. The 'International Style' brought to America by the Bauhaus innovators, demonstrated fashion-inoculation without necessity of knowledge of the scientific fundamentals of structural mechanics and chemistry.

The International Style 'simplification' then was but superficial. It peeled off yesterday's exterior embellishment and put on instead formalised novelties of quasi-simplicity, permitted by the same hidden structural elements of modern alloys that had permitted the discarded *Beaux-Arts* garmentation. It was still a European garmentation. The new International Style hung 'stark motif walls' of vast super-meticulous brick assemblage, which had no tensile cohesiveness within its own bonds, but was, in fact, locked within hidden steel frames supported by steel *without visible means of support*. In many such illusory ways did the 'International Style' gain dramatic sensory impingement on society as does a trick man gain the attention of children…

Bauhaus and International used standard plumbing fixtures and only ventured so far as to persuade manufacturers to modify the surface of the valve handles and spigots, and the colour, size, and arrangement of the tiles. The International Bauhaus never went back of the wall-surface to look at the plumbing…they never enquired into the overall problem of sanitary fittings themselves…In short they only looked at problems of modifications of the surface of end products, which end-products were inherently sub-functions of a technically obsolete world.[49]

For Pawley, as previously for Fuller, 'scientific and technical development is continuous', and inventions pass 'in favour of something cheaper and better, or become part of another composite element in a general process of synergetic fusion into a greater whole'. As a consequence 'it is by truly extraordinary feats of ephemeralizing design – not by tricks of fashion or the luck of production success – that evolving complexes of environmental technology achieve recognition and survive in human consciousness'. Such design 'fits into a recognizable framework, a pattern of mankind-bettering technological advance, instead of an endless spiral of shocks and sensations'. It is only by understanding design as a history-making activity that the flaw in the steel-framed buildings of Mies van der Rohe, the Usonian houses of Frank Lloyd Wright and the concrete villas of Le Corbusier become clear. 'It is a weakness that is in the eye of the beholder, because our way of looking at them has been chained to the classificatory system of art history.'[50]

In addition, Pawley reiterates the point he made in *Theory and Design in the Second Machine Age*, also of 1990, by recognising Banham's dating error in the otherwise scholarly *Theory and Design in the First Machine Age*:

> The only noble exception among art historians is Reyner Banham. In 1960, in *Theory and Design in the First Machine Age*, Banham does experimentally project Fuller into his rightful place as the most farsighted of all the modern functionalists of the pioneering generation. But, looked at closely, Banham's enthusiasm is only half-hearted. He clearly knows little of Fuller's early years and carefully confines him to a passage or two in the last chapter of his book. Worse still, the quotation that he provides to substantiate Fuller's early dismissal of Bauhaus Modernism was actually written 28 years later than he claims. But despite these limitations, Banham does see that the pioneers of Modernism and Buckminster Fuller correct two different value systems. If the theory of 'ephemeralization' is represent [sic], then 'functionalism' is at best a small part of it, not an alternative theory.[51]

Moreover, Pawley noted that by turning to Fuller in 1960 Banham had 'offered a brief obituary for the first generation of Modern architects that was in the nature of a warning of disaster. Despite the brevity of this prediction – it is limited to four speculative pages at the end of a 330-page book – the fact that Banham addressed himself to the possibility of defeat at the height of the global victory of Modernism is what makes *Theory and Design in the First Machine Age* important today'.[52]

> It may well be that what we have hitherto understood as architecture, and what we are beginning to understand of technology are incompatible disciplines. The architect who proposes to run with technology knows now that he will be in fast company, and that, in order to keep up, he may have to emulate the Futurists and discard his whole cultural load, including the professional garments by which he is recognised as an architect. If, on the other hand, he decides not to do this, he may find that a technological culture has decided to go on without him. It is a choice the masters of the Twenties failed to observe until they had made it by accident, but it is the kind of accident that architecture may not survive a second time – we may believe that the architects of the First Machine Age were wrong, but we in the Second Machine Age have no reason yet to be superior about them.[53]

Banham underestimated how architects were constrained by the construction industry, itself a function of the wider political and economic context. He also overestimated the success of the Futurists in rejecting the past, and the stupidity of doing so in all regards. Nevertheless, Banham helped to establish Fuller's strategy of ephemeralisation, and the principle of doing more with less as the history-making human-centred architectural theory modernism lacked.

> To understand what went wrong and what went right with the Modern Movement we must still understand, even try to re-experience, the revolution in sensibility which was wrought by, and upon, the Futurists and their contemporaries like Le Corbusier and Mies van der Rohe; we must understand the irrational mechanistic urges that underlay the rationalist platitudes with which the Bauhaus has been justified to later generations; what romantic dreams of prismatic crystalline splendours, cathedrals of light and colour, are imprisoned in the snug and inexpensive towers of glass that form our current downtown scenes.

> For these are the true 'ghosts in the machine' of the Twentieth Century, faint echoes of a far from faint-hearted epoch when men truly tried to come to terms with 'the Machine' as a power to liberate men from ancient servitudes to work and exploitation.[54]

From 1960 *Theory and Design in the First Machine Age* became one of the seminal texts for a debate among practitioners, academics and students on how the environmental professions could better society, or whether they could determine social change at all through their professional lives.

HISTORIC MOMENTS IN TECHNOLOGICAL ADVANCE

It remains a mistake to attribute change to technology alone, and an oversight to ignore the capacity of people to make history. Alan Hudson has argued for a sense of human agency, backed up with an appreciation of the potential of science and technology:

> The function that modernity plays is that it presents historical change as a result of progress in the abstract – rather than through human intervention. Social relationships become fixed and naturalised and technological innovation constitutes the dynamic of substantive change. In the process of separating social change and technological innovation a strange thing happens. The development of capitalist society is described but – and this is the source of confusion in modernity – the social contradictions inherent in the capitalist relationship vanish. Modernity is essentially an ahistorical concept.[55]

What is interesting is that the technocratic presumptions of planners advocating Urban Task Force density prescriptions are the anti-machine age companion to the earlier technological determinism of Banham and Fuller. Where planners wish that people would match their aspirations to the development plan, technological determinists consider that populations only need better products for social progress. Both the demand-side managers of sustainable development and the supply-side technologists of the machine age make the mistake of treating people as passive participants in a technocratic project of modernisation. Pawley understands that it will take political will, a willingness to take risks on a return on capital investment, and the commitment of well-paid and skilled labour to produce the special rural dwellings (SRD) programme he sketches in Chapter 13. Architects can plan all they like, or investigate any technology, but the SRD programme rests on the ability of capitalism to raise the productive capacity of society. Advocates of sustainability suggest that rather than raising production it is consumption that must be constrained and the countryside held in stewardship.

The SRD programme is a timely updating of the scientific dwelling service that Fuller proposed in his *Nine Chains to the Moon* of 1938, which only gained a wider audience from the 1963 reprint. For Fuller there were 'four overlapping applications and conflicting interpretations of the phrase MASS PRODUCTION HOUSE'. These are paraphrased as:

- Repetition of a number of standard house types by site-based building trades.
- Erection on site of sectional assemblies and integrated components from a catalogue.
- Delivery of a volumetric unit prefabricated to be installed on a prepared site.
- Supply of a production-run house with full dwelling service including a finance package.
  A competitive shelter service industry, similar to the hotel industry, and of the mechanical standard, scope, and integration of the automobile industry, engaged in furnishing on a RENTAL basis complete scientifically-evolved individual-family dwelling machines, whose design, economy, standard of adequacy, equipment, production, erection, land rent, service, maintenance, moving and removal, improvement and replacement rate are THE ENTIRE RESPONSIBILITY OF THE INDUSTRY'S CENTRAL COMPETITIVE CORPORATIONS, and are all included in one monthly rental charge.[56]

The financial arrangements would be much more sophisticated today, and yet the historic problem remains: who is to lead, fund, produce and live in this architectural advance? As Pawley knows, Fuller himself had flinched at the historic moment in the 1940s when faced with the chance to mass-produce a complete house as part of a postwar 'reconversion programme' for the Beech Aircraft Corporation of Wichita, Kansas.

Both the demand-side managers of sustainable development and the supply-side technologists of the machine age make the mistake of treating people as passive participants in a technocratic project of modernisation.

When it was finally unveiled, the first 'Wichita' prototype was universally praised as a masterpiece of design...The house really did look as though it was a product of the same industry that had manufactured the P-38 and the B-29 and had none of the compromised appearance of the British AIROH house, an uneasy exercise in conventional housing in bolt-together aluminium sections that was going into production on a former bomber production line in England at the same time. In all the public reactions evoked by the 'Wichita' house there was no sign of the supposed conservatism and preference for traditional styling that had influenced the American housebuilding industry's pre-war attempts at prefabrication. Like the Airstream Trailer, a more fortunate design of the period, the 'Wichita' house proved that the public enthusiasm for innovation and performance that had for so long underpinned the research and development of the motor industry, could be ignited in the housing market too.[57]

Pawley shows that despite a healthy order-book, Fuller seemed to lose his nerve. He refused to go into production, missing the opportunity to improve the design over time. The co-incidence of housing demand and available agricultural land again raises the prospect of a historic technological advance for labour-saving architecture, built on capital-intensive production lines. There is no particular need to limit this approach to low-density development, and audacity.org is interested in the architectural opportunities for raising labour productivity and gaining resource efficiencies through the transfer into hydrogen as a clean fuel. Where Pawley gives the low-density prospect for raising the quantity and quality of architectural production, Shane Slater, Ben Madden and Duncan Price of Whitby Bird and Partners argue for an urban application of hydrogen-fuelled technologies in Chapter 14, 'Revolutionary Energy'. Conversely, there is no particular need to limit hydrogen fuel cell use to higher-density development.

The prospect of raising production, lifting planning constraints, and starting the hydrogen-fuelled future present architects with a historic opportunity that might be considered sustainable – that is, if Britain were not about pursuing sustainability through a reliance on labour-intensive construction, adding to planning difficulties, and obsessed with reducing the consumption of fossil fuels in an ageing building stock. Hydrogen technologies also render the criticism of suburbia and car-based mobility technologically obsolete, contrary to Pawley's view that dispersed development into a diversified countryside heralds an age of immobility made possible by telecommunications. Just because we are better able to communicate virtually is no reason to abandon the mobility provided by the private car. The Institute of Public Policy Research (IPPR) briefing document *H2 – Driving the Future*, discusses the policy implications of developing hydrogen as a fuel for road vehicles.[58] It remains to be seen whether the report predictions for motive power hydrogen applications coming to market are pessimistic and overly reliant on government intervention. At the time of writing a companion report on static – or architectural – fuel-cell applications was expected in the autumn of 2001.

CONSEQUENCES OF THE LACK OF ARCHITECTURAL MANUFACTURING

If British developers fail to realise manufactured architectural production on a large scale, and fuel it through the hydrogen-producing economy (rather than the carbon-reducing economy of managed consumption), economic, social and environmental sustainability are likely to be reduced to design themes. This is the approach taken by the Prince of Wales in Poundbury, Dorchester, developed in Canada as New Urbanism and revamped in the urban village ideas of the Urban Task Force. In Chapter 15 Sean Stanwick explores how the resultant 'Smalltowne' is little more than a themed suburbia bound up with voluntary but nonetheless intrusive codes of personal behaviour. Missing the opportunity to produce our way out of fossil-fuelled site-based construction may mean an increasingly thin architectural façade over a stifling parochialism morally justified as sustainable development. Does Smalltowne promise the sense of 'dwelling' that Phil Macnaghten argues for in Chapter 6, and is that the appeal?

We can, of course, continue to design housing or other repetitive forms of accommodation on a bespoke basis, but to date this has not sustained the status of the architectural profession within the construction process. The *Architects' Journal* survey of the top-100 practices revealed that 20 per cent were most concerned that architects are no longer lead consultants, 24 per cent were concerned that the public does not understand what architects do, 25 per cent worried about a lack of skilled staff, and 31 per cent about poor fee levels.[59] In Chapter 17, 'From Strategic Adviser to Design Subcontractor and Back Again', Peter Walker notes the drift of the architectural profession into design sub-consultancy, away from a position of influence between client and contractor. *Constructing the Team*, the Latham report of 1994,[60] and the Construction Task Force report *Rethinking Construction* under Sir John Egan,[61] have exacerbated this drift, but were not the cause. The SRD programme may suggest another option for some architects other than attempt to recover lost status in the construction process. Perhaps there is a route for some to become the employees of building-product manufacturers, and to take the drift toward sub-consultancy to its logical extreme.

Airstream caravan.

There are already contradictions in team-working and partnering introduced from manufacturing, as Daniel Lloyd and Deborah Brown recognise in their joint Chapter 16, 'Architecture or Clerkitecture?'. The construction industry works best with contractual arrangements because no contractor can dominate sub-contractors as a manufacturer can dominate suppliers. Construction management firms attempt to repli-cate those relationships of mutual dependence. However, firms of managers lack the element of long-term risk that moderates the behaviour of product manufacturers, and the construction subcontractors have no capital to lose by underperforming as might a manufacturer's supplier. This suggests architects should delineate their work between contractual-based construction for bespoke projects of cultural sig-nificance that explicitly exclude third-party interests, and Latham- or Egan-style arrangements where archi-tects are employees of product manufacturers providing consumers with incrementally improving goods and services.

It is interesting to read Chapter 16 and Chapter 17 together and to understand the turmoil in contract-ing arrangements as the frantic effort of all parties not to share in the risk of development, but to dump it on each other. For all the talk of teamwork or partnership the contract-based construction industry remains risk averse in a way manufacturers cannot be when mass-producing products.

AN AFFORDABLE POLICY OPTION

For Clough Williams-Ellis it was evident in 1928, that 'the Americans are more logical and realise that, given a really good original, the more it is multiplied the better'.[62] The problem, obviously, is that these architectural manufacturers do not yet exist. They never will if labour productivity in construction contin-ues to be held down in the one-sided pursuit of resource efficiencies; meaning that construction output per employee remains low. In Chapter 18, 'Development Rights for the Hydrogen-fuelled Future', I raise the possibility of encouraging manufacturing production across the range of densities by returning devel-opment rights to all landowners. This is a reprise of 'Non-Plan', the idea raised in *New Society* in 1969 by Reyner Banham, Paul Barker, Peter Hall and Cedric Price.[63] It is suggested that this democratisation will multiply construction activity to ensure a higher rate of environmental renewal. There is no reason why sustainability should mean a low-growth economy with low rates of building replacement and poor prospects for architects. As Paul Hyett institutes sustainability, he needs to do so without rendering the profession of architecture unsustainable:

> The basic objectives remain the same: establish the brief; prepare accurate and reliable informa-
> tion; plan the critical path through the job; resource appropriately; and deliver a project that is
> technically sound, to programme and within cost targets. And, of course, make it architecture.[64]

There is the additional problem, (for directors and associates with a stake in the practice) of sustaining themselves in business and avoiding legal action. In the RIBA *Small Practice Survey 2000* nearly 10 per cent of the profession were earning less than £10,000 a year, more than 25 per cent of small practition-ers were earning less than £20,000, with 7 per cent hiring themselves out for less than £25 an hour. The British construction industry employs about 7 per cent of the workforce, or around 1.4 million people, who generate about 9 per cent of gross domestic product (GDP), or just under £60 billion. The majority of con-struction firms are small, with 90 per cent of work being undertaken by firms employing less than 10 oper-atives.[65] Dependent on that activity are the 63,000 or so professionally registered construction consultants with an 87,000-strong support staff spread across 19,000 practices earning total annual fees of £6.7 bil-lion, with £1 billion from overseas, according to the 1997 *Survey of UK Construction Professional Services*. As I mentioned earlier architects had 22 per cent of that fee income.[66] If these figures are divided across 30,000 registered architects at home and abroad,[67] each earns more or less than an average of £49,100 annually in professional fees, including any overseas income. No director or associate can draw a dividend out of that income until the architect's salary and that of the shared support staff is paid, and the practice expenses covered. This is immediately strained by the fact that the top-25 practices had a yearly average practice fee income per qualified architect ranging rapidly down from Foster and Partners at over £260,000 to just under £90,000.[68] While writing this book Martin Pawley pointed out that the title *Sustaining Architecture in the Anti-machine Age* is comprised of two ideas he has never argued:

> First that architecture should be 'sustained', and second that we live in an 'anti-machine age'. In
> my view architecture sustains itself and, where there is hostility to machines, we all know we
> live in an age more totally dependent on them than any previous era.[69]

The profession is barely sustaining itself on this basis, but still has to cope with the delusions of the anti-machine age. In Britain, economic inertia has been a fact since the 1970s, and as an exercise in demand management, sustainability is the theoretical expression of that underlying economic decline. Low eco-nomic growth has never been a mandate for architecture, and we should be clear that in Britain sustain-ability tries to reconcile architects to the loss of an industrial dynamic. For those architects who believe in

There is no reason why sustain-ability should mean a low-growth economy with low rates of building replacement and poor prospects for architects.

...economic inertia has been a fact since the 1970s, and as an exercise in demand manage-ment, sustainability is the theoretical expression of that underlying economic decline.

the possibility of social progress through the development of science and technology, the anti-machine sentiment within sustainability needs to be challenged.

Since Banham wrote *Theory and Design in the First Machine Age* in 1960, British architects have faced that additional problem of a dwindling manufacturing industry. The recent decline in the economic fortunes of the information technology and communications industries has revealed the underlying weakness of the rest of British manufacturing. As Lea Paterson noted in *The Times*: 'If you strip out the technology and telecoms sectors, the figures suggest that "old economy" manufacturing has been in recession for much of the last decade'.[70]

For larger contractors the decline in the supposed 'new economy' has meant that City investors have once again reappraised the construction industry, as Gordon Jon Thompson recognised in the *Building* annual survey of the top 100 firms:

> this year the City has finally woken up to the growing evidence that there is good money to be made from the companies still in construction…The departure of companies for the services sector took some capacity out of the market, and left the firms that stayed with bulging order books. Meanwhile the fall from grace of IT and telecoms companies over the past year has given investors an incentive to appreciate those order books. As a result, contractors, analysts and investors can see that there is a gap in the market.[71]

Being 'flavour of the month' for vacillating investors while another industrial sector is in crisis is no reflection that the construction industry has modernised itself to achieve greater productivity and deliver better service. Where will the speculation be next month? A better appraisal of the project to modernise the construction industry came from Sir Michael Latham in the same issue of *Building*. Basically the Latham and Egan initiatives are in a mess:

> Green issues and sustainability – key messages of the previous DETR – are now with Margaret Beckett's Department of Food and Rural Affairs. Transport, local government, housing and planning, each with a different minister, are in Stephen Byer's ministry, while the regional co-ordination unit and the government offices for the regions are in the Cabinet Office. Patricia Hewitt's DTI has taken over the sponsorship of the Regional Development Agencies and the construction industry. Architecture is somewhere in the culture ministry. Joining all that government up looks like a real nightmare. We can be fairly sure that when the Prime Minister took these decisions to restructure the entire machinery of government, the effect on construction had a very low priority in his mind, if indeed it entered it at all.[72]

Basically the Latham and Egan initiatives are in a mess.

Certainly the Latham and Egan initiatives have been dislocated by recent institutional reorganisation, but they were themselves preoccupied with managerial reform, and hardly resulted in the investment required to remove architectural production from site and into new production facilities. The coercive partnership that exists in the capital-intensive manufacturing industry among component suppliers, the assembly corporations and their end-product service providers simply does not work in the fragmented and largely labour-intensive construction industry.

On a building that is supposed to be more a work of art than most accommodation, the extraordinary and considerable expenditure of time and effort is culturally and socially justified. For the production of everyday, repetitive buildings that are also architecture, low labour productivity is a problem.

More government control, whether demonstrating 'joined up' thinking or not, is not the answer to the problem of architectural production. Nor will fashions in forms of contract or the jargon of experimental project management arrangements make up for the fact that site-based construction is inherently unproductive and time consuming. On a building that is supposed to be more a work of art than most accommodation, the extraordinary and considerable expenditure of time and effort is culturally and socially justified. For the production of everyday, repetitive buildings that are also architecture, low labour productivity is a problem. In reviewing *Factor Four – Doubling Wealth, Halving Resource Use*[73] for *Prometheus* magazine, John Gillott drew the link between labour productivity, the resource efficiency that proponents of sustainability are concerned with, and social progress that Paul Hyett considers in Chapter 1.

> Increasing the productivity of human labour was and should remain a key goal of human progress because it is intimately tied up with increasing both the goods available to people (which increased resource productivity will also allow, which is why the two should not be counterposed), and the amount of time available to people to pursue a range of options in life. *Factor Four* correctly notes that increased labour productivity can be associated with unemployment. But it is a perverse form of make-work to think that the solution to this is less efficient, more labour intensive work, rather than reduced hours with higher living standards.[74]

That really is the question. Should sustainability mean reduced living standards? This book compares arguments for reduced consumption with those for raising production in the pursuit of resource efficiency and a better life. It contrasts those arguing for more regulation in the law, within environmental institutions, through planning or within construction practice, with those advocating that greater freedoms are required. I argue in Chapter 18 that less governmental or legal control of development is required to deliver the sorts of initiatives that both Latham and Egan pointed towards. The entire system of development control predicated on the denial of development rights could be democratised to confront the growing demand for and expectation of public participation in planning. By pursuing immediate democratic freedoms rather than remote legal duties of care we might also avert the hardening of the morality of sustainability into law. Such a shift in emphasis might encourage an architectural manufacturing industry that will help extend the 'amount of time available to people to pursue a range of options in life'.

A consequence of manufacturing architecture might be an increase in society's resources for creating extraordinary architectural works of art and landscape in the twenty-first century. After half a century of planning it may be that the time has come to find a more democratic way out of the mess of policy and institutional initiatives that Latham recognises as a frustration to modernisation. It may be the current crisis in agriculture that provides another opportunity to transform architecture into the manufacturing industry it should have become in Banham's time.

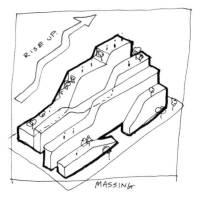

MASSING

That will take capital investment in production on an unprecedented scale, and would be highly unlikely in the present circumstances. Roger Trapp interviewed Paul Hyett for a Design Council supplement in *The Independent*, anticipating sustainability to be more than a passing architectural fashion. Hyett noted that after the demise of Modernism 'architecture needs a new ideology, and sustainability may be that ideology.'[75] Leaving aside the fact that twentieth century architectural Modernism was 'fashion-inoculation' and not substantially ideological, it may yet be that the current morality of sustainability will harden into an ideology. However it will be one that makes a virtue out of failing to raise the level of machine age industrial development around the world, and one that advocates ever more self-restraint and regulation. It will be a crisis of confidence to heighten any underlying crisis of profitability, at the very moment when there is no real political opposition to capitalism, and when life for the vast majority has never been so good. Preferring to anticipate environmental collapse as a consequence of materialism, advocates of sustainability have dismissed the extensively researched message of *The Skeptical Environmentalist*, written by the Associate Professor of Statistics in the Department of Political Science, Aarhus University, Denmark, Bjørn Lomborg.

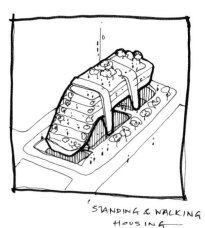

> We are actually leaving the world a better place than when we got it and this is the really fantastic point about the real state of the world: that mankind's lot has vastly improved in every significant measurable field and that it is likely to continue to do so. Think about it. When would you prefer to have been born?[76]

Unfortunately the morality of sustainability seems well suited to become the ideological expression of a self-doubting and underachieving twenty-first century capitalism. New restrictions are promoted and expectations are being lowered at the very moment that the quality of life for the majority of six billion people is better than ever before, working against the achievement of ever-greater freedoms and prosperity.

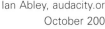

'STANDING & WALKING' HOUSING

'Creature-living' proposal for housing.

Ian Abley, audacity.org
October 2001

Notes

1. World Commission on Environment and Development, *Our Common Future*, commonly known as the Brundtland Report (WCED, Oxford: Oxford University Press, 1987), p. 32.
2. Catherine Slessor, 'Physics and phenomenology', *The Architectural Review*, January 2000, p. 17.
3. John Gillott and Manjit Kumar, *Science and the Retreat from Reason* (London: Merlin Press, 1995), p. 139.
4. Richard Rogers in Philip Gumuhdjian (ed.), *Cities for a Small Planet* (London: Faber and Faber, 1997), p. 3.
5. Anthony Giddens, *Modernity and Self Identity – Self and Society in the Late Modern Age* (Cambridge: Polity Press, 1991), p. 183.
6. Paul Hyett, 'Sustainability issues will grow in the new warmer millennium', *The Architects' Journal*, 13 January 2000, p. 18.
7. Brian Edwards, *Green Architecture – An International Comparison* (Chichester: John Wiley and Sons, 2001).
8. Brian Edwards and Paul Hyett, *Rough Guide to Sustainability* (London: RIBA Publications, 2001).
9. Professor Brian Edwards, 'Letters', *Architects' Journal*, 11 January 2001, p. 23.
10. Allan Ashworth and Keith Hogg, *Added Value in Design and Construction* (Harlow: Longman, 2000), p. 31.
11. Rab Bennetts interviewed by Elaine Knutt, 'Wessex man', 'The Green Century', *Building*, 5 January 2001, p. 20.
12. Brian Edwards and Paul Hyett, *Rough Guide to Sustainability* (London: RIBA Publications, 2001), p. 1.
13. Sir Michael Latham, *Constructing the Team – Final Report of the Government and Industry Review of Procurement and Contractual Arrangements in the UK Construction Industry* (DETR, London: HMSO, 1994).
14. Sir John Egan, *Rethinking Construction – the Report of the Construction Task Force* (London: HMSO, 1998).
15. Sean Barry, 'Clients wield the knife', *Construction News*, 26 April 2001, p. 12.

16. John Gummer, 'Headline', *Construction News*, 26 April 2001, p. 1.
17. Phil Macnaghten and John Urry, *Contested Natures* (London: Sage Publications, 1998), p. 16.
18. RIBA, *Meeting the Challenge – RIBA Strategy for Architecture and Architects 1999-2003* (London: RIBA Publications, April 1999), Section 1.0.
19. David Taylor quoting Marco Goldschmied's inaugural address as President of the RIBA, 'Goldschmied calls for sustainable cities', *Architects' Journal*, 14 October 1999, p. 20; Marco Goldschmied commenting on The President's Medals entrants, *Architects' Journal*, 16 and 23 December 1999, p. 25.
20. Paul Hyett, 'Awful warnings on the pressing need for sustainable cities', *Architects' Journal*, 8 July 1999, p. 18.
21. Paul Hyett, *In Practice* (London: Emap Construct, 2000), p. 10.
22. Paul Hyett, speaking at the Building Audacity conference at The Building Centre, London, 10 July 2000.
23. RIBA, *Meeting the Challenge – RIBA Strategy for Architecture and Architects 1999–2003* (London: RIBA Publications, April 1999), Section 4.0.
24. *Housing Grants Construction and Regeneration Act* (London: The Stationery Office, 1996), Part III, The Architects Registration Board, paras. 118–125, p. 67.
25. Architects Registration Board, *Architects Registration Board Annual Report – 1999-2000* (London: ARB, 2000).
26. Royal Institute of British Architects and Architects Registration Board Joint Validation Panel, *Criteria for Validation* (London: RIBA Publications, 1997).
27. Architects Registration Board, *Architects Registration Board Annual Report – 1999-2000* (London: ARB 2001).
28. Davis Langdon Consultancy for the Construction Industry Council and the Department of the Environment, Transport and the Regions, *Survey of UK Construction Professional Services – Survey Results*, Part 1 (London: CIC, 1997), headline findings.
29. European Commission, *Commission Communication to the Council and European Parliament on Remedying Environmental Damage, COM(93)47fin* (Brussels: EC, 1993), at point 2.1.7.
30. Martin Hedemann-Robinson and Mark Wilde, 'Towards a European Tort Law on the Environment?', in John Lowry and Rod Edmunds (eds), *Environmental Protection and the Common Law*, (Oxford: Hart Publishing, 2000), p. 215.
31. Hewitt Roberts and Gary Robinson, *ISO 14001 – Implementation Handbook* (Oxford: Butterworth Heinemann, 1998), introduction, p. xiv.
32. International Organization for Standardization, *ISO 14001 Environmental Management Systems – Specifications With Guidance for Use* (Geneva: ISO, 1996).
33. European Community, *Community Eco-Management and Audit Scheme,* Council Regulation 1836/93, 29 June 1993, in *Official Journal of the European Communities*, OJ 10.7.93 L 168, 10 July 1993.
34. Hewitt Roberts and Gary Robinson, *ISO 14001 – Implementation Handbook* (Oxford: Butterworth Heinemann, 1998), p. 168.
35. Christopher Booker and Richard North, *The Mad Officials – How the Bureaucrats are Strangling Britain* (London: Constable, 1994), p. 89.
36. Paul Hyett, speaking at the Building Audacity conference.
37. Ibid.
38. Ibid.
39. Martin Hedemann-Robinson and Mark Wilde, 'Towards a European Tort Law on the Environment?', in John Lowry and Rod Edmunds (eds), *Environmental Protection and the Common Law* (Oxford: Hart Publishing, 2000), p. 212.
40. Karen Morrow, 'Nuisance and environmental protection', in John Lowry and Rod Edmunds (eds), *Environmental Protection and the Common Law* (Oxford: Hart Publishing, 2000), p. 139.
41. Paul Hyett, speaking at the Building Audacity conference.
42. Martin Pawley, *Theory and Design in the Second Machine Age* (Oxford: Basil Blackwell, 1990).
43. Martin Pawley, *Buckminster Fuller – How Much Does the Building Weigh?* (London: Grafton, Trefoil Publications, 1990), p. 174.
44. 'R Buckminster Fuller – The Art of Design Science', symposium at the RIBA, 16–17 June 2000, and exhibition at the Design Museum, London
45. Claude Lichtenstein and Joachim Krausse, 'How to make the world work', in *Your Private Sky – R. Buckminster Fuller – The Art of Design Science* (Baden: Lars Muller Publishers, 1999), pp. 11 and 18.
46. Martin Pawley, *Buckminster Fuller – How Much Does the Building Weigh?* (London: Grafton, Trefoil Publications, 1990), p. 39.
47. Peter Reyner Banham, *Theory and Design in the First Machine Age*, first published Reed Educational and Professional Publishing, 1960, ninth reprint of paperback edition (Oxford: Architectural Press, 1997).
48. Martin Pawley, *Theory and Design in the Second Machine Age* (Oxford: Basil Blackwell, 1990), pp. 8 and 9.
49. Richard Buckminster Fuller corresponding with John McHale, January 1955, quoted but not identified or dated by Peter Reyner Banham, *Theory and Design in the First Machine Age*, first published Reed Educational and Professional Publishing, 1960, ninth reprint of paperback edition (Oxford: Architectural Press, 1997), pp. 325–26.

50. Martin Pawley, *Buckminster Fuller – How Much Does the Building Weigh?* (London: Grafton, Trefoil Publications, 1990), pp. 172 and 175–77.
51. Ibid., p. 180.
52. Martin Pawley, *Theory and Design in the Second Machine Age* (Oxford: Basil Blackwell, 1990), p. 7.
53. Peter Reyner Banham, *Theory and Design in the First Machine Age*, first published Reed Educational and Professional Publishing, 1960, ninth reprint of paperback edition (Oxford: Architectural Press, 1997), p. 329.
54. Ibid., p. 12.
55. Alan Hudson, 'The interruption of history', *Prometheus*, No. 2, Spring 1999, p. 48.
56. Richard Buckminster Fuller, *Nine Chains to the Moon*, first published 1938, first reprint (London: Feffer and Simons Inc, 1963), fifth reprint June 1970, p. 327.
57. Martin Pawley, *Buckminster Fuller – How Much Does the Building Weigh?* (London: Grafton, Trefoil Publications, 1990) p. 104.
58. Julie Foley for the Institute of Public Policy Research, *H2 – Driving the Future* (London: IPPR, July 2001).
59. David Taylor, 'AJ One Hundred', *Architects' Journal*, 22 March 2001, p. 76.
60. Sir Michael Latham, *Constructing the Team – Final Report of the Government and Industry Review of Procurement and Contractual Arrangements in the UK Construction Industry* (London: HMSO, 1994).
61. Sir John Egan, *Rethinking Construction – the Report of the Construction Task Force* (DETR, London: HMSO, 1998).
62. Clough Williams-Ellis, *England and the Octopus* (London: Geoffrey Bles, 1928), facsimile edition (London: Council for the Protection of Rural England, 1996), p. 175.
63. Reyner Banham, Paul Barker, Peter Hall and Cedric Price, 'Non-Plan – an experiment in freedom', *New Society*, 13, no. 338 (20 March 1969), pp. 435–43.
64. Paul Hyett, *In Practice* (London: Emap Construct, 2000), p. 6.
65. Construction Industry Training Board, *Construction Workforce Development Planning Brief – 2001–2005* (London: CITB, 2001), pp. 10–13.
66. Davis Langdon Consultancy for the Construction Industry Council and the Department of the Environment, Transport and the Regions, *Survey of UK Construction Professional Services – Survey Results*, Part 1 (London: CIC, 1997), headline findings.
67. Architects Registration Board, *Architects Registration Board Annual Report – 1999–2000* (London: ARB, 2000).
68. David Taylor, 'AJ One Hundred', *Architects' Journal*, 22 March 2001, p. 53.
69. Martin Pawley in correspondence with Ian Abley, 14 May 2001.
70. Lea Paterson, 'Sterling is not the only suspect to blame for manufacturer woes', *The Times*, 7 August 2001, p. 18.
71. Gordon Jon Thompson, 'Flavour of the Month', in '100 Top Bananas', *Building*, 20 July 2001, p. 40.
72. Sir Michael Latham, 'Picking up the pieces', *Building*, 20 July 2001, p. 31.
73. Ernst von Weizsäcker, Amory B. Lovins and L. Hunter Lovins, *Factor Four – Doubling Wealth, Halving Resource Use* (London: Earthscan, 1997).
74. John Gillott, 'The (New) Limits to Growth', *Prometheus*, No. 2, Spring 1999, p. 138.
75. Paul Hyett interviewed by Roger Trapp, '"New Ideology" set to transform profession', *The Independent*, 2 October 2001, p. 3 of the Design in Britain supplement produced in association with the Design Council.
76. Bjørn Lomborg, *The Skeptical Environmentalist – Measuring the Real State of the World*, (Cambridge: Cambridge University Press, 2001) p. 351.

Chapter 1

If Sustainable Design isn't a Moral Imperative, What is?

Paul Hyett, Ryder

Paul Hyett collaborated with service engineer Max Fordham to produce a low energy headquarters building for the Atlantis Paper Company (completed 1991)

The particular difficulty for America is...that her economy has become so effective and powerful that it has created the wealthiest society on earth.

HUMAN EXPECTATION AND GREED

Everyone will remember where they were and what they were doing when their lives were rudely interrupted by the horrific images of the civilian airliners hurtling into the World Trade Center. And no civilised person will ever forget the dreadful horror of watching first one, then the other tower collapse – all 110 storeys – into the densely populated streets below. Like the death of president Kennedy, and the "one small step for man and one giant leap for mankind" message of Neil Armstrong as he walked onto the moon, the collapse of the World Trade Center is an inevitable milestone in our shared history.

This terrible destruction, an act of merciless and ruthless aggression against innocent civilians within an unprotected target, has come at an increasingly difficult time for the so-called developed countries: world opinion is evermore intolerant of the apparently irresponsible exploitation of the earth's resources for which we are collectively responsible. Unfortunately America, a country so deservedly associated with progress and opportunity, has at the dawn of the 21st century come to symbolise the greed, waste, and environmental damage that all first world and many second and third world countries contribute to. This is as relevant to the construction and operation of buildings as it is to other demands such as transportation and manufacturing services. The particular difficulty for America is however that her economy has become so effective and powerful that it has created the wealthiest society on earth. That society has, perhaps inevitably, become the most demanding and damaging in terms of its impact on our host planet. That is the inevitable legacy of America's success.

With her founders' ambitions of creating a 'new world' free from the misery and conflict of the 17th and 18th century Europe, America had quickly established herself as a symbol of hope for mankind. But, as we now face the awful problems that arise out of environmental damage, we must ask ourselves whether hope can continue to be represented by a community that is knowingly consuming resources and generating waste at a rate that ultimately threatens the very survival of our planet.

It is of course unfair to focus criticism exclusively on a people who have contributed so richly to the cultural and scientific development of the modern world, and who have given so generously in terms of aid to less fortunate nations. We could equally look to the excesses of the Stalinist cotton irrigation schemes that have left the Aral Sea as a dry and dangerous bowl of polluted dust, or the appalling damage to human and animal reproduction systems consequent upon the heavy radiation emanating from the Soviet nuclear testing programmes carried out in East Kazakhstan since the Second World War? Then there is Chernobyl, and further west the filth produced by the hopelessly inefficient processes of the old Eastern bloc industrial programmes. We could also look at the uncontrolled growth of developing cities with their crippling demands on resources and unchecked emissions and wastes, or to China, which is apparently now shedding the strict disciplines associated with the Mao Tse-tung era and embarking on programmes of so-called development that will place further impossible demands on our environment.

And, against this broader scenario, we ourselves cannot become too complacent. We have only to look at Britain's track record: during the Thatcher era Britain gained the unenviable position of being the European Economic Community's (EEC's) largest producer of sulphur dioxide (SO_2)– the primary cause of acid rain. Our network of giant tall-stack power stations, designed to pass fumes into the higher atmosphere, effectively 'export' acid rain to neighbouring countries. Indeed, Drax power station in Yorkshire produces more sulphur dioxide – the main component of acid rain – than Sweden and Norway put together.

CONSEQUENCES AND BLAME

The Drax figures are astounding: in 1987 Drax emitted 321,000 tonnes of sulphur dioxide compared with Sweden and Norway's entire output of 200,000 and 70,000 tonnes respectively. And it is not just other countries that suffer: in 1989 sewage bacteria was reported to be 'raining' down as a fine dust on the houses around Drax.[1] This threat to health had arisen due to the steam-producing cooling towers at Drax taking water from the River Ouse, which had deteriorated to a point of being 'biologically dead'. Indeed, throughout the 1980s water standards in rivers across Britain had been allowed to fall. According to Chris Rose, this was a consequence of the actions of a government that had 'systematically fiddled the pollution rule books by changing "consent conditions" for sewage works'.[2] The result was a frequent doubling or even trebling of the volume of urine and faeces poured into our rivers under so-called, albeit revised 'legal targets'. Rose alleges that these circumstances were a deliberate consequence of Department of Environment (DoE) policies that were brought to light only through the privatisation programmes of the later Thatcher era.

Furthermore, Britain's record of rule-bending and resistance towards international efforts to curb pollution is shameful. Its farming activities have generated intense pesticide and nitrate outputs. The country also gained a poor record during the 1980s through the continued practice of pumping raw sewage into its coastal waters while dumping chemically contaminated sewage sludge at sea – the practice of which had long since ceased in neighbouring countries.

Guthrie Pavilion, by T. R. Hamzah and Yeang

So again why, against the poor record of other countries, dare this chapter focus criticism on the US? It does so for three reasons. First, the US standard and way of life has come to represent an ideal that sets the targets and direction by which other countries all too often measure their own progress and achievement. Second, while other countries through their own association with unsustainable lifestyles cannot be free of criticism, it is the US, through its excesses of consumption and pollution, that most clearly epitomises the irresponsibility of modern humanity towards its host and definitively finite environment: mother earth. And finally, through a combination of the self-acclaimed power and indisputable authority and influence of the US, the country has a moral responsibility at least to join, if not lead, the struggle towards a more responsible management of the planet's resources.

But despite continued claims that its system of government – market democracy – is superior, the US continues to encourage unfettered growth in consumer demand while cynically turning its back on international efforts to introduce restraint. This was evidenced recently by the US refusal to limit the consumption of non-renewable energy forms, or the consequent damaging production of carbon dioxide (CO_2) emissions, through its recent decision to abandon the Kyoto agreement. All this from a country that, with only 4.6 per cent of the world's population, generates 9 per cent of the world's CO_2 emissions from its buildings alone! The American Institute of Architects (AIA) is among many organisations within the US that are seeking to address this problem. However, its efforts to date have had negligible effect on the energy demands of buildings.

THE LEGACY OF 'PROGRESS'

It is not known who first discovered America. Danes, Swedes and Norsemen colonised Iceland and Greenland in the tenth century AD and journeyed on into the territories now known as Nova Scotia in the early years of the eleventh century. But it was not until the seventeenth century that any determined effort by Europeans was made towards the colonisation of the North American continent. The path towards the independence of that part of North America, which now constitutes the US, is of course well known – that independence being proclaimed on 4 July 1776. A brave new constitution that has since provided hope for generations of immigrants established the US as a land of freedom and opportunity, one that has seen unprecedented levels of development.

Increasingly we must challenge whether this development does properly constitute *progress*. Indeed, when one considers that the vast land occupied by the first European settlers was, upon their arrival, as pure as the driven snow, it is alarming that after 300 years of settlement the US today consumes and pollutes at such a rate that it threatens the future existence of mankind. This threat, by way of both emission outputs and the continued incitement for the rest of the world to emanate its own political and economic model, is what brings the US into sharp relief as a target for criticism. Can such a passage towards disaster really constitute progress?

...the US continues to encourage unfettered growth in consumer demand while cynically turning its back on international efforts to introduce restraint.

The challenge for the human race at the beginning of the twenty-first century must clearly be to achieve the standards of living to which the Americans aspire, within a political freedom that the Americans enjoy, but in the context of technologies and forms of development that are sustainable within the world's threatened eco-system. The question is whether this can be achieved under the political system of 'market democracy' now so prevalent worldwide? Is it possible to curb the voracious and short-term demands of the market when presidents and senior politicians so often owe their success in gaining office to the funding provisions of their corporate sponsors (for example, President Bush's campaign-dependence on the financial support of the oil companies)? This is the context within which the architectural profession, both here and abroad, must operate in its endeavours to promote safer and sustainable forms of building and human settlement.

ARCHITECTURE'S SCOPE FOR ALLEVIATING ENVIRONMENTAL DAMAGE

Buildings and cities, in terms of the way they are arranged and serviced, and the methods by which they are constructed, have an enormous impact on the world's eco-system. The creation and operation of buildings accounts for some 50 per cent of all energy resources consumed across the planet, making the construction industry 'the least sustainable industry in the world'.[3]

Within the developed world, transport accounts for around 30 per cent of energy consumption, while manufacturing demands some 20 per cent. Despite the fact that transport and manufacturing are becoming increasingly efficient in terms of energy usage, the situation is worsening as buildings, towns and cities are, in contrast, becoming more demanding – especially those designed to meet the requirements of tomorrow's world. For example, towns and cities are being arranged in ways that place heavier demands on the use of the motor car and, to compensate for deep plan building arrangements, modern buildings rely more heavily than their predecessors on mechanical servicing for cooling, ventilation and artificial lighting.

The above can be seen in the case of Los Angeles, where the apparently insatiable demand on global resources has been documented by Mike Davis,[4] who examines the *imagination* and dread within the city of the potential disasters that threaten it as a consequence of man's abuse of the environment. In Los Angeles, as in cities the world over, the reconciliation of land-use and transport planning is an increasingly elusive goal against which a very heavy price is being paid.

But it is not the consumption of energy within our buildings and cities that is the problem. The threat to our existence and that of our host environment is the consumption of *non-renewable* forms of energy, and the production through energy generation of environmentally damaging by-products, such as CO_2 emissions. The challenge is, therefore, to utilise as far as possible renewable forms of energy that do not produce adverse consequences, at the same time providing for the urban lifestyles expected by 'advanced' societies and demanded by communities across the developing world.

The construction and development industries have a major role to play in meeting this challenge but are heavily dependent on the economic and political systems within which they operate. This is the dilemma for architects and other members of the design team in addressing the sustainability agenda. The remainder of this chapter considers recent progress in this field within British architecture, looking in particular at the work of the Royal Institute of British Architects (RIBA), for which I was Vice-President with responsibility for education for three years prior to being elected President for the two-year period from 1 July 2001. That said, I must qualify these remarks as my own, and not necessarily those of the Institute.

The Goldschmied Era

Shortly after taking office on 1 July 1999 as RIBA President, Marco Goldschmied, in referring to the issue of ecological sustainability, was reported as saying:

> Architects have a duty beyond individual projects to participate in this 'human debate', bringing their vision, energy and intuition to work for mankind.
>
> The profession does not deserve to survive unless we do. The planet will not survive if we don't.[5]

These words presumed an extraordinary level of responsibility both upon the profession collectively and on individual architects. However, the views were personal: Goldschmied did not possess the authority to commit the RIBA or its membership to such an agenda: he boldly offered this as a clarion call following his successful campaign for the presidency. His Council duly accepted the 'call to arms'.

During his subsequent two years in office, Goldschmied never wavered from this task. He immediately appointed Professor Peter Smith to the new office of RIBA Vice-President for Sustainable Development, and RIBA house architects Allies and Morrison were instructed to prepare designs for a wind turbine generator on the roof of 66 Portland Place – immediately running into a very public dispute with English Heritage over the allegedly damaging impact of the proposal on the appearance of the Institute's listed headquarters building. Nowhere has the *reactive* nature of the planning system in this respect been more evident than in Norfolk, where preservation orders exist on old and defunct windmills (which many consider ugly), while consents have been refused for modern turbine 'wind farms' (which others would describe as beautiful) due to their allegedly damaging visual effect on the landscape.

Despite being warned of the likely response of the conservationist lobby to the proposal for a wind turbine at Portland Place, Goldschmied characteristically pushed ahead, making the process of obtaining consent symbolic of the problems with the planning system with regard to sustainable architecture. At the time of writing this planning dispute looks set to continue, but as stated in an interview reported in the *Architects' Journal*:

> I don't like reactive planning. Every initiative should be considered in its own right, and we must embrace the future with confidence. I will press the government to review English Heritage…(it) has had, and does have, a crucial role but the balance has now been lost.[6]

Sustainable design can have an even greater impact in curtailing pollution through the retrofitting of existing buildings than via new work, which represents only a fraction of our built stock. However, the

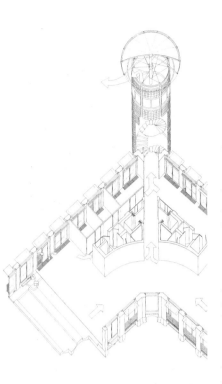

Axonometric showing the air flows through the Inland Revenue Centre by Michael Hopkins & Partners

The Inland Revenue Centre relies on the mass of the brick and concrete construction as a thermal flywheel, tending to maintain an internal climate. Heating and ventilation are arranged by drawing air into the building through a small duct in each bay. Underfloor fans, which can be adjusted individually, control the rate of air flow up over heat exchangers through continuous grilles on the perimeters of the floors. In winter hot water is circulated to warm the air, and in summer cold water is circulated to provide some cooling. Heat is extracted from all but the top floor of the offices through the cylindrical corner stair towers. Acting as chimneys the stairs have roofs that can be automatically raised or lowered according to the rate of draw of air required through the offices, which varies with the internal and external conditions.

progress of sustainability in this field will be severely frustrated if the authorities and lobbyists can block initiatives at every turn in an attempt to rigidly maintain the status quo. Which is the more beautiful: the listed but redundant Battersea power station, which polluted the atmosphere for decades, or a series of wind turbines along the entire central Thames shoreline? Beauty is in the eye of the beholder. Unfortunately, as far as sustainable development is concerned, progress is all too often at the mercy of the Luddites.

VALIDATION

In another sphere, the RIBA Education Department introduced, with the help of past president of the Malaysian Institute of Architects Ken Yeang and others, a paper setting out requirements for sustainable design to become a mandatory part of the curriculum within all schools of architecture validated by the Institute. Charismatic by nature, Ken Yeang is a RIBA member who has developed an international reputation for his work on the bioclimatic skyscraper. His projects, most notably the Tokyo Nara building and Guthrie Pavilion, have established a unique new aesthetic entirely consequent on the architect's technical response to the sustainability agenda.

The proposal to incorporate sustainability as an issue during school validation processes gained the full backing of the Architect's Registration Board (ARB) which, with the RIBA, undertakes validation of British schools. The impact of this initiative cannot be underestimated. Some 75 schools of architecture around the world, in locations from Helsinki to Johannesburg and Santiago to Singapore, as well as Maryland in the US and Moscow (which together with the 35 British schools account for some 20 per cent of the world's graduates in architecture each year) must now address this subject head-on. However, talented Scottish architect Richard Murphy, whose reputation is based on a series of outstanding built projects, was a notable critic of the proposal.

CONTINUING PROFESSIONAL DEVELOPMENT AND GOOD PRACTICE

The RIBA Practice Department has, in parallel, encouraged practising architects to address sustainability through continuing professional development (CPD) programmes, but it has (so far) stopped short of making this a mandatory requirement (possibly with tests) for professionals 'in the field'. Mandatory CPD with respect to particular subjects such as sustainable design would, of course, meet predictably heavy resistance among any profession, but a precedent is currently being set by the General Medical Council which has initiated a programme to 'reassess' all British doctors on a regular basis. Effectively this ends the principle of a right, from initial registration, to practice for life, and introduces the concept of a licence, the renewal of which is subject to periodic compliance with ongoing testing procedures. Such drastic action, claims Robin Vaughan of the ARB, has been necessitated by the dramatic loss of public confidence in the medical profession following a series of highly publicised 'errors' among its members. At the time of writing, the latest of these, reported nationally in June 2001, involved an unfortunate doctor who despite undoubted good intention and integrity had seemingly failed to keep up with medical progress in the area of bladder cancer. His alleged ignorance had led to some 12 patients being denied recently developed forms of treatment which may have been beneficial. Sadly, 10 of these had since died.

Speaking at a meeting between the Royal Incorporation of Architects in Scotland (RIAS) and the ARB in Edinburgh on 27 June 2001, I argued that the notion that architects have an ongoing right to practise should be challenged: we live in a fast-moving age and architects have a duty to keep abreast of new developments. In this context the privilege of being an architect brings with it certain obligations to both the profession and the wider community. Indeed, if the profession is serious about its response to the sustainability agenda, it must make sure that its members develop the appropriate awareness and skills to deliver the RIBA's stated ambitions.

The ARB, supportive of this view, intends to conduct a review of CPD, with the intention of working with and through the RIBA. As Barbara Kelly, chairperson of the ARB pointed out, the evidence of the medical profession's recent experience clearly shows that properly managed CPD is essential for the ongoing protection of the reputation on which all professions must rely. Characteristically the RIAS, though understandably not willing to endorse such initiatives, was firm in its view that the profession needs to treat technical training and CPD more seriously. It is of course easier for a regulatory body to enforce a more serious approach to CPD than it is for a professional institute and in this respect it is particularly important to note that the RIAS and AIA require that all of their members are registered with the regulatory body, which provides for a greater level of influence over CPD. The RIBA does not require this and accordingly has less influence in this respect, though at the time of writing this issue is being reviewed. One argument here is that consumers assume that the suffix 'RIBA' denotes that its user is entitled to adopt the title 'architect'. It does not.

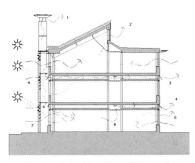

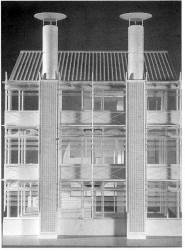

New Environmental Office by Feilden Clegg Bradley Architects

The New Environmental Office at the Building Research Establishment is a cutting edge project to demonstrate a wide range of sustainability issues.

Feilden Clegg Bradley Architects was appointed from an initial 115 applicants to develop a design that significantly improved on previous best practice delivering energy consumptions approximately 30% better than any previous equivalent building while maintaining accepted standards of comfort for occupants. Max Fordham and Partners were the services engineer, and Buro Happold were the structural engineer. The contractor was J Sisk & Son Ltd.

The project uses a combination of controlled natural lighting, controlled ventilation and 'solar stacks'. Floor slabs were used to provide thermal mass reducing temperature fluctuation. The scheme has achieved all of its design targets and been widely published both in Britain and elsewhere. It has won a large number of design awards including an RIBA award, a Concrete Society Award and Institute of Architectural technologists Award for Supreme Technical Excellence. The BRE has long been a champion of energy efficient design, with a tradition of putting design theory into practice in its own buildings.

Hope House is the prototype live/work unit within a theoretical solar city that places workspace (IT uses need cool north light) in the shade of housing which can benefit from winter and spring sunlight providing increased daylight and useful passive solar gain. The south facing glazed sunspace is equipped with photovoltaic panels sufficient to run the electric car and solar hot water collectors for all domestic needs.

Urban Loft Farm is a design for an Innovation in Housing Competition issued by the Housing Association Circle 33. The carbon emissions from the average British family are a third to power their home, a third on travel, and a third on foodmiles. It is as important to make it easy to reduce travel and food miles as it is to design energy efficient homes. With the allotments and conservatories on the roof of the Urban Loft Farm, the motivated resident has the opportunity to reduce their ecological footprint.

Flower Tower – concern for the negative environmental impact of high rise developments, lead BDa to propose a mixed use tower community that actually generates its own energy. Towers also rob sunlight from neighbours, so a 200 sq m urban block incorporating Landzed and Skyzed urban models; sport and park facilities in the shade zone and schools, nurseries and community centres to complete the solar urban village.

EXPANDING THE MESSAGE

Goldschmied has also tirelessly raised the profile of sustainability in the national press, on radio and TV. Under his presidency, the RIBA hosted Herbert Girardet's exhibition on sustainable cities, which attracted large audiences and considerable publicity. Many other architects have, of course, contributed substantially to this debate, including academics such as Tom Woolley at Queen's University, Belfast, and practitioners such as Feilden and Clegg, Michael Hopkins and Rick Mather with such projects as the Building Research Offices at Watford, the Inland Revenue Headquarters building at Nottingham, and student residences at the University of East Anglia. In addition, the great might of the Foster Office has, albeit some might say belatedly, turned its attention to this subject as evidenced in its new project for the Greater London Assembly Building. Most encouraging, however, is the work of younger practices such as that started by Bill Dunster which has placed sustainability at the centre of its agenda, and the work of recent research graduates including Jude Harris who is now developing his interests in this field through built projects courtesy of Jestico + Whiles.

One highly respected architect, Nicholas Grimshaw, has recently chosen to publish his firm's manifesto on sustainable design[7] (see the Eden Centre case study on page 32). There is also a growing body of literature on this subject, with academics such as Brian Edwards producing highly informative guides to sustainable design for both student and practitioner use. Clients, local authorities and indeed their own staff will no doubt increasingly expect architectural practices to establish and maintain a policy statement on sustainable design. And we must not forget the contributions made by those within the engineering disciplines – for example Whitby Bird and Partners, Max Fordham LLP, Battle McCarthy and Fulcrum Consulting – or the work of people such as Robin Nicholson during his period as Chairman of the Construction Industry Council (CIC), and civil servant Phillip Ward of the Energy and Waste Directorate at the DETR. However, the combined influence of all professional disciplines within the construction industry, including the quantity surveyors and those other advisors who so often hold significant influence over client decision making (such as accountants, estate agents, valuers, estate managers and facility managers), is crucial to real progress in this area.

INCONSISTENCIES

To date, Goldschmied has been the most prominent leader of a professional institute to address the sustainability issue. As a powerful spokesperson for one of the most influential professional bodies he has accordingly achieved monumental progress: sustainability is at last formally on the institutional agenda, and now lies at the very heart of all RIBA policy.

Nevertheless, there have been inconsistencies that demonstrate the need for 'joined-up' thinking, and setbacks that illustrate the many difficulties thrown up by the sustainability agenda. For example, during Goldschmied's first year of office, the Stirling Prize (British architecture's most prestigious award) was granted to the Future Systems' partnership of Jan Kaplicky and Amanda Levete for their commentator's stand at Lord's Cricket Ground. Undoubtedly a building of high architectural quality, it is vulnerable to criticism regarding ecologically responsible design in terms of its form of construction and its operational performance. A future RIBA awards panel would surely be expected to demonstrate more 'joined-up' thinking in order to ensure compliance with the RIBA's stated intentions under its sustainability agenda.

In another arena, the English schools of architecture (and I mean English as opposed to schools in Scotland, Wales, Northern Ireland or overseas) have proved characteristically difficult, demanding on the one hand clear guidance on how sustainability should be taught while maintaining, quite rightly, that the RIBA should not be prescriptive in terms of its curricula requirements. There have also been disputes among schools over the definition of sustainable design, and the insistence that existing teaching programme obligations provide no room for additional subject matter. Such responses have been met with a robust insistence by the RIBA and the ARB that it is for the schools to explore and extend the debate on what constitutes 'sustainable design', and determine how it should be incorporated into their teaching programmes. The RIBA and ARB demand only that the *results* of the schools' work must be evidenced in the students' portfolios which, through project activity, form the basis of assessment under the validation system. Thus the RIBA sees the student project and the teaching studio as a fundamental tool of research. As eloquently argued by Eric Parry,[8] the output of the student/tutor collaboration should inform and influence mainstream practice both by example, and by the contribution of graduates within the workplace in the years ahead.

There have also been other, not unexpected, disappointments. For example the ARB, of which Goldschmied has been an elected Board member throughout his RIBA presidency, evidently weakened in its will to address the sustainability agenda. Its initial Code of Conduct addressed sustainability with respect to environmental design fair and square:

5.11: In meeting his obligations under this Code an architect should have due regard to the need
    to conserve and enhance the quality of the environment and its natural resources.

In this clause, 'should', as the first registrar of the ARB pointed out, means 'must'. But it seems the ARB got cold feet and backed down with the publication of its second code in December 1999, which qualifies this obligation by stating:

whilst architects' primary responsibility is to their clients, they should nevertheless have due regard to their wider responsibility to conserve and enhance the quality of the environment and its natural resources. (author's italics)

Clearly, as far as the ARB is concerned, the obligation to clients has again moved to the fore. In its amended form this clause has no teeth whatsoever: it exists as a token gesture that is wholly unenforceable. The pathetic cries of 'my client made me do it!' can be anticipated to echo down the corridors of any disciplinary hearing the ARB may attempt to set up on this subject.

PROTECTION OF TITLE IS WORTHLESS...

The obvious difficulties in imposing any form of 'professional' obligations on architects particularly highlight the problems caused by the lack of protection of function for architects in their work. As previously stated, under Britain's registration laws architects only enjoy protection of title. Accordingly, anyone can act as an architect, however only those qualified to the ARB's stipulated requirements, and registered by the Board, can use the title 'architect'. This is in direct contrast to the medical and legal professions in Britain, under which there is protection of function not title. Anyone can use the title 'doctor' or 'lawyer', but only those appropriately qualified and registered can deliver specified medical or legal services.

With regard to what is increasingly seen as a highly unsatisfactory piece of legislation, it must be noted that while the RIBA's duty under its charter is to advance and promote architecture, it has an implicit obligation as a professional organisation to service and support the interests of its members. There are currently around 34,000 RIBA members, of whom about 4,500 are based outside Britain. The influence of the Institute is threatened if the size of its membership is eroded. Membership is not compulsory and architects will inevitably leave if the Institute imposes unacceptable rules on their conduct.

A more constructive way forward is for the RIBA to influence government in the development of legislation that will ensure the ecological agenda is properly addressed in the design of buildings. The RIBA can also encourage the public to demand that the sustainability issue be included as an intrinsic part of the client's design brief (see below). In summary, it is clear that while it is appropriate for the RIBA to act boldly, it must be careful to 'take its membership with it'.

Let us now consider two areas of competition for British architects. First, many US firms have set up large offices in Britain. This has been relatively easy because there is no protection of function under British law for architects, there is no restriction on the freedom of any architect from overseas (subject to appropriate work permits etc.) to design buildings, make planning applications or oversee construction. US architects, in contrast, enjoy strict protection of function in the USA through the 'Certificate of Record' obligations that require a registered architect to 'sign off' project drawings prior to occupation of a building. Because architects in Britain have no such protection, even unskilled people, with no training whatsoever, are entitled to design buildings on behalf of 'clients': provided that they do not use the title 'architect' such action is perfectly legal. US firms currently carry out an estimated £540 million of construction in the British home market annually just to service American staff operating from American offices based in Britain. With an estimated ratio of at least 10 'other' staff to Americans in their British offices, these firms are responsible for an estimated £5.4 billion of construction in Britain per year.

When a columnist for the Architect's Journal, I named ten Americans who, by entering their names into the RIBA *Directory of Practices* whilst not registered, had clearly breached the British registration laws by holding themselves out as architects. Despite considerable pressure, the ARB chose only to warn the individuals concerned. This issue is directly relevant to sustainable design: the architects concerned each hold senior positions in offices which have a history of producing large commercial projects that have tended (like the gas-guzzling cars produced by the US automobile industry in the 1950s, 1960's and 1970s) to be the most demanding and least responsible building type in terms of energy consumption. As mentioned above, the US, despite the AIA's attention to the sustainability agenda, all too often produces very *unsustainable* architecture.

According to RIAS past president George Wren, the inability of the ARB or RIBA to curtail the extensive US operations within Britain that are manifestly breaching the 'spirit', if not the letter, of our legislation 'makes a complete mockery of our registration laws!'. Indeed, it also has dangerous consequences for our own environment: effectively we encourage the US to export its bad practices to this country.

Under such circumstances could the RIBA really make its members less competitive by regulating design with respect to environmentally sustainable objectives when the Americans are free, having accept-

BEDZED is an integrated live/work urban village for the Peabody Housing Trust. Workspace is placed in the shade zones of south facing terraced housing, with sky gardens on the workspace roofs, enabling all flats to have outdoor garden areas, good access to sunlight. The combination of high insulation and wind driven ventilation with heat recovery enables the whole scheme to be powered by a CHP plant running on wood chip from urban tree waste. BEDZED is only Zero 'fossil fuel' Energy development of its kind. To keep travelmiles down, all the materials specified were sourced, wherever possible, within a 35-mile radius of the site.

House for the Future, Museum of Welsh Life in South Wales, by Jestico + Whiles

The project has received Special Prize for Innovation in the June 2001 Aluminium Imagination Awards at a Gala Ceremony held at the Nat West Media Centre in Lord's Cricket Ground. This recognises the innovative use of a standing seam recycled aluminium roof to support a sedum-planting layer as a lightweight alternative to 'greening' the roof.

The project has also won the 'Best House for the Future' category in the National Homebuilder Design Awards 2001 sponsored by the Britannia Building Society and the Guardian newspaper. The judges praise Jestico + Whiles' entry by stating that "...the housebuilding industry is a long way from understanding the concepts of innovative design and sustainable construction, which explains why the entries for this category were so disappointing this year, with the single – and outstanding – exception of this award winning entry".

The House is commissioned by the National Museums and Galleries of Wales and BBC Wales to stand alongside the collection of domestic Welsh buildings through history which comprise the Museum of Welsh Life at St Fagans near Cardiff. Jestico + Whiles' winning entry was selected through an international architectural competition held in the Spring of 1999, providing an opportunity for architects to portray their vision of the way housing would evolve over the next fifty years. The House has had to be self-contained, yet flexible so that although initially it should house a family of 4-5 people, it might address the changing needs of its occupants over time. In order to reflect this realistic brief, the construction cost of the house was limited to £120,000. The House eschews high-energy technology and embraces appropriate sustainable technologies incorporated within a contemporary design, built by Redrow Homes Ltd.

ed an appointment from a developer who demands that such an agenda is ignored, to practise in this country without being registered with the ARB or being a member of the RIBA? Again, it is notable that AIA membership is contingent on that member being 'licensed' with the State Licensing Board – something the RIAS, but *not* the RIBA, also requires with regard to corporate membership of its respective organisations.

Sadly, because British architects do not enjoy protection of function, most building 'design' is carried out by untrained designers – only 30 per cent of British planning applications last year were submitted by architects – and the figure was a mere 20 per cent in Manchester. Again, can the RIBA contemplate making its members even less competitive against the services of non-qualified 'home-based' designers and technicians who compete for architectural work? As stated in the *Rough Guide to Sustainability*:

Ethics and codes of conduct cut little ice when viewed through the lens of competitiveness.[9]

This takes us back to the issue of operation within a free market economy, the most extreme version of which is manifest in the US. Essentially, without strict rules to protect the profession in terms of function, the ARB and RIBA are powerless to do much towards securing a more responsible programme of building work. It is increasingly a 'free for all' in Britain and the market will demand, and get, what it wants. In the context of an unmanageable law governing regulation of title, the only effective instrument is, as mentioned above, legislation. By controlling building construction through the Building Acts, those who design and make buildings, whether trained, registered or neither, must respond.

Despite the apparent inconsistencies and setbacks described above, the record on the sustainability agenda under the Goldschmied presidency is robust and hopeful, especially when some of the broader political issues that compromise the Institute's capacity to make progress in this area are considered. In short, the legacy of the Goldschmied era is that the sustainability agenda now lies at the very heart of the RIBA's work: the Institute, and increasingly the profession in general, are committed to the continuous promotion of the sustainability issue within the development and construction industry and the broader political and public arena. There can be no turning back.

SO WHERE NOW?

The opening section of this chapter outlined the difficulties within a market democracy of curbing the voracious instincts of human beings to consume and pollute. The US was charged with being at the vanguard of this process: the US population emits 5.85 tonnes of CO_2 per person year compared with Britain's 2.92 tonnes, 2.31 tonnes generally within the EU, and 0.65 tonnes and 0.23 tonnes respectively for China and India.[10] As Brian Edwards says:

Lifestyle is clearly a related issue. As we become more prosperous, we desire and consume more. Consumption carries a corresponding burden of resource use, waste generation, and ultimately, CO_2 production. Buildings...could, through better design, reduce adverse ecological impacts.[11]

Indeed, we could even achieve new forms of architecture that require 'zero-take' in terms of demands on non-renewable energy sources. However, the social, political and economic context for improving our performance is difficult. No doubt we need to increase awareness (among professionals and the public) of the need for more ecologically responsible architecture in all its aspects from 'cradle to grave' in the life of a building. But we also need to increase professional skills, and advance research, so that we can posit alternative and more cost-effective solutions.

But despite the important contribution that can be made through the construction and development industry, this forms only a small part of the overall sustainability agenda and, anyway, architects enjoy only a limited sphere of influence within the building process. Nevertheless, it was right to support Goldschmied's inspirational lead, and we must continue to do so. At one extreme we must increase the awareness of land-use and planning issues: low-density sub-suburban residential arrangements, remote from the workplace and amenities, impose a huge demand on resources. Architects, urban designers and planners have a duty to offer alternative and persuasive 'settlement' models that provide for more eco-responsible lifestyles. At the other extreme, the detail of our design work for even the smallest projects, in terms of materials chosen, the energy 'take' in use and, finally, the demolition of buildings, is crucial to the success of the sustainability agenda.

THE CONTEXT FOR PROGRESS

We must recognise the constraints of the political system within which we operate. Essentially, development is delivered through three 'agencies': the *initiators*, the *facilitators* and the *officiators*. Recent shifts in our economic-political system have led to a transfer of power and influence in each of these three areas.

For example, the state increasingly procures its buildings through the private sector, leaving the market to determine what, where and how development should be shaped. Private Finance Initiatives (PFIs) are the extreme form of a system that is now expected to fund, deliver, maintain and own such infrastructures as schools, hospitals, universities and facilities for the fire, police and ambulance services. No longer does the state deliver, through its own resources, the large housing programmes and building infrastructure of the postwar welfare era. Accordingly, state influence has diminished as its function has shifted from a proactive to a reactive role.

Similarly, corporations and companies increasingly look to the developer to fund and deliver property, be it commercial office space, research parks or lower-grade so-called 'industrial' accommodation. These projects are proposed by developers and built either speculatively or, more commonly, against secure letting covenants, before being sold on to institutional investment funds. Increasingly, conservative bankers, operating against the advice of surveyors, prefer to lend to 'professional developers', making it even more difficult for individual (particularly smaller) companies to raise finance for their own projects. Such companies must therefore accept the market's offerings. These changes to the initiators' character in both state and private sectors not only have a profound effect on the type of construction that takes place, but also distance the community from responsibility for the delivered development.

Under the second category, *facilitators*, there has been a significant change of roles among the suppliers of buildings, as first the development industry, then the government have adopted new forms of procurement. The division between professional disciplines and the construction teams has blurred, with building contractors even emerging as team leaders responsible for managing the design element as well as the construction process (design and build etc.). Initially a response to the effects of high inflation (peaking at 27 per cent in the early 1980s), 'one-stop shop' prime appointment arrangements aim to provide for early construction starts (without full design and/or specification information), with correspondingly greater control on out-turn costs through reduced 'claims' opportunities. The disadvantage here is the diminishing authority of the design team and a general curbing of opportunities for architects to inform the design process with regard to the project brief and agenda: the developer-contractor can effectively eliminate any opportunity for addressing an issue, such as ecological sustainability in design, by refusing time for its development or opportunity for its discussion with the client.

Finally, the effectiveness of *officiators*, including such agencies as building regulations officers and planning departments, has been reduced. Indeed the latter group, the planners, have virtually been denuded of any opportunity to plan at all. Once great departments within local authorities have now been reduced to reactive agencies, dependent on proposals from the private sector against which they can only comment and attempt to negotiate improved outcomes.

These changes in roles do, however, produce significant opportunities provided that we are willing to shape new and effective relationships. If we accept that the government, while committed to enormous spends of some £12.1 billion, £4.1 billion and £3.3 billion in transport, education and health building infrastructure respectively during the next Parliament will, quite rightly, not countenance the kind of laissez-faire attitudes to programme and cost control that were endemic in the 1960s and 1970s, we are at least on the way to acknowledging the need for new forms of procurement. The architectural profession, along with the other members of the design team, should embrace these changes with confidence and shape new opportunities through which our services can be delivered effectively. Architects in particular have little to fear: they possess the ability to *shift and manipulate space*. This is a unique skill and architects should ensure that they secure circumstances in which their services can be delivered effectively. But we must accept that there is no automatic right to design or preside over the delivery of buildings. If we do not carry the skills to do it, or refuse to adapt to new forms of procurement that reflect the changes of recent years, we will be left as 'gooseberries' while others join the party.

Constable Terrace, University of East Anglia student residence, by Rick Mather Architects

Planning the development and expansion of the University of East Anglia campus for 25 years from 1988 onwards, Rick Mather Architects' masterplan identified sites for new construction including several residential buildings. Catering for no less than 800 students, new low energy accommodation and communal facilities were constructed on two of these sites, one of which is Constable Terrace. Consisting of three-storey units of student study bedrooms, and a fourth floor, with two-person flats, the living rooms and kitchens face a southerly terrace and a pedestrian street. Energy conservation is recognised as a priority. Carefully conceived and detailed, the scheme is so energy efficient that no central heating is required. In addition to the new residences earlier work on the campus includes the Climatic Research Unit.

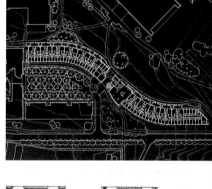

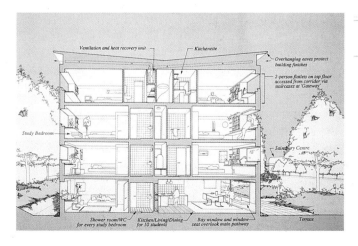

GROUND FLOOR PLAN   FIRST FLOOR PLAN   SECOND FLOOR PLAN   THIRD FLOOR PLAN

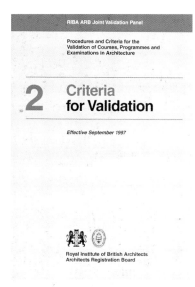

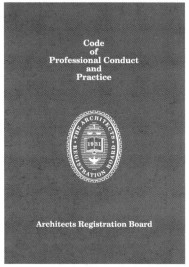

TOP TO BOTTOM:

RIBA ARB Joint Criteria for Validation;
ARB Code of Conduct 1997; ARB Code
of Conduct 1999

NO GOING BACK

The above is a particularly sobering warning for a profession that has embraced new forms of technology in both construction techniques and communication methods (high-tech and CAD respectively) but which continues, especially in the smaller scale of office that makes up some 65 per cent of architectural practice, to cling to the belief that traditional forms of appointment and contract can be maintained. We do need to protect the workloads of smaller practices and the right of communities to use local, smaller firms for public-sector projects, but it is for us to achieve such protection and opportunity *within* the constraints of new procurement methods. Despite the fact that many problems associated with increased costs lie outside the architect's control, it is futile to imagine that there will ever be a return to the sloppy old ways of delivering late and over-budget projects – particularly for state-funded projects such as primary schools that have for so long been an essential part of the workload of smaller firms.

So if our profession is to make an influence on new development in both the state and private sectors it must be willing to identify market changes and gain the skills to operate effectively in the new conditions that shape the way we must work in future to deliver buildings.

EDUCATION, EDUCATION, EDUCATION...

For too long there has been a general shift within our schools of architecture away from interest in, and teaching of construction technology. We must remember that architecture should remain an essentially vocational course: graduates need to be equipped with appropriate knowledge and skills for practice and they need to assume a 'professional' culture. They are expected to design functional buildings, effective in technical terms, and deliverable within predetermined parameters of cost and programme. It is a serious business and after seven years of training, students, sponsors, future employers and the construction industry expect a high level of 'rounded' competence.

If architects are to achieve what is demanded of them in the emerging territory of sustainable design, they will need to deliver technical competence. Being 'signed up' to the intention is not enough: architects must be able to demonstrate how sustainable buildings will be delivered.

It is therefore essential that students are supported by competent and inspiring teachers so that, particularly through their project work, they can explore and develop the necessary skills and gain the appropriate knowledge to deliver sustainable buildings. A brief look at the 'contents' section of Peter Smith's new book *Architecture in a Climate of Change*[12] reveals that the subject is vast: passive and active solar energy, the 'solar chimney', wind power, photovoltaics, super-insulation, natural ventilation and cooling strategies, life-cycle assessments, and so on. We should be able to set appropriate targets for energy use, incorporate 'smart' integral management systems within our buildings, and predict their performance in terms of energy use and emissions. If we develop the knowledge and skills, the market will turn to us to deliver, as it faces the inevitably increasing demands of society for ecologically responsible design.

OTHER SPHERES OF INFLUENCE

The RIBA has a substantial influence on research, itself sponsoring individual programmes. Applications for research into aspects of sustainable design will receive growing support. The Institute's work in exhibitions will continue and its advancement of the sustainability agenda through the media must expand. Competition briefs will routinely incorporate a sustainability component, and support for and co-operation with other groups and disciplines active in the field will be expanded.

CODES OF CONDUCT AND REGULATIONS

But whilst the RIBA can encourage and inspire its members, it cannot impose effective codes or regulations on practice in the performance of its duties to clients. Only government can achieve this, by introducing legislation to which those responsible for delivering projects must respond. The RIBA certainly has a major role in assisting government in the shaping of codes of practice, and helping government in developing new legislation, but that role must be imposed evenly across all projects if the market place is to be forced to behave responsibly. Our job as architects is to show what can be achieved, to publicise the results of our research, to encourage the market to demand ecologically sustainable design, and persuade the government to legislate for it.

RESPONDING TO NEW PRESSURES AND A NEW AGENDA

Food retailer Sainsbury's has shown what can be achieved in this area through its patronage of ecologically responsible design and smart building-management systems. Its work continues to be particularly successful in raising public awareness of the sustainability agenda, as demonstrated by the recently completed Greenwich superstore. Shortlisted for the 2000 Stirling Prize, the building was designed by its architects and service engineers (Chetwood Associates and Oscar Faber respectively) to a serious environmental agenda. It is claimed to be the most energy-efficient supermarket ever built, using some 50 per cent less energy than a standard store, and has achieved an 'excellent' rating by the BREEAM assessment method.

Sainsbury's has taken a responsible role that is exemplary in its research and development work on sustainability in buildings: indeed it has broken new ground in ecologically sustainable design. In time the public will increasingly learn from Sainsbury's instructive buildings and, as consumer awareness of the sustainability agenda increases, so they will demand more responsibility from the marketplace in its patronage of architecture. Architects and their colleagues within the other 'sister' professions having inspired this more responsible agenda, will in turn be obliged to respond to ever more demanding requirements in terms of sustainable design as their clients realise that the sale or supply of products and services from a 'sustainable' building is a prerequisite of meeting their customer preferences. 'We only buy from ecologically responsible suppliers' will be the cry of the enlightened consumer. This is the marketplace operating in its most sophisticated form.

In support of this example we must look to a whole generation of architects to develop a completely new architectural method in response to the sustainability agenda. Ultimately, this will lead to a new aesthetic within a wholly new architectural movement – Sustainable Architecture – a movement that will at last be worthy enough in terms of substance and ideology to replace the modern movement in architecture that has effectively dominated the discipline for the last 70 or so years.

The World Trade Center towers were a symbol of free markets and international trade. The terrorist attack has produced devastating results: the world's single most important piece of commercial infrastructure has been destroyed with huge loss of life and the cruel images of its collapse have been etched forever into our memories.

But despite the terrible physical damage and the awful human suffering that has been inflicted new buildings must be constructed. This provides an extraordinary opportunity for our American friends to create an architecture that puts sustainability to the fore of its agenda – an architecture that symbolises for the world a new way of building and living in harmony with nature. No more fitting tribute could be paid to the innocent people whose lives were cut short in this savage attack, and no more fitting monument could be constructed to symbolise the ideals which continue to underpin the American dream: *freedom* to live in harmony with nature, and *prosperity* for future generations who will not have to face the legacy that will otherwise arise through our misuse and abuse of the earth's resources.

As Peter Smith once said: 'If sustainable design isn't a moral imperative, what is?'.[13]

Notes

1. Paul Brown, *The Guardian*, 23 October 1989.
2. Chris Rose, *The Dirty Man of Europe – The Great British Pollution Scandal* (London: Simon and Schuster Ltd, 1990), p. 1.
3. Brian Edwards and Paul Hyett, *Rough Guide to Sustainability* (London: RIBA Publications, 2001), p 1.
4. Mike Davis, *Ecology of Fear – Los Angeles and the imagination of disaster* (Canada: Fitzhenry & Whiteside Ltd, 1998) Also (New York: Metropolitan Books, 1998).
5. Marco Goldschmied's inaugural address as President of RIBA, October 1999.
6. Paul Hyett quoted in David Littlefield, 'Hyett set to tackle "reactive" EH', *Architects' Journal*, 28 June 2001, p. 4.
7. 'Grimshaw's sets green standard', *Building Design*, 12 January 2001.
8. Eric Parry in *Architectural Research Quarterly (ARQ)*, Vol. 1, University of Cambridge Department of Architecture, EMAP, Winter 1995.
9. Brian Edwards and Paul Hyett, *Rough Guide to Sustainability*, (London: RIBA Publications, 2001), p. 17.
10. Adapted from Peter F. Smith, *Options for a Flexible Planet* (Sheffield: Sustainable Building Network, Sheffield University, 1996), p. 38, in Brian Edwards and Paul Hyett, *Rough Guide to Sustainability* (London: RIBA Publications, 2001), p. 4.
11. Brian Edwards and Paul Hyett, *Rough Guide to Sustainability* (London: RIBA Publications, 2001), p. 4.
12. Peter F. Smith, *Architecture in a Climate of Change – A Guide to Sustainable Design* (Oxford: Architectural Press, 2001).
13. Peter F. Smith in debate at RIBA Council during Paul Hyett's presentation of proposals for curricula adjustments to incorporate mandatory teaching of 'sustainability' in RIBA validated courses.

Sainsburys, Greenwich, by Chetwood Associates

ISO 14001 AND THE ARCHITECTURAL IMAGINATION

The Eden Project
Nicholas Grimshaw & Partners

The Eden Project, a £57m showcase for global bio-diversity, consists of three principal structural elements brought together in a 15-hectare landscaped site, formerly a worked out Cornish clay-pit. These elements are the 'biomes', a sequence of transparent domes that encapsulate humid tropic and warm temperate regions. Now complete, it represents the perfect fulfilment of Richard Buckminster Fuller's vision of the maximum enclosed volume within the minimal surface area. The biomes are a sinuous sequence of 8 inter-linked geodesic domes threading around 2.2 hectares of the site. These 'Bucky balls' range in size from 18m to 65m radius in order to accommodate the varying heights of the plant life.

The exact location of the biomes on site has been determined by Solar Modelling, a sophisticated technique that indicates where structures will benefit most from passive solar gain. The architects have capitalised upon this gain by cladding the biomes with ETFE (Ethylene Tetra Fluoro Ethylene) foil. ETFE is highly transparent to a wide spectrum of light and as a lightweight material, it is capable of covering wide spans supported by the most minimal of structures. This ensures that the maximum amount of daylight filters through the biomes' skin to nourish the plant life within and, as the foil is triple-layered within the frame of each hexagon, that its heat is retained.

There is an 'active' heating system in place in the biomes, but this is supplementary: a means of 'fine-tuning' the natural passive system. Similarly, ventilation and water strategies have been devised with the aid of innovative Computational Fluid Dynamic Studies to minimise natural wastage. Rainwater is recycled for humidification. Even ground water seepage, a potential problem in other circumstances, has been transformed into a positive resource, being distributed within the envelope for irrigation purposes.

The Visitors' Centre opened to the public on 16 May 2000 and whole project opened on 17 March 2001. To date Eden has had upwards of 1,000,000 visitors and has won seven architectural awards. The project is also a good example of how an environmental management system can be used to assess design development. Nicholas Grimshaw & Partners has certification to ISO 14001, the international standard for environmental management systems. To date, the standard has been adopted mainly by the manufacturing industry and Nicholas Grimshaw & Partners has therefore become the first major firm of architects to obtain certification. The International Standard states that its aim is to support environmental protection and prevention of pollution in balance with socio-economic needs.

Nicholas Grimshaw & Partners has developed a system that assists architects in controlling the impacts that projects may have on humans, flora, fauna and natural resources; water, air and atmosphere, land and soil, local community and cultural features. Generic design clauses in the system provide measures for controlling the impacts and can be adapted to suit individual projects. The assessment system has been designed with ease of use in mind and the rose diagram forms an integral component. As a tool it provides a quick pictorial representation of the assessment results for that particular stage of the project. From this concise information design leaders will be aware of any potential shortcomings as well as successes and make the corrective decisions.

An assessment method allows design inputs to be categorised as dark green (best practice), mid green, light green (a minimum target for all projects

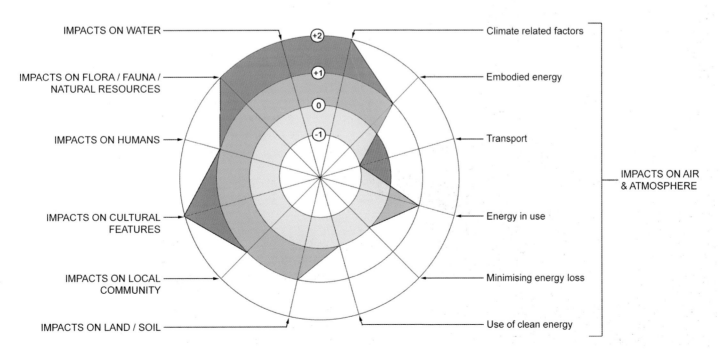

to achieve) or red (substandard). Environmental reviews are carried out at key project stages and any areas that show up as 'red' must be addressed by the project architect before proceeding to the next stage. The project architect, before proceeding to the next stage, addresses any areas that show up as 'red'. By attributing a score of +2 for dark green, +1 for mid-green, 0 for light green and –1 for red the assessment allows an overall score to be calculated for a project and consequently target figures can be set. The assessment system allows an overall score to be calculated for a project and consequently target figures can be set. The intention is that the targets will be raised every year to encourage continual improvement.

The system aims to make it easier for architects to design in an environmentally sustainable way and encourages a thoroughness of approach to the subject by identifying all the main impacts together with proposed measures for controlling them. By analysing and comparing the performance of projects within the practice, areas for improvement can be noted and addressed by means of additional research or training as appropriate. Achievements can also be identified and the knowledge shared.

First point of contact documents now contain environmental statements and the means by which all potential projects are assessed now include environmental sustainability as a key criterion. The system will be used on all new projects and will assist in greening schemes such as speculative offices where conditions can make the incorporation of sustainable design very difficult. A research team is continuing to develop the ISO 14001 system to give rapid access to design advice and background information.

First point of contact documents now contain environmental statements and the means by which all potential projects are assessed now include environmental sustainability as a key criterion. The system will be used on all new projects and will assist in greening schemes such as speculative offices where conditions can make the incorporation of sustainable design very difficult. A research team is continuing to develop the ISO 14001 system to give rapid access to design advice and background information.

For further information on ISO 14001 and practice projects please contact Nicholas Grimshaw & Partners on 020 7291 4141 or by email at communications@ngrimshaw.co.uk. The rose diagram and text are reproduced courtesy of Nicholas Grimshaw & Partners.

PHASE CHANGES

Explore at Bristol
Wilkinson Eyre Architects

The technique of thermal storage is interesting at Explore at Bristol, by Wilkinson Eyre Architects. The project was completed in 2000 with Woolf Ltd, Ove Arup and Partners, Symonds Projects, Davis Langdon & Everest, Arup Associates, Arup Fire and WS Atkins. It consists of a 7-metre-high clear acrylic cylinder filled with hundreds of tennis ball sized plastic spheres containing eutectic salts. The salts change from solid to liquid at 27°C, thus cooling or warming the surrounding water. The balls also contain a thermochromatic resin that changes colour as their temperature rises and falls – changing gradually from pink to white and back again. The tank provides the building's main energy store for heating and cooling. On summer nights, electric heat pumps on the roof will freeze the eutectic solution using cheap-rate electricity, and the freezing point of 27°C matches the maximum pump operating efficiency. The pumps work much the same way as a domestic fridge, cooling the tank by taking heat out. In the winter the system works in the opposite mode by warming the eutectic solution as a storage medium. Eutectic systems are rare outside large manufacturing facilities and processing plants.

BEAUTIFULLY SIMPLE

Gateshead Millennium Bridge, Gateshead
Wilkinson Eyre Architects

The design is the winning entry to the 1997 competition for a major new crossing over the Tyne. The project, promoted by Gateshead Metropolitan Borough Council, links the newly developed Newcastle Quayside with the ambitious plans for redevelopment of east Gateshead. The idea is beautifully simple; a pair of arches, one forming the deck and the other supporting it, pivot around their common springing point to allow shipping to pass beneath. The motion is efficient and rational, evoking the action of a closed eye slowly opening. It is dramatic beyond the capabilities of previously explored opening mechanisms. The £14.5 million project has involved structural and services engineers Gifford & Partners, with Harbour & General/Volker Stevin as main contractors. Subcontractors included Kvaerner Markham, Watson Steel Ltd and Jonathan Speirs & Associates for Gateshead MBC.

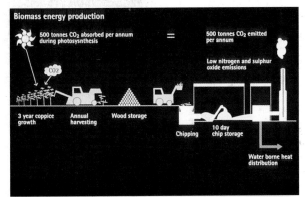

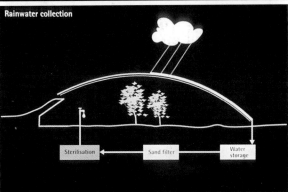

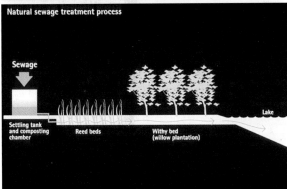

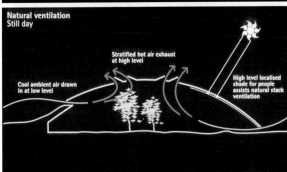

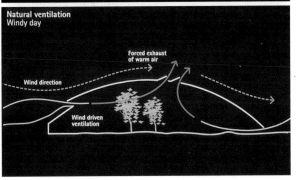

THE UNDULATIONS OF THE SURROUNDING LANDSCAPE

The Great Glasshouse
National Botanic Garden of Wales, Carmarthenshire
Foster and Partners

The Great Glasshouse in the National Botanic Garden of Wales reinvents the glasshouse for the twenty-first century, offering a model for sustainability. Costing £8 million and open to the public since May 2000, this is the largest single-span glasshouse in the world. It contains more than a thousand plant species – many endangered – and conserves specimens from Mediterranean climates around the globe.

Set in hills overlooking the Towy Valley in Carmarthenshire, the building forms the centrepiece of the 230-hectare park of the former Middleton Hall. Its tilted, elliptical plan creates a toroidal form for the roof, measuring 99 by 55 metres, which swells from the ground like a glassy hillock, echoing the undulations of the surrounding landscape. Landscape architects for the glasshouse are Gustafson Porter, and for the gardens Colvin and Moggridge. Construction and project managers were Schal, with structural engineers Anthony Hunt Associates, mechanical and electrical engineers Max Fordham & Partners, and quantity surveyors Symonds Ltd.

The aluminium glazing system with its tubular-steel supporting structure is designed to minimise materials and maximise light transmission. Twenty-four arches spring from a concrete ring beam, rising to 15 metres at the apex of the dome. Because the roof curves in two directions, only the central arches rise perpendicular to the base; the outer arches lean at progressively steep angles.

To optimise energy usage, conditions inside and outside are monitored by a computer-controlled system, which adjusts the supply of heat and opens the glazing panels in the roof to achieve desired levels of temperature, humidity and air movement.

The building's concrete substructure is oriented to provide protection from cold northerly winds and is concealed by a covering of turf so that the three entrances on the northern side appear to be cut discreetly into the hillside. Within this base are a public concourse, a cafeteria, educational spaces and services installations.

The principal heat source is a biomass boiler, located in the Park's Energy Centre, which burns timber trimmings. This method is remarkably clean when compared with fossil fuels, and because the growing plants absorb as much (CO_2) as is released during combustion the CO2 cycle is broadly neutral. Rainwater collected from the roof supplies 'grey water' for irrigation and flushing lavatories; waste from the lavatories is treated in reed beds before release into a watercourse.

TOP TO BOTTOM:
Biomass energy diagram; Natural sewage treatment diagram; Rainwater collection diagram; Natural ventilation diagram for a still day; Natural ventilation diagram for a windy day.

Chapter 2

Zen and the Art of Life-Cycle Maintenance

Austin Williams, *Architects' Journal*

Statue of Liberty

SELF-SUFFICIENCY

Bodhgaya is a small rural setting in Bihar, one of the most deprived areas of India. Located about 195 kilometres southeast of the Hindu holy city of Varanasi, Bodhgaya is the site of a totally separate Indian tradition, the place where Buddha is deemed to have found Enlightenment some 2,500 years ago. While Varanasi has thrived (it is one of the most populous places in India), Bodhgaya is essentially a village. The main attraction has been the ancient Bodhi tree, under which Buddha is reputed to have sat for 90 days before finding himself. But with the commencement of one of the largest and most dramatic construction projects in Asia, scheduled for completion in 2006, things are about to change for this rural backwater.

While international media has focused on the desecration of Buddhist iconography by the Taliban of Afghanistan, a five-year construction project has begun. The Maitreya project will make Bodhgaya the site of one of the true wonders of the world. The 'building' is a giant Buddha, awesome in its dimensions. At 152 metres high, or half as high again as the Statue of Liberty and larger than the London Eye, it will contain internal areas of cathedral-like proportions. The scheme is part of a £100 million, 16-hectare masterplanning exercise in the region, involving monastic quarters, offices and ancillary accommodation for Buddhists and tourists alike, all within a three-storey perimeter 'living wall'.[1]

It might seem churlish to criticise such an impressive and challenging scheme as the Maitreya project, and it is not the intention to promulgate the type of disapproval levelled at the Millennium Dome, for example that the money could have been better spent on poverty alleviation or social welfare programmes.[2] Indeed, the clients of the Maitreya project have already provided much praiseworthy knock-on benefit with, among other things, the construction of medical facilities and a new airport terminal. Regardless of this regeneration-by-default, the ethos of sustainability is a pervasive feature of the scheme – an ethos that prioritises 'the self', even when issues are presented in terms of 'the social'.

Situated in a remote region of rural India, the self-sufficiency of the Maitreya project is an understandable reaction to the untrustworthiness – or non-existence – of mains backup services. The architects have therefore designed-in a massive underground aquifer that provides potable water for the compound to see it through the drought months, solar collectors to provide all of the electricity needs, and reed beds to treat the waste produced. While it would be unreasonable to demand that the architect or the client solve the infrastructural deficit of Bihar province, it is a shame that their 1,000-year vision is based on no improvement in the extant Third World conditions. Providing mains infrastructure, or extending some of the infrastructure from the scheme-works, could have benefited more than just the compound. Yet the fact that the design team is building-in self-sufficiency, on the assumption that there will be no change for the better for the surrounding area in future, says it all. Sustainability is indeed a bleak vision.

Take, for example, the views of Brian Marks, partner at Fulcrum Engineering, environmental consultant to the Maitreya project, who says: 'the living wall is the modern equivalent to a castle wall...designed to withstand attack from 200 armed raiders'. He continues, 'for Marks the wall will also define the boundary within which the complex will have to be self-sufficient in water, power and waste. This is partly to satisfy the client's sustainability agenda, and, more conjecturally, to safeguard the statue against any future breakdown in society during its millennial lifespan. One of the main parameters in designing the monument for a 1,000-year life is what is going to happen to Bangladesh – if the country floods, the inhabitants have to go somewhere.[3] So even such an exciting project as this is premised on a depressingly negative worldview that if global warming doesn't get you the invading hordes of the disenfranchised will.

The building, therefore, can be seen as the material and philosophical embodiment of Buddhist dharma, but in a way that captures the very Western precautionary paranoia of the twenty-first century. The architects have been keen to promote and unify the client's moral ethos with the sustainable credentials of the scheme. Nick Readett-Bayley, design architect at Aros in London, is understandably reticent about defining the scheme as a model of appropriate technology, although he describes the project in recognisably similar terms. The Buddha project has maximised waste disposal, water catchment and energy generation to serve its own site, and no connection of infrastructure has been developed to satisfy the needs of the villagers living outside its boundaries. In other words, even though it is a magnificent engineering feat, it reinforces E. F. Schumacher's philosophy of learning 'to recognise the boundaries of poverty'.

For Schumacher, 'a project that does not fit educationally and organisationally into the environment, will be an economic failure and a cause of disruption'.[4] This interpretation of the word 'environment' portrays a static snapshot of the world, rather than a fluid moment in the history of development.

The concept of stasis is central to the debate over environmental efficiency. Readett-Bayley explains that the completed scheme will have 'the same environmental impact as if the site had remained virgin paddy field'. In essence, this means that there is equilibrium between energy used and produced in the project, with no 'detrimental environmental harm'.[5] This is quite a staggering claim for such a vast structure. Can it be that such a scheme, of such proportions, can have a limited detrimental impact? And why has that become such a proud boast anyway?

ENVIRONMENTALLY HARMLESS BUILDING

We should remember that the concept of what is meant by 'detrimental' has shifted dramatically from the recent past of eco-zealotry, when building per se was portrayed as a harmful activity. Reactions such as that of Dale Bates, who claimed it was 'after visiting a construction site that I realised that the "new and improved" building materials were making me sick',[6] are now few and far between. There is now an acceptance of the inevitability of changes to the material world, though this is tempered by a clamour for a simpler life. However, the majority of architects recognise that they cannot follow the mysticism proffered by Prince Charles, when he suggested working 'with the grain of nature'.[7] In *What is Nature?* Kate Soper usefully conjectures that 'the one thing that is not "natural" is nature itself';[8] there is no timeless way of building any more than there is a timeless way of rural existence. The bucolic charm of the British countryside has been thoroughly transformed from its previous wilderness by the development of farming processes over the centuries. Dame Mary Warnock argued convincingly that 'it cannot be intervention (in the environment) as such that is held to be against nature…that is no more relevant an argument…than it would be to claim that a replacement hip joint is against nature'.[9]

Clearly the argument that ecological building means not building at all has become a bit of a straw man. Environmentalists now accept that 'economic growth requires more and more buildings', but they advocate that this can be 'challenged by the development of interest in the use of natural materials that are fully renewable with only limited amounts of manufacturing and processing'.[10] We are supposed to be able to build without detriment to (or any effect on) the natural environment, using supposedly natural materials – those that are defined as minimally modified by the human hand. The objective of sustainable architecture now tends to mean at the very least 'responsible' building processes and typologies that minimise the resultant and unavoidable impact on the natural environment.

The old assumption that sustainable architecture is about small, vernacular buildings no longer holds true, and through people like Ken Yeang's promotion of the 'Bioclimatic Tower', even the more reserved eco-architects now tend to embrace high-rise construction:

> On the premise that both intensive developments and tall buildings are inevitable in our cities, the bioclimatic skyscraper will contribute to reduced energy consumption in the built urban environment and will be more ecologically beneficial than the conventional skyscraper since it achieves this *passively*. At the same time, the bioclimatic skyscraper provides a more aesthetically fulfilling, human and safer high-rise built environment for its occupants.[11]

Although these days it is unusual to suggest that we should not build on a large and visually intrusive scale, the belief is that whatever the size, design and location of the building its environmental impact should be kept as small as possible – what Herbert Girardet calls 'steady-state' design.[12] This conceptualisation is more than simply about the physical building – it is about accountability. In fact, 'steady state', 'minimal impact', 'environmentally benign' or 'passive processes' are all mantras of zero-impact ecological accounting, through which sustainable architects make apologies for the fossil-fuelled, industrial misdeeds of others, and promise not to stray from the environmental straight-and-narrow in the future.

Considerations about sustainability today differ dramatically from the design efficiencies of the past. The twentieth century specifically saw a rise in conflicting architectural aspirations determined by the reaction to the onset of modernity. Very little was sacrosanct and it was quite common for leading architects to challenge the notion of the restraining influence of 'the detritus of dead epochs', as Le Corbusier defiantly called it. 'The great task incumbent on us,' he wrote, 'is that of making a proper environment for our existence, and clearing away from our cities the dead bones that putrefy in them'.

> We must construct cities for to-day…The machine age…has not yet achieved that architectural style by means of which it will gratify its material needs.[13]

Many advocates of sustainability have attempted to reclaim the great modernist or technocratic dream as their own.[14] Unfortunately, Le Corbusier's refreshing boldness is sadly lacking today, when even the most high-profile designers have cause to express themselves in mystical terms, relying on uncharacteristic

We should remember that the concept of what is meant by 'detrimental' has shifted dramatically from the recent past of eco-zealotry, when building per se was portrayed as a harmful activity.

restraint rather than on confident authority. 'Nature is seldom clumsy,' says Chris Wilkinson, of Wilkinson Eyre. 'It is a pity, therefore, that many of our man-made structures are so heavy and monumental. I prefer the aboriginal concept of treading lightly on this earth'.[15]

This ironic aspiration for design at the start of a new millennium represents a new phase for architects; architects are looking beyond the post-modern rejection of the Big Idea, and instead for the small idea. As distinct from the various movements of the last century, architects are providing themselves with more constraints, rather than seeking to rid themselves of restrictions. The autonomy of an architect's role is now subsumed in a bewildering array of third-party interventions, and architecture is prone to a minefield of dos and don'ts from Quality Assurance auditors, health and safety professionals, management consultants and government design quangos. And perhaps more worrying is the tendency for architects to self-regulate in the name of environmental protectionism.

Ultimately, the restrictions on architects are severe enough, and calling for more is perverse. We may admire John Pawson's minimalist approach, but to be told that his philosophy should infuse all of our responses to architectural challenges would be a depressing thought for many. While lots of materials, time and money may not necessarily produce good architecture, they certainly provide more opportunities – by definition.

A PURPOSE FOR DOING MORE WITH LESS

Admittedly achieving more with less has always been a badge of honour for architects, and a building done well with fewer resources will usually be better regarded than an equivalent building that uses many. But even though this sounds simplistic, it reflects an understandable appreciation of efficient design. The problem is that the resultant canonisation of achievement through adversity risks demeaning the transformative potential of architectural aesthetics. Even though Buckminster Fuller coined the phrase 'ephemeralization'[16] as the concept of doing more with less, he still used it as a starting point for doing yet more. This is not the premise today. We are now enjoined to use limited resources 'imaginatively'. The idea that people should push for more resources is anathema to the current focus on 'realism':

> In the lobby of the lavish UN building, an exhibition of best practice developments was displayed showing 'responsible' low-cost urban management proposals. The most visited attraction was a plaintive display by the Slum Dwellers Association who noted that 'most housing stock in the world today is designed, constructed and financed by the poor. Do governments want to support it or negate?' They had mocked up a humble slum shack and had costed it out to $878.50. They asked, 'Is this too much to ask for?' No, as a matter of fact, it is far too little to ask for. Unfortunately, as stakeholders in partnering relationships with government for the stable management of their fragile domestic economy, they don't think it reasonable to ask for any more.[17]

Coincidentally, architects too seem to have lowered their aspiration for development. Even Jean Nouvel, the recent Royal Institute of British Architects (RIBA) Gold Medal winner, points out that on 'the other side of the glorification of Western "progress"…it is possible to use local resources (wind, sun, ocean), before it is attempted…to offer development help with exorbitantly expensive infrastructure systems of Western buildings and ways of thinking'.[18] Certainly it is probably cheaper to construct from indigenous materials, but Nouvel's comment represents more than that. It represents a game of presenting limitations as positively beneficial – both to the designer and to society as a whole. It is simply a variant of the wartime 'tighten your belts' policy for the new millennium, which has a direct memory for the western world, as recognised in an article in *The Guardian* subtitled 'Lessons from the Second World War are inspiring environmentalists':

> The government's propaganda hinged on this ability to make people feel they had to contribute to the war effort. One poster urged: 'Buy nothing for your personal pleasure or comfort, use no transport, call on no labour – unless urgent necessity compels. To be free with your money today is not a merit. It is contemptible. To watch every penny shows your will to win'.[19]

Katherine Shonfield also makes positive comparisons with the dynamics of the western war economy in *Walls Have Feelings*, where she supposes that 'the effective suspension of the market during wartime leads to the most efficient use of resources possible'.[20] There is a creeping tendency to strive for maximum inconvenience as a shock tactic to convince people of the urgent need to adopt sustainable lifestyles. However, because of the difficulty in creating a believably positive reminiscence of the wartime experience for us in the West, most of the discussion revolves around the closest thing – the 'prudent' poverty of the developing world, where the sustainable noble savage lives.

> Knowing the limits of one's discipline may be positive in itself, and there are many ways in which architects can provide enabling strategies to help people make better use of their resources. And in spite of the crime, drugs and insanitary congestion there's a spatial richness in places like

Mathare (a Kenyan 'community' of some 400,000 people crammed into an a abandoned quarry) and a dynamic attitude to shelter which, to those used to a more product-oriented building industry, can seem quite refreshing.[21]

Attempting to turn around the power relationship between the First and the Third World, Robin Nicholson, Director at Edward Cullinan Architects says, in 'learning from their simplicity…it's the first time that the developed nations need something from the developing ones!'[22] This presumably means we are supposed to learn the benefits of living within pressing limits, even though the malnutrition and insanitary conditions that come with underdeveloped status shatters the romance a little.

Despite the fact that the mainstream glorification of architectural constraints is only a recent phenomenon, it has been bubbling under for a considerable amount of time. Writing about Egan-style partnering, *Architects' Journal* editor Isabel Allen says 'constraints can be inspirational…There are few things more stultifying than sitting alone with infinite possibilities and a blank piece of paper.'[23] While this might be true (anecdotes about novelists' and architects' mental blocks when confronted with a virgin sheet of paper are legend), we should be honest in stating that a reduced palette is just that. To pretend otherwise is to parrot the mock-Eastern philosophy, which suggests that 'the more we know, the less we know'.

However, less is not more. Having a blacklist of unacceptable specification items, as do many housing associations, local authorities and developers, or ruling out certain materials because of their high quotient of embodied energy, reduces the opportunities for a full exploration of the design and detailing potentials of a scheme. It may consequently concentrate the mind to dream up alternatives or to make do and mend, but this is certainly not a progressive perspective, or a desirable starting point. This is the architectural equivalent of the UK transport 'policy' that restricting car use will mean people use alternative modes of transport. Unfortunately, it tends to mean that people simply have to cram themselves into the only available, overused and generally unsatisfactory alternatives. Similarly, design potential is denied.

Much of this shift in emphasis should be laid at the door of the construction radicals themselves: the very people who are now continuing the policies of sustainable restraint with a renewed fervour. In the 1960s and 1970s, in an era of rebelliousness, DIY and self-build protest action was a dynamic counter-cultural activity. Peter Ward presents self-help as an example of 'freeing oneself from the interference from the state.[24] After years of rebelling against inadequate and unresponsive state provision, activists began 'providing for themselves'. However, in today's climate, criticism of state provision has become a mainstream activity indulged by the state itself. It is not just cash-starved authorities that are pleased to see people provide for themselves – the United Nations (UN) convenes global conferences on the subject. The community ethos thus generated is a fundamental aspect to the social policy of the built environment, and has had a debilitating influence on the architectural debate as well as, more worryingly, in the political arena.

The connection with Third World 'prudent consumption' is apposite. In the mid-1980s, John Turner, icon of the self-build movement and Third World aid, redefined the housing problem in terms of 'attainable and available resource use instead of the conventional and unattainable unit production targets'. Instead he argued for 'a new focus…on ways and means of complementing and supporting local initiatives, rather than "mobilizing" or directing it through co-operation by either the state, as in the east, or the market, as in the west'. He preferred 'the current emphasis on negotiation and mediation'.[25] Coincidentally, sustainability thrives on a conciliatory approach to architectural issues.

In the 1960s and 1970s, in an era of rebelliousness, DIY and self-build protest action was a dynamic counter-cultural activity…However, in today's climate, criticism of state provision has become a mainstream activity indulged by the state itself.

THE SUFFERING WORLD

Maybe the Buddhist iconography is apposite. In *The Green Skyscraper* Ken Yeang requires that, 'the designer must be aware of entropy in natural systems in the biosphere and not contribute by his designed system to further accelerating the entropic processes in the natural environment' because 'human activity throughout history has expropriated natural resources', and has 'eroded much of the biosphere's natural self regulating system (its ability to heal)'.[26] This anthropomorphic rhetoric conjures up images of Gaia on a heart monitor. The challenge, as Zen Master Seung Sahn says, is this:

When enlightenment and correct life come together, that means your life becomes truth, the suffering world becomes paradise. Then you can change this suffering world into paradise for others.[27]

Sustainable architects may no longer use hippie phrases, but they continue to situate themselves at the forefront of a damage-limitation crusade, aiming to save the planet in order to save themselves.

Respect relationships between spirit and matter. Consider all aspects of human settlement including community, dwelling, industry and trade in terms of existing and evolving connections between spiritual and material consciousness.[28]

Or vice versa. Or maybe just trying to rationalise their purpose beyond mere self-indulgence. Whatever the reasons (which are fairly indeterminate), the abstract desire to modify our individual actions in deference to the planet reveals itself as a codified way of trying to give ourselves, and humanity, meaning.

Other people can talk about how to expand the destiny of mankind. I just want to talk about how to fix a motorcycle. I think that what I have to say has more lasting value.[29]

In retrospect, Robert Pirsig's philosophical pretensions were precursors of the post-modern era, capturing a mood that says 'the truth is indefinable and can be apprehended only by non-rational means'. As Allmendinger puts it, 'truth has no correspondence to reality but is merely a matter of convention in post-modern eyes'.[30] Pirsig presented an opt-out rather than a programme of change, but by decrying the duality of subject and object, demeaned both.

Pirsig's classic *Zen and the Art of Motorcycle Maintenance*, his 'inquiry into values', written in the mid-1970s was of, and ahead of, its time. As a quirky bestseller, it never really represented any mass defection to Eastern mysticism, except by a minority of devotees, but it did key into the general frustration among an audience at a market-driven and polarised society – one in which tension between classes and geopolitical interests was unmediated. Its equal relevance today is in the glorification of political disengagement as the precursor to political change. Saskia Sassen calls it the 'dynamics of the disenfranchised',[31] and it clearly resonates with the sustainable objectives of the sustainable chattering classes.

In a similar way, the theoretical engagement of Lord Rogers with the disenfranchised represents the changing face of the debate. The different emphasis between both of his most recent books indicates a move from a call for moral rectitude to a demand for self-awareness and self-restraint. There are also fewer demands for proscriptive policy-making in his later work. In *Cities for a Small Planet*,[32] the edited transcripts of his influential Reith Lecture series, Rogers cites 'sustainability' (or derivatives) on 97 out of 175 pages. Three years later, in *Cities for a Small Country*,[33] the update written during work on the Urban Task Force, sustainability was not to be found anywhere in the book. Instead, a new set of generic descriptors had taken its place, which might be labelled the 'social responsibility indicators'. These included the promotion of 'social integration', 'social change', 'social cohesion' and the campaign against 'social polarisation' which were mentioned on at least as many pages as sustainability had been in his previous text. Sustainability is no longer about what you do, but what you try to do; it is about what you are. This is architecture as social policy with sustainability as the new secular religion.

The correlation between sustainability, moral restraint and mysticism has been evident for years, from the abstemious sense of guilt in *Beyond the Limits*,

> The human world is beyond its limits...the future, to be viable at all, must be one of drawing back, easing down, healing.[34]

as penitence for the sin of modernity in *The Gaia Atlas of Cities*,

> Le Corbusier planned only one real city, Chandigarh, a new capital for India's Punjab. He designed it as an American or European city, suitable for the routine use of cars. Chandigarh's spatial arrangement is for the machine age, not for the traditional Indian way of life.[35]

and to the work ethic of material sacrifice to facilitate a better world in *Factor Four*:

> the World Bank and other lending institutions should swiftly stop most of those destructive schemes for further resource exploitation which tend to depress world market prices for the respective commodities. That mechanism benefits the North more than the South to whom the benefits allegedly are meant to accrue...It is the message from Rio de Janeiro, sustainable development, which will very likely induce the world to stop overexploiting resources and underusing human labour.[36]

While Brenda and Robert Vale, gurus of 'green buildings', intersperse their text with Hindu allegories,[37] Ted Trainer puts forward an evangelical case for a 'radical conserver society'.[38]

Though generally cynical about the motivation behind many environmentalists, Matt Ridley pertinently observes that 'it is now theology, not science, that drives global warming alarmists'.[39] The same could be said of past sustainability advocates. Whether it is the fundamentalism of eco-warriors or the pulpit of environmental advocacy, each has an unmistakable whiff of sermonising.

ARCHITECTURAL SELF-RIGHTEOUSNESS

As relatively free-spirited individuals, however, architects do not tend to want to be bounced into eco-compliance. Naturally they want to believe that it has been their decision to accept the environmental parameters regardless of the fact that demands for sustainable design are everywhere. The omnipresence of self-righteous sustainability has allowed space for government agencies and lobby groups to ease off a little – to no longer preach or moralise but to allow each to find their own path. The passivity of achieving social relevance from individual actions – or the global significance of local issues – is often taken to exemplify the sustainability agenda:

> The three directors at Leeds Environmental Design Associates live and breathe sustainability. Not only do they cycle to work, but they run gas-powered cars for longer journeys. One of the three,

The omnipresence of self-righteous sustainability has allowed space for government agencies and lobby groups to ease off a little – to no longer preach or moralise but to allow each to find their own path.

James Haigh, even measures his daily carbon dioxide emissions as a way of monitoring how much his actions have contributed to the greenhouse gases that cause global warming.[40]

Not everybody goes to this extreme, but Rab Bennett's Wessex Water Headquarters, for example, exemplifies the design-as-individual-duty concept, taking a perverse interest in the building's environmental credentials. Since some elements of the structure had to be imported from abroad, Bennett ensured that they were manufactured from a region that used energy from renewable sources, in order to minimise the use of non-renewable resources! The ability, by some, to indulge in an almost yogic posturing of purity of purpose and hence achieve absolution from culpability, is a luxury not available to most people operating on the less spiritual plane.

The Straw Bale House in London by Sarah Wigglesworth and Jeremy Till, and the House for the Future by Jestico + Whiles, are two more high-profile, pseudo alternative-technology 'solutions' to environmental problems – costing significant amounts of money. These styles of architecture earn large quantities of EcoHomes points for 'verifiable' environmental performance, and even more brownie points for moral rectitude.[41]

THE SEARCH FOR MEANING

In fact, very few commentators disagree with the notion that the old energy-intensive ways of building need to change, although no one seems to know with any certainty what the new way of building should be. The only certainty seems to be the need to change our ways; to what is less clear. It is this lack of direction (celebrated by sustainability advocates) that is reinforcing a sense of uncertainty in architectural practice. Al Gore suggested in his book *Earth in the Balance* that 'we must make the rescue of the environment the central organising principle for civilisation'.[42] Meanwhile, Warwick Fox, writing in *Ethics and the Built Environment*, says:

> the 'green' imperative of sustainability…links directly to issues of human intra-generational justice, human intergenerational justice, the ethics of the human-non-human relationship (including the preservation of global diversity) and, ultimately, questions concerning the richness, beauty and even survival of life on Earth.[43]

Each attempts to give meaning to a resolutely unquantifiable concept of sustainability. But by making sustainability (whatever that is) an ethical imperative, good architects, whose job it is to compound 'individual effort with social needs and desires',[44] are now placed centre-stage in a battle to prove themselves worthy of their title. Brian Edwards notes: 'no architecture has moral validity unless it addresses…being environmentally sustainable'.[45] There are still some who 'refuse to be the world's environmental policeman',[46] but sadly, even this type of critical response is one of exasperated evasion, rather than confrontation. With moral pressure forcing the hand of architects, it is easy to portray those who continue to build 'in the old way' as no better than environmental vandals.

It is now commonplace to accept that 'solutions to problems in one area can create problems for someone else to solve in another.'[47] In this scenario, architects are labelled with greater potential for doing harm, through the 'connexity'[48] of their actions. The formalisation of these unknowable detrimental harms, via the standardised prism of risk-management and litigation, has left many architects uncertain about the unforeseeable knock-on effects of their actions. We are told to be eternally vigilant.

But it is not a logical process of cause and effect. Sustainable architects have to participate in the never-ending process of assessing the interconnections between actions and consequences. In any given project one could consider a vast range of issues *ad nauseam*, from the amount of energy embodied in the materials, the transportation implications on non-renewable diesel stocks, CO_2 emissions resulting from the travel patterns of millions of construction workers and end-users, or the costs to the nation in health-care treatment arising from industrial and traffic accidents.

It should be mentioned that the inability to define sustainability, sustainable development and sustainable architecture has spawned an industry in formulating ways of supporting and disproving claims of eco-friendliness. Just one year after the Brundtland Report, 23 different interpretations of sustainability were detailed in *Blueprint for a Green Economy*, from a range of ecologists as well as the World Bank and Margaret Thatcher.[49] A brief snapshot of guidelines and advice currently on offer today include Building Services Research and Information Association conferences, Construction Industry Research and Information Association documents, ISO 14001, Quality Assurance criteria, Building Research Establishment brochures, Construction Industry Council advice, and the Royal Institution of Chartered Surveyors (RICS) *Comprehensive Project Appraisal*. There is rivalry between the Steel Construction Institute and the Concrete Society to demonstrate whether steel or concrete is the more sustainable. There is Ove Arup's SPeAR programme, and myriad other professional consultancies as diverse as Llewelyn-Davis, WS Atkins, Oscar Faber or Buro Happold, quangos like the Environment Agency, and the reorganised government ministries.

Sustainable architects have to participate in the never-ending process of assessing the interconnections between actions and consequences.

To those third parties who have carved a niche for themselves as sustainable paragons, whether as commercial consultants or moral guardians, the more regulatory the criteria the better. The dangers of the infatuation with sustainability indices are threefold:

- First, architects should not even concern themselves with the ethics or production values of subcontractors or suppliers. Even so, the idea that architects should research the manufacturing processes behind a given product (or even worry about it) is a means of inputting (or interfering) in the business practices of others.

- Second, insistence on indicators and transparency means that we will inevitably begin to develop architecture inured to bureaucratic intervention and immunised from real innovative design applications. Inevitably, the tick-box will become a more common feature of architectural practice, and indicators will become a mainstay of architectural education, where form-filling gurus will impart their karma to impressionable students.

- Third, the developmental model that says that humankind has a historical duty to maximise its impact on the natural environment is being shelved. Learning to live with less – the *cri de coeur* of sustainability – has created a paranoid and stultifying climate that ultimately slows down a process of change and puts real development on the back-burner. Ultimately, with precaution its watchword, sustainability indicators lead to proscriptive regulation, or worse, self-proscription; lowering one's sights to that deemed achievable rather than elevating our gaze to the higher goal of what is desirable.

Obviously not all sustainability indicators are presented in terms of restraint. Fortunately, not everyone accepts the logical conclusions put forward by Janine Benyus, who advocates that we should 'respect nature's limits or pass up what technology promises, be it convenience, wealth, power, predictability or cheap food'.[50]

FORM-FILLING FUNCTIONARIES

...those companies not buying into environmental markets will become uncompetitive as the market moves towards ethical or environmentally responsible business practice...

Indeed, many key architectural schemes today are thought of as imaginative and radical, causing many to espouse a belief in a new ecological design paradigm. Bill Dunster's BedZed development, for example, the latest in a long list of projects praised for its prima facie ecological aesthetics. And most advocates of sustainability see themselves as propagating new and exciting avenues of architectural or technological experimentation. The evident dynamic behind products and processes like photovoltaics, fuel cells, climatically responsive materials, geothermal heat sinks and energy efficiency, for example, once dismissed as minority interest or cranky, seem to contradict the charge that environmentalists are backward-looking. David Rice, Director of Policy at BP (now rebranded as Beyond Petroleum), says 'BP is a growth company, though when you look at the figures, oil is growing by 3 per cent, gas by 8 per cent, solar is a different story – here we're looking at 25–30 per cent growth, that is why we think this is bigger than a dotcom'. In 1998, BP *sales* of photovoltaics reached $95 million, up 19 per cent on the previous year.[51] Alternative energy and recyclable materials is definitely a growth sector.

> The simple reason is that increasing resource productivity can be a highly profitable strategy, and 'picking up £20 notes from the street' has been our expression for much of this agenda.[52]

In *Factor Four*, Amory Lovins points out that those companies not buying into environmental markets will become uncompetitive as the market moves towards ethical or environmentally responsible business practice; with myriad environmental projects to buy into. For others, sustainability is engaged with in a cynical way, and this only serves to reinforce the cynicism within the profession. Many projects claiming sustainable credentials are familiar commercial projects, built as they always have been, but provided with a sufficiently robust rationalisation of design intent to justify the label 'sustainable'. However, sustainability is a principle, which even the cynical do not challenge, infusing the architectural project team from inception to completion and beyond. As Manfred Wolff-Plottegg argues, 'sustainability (represents) a shift from object to process'.[53] This, therefore, is more than simply a debate about design or new products; it is much more solidly rooted in the new paradigm of demand management and restraint, or at least a modification or a reappraisal of absolute attainment targets. Before the British government thought of Quality of Life Indicators, people like Victor Anderson were *Redefining Wealth and Progress*, while holding out the belief in future good. It is a lifestyle thing.

> If governments of the South can create a consensus amongst themselves around lists of indicators such as ('net forest destruction', 'extinction of species', secondary school enrolment ratios, etc) which are ways of measuring social development and environmental quality and sustainability, they will be creating something which can rival orthodox ways of measuring 'progress', such as growth in GNP.[54]

This is life-cycle analysis that happens in real time. What you measure is not meant to be any universal criteria, but your contribution to sustainability. Duncan Baker-Brown of Baker-Brown McKay, winner of the RIBA's sustainable schools competition, says that designers 'should look more to embodied energy and specifying environmentally friendly materials rather than employing sustainable design "gestures".'[55] But factored in over the lifespan of a normal building, some argue that 'embodied energy is a marginal factor compared to the energy in use',[56] although there is clearly some debate about this point. That the path of sustainability will lead towards some kind of individual enlightenment now goes unquestioned.

The means by which we get there is for each of us to decide individually, although an entire self-promoting industry exists out there to give us the benefit of their enlightened opinion, for a substantial fee. Their educational remit is to advise on how best to complete the next questionnaire, or fill in the next pro-forma to show that you have a transparent paper-trail legitimising your decisions. The 'eco-Nazis', as Richard Murphy calls them[57] – while the new unter-Menschen are those who don't believe in the value of 'The Form'.

Ove Arup's SpeAR (Sustainable Project Appraisal Routine) consultancy best sums up the pervasive logic of sustainability as a process, rather than a goal. By means of a diagram comprising concentric circles of varying tones from the perimeter red to a green bullseye, and segments representing themes such as 'transport', 'embodied energy', 'cost', 'lifespan', etc, the objective is to judge various aspects of a given project to see how red or green it is. What is interesting is that there are no values attached to each coloured ring. Ove Arup uses its skill and judgement to place each assessed element in the appropriate coloured zone; the nearer the green the better. The consultancy recognises that adjusting one to perform better may adversely affect another, but the fact that some sectors may be further into the red than others is intended to be a graphic reminder to do better in the future. There is no blame or criticism intended – no value or critique – the diagram simply serves as a visual mnemonic of the failings of a building's architectural sustainability criteria. Each year the diagram is reviewed and modified to achieve a kind of optimum status.

Assessing the amount of energy used in a building, especially over its lifetime, may, in some circumstances, be a sensible thing to do, in the same way that one might monitor any prototype. Similarly, improved fabrication techniques and detailing ought to ensure that in the future not every building is a prototype in need of testing. However, monitoring is not a new idea; it reflects a common-sense search for efficiency, which has been carried out by industries and homeowners alike since time immemorial, equating to Mr Micawber's search for happiness:

> Annual income twenty pounds, annual expenditure nineteen nineteen and six, result happiness.
> Annual income twenty pounds, annual expenditure twenty pounds ought and six, result misery.[58]

Automotive designers, for example, have always sought ways to maximise a vehicle's aerodynamics by improving the designs to reduce drag and fuel consumption to improve performance; but it is only relatively recently that car manufacturers have realised the benefits of marketing these 'sustainable' credentials. It hardly goes without saying that efficiency drives for better, more productive modes of energy are sensible advances over wanton modes of energy production and distribution. Few people would argue that profligacy is a good thing, per se. But the amount of time, energy and effort expended in complying with the proliferation of ephemeral sustainability criteria is a visible example of the preference for resource efficiency over labour productivity as argued for in Factor Four. Amory Lovins expected that 'sustainable development…will very likely induce the world to stop overexploiting resources and underusing human labour.'[59] Making products work harder for you regardless of the amount of time you have to put in to justify their use is a poor kind of efficiency. Unfortunately, the proliferation of assessments, pro-formas, audit trail synopses and spreadsheets make an otherwise straightforward exercise into a straitjacket.

DISEMBODIED ENERGY
Imaginative architecture will continue to thrive, but given the self-imposed constraints, only in the same way that the UN Habitat Declaration concludes: 'those living in poverty are in fact rich in innovative faculties'.[60]

The logical consequence of an unquestioning acceptance of limits, reduced resource use and individual responsibility – the essential ingredients of architectural sustainability – is a tendency towards small-thinking, while pretending that we are looking at the Big Picture. Unfortunately, without a critical appraisal of sustainability, we are led to believe that nirvana – unfettered by worldly concerns – beckons:

> Peace of mind produces right values, right values produce right thoughts. Right thoughts produce right actions and right actions produce work which will become the material reflection for others to see of the serenity at the centre of it all.[61]

Sustainable architecture, like Buddhism, now argues that we can reach enlightenment through programmes of transcendent individual action. However small our actions, the fact that we have an individual part to play – a responsibility to participate – is given. Hopefully this chapter goes some way to undermine this belief, to challenge the current positive perceptions about the religion of 'sustainability' in architecture.

The logical consequence of an unquestioning acceptance of limits, reduced resource use and individual responsibility – the essential ingredients of architectural sustainability – is a tendency towards small-thinking, while pretending that we are looking at the Big Picture.

Notes

1. Austin Williams, 'Bigger, better, cooler karma', *Architects' Journal*, 12 April 2001, p. 40.
2. Penny Lewis, Vicky Richardson and James Woudhuysen, *In Defence of the Dome – the Case for Human Agency in the New Millennium* (London: ASI (Research) Ltd, 1998).
3. Brian Marks quoted in, *Building*, 5 January 2001, pp. 37–38.
4. E. F. Schumacher, *Small is Beautiful – A Study of Economics as if People Matter* (London: Sphere Books, 1974).
5. Nick Readett-Bayley interviewed by Austin Williams, 22 March 2001.
6. Dale Bates, interviewed in 'First person: Dale Bates and living architecture', *Environmental News Network*, 19 December 1999, www.enn.com.
7. Prince Charles, BBC Reith Lecture, 17 May 2000.
8. Kate Soper, *What is Nature?: Culture, Politics and the Non-Human* (Oxford: Blackwell, 1995).
9. Dame Mary Warnock, Gresham College Visiting Professor of Rhetoric, quoted in *The Independent*, 18 May 2001.
10. Tom Wooley and Sam Kimmins, *Green Building Handbook*, Vol. 2 (London: E&FN Spon, 2000), p. 7.
11. Ken Yeang, *The Skyscraper Bioclimatically Reconsidered – Design Primer* (London: Academy Editions, 1996), p. 21.
12. Herbert Girardet, *Earth Rise – Halting the Destruction. Healing the World* (London: Paladin, 1992).
13. Le Corbusier, *The City of Tomorrow and its Planning* (London: The Architectural Press, 1971), third edition.
14. Sigfried Giedion, *Walter Gropius* (New York: Dover Publications Inc, 1992).
15. Chris Wilkinson, *Building Design*, 6 April 2001.
16. J. Baldwin, *Bucky Works – Buckminster Fuller's Ideas for Today* (Chichester: John Wiley & Sons, 1996).
17. Austin Williams, 'The poor will always be with us', *Architects' Journal*, 28 June 2001, pages 20 to 23.
18. Jean Nouvel, quoted in the Official Compendium of the 'Global City versus Local Identity' conference, Third International Architecture Symposium, Pontresina, 13–15 September 2000.
19. Joe Drury, 'War on waste', *The Guardian*, 'Society', 16 May 2001, p. 6.
20. Katherine Shonfield, *Walls Have Feelings – Architecture, Film and the City* (London: Routledge, 2000), p. 76.
21. Martin Valatin, *Building Design*, 11 August 1995.
22. Robin Nicholson, quoted from 'The Challenge of Climate Change' luncheon, House of Lords, 3 October 2000.
23. Isabel Allen, editorial, *Architects' Journal*, 1 March 2001, p. 22.
24. Peter M. Ward (ed.), *Self-Help Housing – A Critique* (London: H. M. Wilson, 1982).
25. John Turner, 'Human settlement issues', Occasional Paper No. 38, University of British Columbia, 1985.
26. Ken Yeang, *The Green Skyscraper – The Basis for Designing Sustainable Intensive Buildings* (London: Prestel, 1999), pp. 43–44.
27. Zen Master Seung Sahn, *The Purposes of Buddhism* (Kwan Um School of Zen, www.kwanumzen.com.)
28. William McDonough Architects, *The Hanover Principles* – Design for Sustainability (Washington: AIA Publications, 1992) prepared for EXPO 2000, p. 6.
29. Robert M. Pirsig, *Zen and the Art of Motorcycle Maintenance – An Enquiry into Values* (London: Vintage, 1974), pp. 300–301.
30. Philip Allmendinger, *Planning in Postmodern Times* (London: RTPI Library Press and Routledge, 2000) p. 222.
31. Saskia Sassen quoted in Austin Williams, 'Sassen and the city', *Architects' Journal*, 17 May 2001, pp. 16–17.
32. Richard Rogers in Philip Gumuchdjian (ed.), *Cities for a Small Planet* (London: Faber and Faber, 1997).
33. Richard Rogers and Anne Power, *Cities for a Small Country* (London: Faber and Faber, 2000).
34. Donella H. Meadows, Dennis L. Meadows and Jorgan Randers, *Beyond the Limits – Confronting Global Collapse, Envisioning a Sustainable Future* (New York: Universe Books, 1992) and (London: Earthscan, 1992).
35. Herbert Girardet, *The Gaia Atlas of Cities – New Directions for Sustainable Urban Living* (London: Gaia Books Ltd, 1996), p. 56.
36. Ernst von Weizsäcker, Amory B. Lovins and L. Hunter Lovins, *Factor Four – Doubling Wealth, Halving Resource Use* (London: Earthscan, 1997), p. 208.
37. Brenda and Robert Vale, *Green Architecture – Design for a sustainable future* (London: Thames & Hudson, 1996).
38. Ted Trainer, *Towards a Sustainable Economy – The Need for Fundamental Change* (Oxford: Jon Carpenter, 1996), p. 1.
39. Matt Ridley, *The Melbourne Age*, 22 September 2000.
40. *Building Design*, 18 May 2001.
41. Susheel Rao, Alan Yates, Deborah Brownhill and Nigel Howard, *EcoHomes – the Environmental Rating for Homes* (Watford: Building Research Establishment, 2000).
42. Al Gore, *Earth in the Balance – Ecology and the Human Spirit* (Washington, DC: Plume, 1993). British title *Earth in the Balance – Forging a New Common Purpose* (London: Earthscan, 1992), p. 269.
43. Warwick Fox (ed.), *Ethics and the Built Environment* (London: Routledge, 2000), p. 5.

44. Saul Fisher, 'How to think about the ethics of architecture', in Warwick Fox (ed.), *Ethics and the Built Environment* (London: Routledge, 2000), p. 171.
45. Brian Edwards and Paul Hyett, *Rough Guide to Sustainability* (London: RIBA Publications, 2001), p. 83.
46. Richard Murphy, speaking at the RIAS annual conference 2001, reported in *Architects' Journal*, 24 May 2001, p. 18.
47. Bob Fowles, 'Transformative architecture – a synthesis of ecological and participatory design', in Warwick Fox (ed.), *Ethics and the Built Environment* (London: Routledge, 2000), p. 103.
48. Geoff Mulgan, *Connexity – How to Live in a Connected World* (London: Chatto and Windus, 1997), with *Connexity – Responsibility, Freedom, Business and Power in the New Century* (London: Vintage, 1997).
49. Pearce, Markandya and Barber, *Blueprint for a Green Economy* (London: Earthscan, 1989).
50. Janine M Benyus, *Biomimicry – Innovation Inspired by Nature* (New York: Quill, William Morrow, 1997), p. 46.
51. BP, *Business and Operating Review*, 2000
52. Ernst von Weizsäcker, Amory B. Lovins and L. Hunter Lovins, *Factor Four – Doubling Wealth, Halving Resource Use* (London: Earthscan, 1997), p. 249.
53. Mark Hewitt and Susannah Hagan, *City Fights – Debates on urban sustainability* (London: James & James (Science Publishers) Ltd, 2001), p. 15.
54. Victor Anderson, 'Alternative economic indicators', in *Redefining Wealth and Progress – New ways to Measure Economic, Social and Environmental Change*, the Caracas Report on Alternative Development Indicators (TOES Books, The Bootstrap Press, 1989), p. 89.
55. Duncan Baker-Brown quoted in 'News', *Architects' Journal*, 19 April 2001, p. 8.
56. Quote from unattributable source at DETR launch briefing of Department of the Environment, Transport and the Regions, *The Building Regulations Approved Document Part L – Conservation of Fuel and Power*, Interim Draft, DETR, dated March 2001, launched 9 April 2001.
57. Richard Murphy, speaking at the RIAS annual conference 2001, reported in *Architects' Journal*, 24 May 2001.
58. Charles Dickens, *David Copperfield* (London: Penguin Classics, 1997), ch. 12.
59. Ernst von Weizsäcker, Amory B. Lovins and L. Hunter Lovins, *Factor Four – Doubling Wealth, Halving Resource Use* (London: Earthscan, 1997), p. 208.
60. Austin Williams, 'The poor will always be with us', *Architects' Journal*, 28 June 2001, pp. 20–23.
61. Robert M. Pirsig, *Zen and the Art of Motorcycle Maintenance – Enquiry into Values* (London: Vintage, 1974), p. 300.

The Great Glasshouse
National Botanic Garden of Wales
Foster & Partners

Chapter 3

The Popular Legal Fiction

Daniel Lloyd, Freedom and Law

...a duty of care to the environment is a legal nonsense, and any such duty of care would inevitably be used to further regulate the activities of architects.

AN ENVIRONMENTAL PREFIX TO THE DUTY OF CARE

In negligence the duty of care is the legal codification of the non-contractual civil obligations that arise between citizens. An environmental duty of care based on sustainability as defined in the Brundtland Report would not protect the living citizen but the natural and built environment for anticipated future citizens:

> Development which meets the needs of the present without compromising the ability of future generations to meet their own needs.[1]

There are a number of legal problems bound up with the creation of an environmental duty of care. The law is man-made. The common law exists to resolve competing claims between legal subjects. Legal subjects are human beings. As human beings we all have rights and responsibilities that can be enforced in law. The 'environment' on the other hand has no rights or interests. It is not a conscious legal subject, therefore in law the 'environment' has no legally enforceable rights or responsibilities. How does the law regulate the way humans interact with the environment? Today sustainability is all the rage and is the moral imperative that informs contemporary social attitudes to the environment. Many are now lobbying for a legal recognition of the importance of sustainability, arguing that where human beings fail to act in line with the dictates of sustainability they should be held legally accountable. They argue, then, for the creation in law of an environmental duty of care.

This chapter investigates some of the problems that may arise from the creation of such a duty. The argument will be that a duty of care to the environment is a legal nonsense, and that any such duty of care would inevitably be used to further regulate the activities of architects. We make the point that a duty of care to the environment can never have a universally accepted definition. To appreciate the nature of these problems and some of the consequences such a duty of care may have on the practice of architecture, it is first necessary to develop an overall understanding of the law as it currently stands.

First, the main elements in the law of negligence will be traced, followed by an examination of how the law of negligence is applied today. Recent developments in the law of nuisance that may have some bearing on the practice of architecture are then outlined, before a look at the implicit subjugation of real and competing social interests to the notional consensual interest of future generations, inherent in the creation of an environmental duty of care.

THE TORT OF NEGLIGENCE

In the law of negligence, liability arises from acts or omissions breaching a duty of care to avoid injuring someone, damaging their property, or causing financial loss due to inadequate expert advice. Negligence may be defined as 'the breach of a legal duty to take care which results in damage, undesired by the defendant, to the plaintiff'.[2] The modern law of negligence has its genesis in 1932, in the case of *Donoghue v. Stevenson*:

> The rule that you are to love your neighbour becomes in law, you must not injure your neighbour; and the lawyer's question, Who is my neighbour? receives a restricted reply. You must take reasonable care to avoid acts or omissions which you can reasonably foresee would be likely to injure you neighbour. Who then in law is my neighbour? The answer seems to be – persons who are so closely and directly affected by my act that I ought reasonably to have them in contemplation as being so affected when I am directing my mind to the acts or omissions which are called in question.[3]

With these words from Lord Atkin, the modern tort of negligence came into being nearly 70 years ago. In the US, a very similar formulation was developed earlier in 1916 in *Macpherson v Buick*.[4] From the Atkin quote above, there would appear to be two distinct elements to the tort of negligence, namely of reasonable foreseeability and proximity. Where both are present and subject to statutory exceptions a generalised duty of care could be said to exist. In *Donoghue v. Stevenson* Lord Atkin attempted to codify in the law, as opposed to morality, the duties we are bound to observe towards each other in our civil relationships. He recognised that regardless of even widespread moral sentiment over a harm caused in some way, the law may not sensibly expect each of us to anticipate every imaginable consequence of our action or inaction for remote individuals:

acts or omissions which any moral code would censure cannot in a practical world be treated so as to give a right to every person injured by them to demand relief. In this way rules of law arise which limit the range of complainants and the extent of their remedy.[5]

Individuals are not held legally responsible for every careless act that has damaging consequences. Any general liability for carelessly causing harm to others would be too onerous for a rational system of law. Lord Macmillan held that 'the law takes no cognisance of carelessness in the abstract. It concerns itself with carelessness only where there is a duty to take care and where failure in that duty has caused damage'. He went on to recognise that 'human beings are thrown into, or place themselves in, an infinite variety of relations with their fellows', which means that 'grounds of action may be as various and manifold as human errancy'. So for negligence claims to be considered plausible, 'the party complained of should owe to the party complaining a duty to take care, and that the party complaining should be able to prove that he has suffered damage in consequence of a breach of that duty'.[6] This is a civilised principle to adopt.

The possibility of harm to a plaintiff must be foreseeable, be it to either an individual plaintiff or to a class of plaintiffs. Initially the 'neighbour principle' was interpreted restrictively and limited in application. During the postwar years the neighbour principle was extended on a case by case basis as the tort of negligence acquired a new social importance. The open ended language of negligence, as expressed in Lord Macmillan's judgement that 'the categories of negligence are never closed',[7] played an important role in allowing an expansion in remit. At the start of the 1970s the tort of negligence was reaching its legal zenith. Lord Reid held in *Home Office v. Dorset Yacht Co. Ltd* that the 'neighbour principle' might be applied in all cases where there was no argument against it, even though the original Queen's Bench case had made no reference to *Donoghue v. Stevenson* as a precedent.[8]

> there has been a steady trend towards regarding the law of negligence as depending on principle so that, when a new point emerges, one should ask not whether it is covered by authority but whether recognised principles apply to it. *Donoghue v. Stevenson*…may be regarded as a milestone, and the well-known passage in Lord Atkin's speech should I think be regarded as a statement of principle. It is not to be treated as if it were a statutory definition. It will require qualification in new circumstances. But I think that the time has come when we can and should say that it ought to apply unless there is some justification or valid explanation for its exclusion.[9]

The House of Lords went one step further in 1978 in *Anns v. London Borough of Merton*. The following quote from Lord Wilberforce has been taken by many as the high watermark of the neighbour principle developed by Lord Atkin in *Donoghue v. Stevenson*:

> Through the trilogy of cases in this House – *Donoghue v. Stevenson* (1932) A.C. 562, *Hedley Byrne and Co Ltd v. Heller and Partners* (1964) A.C. 465, and *Home Office v. Dorset Yacht Co. Ltd* (1970 A.C. 1004 – the position has now been reached that in order to establish that duty of care arises in a particular situation, it is not necessary to bring the facts of that situation within those of previous situations in which a duty of care has been held to exist. Rather the question has to be approached in two stages. First one has to ask whether, as between the alleged wrongdoer and the person who has suffered damage there is a sufficient relationship of proximity or neighbourhood such that, in the reasonable contemplation of the former, carelessness on his part may be likely to cause damage to the latter – in which case a prima facie duty of care arises. Secondly if the first question is answered affirmatively, it is necessary to consider whether there are any considerations which ought to negative, or to reduce or limit the scope of the duty or the class of person to whom it is owed or the damages to which a breach of it may give rise.[10]

In the years that followed the quote became known as the Wilberforce test. *Anns v. Merton* created considerable scope for plaintiffs to bring new types of action in negligence, developing the neighbour principle in *Donoghue v. Stevenson* into a universally applicable two-stage Wilberforce test of liability.

In this regard, *Anns v. Merton* represents the high watermark of the neighbour principle with what seemed to be a universally applicable test to all situations, but Lord Wilberforce had oversimplified the problem. In the second stage, Lord Wilberforce implies that there are no considerations of policy to be found in the first stage. On the basis of wishing to pursue a very restrictive policy regarding the development of the tort of negligence the judiciary has since embarked upon a systematic attempt to reign in the scope of liability in negligence, reading into the first stage of Wilberforce's test questions of policy. In a line of cases starting with *Peabody v. Parkinson* and finishing with *Caparo Industries plc v. Dickman*,[11] the House of Lords consistently used policy considerations to restrict the development of new duties of care. In *Peabody v. Parkinson* Lord Keith found that in determining 'whether or not a duty of care was incumbent on a defendant it is material to take into consideration whether it is just and reasonable that it should be so'.[12] Lord Keith's comments indicated the beginning of an attack on *Anns v. Merton* and the Wilberforce test. In *Leigh and Sullivan v. Aliakmon Shipping Co. Ltd* Lord Brandon stated that the

The possibility of harm to a plaintiff must be foreseeable, be it to either an individual plaintiff or to a class of plaintiffs.

…the House of Lords consistently used policy considerations to restrict the development of new duties of care.

Wilberforce test could not provide a 'universally applicable test of the existence and scope of a duty of care in negligence'.[13] The attack became more explicit in *Yuen Kun-Yen v. Attorney General of Hong Kong* where Lord Keith held that 'their lordships venture to think that the two stage test formulated by Lord Wilberforce for determining the existence of a duty of care in negligence has been elevated to a degree of importance greater than its merits and perhaps greater than its author intended'.[14]

Lord Keith went on to state that Lord Wilberforce intended to use the concept of proximity or neighbourhood as a composite one, importing the whole concept of necessary relationship between plaintiff and defendant described by Lord Atkin in *Donoghue v. Stevenson*. Hence the factors which would have been considered at the second stage of the Wilberforce test, that were essentially policy considerations, may now be of relevance in determining whether there is a sufficient degree of proximity and forseeability between plaintiff and defendant in the first stage of the Wilberforce test.

In *Caparo v. Dickman* the attack on the Wilberforce test was completed when the requirement of 'just and reasonable' was formalised and insisted upon. So instead of a two-stage test as in *Anns v. Merton* the law lords created a three-stage test. This may seem ironic, in that their principal concern in attacking the Wilberforce test was to decry the notion that there could be a universal test to establish whether or not a duty of care exists in any social situation. Instead the judiciary has substituted one universally applicable test for another. However, this is not the key change that has taken place.

Whereas in *Anns v. Merton* the judiciary was comfortable with a liberal principled approach to the question of liability in negligence, by the 1980s judicial attitudes had changed. Scepticism became the order of the day. New duties of care could only come into existence if they passed stringent policy tests laid down by the higher courts. Otherwise, compensation depended on a plaintiff showing that the case already fell within existing precedent. The test for determining the existence of a duty of care today now comprises three stages, unlike the two-stage test in *Anns v. Merton*.

A duty of care today will arise where:
- there is foreseeability of damage to a citizen;
- sufficient proximity between the parties exists; and
- it is just and reasonable to impose a duty.

This final category is inherently non-justiciable. It is a vessel devoid of legal meaning into which the judiciary can import interpretations of public policy to determine whether or not a duty of care should be found to exist. The three-stage test finalised upon in *Caparo v. Dickman* and applied on numerous occasions since 1990 represents the law today.

If we return to the quote from Lord Atkin at the beginning of this chapter, it is clear that it is worded to allow for the development of many new duties of care in negligence against the criteria of reasonable foreseeability and proximity. On a narrow interpretation *Donoghue v. Stevenson* itself may only be authority for the proposition that a manufacturer of commodities owes a duty of care to the ultimate consumer of that commodity. But with the language used by Lord Atkin and the categories that he developed, the law of negligence has proven very pliable and capable of being applied to a wide range of factual situations.

The story of the tort of negligence encapsulates some of the law's problems in adjudicating private disputes. As soon as the law of negligence was used to overcome basic inequalities inherent in a free market economy, it was possible to see the potential for an endless expansion in the number of situations where the law of negligence could be applied, subject only to the mood of the times. The tension between the formal logic of the law and the uncontrollable nature of the market is neatly expressed in the law of negligence. In *Caparo v. Dickman* the Law Lords attempted to restrict new duties of care to those that could pass stringent policy tests at the discretion of the judiciary, so that there would be fewer victims of careless acts entitled to claim compensation in law. However, the policies favoured by the judiciary are informed by wider social attitudes and at the same time help to shape those attitudes. The contemporary compensation culture, where someone else is always to blame and someone else can always pay, may have been precisely the culture that the judges in *Caparo v. Dickman* wanted to prevent coming into being. But it is now a social reality and one that is in many ways conducive to the creation of a new duty of care to the environment. It is not difficult to envisage the three-stage test in *Caparo v. Dickman* being used to create such a duty. The test could be easily used to create a duty of care to the environment, firstly affecting the present, and then extended as a policy of concern for future generations, in accordance with the Brundtland definition of sustainability.

An environmental duty of care in the present day could arise in the following circumstances:
- that there is foreseeability of damage to the wellbeing of a citizen by development deemed to be unsustainable according to good practice;
- that sufficient proximity between the parties exists; and

New duties of care could only come into existence if they passed stringent policy tests laid down by the higher courts.

- that in an age when sustainability informs social policy, with the architectural profession claiming a duty themselves, it must be just and reasonable to impose a duty.

An environmental duty of care to future generations could arise where:
- there is foreseeability of damage to the wellbeing of future citizens by development deemed to be unsustainable according to good practice;
- sufficient proximity between the parties exists if mediated through an independent environmental agency to ensure the environmental damage is corrected; and
- in an age when sustainability informs social policy, with the architectural profession proclaiming such a duty themselves, it must be just and reasonable to impose a duty.

Future generations obviously cannot sue, but this does not mean that third-party standing could not be extended to environmental groups only too eager to be officially cast as their representatives. The law of negligence has shown itself to be flexible in its development. It has been able to encompass new situations and provide a ready-made regulatory apparatus in the absence of a statutory framework. Architects who argue for the creation of an environmental duty of care do so at their peril. Duty is a precise term for Goldschmied and Hyett to have used, as it is central to the law of negligence and has there its own particular meaning:

> It may be objected that 'duty' is not confined to the law of negligence and that it is an element in every tort, because there is a legal duty not to commit assault or battery, not to commit defamation, not to commit nuisance and so forth. But all that 'duty' signifies in these other torts is that you must not commit them: they have their own, detailed, internal rules which define the circumstances in which they are committed and duty adds nothing to those. But in the tort of negligence, breach of 'duty' is the chief ingredient of the tort; in fact there is no other except damage to the plaintiff.[15]

The new tort of unsustainable development has the potential to be the judiciary's contribution to sustainability. Architects claiming such a duty are presumably able to identify whether a particular development is sustainable, or how it can be remedied to be so. In any case the architectural profession that has publicly called for an environmental duty of care can hardly object to a policy shift in the law when it happens.

Future generations obviously cannot sue, but this does not mean that third-party standing could not be extended to environmental groups only too eager to be officially cast as their representatives.

THE MODERN LAW OF NEGLIGENCE FOR ARCHITECTS

Initially there needed to be 'proximity' in the relationship between the plaintiff and the defendant to positively require a duty of care from the latter to the former. Following *Anns v. Merton* the basis of that proximate relationship had to be considered to negatively limit that duty in the interests of 'fairness' to the defendant. There was an immediate and enthusiastic application of this formulation, leading to *Junior Books Ltd v. Veitchi Co. Ltd*,[16] which seemed to support claims for economic loss, regardless of any liability for injury to persons and damage to property. The earlier case, *Hedley Byrne and Co Ltd v. Heller and Partners*,[17] established a principle on economic losses, and was cited in Lord Wilberforce's judgement in *Anns v. Merton*. Involving negligent expert advice, this case is most significant for professionals, as Vincent Moran explains in the *Architect's Legal Handbook*:

> The first exception to the general rule of there being no duty to avoid causing *pure* economic loss was provided in the area of negligent mis-statement and the line of cases following *Hedley Byrne and Co Ltd v. Heller and Partners*…(the) House of Lords held that a defendant would be liable for such negligent mis-statements if: (a) there was a 'special relationship' between the parties, (b) the defendant knew or ought to have known that the plaintiff was likely to rely upon his statement, and (c) in all the circumstances it was reasonable for the plaintiff to so rely on the defendant's statement.[18]

The distinction between a liability for statements and a liability for acts or omissions is necessary, provided that there is a qualitative relationship between the parties, and not just proximity. This was clearly explained by Lord Reid in his judgement on *Hedley Byrne v. Heller*:

> A reasonable man, knowing that he was being trusted or that his skill and judgement were being relied on, would, I think, have three courses open to him. He could keep silent or decline to give the information or advice sought: or he could give an answer with a clear qualification that he accepted no responsibility for it or that it was given without that reflection or inquiry which a careful answer would require: or he could simply answer without any such qualification. If he chooses to adopt the last course he must, I think, be held to have accepted some responsibility for his answer being given carefully, or to have accepted a relationship with the inquirer which requires him to exercise such care as the circumstances require.[19]

Moreover, the liability in negligent misstatement exists irrespective of whether the parties have a contractual relationship. *Hedley Byrne v. Heller* allowed for claims of economic loss due to an individual's reasonable reliance on advice. An architect's liability is then one where the plaintiff could enjoy the choice of action in contract and tort without a conflict between them.

However, an architect may have liabilities to people other than his or her client. In the expansionist mood after *Anns v. Merton* attempts were inevitably made to establish claims for economic loss in other relationships. The boundaries placed on tort were being tested to the extent that in *Junior Books v. Veitchi*, Lord Roskill could observe 'it is sometimes overlooked that virtually all damage including physical damage is in one sense financial or economic for it is compensated by an award of damages'.[20] That may be true, but the law of tort had previously and sensibly excluded claims for economic loss as a matter of policy.

To remain objective the law has to rule for the generality of cases, and it was necessary to be able to establish a policy between recognising all foreseeable harms as legitimate claims, and recognising none. As Lord Templeman had noted, pleadings in negligence cases were mistakenly assuming 'that we are all neighbours now…that foreseeability is a reflection of hindsight and that for every mischance in an accident-prone world someone must be liable in damages'.[21] Similarly for Jon Holyoak, there must be a clear exclusion on liability for purely economic loss, and a resistance against compensation:

> For negligence to be actionable, damage is needed. This is simple when a workman's leg is broken on a building site, or where a property is demolished by a passing truck. These are clear cases of physical damage. However in some sense, purely economic loss is not really a loss at all, but a failure to make a gain.[22]

The dissenting voice in *Junior Books v. Veitchi* was Lord Brandon, who was concerned not to create obligations in tort that were only appropriate in contract. No plaintiff has won a case based on *Junior Books v. Veitchi*. As Jon Holyoak reminds us, 'to remove even some of the constraints on tortious claims for economic loss was to bring the law of negligence into potential conflict with contract law. Negligence claims might be made to fill in gaps in the contractual provisions, as in *Junior Books*, but also might, if successful, actually end up contradicting the intention of the contracting parties'.[23] That could not be accepted.

For Lord Brandon the precedent was *Donoghue v. Stevenson*, concentrating on personal injury or damage to property, leaving economic matters to contract law, notwithstanding the *Hedley Byrne v. Heller* exception for a duty of care when giving expert advice. Proximity had no literal physical interpretation even in *Donoghue v. Stevenson*, but after *Anns v. Merton* attempted interpretations were becoming potentially onerous. To complicate matters further, the Civil Liability (Contribution) Act 1978 assumes that all the relevant parties to a dispute were there to be sued, or were worth suing. This was a particular problem for Local Authorities after *Anns v. Merton*:

> Builders often became bankrupt and development companies are frequently wound up once the development project is over. Architects…at least when *Anns* first burst into the construction world, were quite often not insured against negligence. Local authorities, however, do not go bankrupt and are not wound up but are insured and it was not difficult to envisage cases, like *Anns* itself, where the local authority is left to face the threat of litigation alone, though only partially to blame for the defective state of the premises.[24]

Life was proving rather more complicated than Lord Wilberforce had allowed for. The mere foreseeability of harm is a prerequisite for a duty of care, but the parties must have a close and direct relationship as required by Lord Atkin in *Donoghue v. Stevenson*. This was stressed by Lord Keith in *Yuen Kun-Yeu v. Attorney General of Hong Kong*. He recognised that if foreseeability were mistaken for proximity, 'there would be liability in negligence on the part of one who sees another about to walk over a cliff with his head in the air, and forebears to shout a warning'.[25] Clearly Lord Wilberforce had not intended *Anns v. Merton* to make us all responsible for one another, but only that we should cause no irresponsible harm.

The situation was becoming unworkable. Cases stretched the narrow *Donoghue v. Stevenson* intention. Lord Bridge played a prominent role in rescuing the *Donoghue v. Stevenson* principle from the apparently limitless two-stage test of *Anns v. Merton*. In *Caparo v. Dickman* Lord Bridge narrowed the interpretation of *Hedley Byrne v. Heller*. He sought to resist the law of tort being used 'to confer on the world at large a quite unwarranted entitlement to appropriate for their own purposes the benefit of…expert knowledge or professional experience attributed to the maker of the statement',[26] no matter who had paid for the advice:

> the concepts of proximity and fairness…are not susceptible of any such precise definition as would be necessary to give them utility as practical tests, but amount in effect to little more than convenient labels to attach to the features of different specific situations which, on a detailed examination of all the circumstances, the law recognises pragmatically as giving rise to a duty of care of a given scope.[27]

In this he concurred with Lord Roskill who, deliberating on the same case, considered that proximity or fairness were 'labels or phrases descriptive of the very different factual situations which can exist in particular cases and which must be carefully examined in each case before it can be pragmatically determined'.[28] Again in *Caparo v. Dickman*, Lord Oliver argued against the myth that *Anns v. Merton* offered

The mere foreseeability of harm is a prerequisite for a duty of care, but the parties must have a close and direct relationship…

principles. According to Lord Oliver proximity was a 'convenient expression so long as it is realised that it is no more than a label which embraces not a definable concept but merely a description of circumstances from which, pragmatically, the courts conclude that a duty of care exists'.[29]

In 1991 the much abused two-stage *Anns v. Merton* test of proximity and fairness was conclusively overruled in *Murphy v. Brentwood District Council*,[30] meaning that pure economic loss had once again become irrecoverable. This was considered a reiteration of the *Donoghue v. Stevenson* approach, where damages as a consequence of injury to persons and property were recoverable. While the precise principle of allowing damages as a consequence of negligent statements in the context of a dependent relationship remained, as set in *Hedley Byrne v. Heller*, there is an anomaly in that the case of *Junior Books v. Veitchi* was not overruled at the same time, but it is widely considered to have established no principle of any consequence for *Murphy v. Brentwood*:

> If a builder erects a structure containing a latent defect which renders it dangerous to persons or property, he will be liable in tort for injury to persons or damage to property resulting from that dangerous defect. But if the defect becomes apparent before any injury or damage has been caused, the loss sustained by the building owner is purely economic. If the defect can be repaired at economic cost, that is the measure of the loss. If the building cannot be repaired, it may have to be abandoned as unfit for occupation and therefore valueless. These economic losses are recoverable if they flow from breach of the relevant contractual duty, but, here again, in the absence of a special relationship of proximity they are not recoverable in tort.[31]

The current limitations on the liability faced by architects, that are now being called into question by the idea of an environmental duty of care, have only been enjoyed since *Murphy v. Brentwood*. In overturning *Anns v. Merton*, *Murphy v. Brentwood* decided that a local authority, under its building control function, no longer owed a duty of care to future owners or occupiers of a building to ensure that the building was properly constructed. Until then local authorities did owe this duty of care, and the *Anns v. Merton* principle had been extended throughout the 1980s to include architects in the list of people who could be sued by subsequent owners or tenants of a building. With *Murphy v. Brentwood* professional liability for pure economic loss due to the tort of negligence was ended, as Vincent Moran explained in the *Architect's Legal Handbook*.

> Although the decision in *Murphy v. Brentwood* eliminated liability in negligence for pure economic loss caused to third parties by defective property, such pure economic loss is still recoverable under the Defective Premises Act 1972. Typically claims against architects involve a large proportion of purely economic losses, therefore attention is likely to concentrate in the future on potential liability under the Act.[32]

For architects, *Murphy v. Brentwood* emphasised the contract as the proper means to anticipate the prospect of economic loss, accepting only a duty of care to cause no foreseeable harm to proximate individuals and their property, while acknowledging the reliance placed on professional advice under specific circumstances. This concerns the client but also anyone close to the project dependent on the architect's expertise, and irrespective of any fee being paid. *Murphy v. Brentwood* has reasserted contract law, and the specific standards of conduct that contracts require. Where it exists in restricted form the law of tort provides a basic duty of care, underlying any contract.

The creation of an environmental duty of care would explode this relatively certain legal environment in which architects have been practising for the last decade. Any environmental duty of care may place architects into a 'proximate' relationship with wider classes of potential plaintiffs, or their representatives, in both time and space. For the tort of negligence the extent of foreseeable damage and the bounds of proximity may be exploded by a judiciary. The courts are being encouraged by the Royal Institute of British Architects (RIBA) to impose a duty on architects professing sustainability that they will find very difficult not to breach. Going back to a restricted duty of care, as is currently enjoyed by architects, will be extremely hard to do.

THE TORT OF NUISANCE

The law of nuisance distinguishes between public nuisance and private nuisance. A private nuisance is defined as 'unlawful interference with a person's use or enjoyment of land, or some right over, or in connection with it'.[33] Lord Lloyd has categorised private nuisance in *Hunter v. Canary Wharf Ltd*:

> They are (1) nuisance by encroachment on a neighbour's land; (2) nuisance by direct physical injury to a neighbour's land; and (3) nuisance by interference with a neighbour's quiet enjoyment of his land.[34]

A nuisance may be deemed a public nuisance if it is 'so widespread in its range or indiscriminate in its effects that it is not reasonable to expect one person to take proceedings on his own responsibility to put a stop to it'.[35] Only the Attorney General or a local authority can bring an action in public nuisance. The character of the neighbourhood may have bearing on whether a particular activity constitutes a public nui-

Any environmental duty of care may place architects into a 'proximate' relationship with wider classes of potential plaintiffs, or their representatives, in both time and space.

sance. For example it has been held that the grant of planning permission for a change of use may have the effect of rendering lawful an activity which would have been unlawful if carried out in an earlier period before the character of the neighbourhood had changed.[36]

In addition to public and private nuisance is the *Rylands v Fletcher* tort.[37] Following *Rylands v. Fletcher* anyone who brings on to their land a dangerous substance that subsequently escapes is liable in damages for all the consequences of that escape. They are thus under a strict liability, in that they bear legal responsibility for the consequences of the escape, even if they are not negligent or not directly at fault for allowing the escape to happen. So in the *Rylands v Fletcher* tort a plaintiff only needs to prove that a dangerous substance has escaped from the defendant's land. He or she does not need to prove that the defendant was negligent or that he or she was responsible. The mere fact of the escape makes the defendant liable for any consequential damage.

The strict liability established in *Rylands v. Fletcher* seems perfectly suited to environmental disputes, as it is concerned with damage caused by dangerous materials used on land. While it would be wrong to read any policy toward 'environmental protection' back into cases like *Rylands v. Fletcher*, it is possible to see how this precedent could be used as legal authority for the idea that the polluter pays. However, *Rylands v. Fletcher* has its limitations. In the process of upholding the original judgement, the House of Lords added the requirement that the defendant must have been engaged in a 'non-natural use of his land'. Quite what this is taken to mean has ever since been uncertain and has always been decided on a case-by-case basis. Human uses for land can be considered non-natural by definition, in that we have intervened in the landscape. On the other hand there is a tendency to naturalise established land uses as though they were distinct from innovative practices.

The most recent authority on *Rylands v. Fletcher* is *Cambridge Water Co. v. Eastern Counties Leather plc.*[38] This case has imposed an additional requirement. The possibility that the material is dangerous, or that if it escaped it could cause damage, must be reasonably foreseeable at the time it was brought on to the land. Thus reasonable foreseeability has been introduced into a tort that was previously based on the principles of strict liability.

Following the decision in *Cambridge Water v. Eastern Counties Leather* it is considered that the law relating to the use of non-natural substances on land is now uncertain.[39] This is reflected in the note of caution given by Lord Goff in *Cambridge Water v. Eastern Counties Leather*. Lord Goff cautioned against extending the common law to tackle environmental problems that would be better dealt with in statute through parliament:

> as a general rule it is more appropriate for strict liability in respect of operations of high risk to be imposed by Parliament, than by the courts. If such liability is imposed by statute, the relevant activities can be identified, and those concerned can know where they stand.[40]

The law of nuisance is an ill-designed tool for dealing with environmental damage, but this will not stop the environmentally minded from trying to use it. In the *Rylands v. Fletcher* tort of private nuisance only the interests of property owners in land are recognised. In public nuisance, where pure economic losses are recoverable, the scope for bringing actions to protect the environment is limited by the consideration of intervening social values. The environmental lawyer's frustration with the social priority in the tort of nuisance is evident in *Environmental Protection and the Common Law*, and particularly from contributors Martin Hedemann-Robinson and Mark Wilde in regard to EC law:

> Behind the Commission's rhetoric of strict liability which has accompanied its proposals on civil liability in respect of environmental harm lies a host of caveats and compromises that raises question marks over whether the European Community-inspired toxic tort law would be able to make a significant contribution in terms of environmental protection. This is all the more concerning, as so much political effort and hyperbole has been invested in this long-awaited addition to the body of Community environmental law.[41]

This social priority severely restricts the ability of environmentalists to use the law to further environmental campaigns. Environmental damage is rightly considered to be a question of social priority in the torts of nuisance. Any extension of liability for nuisance may follow from a growing social commitment to sustainability among property owners, and more widely as public policy in the case of public nuisance. With sustainability established as the new moral imperative, the extension of liabilities in the law of nuisance cannot be ruled out as a possibility. An architect professing sustainability may find that property owners and public authorities attempt to pursue claims for the nuisance of unsustainable development, in an attempt to establish strict liability for some recognised environmental harm.

THE TORTS OF NEGLIGENCE AND NUISANCE COMPARED

It is regrettable that the RIBA chooses to join environmentalists in an effort to reinterpret the duty of care in negligence after a brief decade of legal stability for practitioners. The fact that members may have voted

With sustainability established as the new moral imperative, the extension of liabilities in the law of nuisance cannot be ruled out as a possibility.

The judiciary may take architects at their word.

for such exposure is almost incredible. While there is scope for legal clarification in nuisance to bring it back to strict liability, the tort of negligence is clear as it stands. Extending professional liabilities in negligence will not help strengthen the line between negligence and nuisance, as described by Paula Giliker:

'Reasonable Care' in negligence is an objective standard of care, which pays little attention to the personal characteristics of the defendant. 'Reasonable user', in contrast, is not a standard of conduct, but a rule of give and take by which the courts balance the respective rights of the claimant and the defendant freely to enjoy their land. In this sense the courts have a different focus. Negligence assesses the conduct of the defendant utilising the yardstick of the reasonable person. Private nuisance seeks not to blame the defendant, but to protect the claimant's interest, and is therefore more concerned with the *effect* of the defendant's conduct on the claimant.[42]

Further, the defendant may have created a nuisance regardless of whether the act was deliberate, reckless, negligent or otherwise. Fault-based principles may play a role in nuisance cases, blurring the distinct torts of negligence and nuisance, but they are distinct. The tort of nuisance is said to be a strict liability 'in the sense that the defendant may be held liable notwithstanding that he has exercised all due care'.[43] Consequently there are differences between the torts of negligence and nuisance that are of concern to environmentalists:

Whilst procedurally some problems may be overcome by pleading both negligence and nuisance, the potential remains for losses to fall between either…Nuisance depends upon the reasonableness of the user. Activities, however carefully executed, may give rise to liability, if unreasonable in the locality. Negligence in contrast, holds people liable only if they have failed to exercise reasonable care.[44]

It is possible that individuals will find that neither the tort of nuisance nor that of negligence can offer a satisfactory remedy. The tort remedy is always damages after the event, which for the environment is obviously too late:

For those who have been damaged, whether the damage is in the form of personal injury or damage to property or wealth, tort remains a primary mechanism whereby compensation for those losses can be recovered. Regulatory mechanisms, as currently structured in English law, may operate to prevent losses, to limit any damage which does ensue or to compel remediation, but they have limited capacity for providing compensation for harm which has already been caused. Direct compensation for established damage flowing from the private sector wrongdoer, as opposed to the public sector body only, attracts a remedy through tortious mechanisms.[45]

Only in nuisance cases may these damages be coupled with an injunction to prevent repetition and therefore further damage, but as we have seen, nuisance prioritises social interests over notional environmental interests. Lord Goff in *Cambridge Water* sensibly cautioned against the common law being used to protect the environment. He rightly argued instead for parliamentary legislation for legal protection for the environment.

Environmental protection is a matter of public policy and matters of public policy are not best handed to unelected judges. That note of caution is not deterring enthusiasts for the establishment of a common law environmental duty of care to obviate the need to engage in the inconvenient democratic process of getting parliament to enact legislation to that effect.

As with the tort of nuisance an action citing *Rylands v. Fletcher* can only be brought by landowners directly affected, and not by third parties. Environmentalists wanting to intervene across the legal boundaries of property ownership find this a problem. The law of nuisance only protects the right of property owners to enjoy the use of their land. It does not, nor does it seek to protect the interests of the 'environment':

In nuisance, once a defendant's use of his land is found to be unreasonable, in that it interferes with his neighbour's use of his land in a manner or extent such that no occupier of land could be expected to put up with it, it is no answer for the defendant to say that he exercised all reasonable care and skill in conducting the activity or overseeing the state of affairs that gave rise to the interference. To do that would be the equivalent to claiming that his neighbours must suffer for the sake of his activities, or the current harmful state of his land, so long as he has not been careless in his conduct.[46]

The essence of nuisance is an interference with the rights of use of land, and only those with property rights have any standing to sue. Currently, the social tort of nuisance is insufficient for environmentalists because it can do nothing to prevent an owner of land acting, or allowing his or her neighbour to act, in ways that are considered detrimental to the environment by those with no immediate property rights. No law of tort protecting property rights can transcend the reality that the property owner has a temporary real interest in the land. Environmentalists are not concerned with individual owners conducting specific activity, but with future land use. Present owners are not legally bound to the project of sustaining patterns of land use for the sake of future generations by the tort of nuisance.

Environmental protection is a matter of public policy and matters of public policy are not best handed to unelected judges.

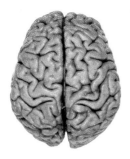

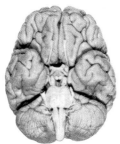

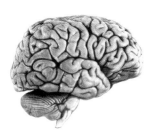

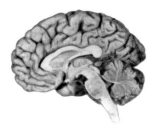

Creating a duty of care to the environment, one that could be actionable in either negligence or nuisance, would therefore challenge many assumptions that underpin the law. The law bestows rights upon human beings, recognises conflicts of interest between human beings and seeks to adjudicate those conflicts through applying well-established principles borne of statute and case law. At the moment the law appreciates that environmental damage is a social question, because harming the environment for one person may be positively enhancing it for another. Compensation in tort follows from the breach of duty. But the law of negligence cannot prevent 'environmental harm' from being done. It can only act as a deterrent to potentially harmful action or inaction. An environmental duty of care to ensure the well being of future generations sounds humanistic, but the people that are being privileged have not been born and we can never know them in advance. It diminishes the rights of human beings alive today. It would need a socially accepted authority to imagine the interests of a future society, and to define environmental damage in the present and the future. Given that the range of the potential harm is spatially and temporally the eco-system of the planet in the present and the future, there will be a massive deterrent to practitioners acting on their initiative and a demand for RIBA-sanctioned good practice guidance to be slavishly adhered to. The introduction of an environmental duty of care is incapable of preventing actual environmental harm, but will stifle architectural design and technological innovation. By inviting the law in to regulate further the practice of architecture, practitioners could be making the world a much drearier place.

An environmental duty of care that incorporates the Brundtland definition of sustainability will create a legal fiction that will not 'protect' the environment. It will instead require an agency or authority to speak for the unborn on environmental matters affecting the living – an agency or authority that society resigns to obey. It would require the law to retreat from reason, and follow instead the doomsday scenarios that environmentalists are so fond of proclaiming.

THE REASONABLE ARCHITECT

Regardless of the differences in negligence or nuisance, we are considered by the common law to be reasonable people among our peers, famously conceptualised by Lord Bowen in the nineteenth century as 'the man on the Clapham Omnibus'.[47] As ubiquitous reasonable men and women we are not imagined to be clairvoyant, but are expected to have learnt from common experience, possibly acquiring a particular level of expertise. The principle for assessing expertise was clarified by Mr Justice McNair in the High Court case of *Bolam v. Friern Hospital Management Committee*:

> The test is the standard of the ordinary skilled man exercising and professing to have that special skill. A man need not possess the highest expert skill; it is well established law that it is sufficient if he exercises the ordinary skill of an ordinary competent man exercising that particular art.[48]

We are not considered to have special insight, unless we profess to be a specialist, and the law requires us to show such skill and judgement as fellow professionals routinely demonstrate in contemporary practice. This temporal component is essential, because each generation finds its predecessor ignorant and there is a steady rise in the standard of competence expected. What is habitual in one generation may be considered negligent by the next, and understood as an advance. This is an entirely sensible approach, having tremendous flexibility when dealing with matters of individual conduct defying precise and fixed social definitions. As Jon Holyoak reminds us, this makes complete sense:

> It is self-evident that building owners expect their buildings to be designed and built with something more than the skill of the ordinary man, and so it is necessary to adapt the test accordingly; the basic approach is to compare the acts of the professional or skilled defendant with the approach of the reasonable practitioner of the particular profession or skill in question.[49]

However, we face the situation that the RIBA wishes architects to be judged against sustainability, which hardly constitutes a body of clear professional knowledge. Sustainability is moral, but not technically or aesthetically defined. Architects may wish to improve the environment, but there is no duty to act for the benefit of anyone. In the case of *Stovin v. Wise* Lord Hoffman reiterated how the law does not positively encourage us to act for the benefit of others, but only discourages negligent acts or omissions:

> It is one thing for the law to say that a person who undertakes some activity shall take reasonable care not to cause damage to others. It is another thing for the law to require that a person who is doing nothing in particular shall take steps to prevent another from suffering harm from the acts of third parties...or natural causes.[50]

We are not held responsible for what others do, but are also not responsible for helping our contemporaries. The law does not positively require us to achieve improvements for others and nor should it. It is debatable whether sustainability requires us to positively improve the environment, rather than to prevent further harm. However, under the common law we are not necessarily expected to avoid making matters worse for our contemporaries. As Jon Holyoak points out, the law is not morality:

It makes good moral sense to penalise careless behaviour, especially careless behaviour that causes damage. Whether to punish the wrongdoer, deter his successors or to compensate his luckless victim (and each of these has been suggested as a justification) it seems right to most people that the wrongdoer should compensate his victim.

Such a broad approach is not, however, that taken by the law.[51]

Until now that is! The category 'just and reasonable' articulated by Lord Keith in *Peabody v. Parkinson* is one that is inherently non-justiciable. It is a category that can have no strict legal meaning.

What is 'just and reasonable' is entirely a social category, the meaning of which will change from one generation to the next. When Lord Keith developed the category his main concern was to keep the floodgates of litigation well and truly closed. However, times have moved on and the floodgates are now well and truly ajar. Sustainability, and with it the idea of environmental protection as a priority, is now accepted public policy. It would therefore take a brave judge, or perhaps one out of tune with the times, to find that it was not 'just and reasonable' for the law to recognise an environmental duty of care, notwithstanding the fact that any such duty would be a popular legal fiction.

It would therefore take a brave judge, or perhaps one out of tune with the times, to find that it was not 'just and reasonable' for the law to recognise an environmental duty of care, notwithstanding the fact that any such duty would be a popular legal fiction.

Notes

1. World Commission on Environment and Development, *Our Common Future*, commonly known as the Brundtland Report (WCED, Oxford: Oxford University Press, 1987).
2. *Winfield and Jolowicz On Tort*, first published 1937, fifteenth edition by W. V. H. Rogers (London: Sweet and Maxwell, 1998), p. 90.
3. Lord Atkin, *Donoghue v. Stevenson (1932) AC 562.*
4. *Macpherson v. Buick (1916) 217 N.Y. 382, 111 N.E 1050.*
5. Lord Atkin, *Donoghue v. Stevenson (1932) AC 562.*
6. Lord Macmillan, *Donoghue v. Stevenson (1932) AC 562 at 619.*
7. Ibid.
8. Lord Reid, *Home Office v. Dorset Yacht Co. Ltd (1970) AC 1004 at 1027* on *Home Office v. Dorset Yacht Co. Ltd (1969) 2 Q.B. 412.*
9. Lord Reid, *Home Office v. Dorset Yacht Co. Ltd (1970) AC 1004 at 1026* .
10. Lord Wilberforce, *Anns v. London Borough of Merton (1978) AC 728 at 751.*
11. *Caparo Industries plc v. Dickman (1990) 2 AC 605.*
12. Lord Keith, *Peabody v. Parkinson (1984) 3 All ER 529,* p. 534.
13. Lord Brandon, *Leigh and Sullivan v. Aliakmon Shipping Co. Ltd (1986) 2 All ER 145.*
14. Lord Keith, *Yuen Kun-Yen v. Attorney General of Hong Kong (1988) AC ER 175.*
15. *Winfield and Jolowicz On Tort*, first published 1937, fifteenth edition by W. V. H. Rogers (London: Sweet and Maxwell, 1998), p. 90.
16. *Junior Books Ltd v. Veitchi Co. Ltd (1983) 1 AC 520.*
17. *Hedley Byrne and Co Ltd v. Heller and Partners (1964) AC 465.*
18. Vincent Moran, 'The English Law of Tort', *Architect's Legal Handbook*, first published 1973, sixth edition edited by Anthony Speaight and Gregory Stone (Oxford: Butterworth Architecture, 1996), p. 19.
19. Lord Reid, *Hedley Byrne and Co. Ltd v. Heller and Partners (1964) AC 465 at 486*, quoted by Jon Holyoak, *Negligence in Building Law – Cases and Commentary* (Oxford: Blackwell Scientific Publications, 1992), p. 20.
20. Lord Roskill, *Junior Books Ltd v. Veitchi Co. Ltd (1983) 1 AC 520 at 545.*
21. Lord Templeman, *C.B.S. Songs Ltd v. Amstrad Consumer Electronics p.l.c. (1988) AC 1013 at 1059.*
22. Jon Holyoak, *Negligence in Building Law – Cases and Commentary* (Oxford: Blackwell Scientific Publications, 1992), p. 18.
23. Ibid., p. 26.
24. Ibid., p. 107.
25. Lord Keith, *Yuen Kun-Yeu v. Attorney-General of Hong Kong (1988) AC 175.*
26. Lord Bridge, *Caparo Industries v. Dickman (1990) 2 AC 605.*
27. Ibid.
28. Lord Roskill, *Caparo Industries v. Dickman (1990) 2 AC 605.*
29. Lord Oliver, *Caparo Industries v. Dickman (1990) 2 AC 605.*
30. *Murphy v. Brentwood District Council (1991) 1 AC 398.*
31. Lord Bridge, *Murphy v. Brentwood District Council (1991) 1 AC 398 at 475.*
32. Vincent Moran, 'The English Law of Tort', *Architects Legal Handbook*, first published 1973, sixth edition edited by Anthony Speaight and Gregory Stone (Oxford: Butterworth Architecture, 1996), p. 21.
33. *Winfield and Jolowicz On Tort*, first published 1937, fifteenth edition by W. V. H. Rogers (London: Sweet and Maxwell, 1998), p. 494.
34. Lord Lloyd, *Hunter v. Canary Wharf Ltd. (1997) AC 655.*
35. Lord Denning in *Attorney General v. PYA Quarries Ltd (1957) 2 QB 169 at 192.*
36. See *Gillingham Borough Council v Medway (Chatham) Dock Co Ltd (1993) QB 343.*

37. *Rylands v. Fletcher (1868) LR3 HL 330.*
38. *Cambridge Water Co. v. Eastern Counties Leather plc. (1994) 2 AC 264.*
39. Sue Hodge, *Tort Law*, first edition (Oxford: Willan Publishing, 2001), p. 121.
40. Lord Goff, *Cambridge Water Co v. Eastern Counties Leather (1994) 1 All ER 53 at 76.*
41. Martin Hedemann-Robinson and Mark Wilde, in John Lowry and Rod Edmunds (eds), *Environmental Protection and the Common Law* (Oxford: Hart Publishing, 2000), p. 211.
42. Paula Giliker, 'The relationship between private nuisance, negligence and fault', in John Lowry and Rod Edmunds (eds), *Environmental Protection and the Common Law* (Oxford: Hart Publishing, 2000), p. 164.
43. Lord Goff, *Cambridge Water Co. v. Eastern Counties Leather plc. (1994) 2 AC 264 at 302.*
44. Keith Stanton and Christine Willmore, 'Tort and environmental pluralism', in John Lowry and Rod Edmunds (eds), *Environmental Protection and the Common Law* (Oxford: Hart Publishing, 2000), p. 99.
45. Ibid., p. 96.
46. J. E. Penner, 'Nuisance, neighbourliness, and environmental protection', in John Lowry and Rod Edmunds (eds), *Environmental Protection and the Common Law* (Oxford: Hart Publishing, 2000), p. 38.
47. Lord Bowen, in *McQuire v. Western Morning News Co (1903) 2 KB 100.*
48. Justice McNair, *Bolam v. Friern Hospital Management Committee (1957) 1 WLR 582 at 586.*
49. Jon Holyoak, *Negligence in Building Law – Cases and Commentary* (Oxford: Blackwell Scientific Publications, 1992), p. 36.
50. Lord Hoffman, *Stovin v. Wise (1996) AC 923.*
51. Jon Holyoak, *Negligence in Building Law – Cases and Commentary* (Oxford: Blackwell Scientific Publications, 1992), p. 1.

MINIMAL IN THE EXTREME

Royal Victoria Dock Demountable Transporter Bridge
Techniker and Lifschutz Davidson

Poised 15 metres above the water, the bridge structure takes the form of a Fink truss spanning 130 metres and supported at each end by a pair of trestles. Six tapering conical steel masts of varying lengths are linked by cables to tie-down points along the length of the deck. At each end of the bridge, another cable carries tension forces to the ground through an angular bowsprit, adding to the overall dynamism of the composition. The pin jointed bridge sections allow for full demountability and reuse of the superstructure. Materials have a functional maritime rigour, and at night the bridge is magically illuminated.

Chapter 4

Ecological Frequencies and Hybrid Natures

Pamela Charlick and Natasha Nicholson, charlick + nicholson

AN ALTERNATIVE VIEW OF REALITY

As new cultural and technological transformations collide with contemporary debates about the environmental challenges we face, radical shifts in the relationship between the human species and both nature and technology are emerging. New scientific discoveries lead us away from the reductionist thinking of the Cartesian model and towards a more inclusive thinking, based on networks rather than the separation of entities, which has more in common with the organism than the machine:

> There is an alternative view: reality is a single vast flow in which eddies and cascades of eddies form and re-form, never quite the same, yet some lasting so long as to seem permanent. They have no existence separate from the overall flux, which gives birth to them and which swallows them up, and they acquire their character from their interactions. Effects feed back into their own causes, and causation loops and spirals and tangles. The whole explains the parts as much as the parts explain the whole.[1]

This convergence constitutes a paradigm shift of global proportions, a change in our understanding of the underlying pattern of the world. The appearance of the concept of sustainable development is an indicator of a fundamental shift. This is a chance to refocus the lens and zoom out to a wider landscape. From this new perspective, an agenda for change emerges and opportunities for architecture to both reposition and redefine itself.

The built environment is at the centre of the challenges and opportunities facing us. A human population of six billion inhabits the earth and it is caught on a tidal wave of urbanisation. As more people are pulled towards the cities, they are increasingly connected by globalisation and the Internet but divided by disparity of wealth and opportunity. The past one hundred years have seen urbanisation coupled with rapid population growth inflicting the greatest changes on the environment by any one species. These changes have been driven by a combination of the use of fossil fuel based energy and an ideological and political commitment to economic growth and military power. At the same time cities have created a psychological distancing between people and the natural environment.

The construct of man versus nature is deeply embedded in western cultural history, and architecture, as the built affirmation of the economic, social and political status quo, has reflected this. As oppositions dissolve between nature and technology, simulation and reality, individual and collective, new evolutionary orders are growing. Factors like globalisation, ethics, information and knowledge-based economies are reshaping our world and new insights are needed to accommodate the dynamic conditions that are emerging. Architecture needs to move beyond the component solution to sustainable building, where the inclusion of photovoltaic panels is a signifier of a building's sustainable credentials, to embrace these more profound changes.

From a western cultural perspective the Cartesian paradigm has dominated our understanding of the world since the seventeenth century, and left its mark on our institutions, our technology and our ideology. For hundreds of years Western science has successfully promulgated the method of breaking down complex objects and processes into simple constituent parts to discover their enduring properties and how they interact. The origins of this thinking appear in Descartes' *Discourse on Method* of 1637. Based on the assumption that the world is comprised of static and discrete elements seen in isolation from their environment, relationships are seen as linear and rest on simple criteria of 'cause and effect'. In the attempt to rationalise and quantify nature, humankind has sought to dominate and control it. It is this determinist, rationalist and hierarchical view of the world based on the logic of the machine that is at the centre of the decoupling of human beings from the natural world.

Increasingly this worldview fails to explain the world we know, or to provide appropriate answers to the questions it raises. An entity-based model of reality does not respond well to systems that have no clear boundaries, for example the weather, a flock of birds or ecosystems. There is a need for a coherent new paradigm that offers more effective and appropriate models for change. This is not a Utopian vision, but is a model that accepts change, diversity and connectivity.

Fundamental discoveries in theoretical physics during the last century have gradually undermined the integrity of the Cartesian worldview. The discoveries of relativity theory between 1905 and 1925, quantum theory from 1930 onwards, and chaos and complexity theories from 1950 have revealed an unpredictable and fuzzy construction of the universe, which is entirely different to that previously supposed:

Fundamental 'particles' are not precisely located but are 'smeared' through space; 'particles' that have interacted continue to be 'entangled', however far apart they are; whole atoms have wave functions which are not just the sum of those of the constituent particles; and the properties of the very small depend on those of the whole universe, and vice versa.[2]

This is the invisible science that underpins our world, and increasingly this knowledge is filtering through into the popular consciousness. Quantum mechanics reveal behaviour of matter at the micro-scale, and at the macro-scale which scientists have not been able to reconcile with Cartesian logic. In a sense we are living in an overlap between two fields of understanding.

Driven by advances in computing, the study of living systems is provoking a radical rethinking of the way life works and how living organisms function, particularly in the fields of evolutionary theory and genetics. This has led to a reassessment of the basic principles of Darwinism. A living system is fundamentally different from a machine, but from the dominant determinist viewpoint it is seen in machine-like terms; composed of discrete and unchanging elements, acting independently of the environment. David Korten describes this as leading to an 'assumption of a non-democratic hierarchy of control dictated by predetermined and unchanging genetic structures that deny life's consciousness, intelligence, freedom to choose, and capacity for intentional co-operation – which are among life's more important defining features.[3] Increasing awareness of the co-operative nature of organisms is a further challenge to the Darwinian model of evolution, in which genes are not affected by environmental conditions and competitive struggle for survival is a central tenet. Complex systems from economies to organisms are all self-organising assemblages that have processes of growth, evolution and learning in common. These processes are piecemeal, discontinuous and bottom-up.

The dynamic web of living systems is at odds with Cartesian thinking. The organism is not fixed; it cannot be considered in isolation from its environment; it evolves or adapts to suit changing external conditions. It creates itself (autopoesis) and evolves through transformation of flows of matter, energy and information. The organism co-evolves in a co-operative dance with other organisms and systems in the biosphere. A repetition of the same action can lead to a dramatic non-linear change, a jump that leads to a new phase of evolution. The power of computing technology to simulate the patterns of self-organising assemblages of organisms, or any other non-linear system, is helping to define the new paradigm. As these research methods spread across disciplines our ability to perceive the complexity of the world as a dynamic network of processes is leading to what Sadie Plant recognises as 'an emergent connectionist thinking'.[4]

The shift from the metaphor of the machine to the metaphor of the organism is evident. The World Wide Web is a self-organising system with which millions of the global population interact every day. Viral marketing uses the Internet to seek out customers, by producing messages that people choose to pass

The shift from the metaphor of the machine to the metaphor of the organism is evident.

Internal view of computer modelled lattice structure for Airlander by Jonathan Schwinge

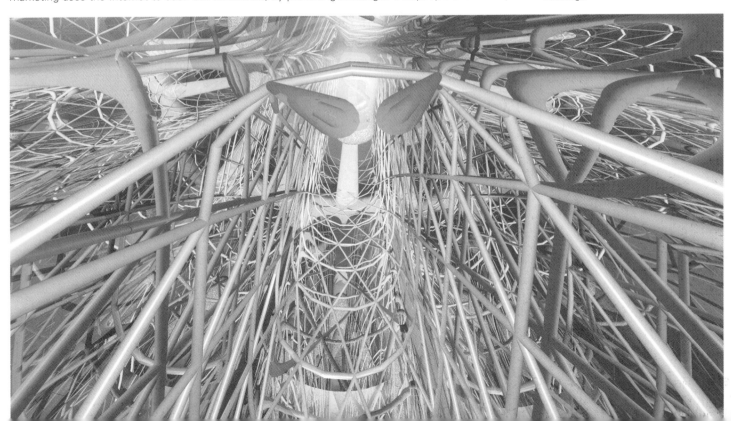

on through their own networks. This is intelligent and fast, and the spread is limited only by the power of the message to communicate. The language of participation, consultation and 'bottom-up' solutions is ubiquitous at all levels of government even if the application is still patchy. London's fledgling Greater London Authority (GLA) has policy agendas to maximise participatory processes, to promote informed communication and interaction between the public and administrators. When business and marketing start using the language of new science it is clear that this thinking is filtering into culture. In this transition phase, the distinction between the two paradigms is exemplified by debates about the human genome project. The premise of the mapping of the human genome is narrow, mechanistic and determinist in nature. Genetic determinism is increasingly undermined by the recognition of the importance of environmental factors, the interaction between genes and the behaviour of the organism as a whole.

Sustainable development sits within this larger landscape of change. As a concept it lacks precision and can be used to justify a moveable feast of actions or in-actions. It rests on the assumption that 'sustainable' and 'development' are mutually consistent, just like 'military peace'. Its popularity feeds on this imprecision: to some it is a justification of conservatism, to others it is a clarion call for a technological fix. But anyone looking for a pre-packaged answer to a complicated set of issues will be disappointed. Sustainable development should be viewed as a process. It is not an aim, or the panacea of a utopian vision. Instead of rushing to find the definitive answer to fill the space that these words have created, we should use the latitude that this allows us to rethink our frame of reference.

Sustainable development should be viewed as a process. It is not an aim, or the panacea of a utopian vision.

Architecture is perhaps one of the last true polymath jobs. Architects are, by training, well suited to the idea of thinking broadly across disciplines. As a profession, architecture should not fall into the trap of confining sustainable development to a box, a subject to be taught in isolation, or developed into yet another specialism. The fragmentation of knowledge belongs to the old paradigm; equally the isolation of the building as object from its context of complex living systems, does not fit with the idea of connectionism running through the new paradigm. Architects have a role to play in the development of a new conceptual framework that embraces both physical and cultural agendas.

A fundamental reassessment of the relationship between the human species, our technology and nature is required. Amory Lovins describes how, environmentally, we have crossed a significant line, in that 'only once in the history of the planet – now – have total flows and movement of materials by one species matched or exceeded natural planetary flows'.[5] The idea of a 'first nature', an unviolated and sacred nature distinct from ourselves is lost. Equally, the utopian vision of a harmonious idyllic nature has been supplanted. The impact of our intervention has produced a hybrid nature, a 'second nature', and there is no possibility of rewind. As our ability to simulate natural systems increases, the hybrid that develops will continue to blur the boundaries between nature and technology. A move towards an integrated understanding of planetary systems, and our place within them, will direct realignment with nature. This will have profound implications for our conceptions of structure, pattern and organisation, the city and use of resources.

As our ability to simulate natural systems increases, the hybrid that develops will continue to blur the boundaries between nature and technology.

The paradigm shift removes antagonistic dualities like city versus country. The city is no longer seen as an independent entity, separate from its environment. Urban and non-urban, or rural conditions exist on a unifying surface. They are differentiated by patterns of intensity and density. The urban condition is characterised by concentration of population, consumption and connectivity, and so there are particular opportunities for positive change, to take advantage of high densities and economies of scale. Around half the world's six billion people live in cities. Collectively, they consume 75 per cent of the world's resources and produce 75 per cent of waste, but consumption is highest in the richer countries of the North. The United Nations (UN) predicts that more than three-fifths of the global population will live in cities by 2030. Almost all these new urban dwellers will be in the new megacities of Asia, Latin America and Africa.

Radical change in the urban condition worldwide, the 'urban network', is a key to an acceleration towards global sustainability. A clue to the development of any ecologically adapted community lies in David Korten's description of the biological community:

> They are inseparable from place as they are exquisitely adapted to the most intricate details of their geographical habitat. They keep supply lines short by positioning each organism near its food supply, and take optimal advantage of whatever opportunity the habitat offers to sustain life on an ongoing basis.[6]

The co-evolution of species is based on both competition and co-operation, similarly with the 'urban organism'. Urban initiatives can be shared and promoted locally and globally. Competition between 'world cities' to achieve sustainability will stimulate positive change.

A confluence between urban and natural environments is significant in the sustainable development debate. The urban system is integral to the bioregion. Cities and the built environment have a vast environmental impact, but are often perceived as either irrevocably bad, or fall outside the scope of discussion. The built fabric is seen as the backdrop against which our other activities are played out. The fact is that buildings account for 50 per cent of Britain's carbon dioxide (CO_2) emissions. How, what, and where we build matters.

Why bother with a thinking which concerns itself only with 'legitimizing what one already knows', when it could 'consist of an attempt to know how and to what extent it is possible to think differently'?[7]

To think differently we need to ask questions in the right way. As new science gradually removes the Cartesian filter, it becomes inappropriate to think in absolutes. The answer to the question is not either/or, but both. Modernism sits firmly in the Cartesian world. It produced the 'fantasy of a universal architecture girdling the globe, doing its bit to produce the socialist "new man". But as Michael Sorkin explains in *Metropolis*, 'Nature – and democracy – prefer more dynamic forms of stability, compounded from order and disorder both'.[8]

In what directions will this new thinking take us? First we need to think more in terms of an 'ecological landscape' than an 'environment'. The former requires us to recognise the existence of multiple relationships, 'a reality of which we are part and of which the essence is taking part'.[9] The latter is removed; it is something we relate to, a reality that exists irrespective of our existence, another 'psychological distancing'. But if we operate within a new framework evolved from the web world of the organism we may find ourselves enmeshed in something quite different.

The 'site' is no longer a static entity but instead is a sea of systems and patterns. Within this context the self-organising assemblages of organisms seek to maintain themselves in a state of health. To do this they will aim for ecological balance, co-operation, dynamics and communications within the system, and in inter-relationships with external systems. The organism is constantly processing energy and matter to maintain life. It will adapt itself as necessary to suit changing conditions. Most existing urban systems could not be described as healthy in these terms. By recognising how networks of processes contribute to the overall wellbeing of the whole we can develop a different way of looking at the site of operations.

This way of looking can start with our own body. Rather than a single entity, the human body is a co-operative multi-bacterial system that forms a coherent whole. Dorion Sagan describes the human body in the following terms:

an architectonic compilation of millions of agencies of chimerical cells. Each cell in the hand typing this sentence comes from two, maybe three types of bacteria. These cells themselves appear to represent the latter-day result, the fearful symmetry, of microbial communities so consolidated, so tightly organised and histologically orchestrated that they have been selected together, one for all, and all for one, as societies in the shape of organisms.[10]

The organism is in a dynamic inter-relationship with its environment. One cannot be separated from the other. The environment modifies the organism as it takes in energy, food and information, and simultaneously it modifies its environment as it outputs wastes. In the natural ecosystem as a whole there is no waste, as the by-product of one system provides a resource for another system. Like an organism within an ecosystem, the city can be said to have a metabolism. A sustainable urban system aspires to the circular metabolism of an ecosystem with the result that consumption of new resources, and production of waste, are reduced to a minimum. Closed-loop activities reprocess material within the urban system. Unlike a natural system, a conventional urban system has an impact far in excess of its capacity to provide for its own needs, and this is dispersed around the planet.

The planet is essentially a closed system; James Lovelock's Gaia theory, developed with Lynne Margulis, describes it as a self-organising and self-regulating living organism. Every system is contained within, and interconnected with other systems extending to the global scale, and none can be isolated from the others. The ecological city contains smaller systems, whether individuals, communities or neighbourhoods with distinct identity, and with influence over the larger system. The building is a co-operative entity enmeshed in multiple interactive relationships with its environment.

Living and non-living systems (biotic and non-biotic) are both part of the planetary ecosystem, and cycles of change. Everything is in a state of becoming, but these cycles operate on very different timescales. From source to sink, a building is a transitory assemblage of materials. Buildings have a unique cultural role because they have a different, slower but very public periodicity. Compare the lifespan of a conventional building, often longer than a human life, to the lifespan of email, adverts and much of contemporary culture. Awareness of a broadband of timescales is crucial to an ecological culture.

Global systems are fundamentally dynamic and non-deterministic, and are defined by indeterminate phenomena such as 'strange attractors' and Lorenz's Butterfly effect of chaos theory. Evolution does not progress in a regular and predictable manner. It tends towards complexity, and highly organised and complex structures, such as the human brain, resist entropy. Inter-relationships across the world are intensified by the presence of systems or networks that act globally: environmental and health hazards, information

The planet is essentially a closed system...Every system is contained within, and interconnected with other systems extending to the global scale, and none can be isolated from the others.

and the Internet, and financial markets. When the world was less populated, and there was less traffic of people and goods, there were natural buffers between smaller local systems. Strong local networks, for example local economies, are a stabilising influence on the global system.

Information is a critical aspect of evolutionary dynamics. At planetary scale, there is a parallel between biological and human systems. An interactive web of communicating bacteria encircles the planet. Created three billion years ago, this global communications system works through horizontal gene transfer between single-celled bacteria. The co-operative results of this communication have formed part of our own evolution. The self-organising World Wide Web is our own interactive system for global communication and information exchange.

Because these inter-relationships are so complex and interwoven we cannot engage with them without a technological interface. Cartesian science was limited by available tools, the human brain and mathematical formulae to the study of interactions between two bodies. Computer data-processing enables the study of multiple bodies in self-organisation. In self-organising systems, each individual entity acts according to a simple set of rules, which creates a collective dynamic. This can be anything from the social organisation of people in public space to the behaviour of a pile of inanimate grains of sand. Increasingly, simulations are used to develop new solutions based on natural systems; for example, the co-operative behaviour of ants provides a model for the development of the efficient transfer of telecommunications data. This unfolding area of knowledge and its application breaks down the philosophical barriers between human and natural systems, and provides new insights into integrative strategies.

Developments in the field of scientific knowledge coupled with advances in computer technology, specifically the power of the central processing unit (CPU) and artificial intelligence are producing alternative visions. Supercomputing speed increases exponentially and is estimated to reach 12 trillion calculations per second by 2003. Yet these tools are only beginning to meet the task of unravelling natural intelligence. Mae Wan Ho illustrates the gap:

> Current computation is unable to handle the dynamics of one single protein folding, even given all the information on the amino-acid sequence and the final shape of the folded protein. It takes the computer four hours to find a solution that is at best 70% accurate; whereas the protein itself folds to perfection within a fraction of a second.[11]

Through the filter of the new paradigm, the context for development, 'the site', is almost unrecognisable, and this must lead to new responses. The concept of a static site affected by fixed conditions or constraints is the antithesis of the idea of a multiplicity of interconnected and dynamic relationships that create the site. It demands the simultaneous perception of different scales from micro-scale to macro-scale, and from local to global. Information technology is an essential partner in this dance.

An architectural intervention is an ecological act. Created from the existing environment, it has an impact on the systems of which it is a part. Adopting a strategy as appropriate to its task, it may resemble, for example, a filament, a parasite, a virus or a vital organ. It may be local and specific or may have a global proliferation. The intervention can be seen in terms of its effect within the dynamic system. It may facilitate movement, obstruct free-flow to capture materials and information, connect existing systems, enable communication, incorporate waste or consolidate resources. This is primarily about organisation, rather than form.

Experimental digital architecture is insightful about some of these ideas, and pushes the boundaries of what is possible. Information processing enables intelligent interactions between data flows and real architectural space, between actual and virtual worlds. With continual feedback between real and virtual worlds, each informs the other. Experiments with dynamic and evolutionary models can link into time-based data, such as solar tracking or movement flows. The use of computer technology for design is leading to radical new spatial language, contrasting with the simple geometries of Cartesian space. Simulation of design proposals allows exploration of complexity and innovation in the safe environment of the virtual world.

Architecture can be created, tested and experienced entirely in the virtual realm. In the virtual experience we learn to perceive space differently, from multiple dynamic viewpoints. The formal possibilities of building construction have been revolutionised by the computer, as exemplified by Frank Gehry's Bilbao Guggenheim, and using computer-based manufacturing methods, complex forms can be translated directly into production with minimum wastage.

In the virtual world where anything is possible, an underlying issue is to find meaningful connections. The extraordinary form-making capacities of computing technology are seductive, digital architecture tends to resist engagement with geographical place, and there is some struggle to find meaning from data.

Meanwhile, much 'sustainable' architecture deals in symbolism. The green roof or the solar array represents a 'green' sensibility, which may extend no further than this. Life-cycle studies or impact assessments that engage with the wider issues are opaque to the passer-by. But these are not such difficult concepts

An architectural intervention is an ecological act. Created from the existing environment, it has an impact on the systems of which it is a part.

that they need to be held exclusively by professionals. In fact it is vital that these skills and processes are dispersed. Sustainable architecture, too, struggles to connect.

In this territory of web-thinking and natural systems, there is no prescribed direction or purpose to development. But implicitly, particular value is attached to shared purpose and collective benefit, eliminating waste and curbing excess in use of energy and other resources.

Many people today feel insulated from environmental concerns, but at the same time they are dissatisfied with the conditions of the cities in which they live. In simple terms, lack of access to information, a lack of structures to facilitate change and a lack of connective systems have a paralysing effect. Even lack of awareness of like-minded individuals is a barrier. As there is no masterplan, there is a need for an informed community to create its own agendas for change.

Modelled on the living system, the imperative is the free-flow of information. From this comes a democratic base to decision-making, a diversity of priorities, and a situation where informed consensus is possible. Radical change will not come about without a degree of consensus.

CHANGE THROUGH CONSENSUS

How radical might this be? Leapfrogging the caution of politicians, can we imagine an emerging consensus against consumerism, mobility and capitalism? Architectural practice must change to engage dynamically with these shifting concerns – you might call it popular democratic consciousness – in the real space of the real city. From a new framing of aspirations, there is a potential for major change in the value systems of cities. In order to explode the box of architectural thinking we suggest a number of strategies drawn from the methods of natural systems. All these challenge the traditional Cartesian view of architecture.

They are collaborative, inclusive and interactive, and are applicable from planetary to local scale. They are not bound into high-tech or low-tech solutions. They engage with social, economic and environmental networks and systems, with physical and cultural change. They may not involve 'a building' at all. This is about what we do, but also how we do it.

Communication: exchange of information

Information is the energy of living systems, and the urban fabric must be networked into the flow of information – to accept, process and transmit information. Like the background chatter between microorganisms, international communications networks break down the isolation of buildings and cities. The evolution of the city needs good communicators to advocate change and to inform. Participatory and democratic processes for development must involve professionals removing traditional barriers to engage across disciplines and with the public in open dialogue. The information contained in buildings can become more transparent, from what they are made of to how they work. Interactive communication between people and buildings can produce flexible responsive environments and intelligent use of resources.

Leapfrogging the caution of politicians, can we imagine an emerging consensus against consumerism, mobility and capitalism?

Co-operation: intelligent collective activity

Common-interest communities use Internet and local networks to enable sharing of information without physical or geographical boundaries. Clearly, there is a need for effective co-operation between people with different skills to realise effective change. The development of co-operative structures alters boundary definitions and the dependence on centralised services or even traditional economies. Resources can be shared, and redistributed in flexible ways, and in new symbiotic partnerships. Using new infrastructure, a surplus of solar-generated electricity on a housing scheme can be used by local offices according to demand. Self-organising systems provide new models for co-operative structures. Public spaces and facilities can be designed for 24-hour use and layering of multiple functions. At present, privatisation of space swallows more and more of the city. Could the balance between public and private shift towards the minimisation of privately owned space and a resurgence of activity and collective ownership of the reclaimed public spaces in between?

Adaptation: evolving to suit changing conditions

Floating housing estates in the Netherlands anticipate future sea-level rise. Are our buildings destined for obsolescence, or will they adapt and survive? The redundancy of one element should not lead to failure of the whole system. The failed component is repaired, reused or recycled as a new resource. Evolutionary computing turns computers into automatic optimisation and design tools. Using an artificial neural network, a computer can develop a natural intelligence, which allows it to accommodate and even predict change. Intelligent systems learn from live data such as sensory stimuli, to enable flexible, adaptive responses. This may lead to a gradual evolution in response to changing conditions such as use, occupancy and climate, or a complete morphosis.

Production: restoring and remediating existing environments

This is necessary to create natural capital. An ordinary building, in construction and in use, will consume many times more resources than it produces. Zero-energy development is a proven concept, and increasingly it will be possible to design buildings that, over the whole life-cycle, 'give back' more than they 'take away'. Within the dense urban model, reducing reliance on distant resources is important. Integral production of energy or food growing strengthens local economies and reduces dependency on hard infrastructure.

Incorporation: including or uniting within the body

Marine cells were forced to exude calcium into an exoskeleton to avoid poisoning by the calcium-rich seawater, and our skeletons, made of calcium carbonate, owe their origin to this ancient incorporation. By developing new uses for existing material and techniques for reprocessing waste in physical proximity, the urban system becomes more like a natural ecosystem. The material that would have gone to a remote landfill becomes a new resource for the city. Legislation and policy are instrumental in driving this change and stimulating innovation. If nothing can be thrown away, material is valued on a new scale, and the economy will adapt to accommodate this. Where virtual activities or processes can replace real equivalents, the waste load is reduced.

Specificity: designing to suit a specific condition

The prefabricated standard unit assumes one size fits all, but new manufacturing technology enables economic production of non-standard components and individual configurations to suit particular needs and conditions. We can learn from the precision of natural design solutions, for example the skin of the dolphin. This is ribbed to reduce turbulence, and therefore minimise drag, and to optimise speed of movement through the water. With the help of computers and genetic algorithms, optimal design solutions can be found by feedback, testing for 'fitness' as an iterative process that simulates natural evolution. Specific solutions are resource-efficient. Further economies can be achieved through collaborative organisation. A parallel development may be the gradual elimination of peripheral consumer items, as resources and functions are consolidated in minimal high-density architectures.

Propagation: multiplication of offspring and diffusion of ideas

Architectural culture promotes and values the unique, and this is a force for inertia. An alternative model is the proliferation of a diversity of smaller catalytic projects with the capacity to evolve and adapt intelligently. This is not mass production of a generalised product, but development of a variable family of offspring. A good idea will tend to proliferate, just like a successful natural species, but it will also mutate as it spreads. Most new architecture is a one-off prototype, and there is poor dissemination of results for learning and developing better solutions. Propagation of information, skills and initiatives using hi-tech and low-tech networks is vital.

INTERCONNECTEDNESS

The majority of 'raw' materials for development are all around us in the fabric of the city. Many existing buildings are designed to address a few main issues without regard to intricacies of the wider ecological system. They are often wasteful of resources and difficult to reassimilate. Any intervention is likely to have a remedial aspect, in order to integrate existing built fabric.

It is impossible to build without effecting change. The nature that surrounds us will continue to be a product of our intervention.

Refurbishment is often seen as prosaic in architectural circles. Is this a proposal to reclaim the word and inject it with new energy and creativity? It encompasses this but goes beyond it, because the objectives are more ambitious than a fix or repair. Architectural energy and creativity must be refocused away from the privileging of the new-build and the one-off demonstration project. Invention and intelligent use of our knowledge and technology can be used much more pervasively.

It is impossible to build without effecting change. The nature that surrounds us will continue to be a product of our intervention. The politics encircling it are a complicated tangle of ideology and culture. Our perception of nature is a consequence of myriad social differences. Any definition of sustainable development that implies a romantic universalist view of human society and nature will fail. Underlying the broad picture that has been described is an idea of a move towards our own integration with nature, mediated by technology. In the new paradigm the idea of interconnectedness is paramount.

For a moment in the 1970s the oil crisis prompted a surge in environmentalism. Today global warming is the issue that has focused people's attention, but unlike the oil crisis, it is staying on the agenda. It challenges our ability as a species to respond appropriately. It throws our methods and practices into sharp relief, and shows the limits of existing systems. The increasing potential of computers to reveal previously unseen patterns is shifting the course on which we are travelling. As we tune into new frequencies, different periodicities, time spans and perceptions of interconnectedness and relationship are exposed. Can these insights lead to a new pattern for development, and a model for co-operation – at different scales of implementation, across continents and cultures? Will capitalism survive as the driving force?

The direction we take will pivot on the objectives of the developed world, and the emerging goals of the developing world, and how we all choose to make sense of our situation. Whether or not you believe the world is on the point of dramatic environmental catastrophe, sustainable development will alter the practice of architecture because it is resonating with the bigger story of change we have outlined. It is overtly political as it challenges the precepts on which existing structures are built. Accompanying moments of change are surges of energy. A politicised profession would tap into that energy, revitalise itself, and make itself relevant to the debate.

Notes

1. P. J. Stewart, 'Eddies in the flow. Towards a universal ecology', in Duncan Poore (ed.), *Where Next?* (London: The Board of Trustees, Royal Botanic Gardens, 2000), p. 279.
2. Ibid., p. 279.
3. David C. Korten, *The Post-Corporate World – Life After Capitalism* (San Francisco: Kumarian Press & Berrett-Koehler Publishers Inc., 1999), p. 104.
4. Sadie Plant, 'The virtual complexity of culture', in G. Robertson, M. Mash, L. Tickner, J. Bird, B. Curtis and T. Putnam (eds), *FutureNatural – Nature, Science and Culture* (London: Routledge, 1996), p. 203.
5. Paul Hawken, Amory B. Lovins and L. Hunter Lovins, *Natural Capitalism – the Next Industrial Revolution* (London: Earthscan, 1999), p. 315.
6. David C. Korten, *The Post-Corporate World – Life After Capitalism* (San Francisco: Kumarian Press & Berrett-Koehler Publishers Inc., 1999), p. 111.
7. Sadie Plant, 'The virtual complexity of culture', in G. Robertson, M. Mash, L. Tickner, J. Bird, B. Curtis and T. Putnam (eds), *FutureNatural – Nature, Science and Culture* (London: Routledge, 1996), p. 216.
8. Michael Sorkin, 'Acting urban – can new urbanism learn from modernism's mistakes?', *Metropolis*, August to September 1998, pp. 37–9.
9. P. J. Stewart, 'Eddies in the flow: Towards a universal ecology', in Duncan Poore (ed.), *Where Next?* (London: The Board of Trustees, Royal Botanic Gardens, 2000), p. 279.
10. Dorion Sagan, 'Metametazoa: biology and multiplicity', in Jonathan Crary and Sanford Kwinter (eds), *Incorporations* (New York: Zone, 1992), p. 367.
11. Mae Wan Ho, 'Human genome – the biggest sellout in human history', *ISIS-TWN Report*, Institute of Science in Society and Department of Biological Sciences, Open University, Milton Keynes, 2000.

Lost Exchange – An Icon Economy Reactivator which represents Hope and Optimism to Liverpool's present decline.

Chapter 5

Design Tokenism and Global Warming

Helene Guldberg and Peter Sammonds

CONSENSUS IS NOT A SENSE OF PROPORTION

There is an overwhelming public consensus in Britain that we may be facing a global disaster as a result of a warmer climate. British newspaper columns are filled with warnings about the havoc global warming is expected to cause around the world. Rising sea levels, flooding and stormy weather are anticipated, along with 'invasions of alien species', such as malaria-carrying mosquitoes in the British countryside. Cable Network News (CNN) warned in February 2001 that global warming might bring about 'cyclones, floods and droughts and massive displacement of populations in worst affected areas', with 'enormous loss of both human and animal life due to greater risk from diseases like malaria'. Prime Minister Tony Blair, speaking at a World Wildlife Fund conference in London on 6 March 2001, warned that 'the evidence grows daily all around us of the dangers of indifference to our duty to treat nature with respect, and care for our environment'. The consequence of failing in this duty, he said, is 'increased flooding, soil erosion, decreased crop yields, increased risk of epidemics. Deserts will grow. Disease will spread. Many species of plant and wildlife are expected to become extinct...Some of our most familiar plants will disappear, ones we consider exotic will become commonplace, and many of our animals and insects will be forced to migrate northwards or disappear altogether'.[1]

Architects have less ability to reduce CO_2 emissions than they imagine.

A wet autumn in 2000 led Deputy Prime Minister John Prescott to warn that the flood waters should be 'a wake-up call for everyone on global warming'.[2] He was subsequently 'gutted' at the failure of his attempts to broker a deal between the US and Europe at The Hague convention on climate change, following the 1997 Kyoto convention.

Global warming is an ever-present discussion providing the background to many specific debates, including planning and architectural policy. The 1999 European Commission (EC) publication *A Green Vitruvius – Principles and Practice of Sustainable Architectural Design* demonstrates the centrality of climate change to development policy.[3] Buildings, both in use and in the course of erection, are the biggest single indirect source of carbon dioxide (CO_2) emissions. In Britain, 46 per cent of total CO_2 emissions is caused by energy consumption in the home and in offices. If the 'carbon cost' of the construction is added to this, the proportion of total CO_2 emissions from buildings reaches 50 per cent. Thus there seems to be a persuasive case for finding ways of significantly reducing carbon emissions from buildings.

In *Factor Four*, Ernst von Weizsäcker, Amory Lovins and Hunter Lovins argued that this means 'saving the earth for fun and profit through advanced resource efficiency'.[4] Yet in the absence of widely applied cleaner technologies and a fully upgraded or replaced energy-efficient building stock, doing without fossil fuels means doing without heat and power. While writing in the *Architects' Journal*, and without questioning the supply side prerequisite of profitability, Paul Hyett proposed demand-side restraint on supposedly free consumers to moderate global warming:

> One recent prediction suggested that by the year 2200 – just 200 years – global warming will put Norwich, Cambridge, London, indeed all of Norfolk and Lincolnshire, and most of Suffolk and Kent, under the sea.
>
> Others anticipate the even worse scenario of a destructive 11°C rise in average global temperatures by the end of the third millennium if consumption of fossil fuels continues unabated. However, if carbon dioxide emissions are reduced by 60 or 70 per cent, a mere 2°C rise results – which is apparently tolerable.
>
> Here the twentieth-century's struggle between totalitarian communist regimes and the liberal democracies comes into relief, for it is the pursuit of individual freedom that now drastically threatens our ability to curtail the excessive demands of (free) consumers which spell doom for this planet.[5]

GLOBAL WARMING LINKED TO CAR-BASED SUBURBIA

Architects have less ability to reduce CO_2 emissions than they imagine. The low level of building renewal means that new construction accounts for a small percentage of the total stock. Also, not all buildings are architect-designed. At the 'Building Audacity' conference in July 2000 Martin Pawley suggested that architects are flattering themselves by exaggerating the effect their new designs can have on reducing CO_2 emissions and global warming:

It makes little sense for sustainable development enthusiasts to speak of the requirements of new construction as though they were compatible with sustainability. Due to the enormous back-log of existing built environment, they can never be of more than marginal significance.[6]

This awkward fact prompted alterations to existing buildings to be included in the revision to 'Part L' of the building regulations concerning the 'Conservation of Fuel and Power', excluding only historic buildings. The requirement to upgrade existing property when undertaking refurbishment or alterations is aimed at closing the range of operating inefficiencies between the mass of old and the trickle of new development. Taxation on fuel will perhaps encourage a resurgence of refurbishment or renewal, bringing property owners into the requirements of 'Part L'. How far taxation on periodic fuel bills will have to be increased before expenditure on construction is preferred is an imponderable. If taxation on fuel increases too steeply this hits the new building occupier despite the marginally better energy efficiency of his or her property.

Tenure further complicates the analysis, since landlords will tend not to modernise properties until tenants move to newer accommodation with lower bills, if they can find them. Another desperate idea considered in the *Analysis of the Responses to the UK Government's Consultation Paper on Sustainable Construction* by the former DETR was to involve development finance in the project of energy conservation and carbon emissions reduction:

When asked, a large number of respondents suggest actions by which mortgage lenders, insurers and others might encourage sustainable construction by introducing this as a criteria for lower cost loans and cover. A small number doubt the practicality of these ideas.[7]

Yet none of these initiatives are seriously intended to tackle the intractable problem of the ageing built environment being replaced too slowly, which is where architects would really find a role in carbon emissions reduction. The revised 'Part L' regulation deals with housing and non-domestic building separately, and provides three methods of demonstrating to building control officers that 'reasonable provision has been made for the conservation of fuel and power. These different methods offer increasing design flexibility in return for greater demands in terms of the extent of calculation required. However the overall aim is to achieve the same standard in terms of carbon emissions'.[8] The methods are of increasing mathematical complexity, and if architects want to remain innovative they must quickly master the sort of calculations that building services engineers are best placed to understand at the moment:

- The *Elemental Method*, which simply considers the performance of each type of construction in the building separately, but which severely limits the scope for increasing areas of construction with higher heat losses, such as glazing.
- The *Whole Building Method*, which allows the architect to use any combinations of construction provided the overall energy consumption of heating, ventilation, air-conditioning and lighting systems does not exceed a benchmarked level of CO_2 emission per square metre across the floor area of the building.
- The *Carbon Emissions Calculation Method*, whereby any design is acceptable provided it can be shown that the total annual energy consumption converted into CO_2 emissions will be no greater than that for an equivalent reference building type assuming prevailing weather conditions and normal operation.

As the architect considers the external building aesthetics and the view from inside, the consequences of those design decisions on CO_2 emissions must be calculated. The art of architecture has been subsumed into a convoluted exercise in energy conservation abstracted from building physics with no clear way of linking any of this number crunching to the real-world processes of global warming – themselves over exaggerated or beyond the control of architects. The 2001 'Part L' is the equivalent of putting bottles in bottle banks, except of course that it is a mandatory requirement. At best going through the routine may seem tangibly worthwhile, but there is no way of knowing what the contribution has been to saving the environment. At worst the exercise is a futile gesture. The idea that 'every little helps' is not the basis upon which the 'Part L' regulations are being promoted. These methods claim to be scientific, but are mathematical conventions justified on the basis of global warming, which is itself unpredictable and not necessarily a bad thing.

The problem is that the starting point for discussion has tended not to be considered scientific knowledge but alarmist interpretations. The aim of this chapter is to take a critical look at the evidence behind the global warming projections in order to get a sense of proportion on the issue. The public consensus in Britain, that adverse effects are already evident with worse to come, rests on very shaky scientific foundations.

The problem is that the starting point for discussion has tended not to be considered scientific knowledge but alarmist interpretations.

THE EXTENT OF GLOBAL WARMING DUE TO NATURAL CLIMATE CHANGE

One could be forgiven for viewing with trepidation reports of the temperature rise over the last century, at around 0.6°C, and the projected temperature increases for the current century, predicted to range from

1.4 to 5.8°C. The idea that the earth should operate in some kind of a balanced equilibrium is the foundation of the public consensus. The received wisdom seems to be that the adverse consequences of global warming are already upon us, and that much worse is to come. In fact, the earth's climate is forever changing. We are currently living in what geographers refer to as the Holocene epoch, generally a warmer period that spans back 10,000 years. Prior to the Holocene was the Pleistocene, when the climate alternated between ice ages lasting about 100,000 years and short interglacial ages lasting around 10,000 to 20,000 years.

Change rather than stability is the norm, and nature has no preferred climatic state. There is a case, however, for relative climate stability as desirable from a human-centred view. Human society would find it difficult to adapt to some of the extremities of former climates: for example, reconstructions of palaeo-climates and palaeo-environments show the ice ages as truly dreadful environments in which to live. With mean global temperatures more than 4°C lower than today, ice-age climates were much more arid. There was no Indian monsoon, vegetation only survived in isolated refuges, with the Amazon forest almost wiped out, and there was higher atmospheric circulation.

By contrast, 6,000 to 7,000 years ago, in what geographers call the mid-Holocene thermal optimum, global mean temperatures were 2 to 3°C higher than at present. Warmer climates tend to bring about higher rainfall, and in the mid-Holocene thermal optimum global precipitation was 9 per cent higher than today. The Sahara desert, which was considerably more extensive during the Pleistocene ice ages, effectively did not exist. The savannah, replacing the desert, was far more hospitable to human life. It was only with the general cooling after the Holocene thermal optimum that the Sahara desert grew to its present size. There were some areas of increased aridity, around what is now Turkey and in the Rockies, but in general the warmer climate of the Holocene optimum created a more fertile and productive earth.[9]

Britain has also experienced significant temperature fluctuations. In Roman Britain the climate may have been three or four degrees warmer than today.[10] Just a few hundred years ago, with the Little Ice Age in the northern hemisphere, winter temperatures in London at times fell to −40°C. Ice several feet thick covered parts of the Thames. Since the end of the Little Ice Age there has been a steady warming. There is no reason to think that our present climate is optimal, nor that a future warmer climate would not be more pleasant.

Past climate change

There is an easy assumption in the current debate about global warming that the amount of CO_2 in the atmosphere controls climate change. In fact, during the Pleistocene, the last two million years, climate records show this has never been the case in the past. Other factors have been instrumental in bringing about changes to the climate, and those climate changes have tended to precede rather than follow concentrations of CO_2. On a longer time-scale the warm period at the beginning of the Tertiary period, some 50 to 60 million years ago, occurred when CO_2 concentrations were low.

CO_2 does, of course, play an important role in determining the long-term temperature of the planet. Clearly the earth does experience a greenhouse effect. The surface temperatures would be 33°C colder without our atmosphere. The physical mechanism is straightforward.[11] The earth's surface temperature depends on the balance between incoming short-wave energy from the sun and outgoing long-wave energy emitted from the surface. Some of the gases in the atmosphere, the greenhouse gases such as CO_2, allow short-wave solar radiation to pass through and warm the earth's surface, but at the same time these gases trap some of the long-wave infra-red radiation re-emitted from the ground as heat.

However, as recently explained in *Science* magazine,[12] the record of past climate on a geological time-scale has other important controls. The change in the sun's output is a key factor. Plate tectonics are a crucial factor as they control the distribution of the continents and volcanic activity. Large landmasses have to be at the poles for ice sheets to form. Changes in ocean circulation, due for example to the opening and closing of the Panama straits, can alter ocean heat transport. Volcanism puts natural aerosols into the atmosphere resulting in cooling. However there has to be sustained volcanism for any long-term effect on climate.

The Pleistocene, or the last two million years, has been the period of ice ages. These were extensive worldwide glaciations lasting 100,000 to 150,000 years, punctuated by interglacial periods lasting 10,000 to 20,000 years. It is the present interglacial, the Holocene, that has allowed the development of civilisation. The most important climate control in the Pleistocene has been astronomical. After several false starts the astronomical theory of ice ages finally triumphed in the Milankovitch-Croll astronomical theory. This says that ice ages start when the amount of sunlight on high latitudes in summer is low. Less summer sunlight means more unmelted ice and expanding ice sheets. The intensity of sunlight can be calculated from astronomical observations of the eccentricity of the Earth's orbit, the variation in axial tilt and the precession of the equinoxes. The Milankovitch-Croll theory predicts periodic ice ages, and is a

There is no reason to think that our present climate is optimal, nor that a future warmer climate would not be more pleasant.

prediction found to agree with temperature cyclicity recorded in both sea-bottom cores and ice-sheet cores. These drastic climate changes are not driven by the concentration of CO_2.

It is possible to map the historical relationship between concentrations of CO_2 and climate change by studying ice sheets. As well as recording the past temperature, these also contain a high-resolution record of past atmospheres, thanks to trapped pockets of air. The Vostok ice core drilled in Antarctica shows a strong Milankovitch-Croll temperature cyclicity.

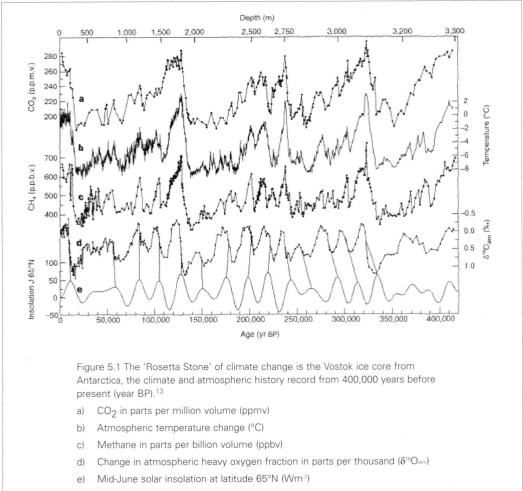

Figure 5.1 The 'Rosetta Stone' of climate change is the Vostok ice core from Antarctica, the climate and atmospheric history record from 400,000 years before present (year BP).[13]

a) CO_2 in parts per million volume (ppmv)

b)   Atmospheric temperature change (°C)

c)   Methane in parts per billion volume (ppbv)

d)   Change in atmospheric heavy oxygen fraction in parts per thousand ($\delta^{18}O_{atm}$)

e)   Mid-June solar insolation at latitude 65°N (Wm^{-2})

Historically, CO_2 concentrations have followed climate change, rather than forcing change.

However, the CO_2 content of the trapped air-bubbles also follows this cyclicity over a long time-scale. Figure 5.1 is often referred to as the 'Rosetta Stone' of climate change because it directly links evidence for changes in temperature to solar insolation and atmospheric composition.

In other words, for palaeo-climates, the CO_2 content of the atmosphere broadly responds to global temperature change. Note the causality. Historically, CO_2 concentrations have followed climate change, rather than forcing change. This is borne out by studying the big picture on the scale of tens of thousands of years. But it is also important to note that, over shorter intervals of a few thousand years, the temperature and CO_2 records can be moving in opposite directions. This needs to be kept in mind when today's meteorologists are making their observations about global warming over decades, and at best hundreds of years.

THE EXTENT OF GLOBAL WARMING DUE TO ANTHROPOGENIC EFFECTS ON CLIMATE

Global warming is happening. The key questions are whether this is going to be a benign warming of up to 2 to 3°C, or more extreme, and what effect human actions have on climate?

The Intergovernmental Panel on Climate Change (IPCC), a United Nations (UN) sponsored group made up of the world's leading atmosphere scientists, puts climate warming over the twentieth century at 0.6 plus or minus 0.2°C. The IPCC *Summary for Policymakers of Working Group I of the Third Assessment Report* prepared in 2001 states that 'most of the observed warming over the last 50 years is likely (66% to 99% chance) to have been due to the increase in greenhouse gas concentrations.[14] Atmospheric content of the greenhouse gas CO_2 has increased from pre-industrial levels of approximately 280 parts per million volume (ppmv) to the current level of around 360 ppmv. CO_2 is the most important greenhouse gas because its residence time in the atmosphere is over a hundred years. Reporting on the publication of the *Summary for Policymakers*, *Science* magazine commented that the IPCC concludes it is not the sun, nor natural climate fluctuations, nor some bug in a computer model that has brought about the changes, but human-induced greenhouse gas emissions, and in particular CO_2.[15] This is a far stronger statement than in 1995 when the IPCC stated, despite remaining uncertainties, that 'the balance of evidence suggests that there is a discernible human influence on global climate'.[16]

IPCC computer models of ocean and atmospheric circulation and the resultant climate when projected back in time support the conclusion that temperature increases over the last one hundred years are due to fossil fuel emissions. Observational studies show the intensification of El Niño, the thinning of polar ice caps and warming of the world's oceans. Few authoritative voices claim that global warming should not be taken seriously. However, some scientists do remain cautious. The global temperature rise last century is relatively small compared to past oscillations. It could be argued that temperature increases in the twentieth century were a result of the northern hemisphere emerging from the Little Ice Age. Most of the warming can be accounted for by increasing output from the sun. There has been cooling too due to volcanic dust.

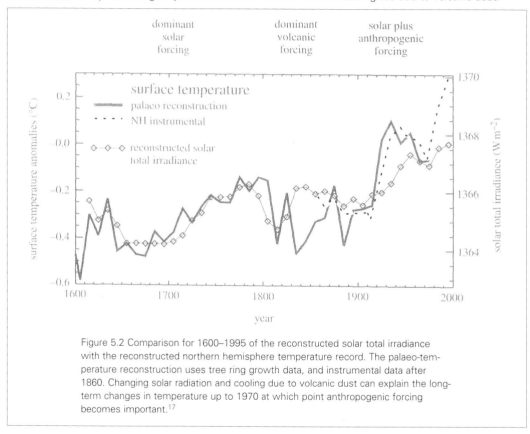

Figure 5.2 Comparison for 1600–1995 of the reconstructed solar total irradiance with the reconstructed northern hemisphere temperature record. The palaeo-temperature reconstruction uses tree ring growth data, and instrumental data after 1860. Changing solar radiation and cooling due to volcanic dust can explain the long-term changes in temperature up to 1970 at which point anthropogenic forcing becomes important.[17]

Over the past 30 years, temperature rise has probably been due principally to anthropogenic effects. In other words, it is due to CO_2 in the atmosphere from the burning of fossil fuels. But the magnitude of this temperature rise is small, even though there has been an increase in CO_2 content of the atmosphere of 30 per cent. So what kind of temperature increases should we anticipate? The IPCC in its 2001 report predict temperatures would increase this century by between 1.4 and 5.8°C. In 1995 its prediction was between 1.5 and 3.5°C.

Much has been made of the increase in the range of the predicted temperature rise, as if things were very much worse than was thought. It is true that as scientists have developed more sophisticated models, taking into account complex physical interactions in the whole climate system, the level of uncertainty in estimates of warming has increased rather than decreased. However, the actual calculated sensitivity of the climate to CO_2 in the atmosphere has not changed that much since the earliest government studies.[18] In 1979, a US National Research Council study by climatologist Jule Charney predicted a 1.5 to 4.5°C increase in global temperatures in the twenty-first century, which was not that different from the majority of current predictions. The real difference between the current IPCC prediction and earlier ones is the variations in patterns of social development that have now been taken into account, as shown in the following schedule:

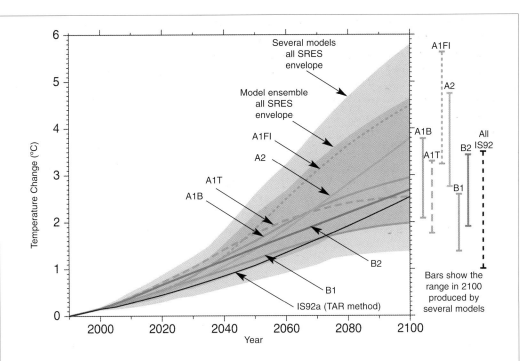

Figure 5.3 Projected temperature rise for the twenty-first century. The 'several models all *SRES* envelope' shows the temperature rise for the simple model when tuned to a number of complex models with a range of climate sensitivities. All *SRES* envelope refers to the full range of 35 *SRES* scenarios. The 'model ensemble all *SRES* envelope' shows the average from these models for the range of scenarios. See below for an explanation of the scenarios.[19]

Table 5.1 IPCC Emission Scenarios of the *Special Report on Emission Scenarios (SRES)*

A1   Scenarios describe a future world of very rapid economic growth, global population that peaks in mid-century and declines thereafter, the rapid introduction of new and more efficient technologies with worldwide economic convergence.

   •A1F1 A fossil fuel intensive scenario

   •A1T   A non-fossil fuel intensive scenario

   •A1B   A balanced fuel scenario

A2   Scenario describes a very heterogeneous world with continuously increasing population, fragmentary economic growth and slow uptake of new technologies.

B1   Scenario features the rapid economic growth and mid-century population peak of the A1 scenario, but with a worldwide move towards a service and information economy, social and environmental sustainability.

B2   Scenario features the heterogeneous world of the A2 scenario, but with a more slowly increasing population, intermediate levels of economic development and localised moves towards environmental protection and social equity.

IS92 Refers to the 1992 studies of projected temperature rise.

These SRES scenarios do not take account of climate change initiatives such as implementation of the emissions targets of the Kyoto Protocol.

For example, the IPCC this time considered scenarios where countries drastically cut emissions of sulphur aerosols, which form a cooling haze over parts of the world. The 1992 *United Nations Framework Convention on Climate Change* signed at the Rio Earth Summit states: 'the parties should take precautionary measures to anticipate, prevent or minimise the causes of climate change and mitigate its adverse effects. Where there are threats of serious or irreversible damage, lack of full scientific certainty should not be used as a reason for postponing such measures'.[20] So although formally independent of the UN, being charged with providing scientific assessments, in practice, and especially through the summaries presented to policy-makers, the IPCC works within this precautionary framework.

   The IPCC is doing nothing more than its job when it presents the worst that could happen due to bad decisions. But should architects be designing for the worst-case scenarios? If such an argument were uniformly applied then no building would be allowed in Tokyo because of the risk of a major earthquake, and Naples should be moved now from the shadow of Mount Vesuvius. If we are to keep a sense of proportion, architects should be planning on a far more benign warming. We need to plan for a steady transition to advanced technologies and building stock replacement, rather than panic ourselves either into punishing fossil fuel use or massive expenditure on marginally beneficial refurbishment programmes that simply prolong the life of inefficient accommodation. Were global warming to be heading to the high end of the IPCC predicted range, then modest reductions in CO_2 emissions through the early introduction of advanced supply technologies and accommodation with operational efficiencies would mitigate the worst effects.

Unfortunately, Peter F. Smith, Royal Institute of British Architects (RIBA) Vice-President and Chairman of the Sustainable Futures Committee, essentially agrees with the energy-conserving intent of the 2001 'Part L' of the building regulations, in the collection of advisory documents published as *Design within a Climate of Change*.[21] In the paper *Climate Change – Still the unanswered question*, Smith argues, like Hyett, that architects need to address 'not the energy supply side, but the demand side', on the basis that this approach 'offers the best opportunities for significant reductions in CO_2 emissions'.[22] Ruling out the research, development and application of cleaner technological solutions for energy supply condemns the British population to restrictions on fossil fuel use. All that will happen with demand-side savings is that the time to develop new energy supply solutions will have been lost, and that advantage will only be harder to recover later when fossil fuels are further depleted. Also, architects have little to contribute to the majority of 'Part L' refurbishment, and everything to offer in a programme of modernisation to exceed 'Part L' performance minima.

The big contributors to CO_2 emissions in Britain are electricity generation, industrial combustion and transport, each producing about 40 million tonnes of carbon per year.[23] This carbon output from industry and power stations has been falling steadily for the last 30 years even though energy demand has been rising steadily. This of course results from the move away from coal to natural gas and nuclear power. Since 1990, total British CO_2 emissions have fallen by 21 per cent, even though the carbon output from transport has been rising steadily. Large reductions in CO_2 emissions from these sectors can be made through the introduction of cleaner technologies. The advantages of hydrogen as the twenty-first century fuel for static electricity generation and motive power is discussed further in Chapters 14 and 18. The Royal Society has also argued in its influential report *Nuclear Energy – the Future Climate* for renewed construction of nuclear power plants.[24]

By contrast, the carbon output from the domestic sector and sundry 'other' sectors has remained static at modest levels of about 20 million and 10 million tonnes respectively over the past 30 years. Within this, energy demands of the construction industry are small and the 'carbon cost' of new construction is only about 4 per cent of total emissions. The level of building renewal is so low that overall gains in energy efficiency will take a long time. Unless the rate of building replacement is increased architects have little role to play in tackling global warming except as apologists for energy or refurbishment cost increases to reduce demand.

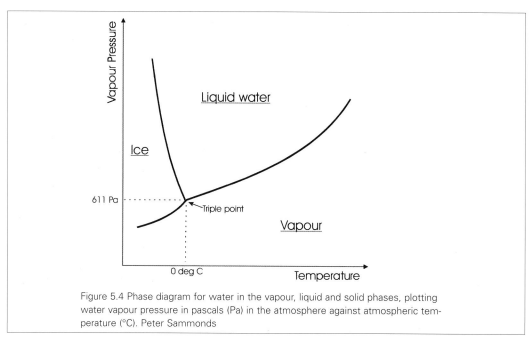

Figure 5.4 Phase diagram for water in the vapour, liquid and solid phases, plotting water vapour pressure in pascals (Pa) in the atmosphere against atmospheric temperature (°C). Peter Sammonds

PHYSICS OF WEATHER AND CLIMATE

The potential for rainfall is determined by atmospheric temperature as described by the Clausius-Clapeyron relation. An increase in atmospheric temperature results in an increase in atmospheric moisture content. It is this relation that explains how rainfall responds to climate change. In the Holocene optimum, when global average temperatures were probably 2 to 3°C higher than they are today, precipitation in the northern hemisphere was about 9 per cent higher.[25] The physics of weather and climate can be found in standard texts.[26]

The line dividing vapour from ice is the saturated vapour pressure, or SVP, over an ice surface. The line dividing vapour from liquid water is the SVP over a plane liquid surface layer. This measures how much water vapour the atmosphere contains at a particular temperature, over ice and water respectively. At temperatures of –50°C, typical of winter time in polar regions, the SVP over ice is only 4 Pa, while at 30°C, typical of equatorial regions, the SVP approaches 4,300 Pa. Between 0 and 30°C, the SVP approximately doubles for each 10°C rise in temperature. This is why cold climates are dry and hot climates are wet.

Aerosols are microscopic solid particles that are injected into the atmosphere either by natural events such as dust storms and volcanic eruptions, or by anthropogenic activities such as burning fossil fuels and biomass. Aerosols block incoming solar energy, so cooling the earth's surface and mitigating the consequences of global warming. The main aerosol source from industrial activity comes from sulphur dioxide (SO_2).

Wind speeds are controlled by atmospheric pressure differences. These pressure differences are influenced by temperature. With global warming, higher latitudes will warm more than lower latitudes. As the temperature differences narrow and the temperature gradient becomes shallower between high and low latitudes then lower average wind speeds and fewer storms would be expected. However, there is another factor. With higher temperatures there would be more energy in the ocean-atmosphere system, which could, for example, generate stronger El Niño events of unusually warm ocean currents in the eastern Pacific. The frequency of Atlantic hurricanes has been linked with El Niño events. However, the suggestion that there are actually more severe land-falling hurricanes in the southeastern US is disputed. From dust found trapped in polar ice cores it has been inferred that glacial periods were far stormier than interglacial. There is 40 times as much dust in glacial cores as interglacial ones.[27] It is for these reasons that the IPCC is so circumspect about predicting severe weather with global warming.

DISPROPORTIONAL ARCHITECTURAL RESPONSES TO GLOBAL WARMING

The Building Research Establishment has published *Potential Implications of Climate Change in the Built Environment* by Hilary M. Graves and Mark C. Phillipson,[28] with a methodology for assessing climate change impacts to inform planning, design and maintenance decisions. As every architect knows, there is a plethora of such advice and guidance, some of it better than other, but all of it tending to overreact to an inherently uncertain situation.

The need to have a sense of design proportion obviously has important implications for architects when considering climate change. Clients expect their properties to withstand the range of elemental forces that could have been reasonably foreseen at the time of designing without incurring unnecessary expense on excessive precautions in the absence of any certainty about the effects of global warming. Architects face a real problem in this regard, and whether construction stays site based, or modernises into manufacturing to increase the output of new accommodation, architects will need better science and not supposition to consider the conditions in which their buildings might need to perform.

Design to the extreme

In *Climate Change 2001 – The Scientific Basis* the IPCC distinguishes between what it calls simple and complex extreme events.[29] We have noted that UN advisors are confident that the earth's surface is going to get warmer over the coming century, but the amount of warming depends upon the initial assumptions made. We can surmise that there will be more days of extreme heat and fewer days of extreme cold. We can also expect increased precipitation globally, and heavier rainfall. These are examples of simple extreme events, but what about complex extreme events, such as storms, droughts and flooding? Most pundits and politicians take for granted that a warmer climate will lead to more complex extreme events, though this is not backed up by the IPCC *Summary for Policymakers*. On the issue of storm activity and drought it says that observed variation shows 'no significant trends evident over the last century'.[30] However, advice given to architects by the RIBA in the collection of papers entitled *Design within a Climate of Change*[31] is that relatively small climate changes could lead to massive outcomes, with a greater intensity and frequency of storms:

> The immediate consequence for architects is that design wind loads should be amended to cope with this progressive change and the fact that buffeting will increase in intensity.[32]

This is not necessarily so. It is not inevitable as heat builds up within the ocean-atmosphere system that this should result in more frequent violent releases of energy. With global warming, the higher latitudes will warm more than lower latitudes. As the temperature differences narrow between high and low latitudes the pressure drive will lessen. In *The Satanic Gases*,[33] Michaels and Balling argue that warmer winters in the polar regions will produce a weaker jet stream with possibly fewer and less powerful cyclones. Also, the general case for more violent atmospheric circulation globally is not borne out by palaeo-climate data, so a warmer climate could lead to fewer complex extreme events, contrary to RIBA advice.

Prepare for local cooling

Design within a Climate of Change also raises the fear that British winters will actually become more severe with global warming due to the demise or rerouting of the Gulf Stream, which is responsible for bringing warmth to northwest Europe. The idea is based on the argument that increased precipitation in the North Atlantic and increased fresh water run-off from melting ice caps would reduce the salinity of ocean surface water. Less saline water is less dense and would not sink so readily. This could reduce or deflect the circulation of warm surface water from equatorial regions.

This is of course scary stuff. While the world warms, Britain could turn into a sub-Arctic wasteland. For Smith, 'the possibility of colder winters adds urgency to the need to tackle the problem of the unacceptable numbers of unfit homes in the UK'.[34] Certainly the bulk of housing is inefficient to heat, but Smith's response is demand-side 'Part L' type refurbishment and not a supply-side replacement of property on a large scale to reduce energy demands in use.

For seasonal cooling to occur, the volumes of fresh water would have to be large. Recent models from the Hadley Centre, the UK Meteorological Office, show that this is just not going to happen, as cited in M. Hulme and G. J. Jenkins in their *Climate Change Scenarios for the United Kingdom – Scientific Report* for the UK Climate Impacts Programme.[35] This suggests that British architects can quite happily plan on continued warming this century.

Take to the high ground

Architects have been given some alarmist reports of what sea-level rise to expect. *Design Within a Climate of Change* cites views of 'Antarctic scientists' that the collapse of the Western Antarctic ice sheet will result in a 6-metre sea-level rise within 25 years.[36]

> It is inevitable that sea levels will rise. Already there are compelling reasons not to develop below the 5 metre contour at or near the coasts. The predictions of rising sea levels are becoming more alarmist, with the doomsday scenario of a 70 metre rise if the ice caps melt. This was the case in the distant past.[37]

This surely is worrying, if it were true. We know of no credible Antarctic scientists holding this opinion. The IPCC *Summary for Policymakers* puts sea-level rise by the end of this century as a global average being between 0.1 and 0.9 metres for a worst-case scenario.[38] The principal contribution to this projected sea level rise is expansion of the oceans as they warm, with a smaller contribution from the melting of ice caps.

Of course the alarmists are right in some very abstract sense. The continental Eastern Antarctic ice sheet has only formed twice since the extinction of the dinosaurs 70 million years ago. It took the exceptional cooling on a geological time-scale at the end of the Miocene about six million years ago for the submarine based Western Antarctic ice sheet to be established and further cooling in the late Pliocene about three million years ago for the onset of northern hemisphere glaciation.[39] The continental Eastern Antarctic ice sheet if anything is growing and is likely to grow with the increased precipitation that global warming would bring. The Western Antarctic ice sheet and the Greenland ice sheet are thinning. The time-scale for melting of the Greenland ice sheet and the 70-metre sea-level rise that would result is thousands of years.[40] We can say that except for those architects with truly dynastic ambition, sea-level rise of this magnitude is not worth considering.

For any particular coastline the question of sea-level rise is quite complex. Sea level will continue to rise in southeast England because of a tectonic response as a consequence of the rebound of the earth's surface following the disappearance of the ice sheet covering Scandinavia more than 10,000 years ago. For this reason alone the Thames barrier is probably inadequate. Climatically related sea-level rise will surely add to these problems. But the suggestion that land areas below the 5-metre contour are under threat is speculation based upon the idea that there will be increased storms with global warming, which we argue against.

Claims that coastal erosion is being driven by sea-level rises have been hotly disputed, and the simplistic geometrical erosion model underpinning this claim, the so-called Bruun rule, derided as having no validity.[41] Geological controls on coastal erosion, that is to say, whether there is a lump of hard rock on

the coastline or soft sand, still seem most important. Even though houses may be falling into the sea at Happisburg in east Norfolk, the other side of the coin is that, along the coast, Wells-next-the-Sea is anything but next to the sea. The process of coastal erosion and deposition further down the coast has been going on for centuries. But this view does not fit in with the apocalyptic global warming scenario.

Heed the flood warning

As Smith notes, 'rainfall patterns will change'. Alarmists claim that in the north of Britain rainfall will rise, increasing the risk of flash floods as rivers rise and the surrounding land is saturated. For the RIBA there is a simple architectural prescription.

> In areas which will increasingly be threatened by flooding, building techniques should change to enable buildings to cope with, say, a one metre flood, either by raising the ground floor level or by ensuring all openings less than 1.5 metres above ground incorporate an effective seal.[42]

It is not necessary to brick up your house just yet, according to Lord Julian Hunt, former Director-General of the UK Meteorological Office. The weather models 'certainly show that there will be periods when you would expect wetter winters. What we can say is that we will have rising sea temperatures. Rising sea temperatures mean more water in the atmosphere. More water in the atmosphere means increased precipitation. But, of course, the rain could come down in a beautiful drizzle every day for three months in the winter, as opposed to a few tremendous events'.[43] Rainfall patterns will change, but that is not necessarily a problem. In a report by the UK Climate Impacts Programme, projected annual rainfall will increase overall by a few per cent across Britain.[44]

Claims that in the south of the country there will be much less rainfall and frequent drought conditions are based on the worst-case IPCC warming scenarios. More benign global warming would result in a 4 per cent drop in summer precipitation, which would be viewed by many as a good thing, against an annual drop in rainfall of only 1 per cent. However, this will lead to increased pressure for water conservation, with harvesting and purification of both rainwater and grey water for use other than human consumption, due to growing population in the south and changing lifestyles leading to more water consumption.

Should Mies van der Rohe have built the Farnsworth House higher?

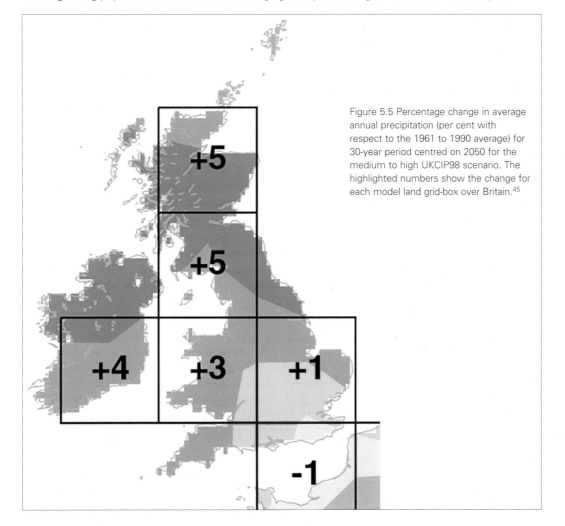

Figure 5.5 Percentage change in average annual precipitation (per cent with respect to the 1961 to 1990 average) for 30-year period centred on 2050 for the medium to high UKCIP98 scenario. The highlighted numbers show the change for each model land grid-box over Britain.[45]

DESIGN TOKENISM AND THE PROFESSIONAL IMAGINATION

Rather than encouraging design flexibility, the revised 'Part L' imposes needless constraints on the architectural imagination. There is no clear linkage between the science of climate change and tinkering with the abstracted building regulations. Architects presumably want to design beautiful buildings that provide shelter from the elements, and did not choose that career because they wanted to perform mathematical acrobatics to demonstrate a concern for global warming. This is design tokenism of the worst kind, and architects need scientific advice on likely climate change to be able to meet their clients' needs with some sense of proportion when thinking globally. As Martin Pawley observed:

> Within 20 years, in a world where, we are told, 60 per cent of the population will live in energy-burning megacities, all of which will be beyond any Western democratic exercise of political power to change, even the most draconian policy of enforced sustainability in Europe must be hopelessly inadequate.[46]

Architects should concentrate on raising the frequency at which the built environment is replaced, to tackle the issue of building more flexible floor area faster and cheaper and to take advantage of the cleaner technologies increasingly available in building services. It makes no sense for architects to become obsessed with the conservation of the mass of inefficient buildings and to push the design of too little new development to extremes of efficiency. To believe that reducing demand for energy can improve the weather is a shared self-delusion that architects should be wary of adopting as a measure of professionalism.

Notes

1. Speech by Prime Minister Tony Blair, 'Environment – the next steps', 6 March 2001, www.number10.gov.uk/news.asp?NewsId=1872&SectionId=32.
2. Deputy Prime Minister John Prescott quoted in *The Times*, www.thetimes.co.uk/article/0,,10-39849,00.html.
3. European Commission, University College Dublin Energy Research Group and Suomen Arkkitehtiliito, *A Green Vitruvius – Principles and Practice of Sustainable Architectural Design* (London: James & James, 1999).
4. Ernst von Weizsäcker, Amory B. Lovins and L. Hunter Lovins, *Factor Four – Doubling Wealth, Halving Resource Use* (London: Earthscan, 1997), p. 144.
5. Paul Hyett, 'Sustainability issues will grow in the new warmer millennium', *Architects' Journal*, 13 January 2000, p. 18.
6. Martin Pawley, speaking at the Building Audacity conference.
7. Department of the Environment, Transport and the Regions, *Analysis of the Responses to the UK Government's Consultation Paper on Sustainable Construction: Executive Summary* (London: DETR, December 1998).
8. Department of the Environment, Transport and the Regions, *The Building Regulations Approved Document Part L – Conservation of Fuel and Power*, Interim Draft (London: DETR, March 2001), p. 35.
9. N. Roberts, *The Holocene – An Environmental History* (Oxford: Blackwell, 1989), pp. 88–92.
10. R. Sterling, *The Weather of Britain* (London: Giles de la Mare, 1997).
11. M. A. Saunders, 'Earth's future climate', *Philosophical Transactions of the Royal Society London A 357*, 1999, pp. 3459–79.
12. T. Crowley and R. Berner, 'Paleo-climate – carbon dioxide and climate change', *Science* 292, 2001, pp. 870–72.
13. J. R. Petit *et al.*, 'Climate and atmospheric of the past 420,000 years from the Vostok ice core, Antarctica', *Nature* 399, 1999, pp. 429–36 (figure 3, p. 431).
14. IPCC, *Summary for Policymakers of Working Group I of the Third Assessment Report of the Intergovernmental Panel on Climate Change* (Cambridge: Cambridge University Press, 2001), p. 10.
15. R. Kerr, 'It's official – humans are behind most of global warming', *Science* 291, 2001, p. 566.
16. IPCC, *The Science of Climate Change – Contribution of Working Group I to the Second Assessment Report of the Intergovernmental Panel on Climate Change* (Cambridge: Cambridge University Press, 1995), para. 2.4.
17. J. Lean, 'The Sun's radiation and its relevance for Earth', *Annual Review of Astronomy and Astrophysics*, No. 35, 1997, pp. 33–67 (figure 10).
18. R. Kerr, 'Rising global temperature, rising uncertainty', *Science* 292, 2001, pp. 192–94
19. IPCC, *Summary for Policymakers of Working Group I of the Third Assessment Report of the Intergovernmental Panel on Climate Change* (Cambridge: Cambridge University Press, 2001), figure 5d, p. 14.
20. UNFCCC, *United Nations Framework Convention on Climate Change*, Article 3.3, United Nations, New York, 1992.
21. Peter F. Smith and the Sustainable Futures Committee, *Design within a Climate of Change* (London: RIBA, 2000).
22. Peter F. Smith and the Sustainable Futures Committee, *Climate Change – Still the Unanswered Question* (London: RIBA, 2000), p. 10.

23. Department of Trade and Industry, *UK Energy in Brief* (London: DTI, 2000).
24. *Nuclear Energy – the Future Climate* (London: The Royal Academy of Engineering and The Royal Society, 1999).
25. N. Roberts, *The Holocene – An Environmental History* (Oxford: Blackwell, 1989), pp. 88–92.
26. N. Wells, *The Atmosphere and Ocean* (London: Taylor & Francis, 1986).
27. W. S. B. Paterson, *The Physics of Glaciers*, third edition (Oxford: Pergamon, 1994), pp. 397–403.
28. Hilary M. Graves and Mark C. Phillipson, *Potential Implications of Climate Change in the Built Environment* (Watford: Building Research Establishment, 2000).
29. IPCC, *Climate Change 2001 – The Scientific Basis*, Draft report by the Intergovernmental Panel on Climate Change, 9 February 2001.
30. IPCC, *Summary for Policymakers of Working Group I of the Third Assessment Report of the Intergovernmental Panel on Climate Change* (Cambridge: Cambridge University Press, 2001), p. 5.
31. Peter F. Smith and the Sustainable Futures Committee, *Design within a Climate of Change* (London: RIBA, 2000).
32. Peter F. Smith and the Sustainable Futures Committee, *Construction within a Climate of Change* (London: RIBA, 2000), p. 1.
33. P. J. Michaels and R. C. Balling, *The Satanic Gases* (Washington: Cato, 2000), pp. 151–5.
34. Peter F. Smith and the Sustainable Futures Committee, *Construction within a Climate of Change* (London: RIBA, 2000), p. 2.
35. *Climate Change – An Update of Recent Research from the Hadley Centre*, UK Meteorological Office, Bracknell, cited in M. Hulme and G. J. Jenkins, *Climate Change Scenarios for the United Kingdom – Scientific Report*, UK Climate Impacts Programme, Technical Report No. 1 (Norwich: Climatic Research Unit, University of East Anglia, 1998), p. 34.
36. Peter F. Smith and the Sustainable Futures Committee, *Climate Change – Still the Unanswered Question* (London: RIBA, 2000), p. 8.
37. Peter F. Smith and the Sustainable Futures Committee, *Construction within a Climate of Change* (London: RIBA, 2000), p. 2.
38. IPCC, *Summary for Policymakers of Working Group I of the Third Assessment Report of the Intergovernmental Panel on Climate Change* (Cambridge: Cambridge University Press, 2001), p. 14.
39. J. Zachos, M. Pagani, L. Sloan, E. Thomas and K. Billups, 'Trends, rhythms, and aberrations in global climate 65 Ma to present', *Science* 292, 2001, pp. 686–93.
40. IPCC, *Summary for Policymakers of Working Group I of the Third Assessment Report of the Intergovernmental Panel on Climate Change* (Cambridge: Cambridge University Press, 2001).
41. A. H. Sallenger, R. Morton, C. Fletcher, E. R. Thieler and P. Howd, *Eos*, No. 81, Transactions of the American Geophysical Union, 2000, p. 436.
42. Peter F. Smith and the Sustainable Futures Committee, *Construction within a Climate of Change* (London: RIBA, 2000), p. 2.
43. Lord Julian Hunt, former Director-General of the UK Meteorological Office, quoted by Helene Guldberg, *Architects' Journal*, 18 March 2001, pp. 44–5.
44. M. Hulme and G. J. Jenkins, *Climate Change Scenarios for the United Kingdom – Scientific Report*, UK Climate Impacts Programme, Technical Report No. 1 (Norwich: Climatic Research Unit, University of East Anglia, 1998).
45. Ibid., p. 22.
46. Martin Pawley, speaking at the Building Audacity conference.

Production house buying for your rural site.

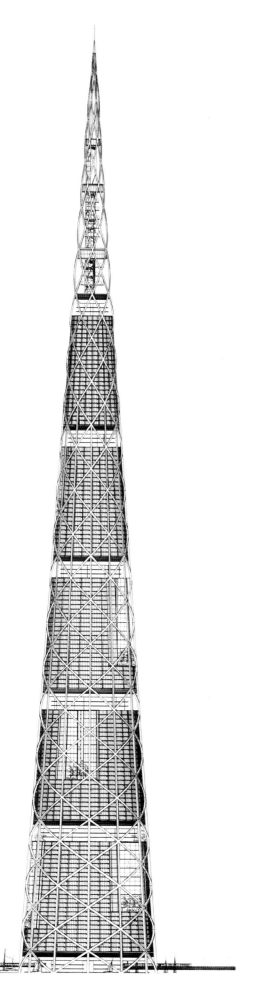

CHALLENGING ASSUMPTIONS ABOUT CITIES OF THE FUTURE

Millennium Tower, Tokyo
Foster and Partners

Commissioned by the Obayashi Corporation, this commercial development offers 1.04 million square metres of space. At 170 storeys high it is the world's tallest projected building.

Rising out of Tokyo Bay, two kilometres offshore, and linked to the mainland by road and rail, the proposed tower takes a traditional city quarter and turns it on its side. Tokyo is among the 'megacities' forecast to exceed populations of 15 million by 2020. Capable of housing a community of up to 50,000 people, generating its own energy, processing its own waste, and with its own transportation system, it is a virtually self-sufficient, fully self-sustaining community in the sky. The tower presents a timely solution to the social challenges of urban expansion on this scale, and to the particular problems of Tokyo, with its acute land shortages.

High-density or high-rise living does not mean overcrowding or hardship; it can lead to an improved quality of life, where housing, work and leisure facilities are all close by. The lower levels accommodate offices, light manufacturing and 'clean' industries such as consumer electronics. Above are apartments, while the topmost section houses communications systems and wind and solar generators, interspersed by restaurants and viewing platforms to exploit the spectacular outlook.

A high-speed 'metro' system – with cars designed to carry 160 people – can track both vertically and horizontally, moving through the building at twice the rate of conventional express lifts. Cars stop at intermediate 'sky centres' at every thirtieth floor; from there, individual journeys may be completed via lifts or escalators. This continuous cycle reduces travel times – an important factor in a vertical city, no less than in a horizontal one. The five-storey sky centres have different principal functions: one might include a hotel, another a department store, and each is articulated with mezzanines, terraces and gardens to encourage a sense of place.

Developed in response to hurricane-strength wind forces and earthquakes, for which the region is notorious, the tower's conical structure, with its helical steel cage, is inherently stable. It provides decreasing wind resistance towards the top, where it is completely open, and increasing width and strength towards the base to provide earthquake resistance.

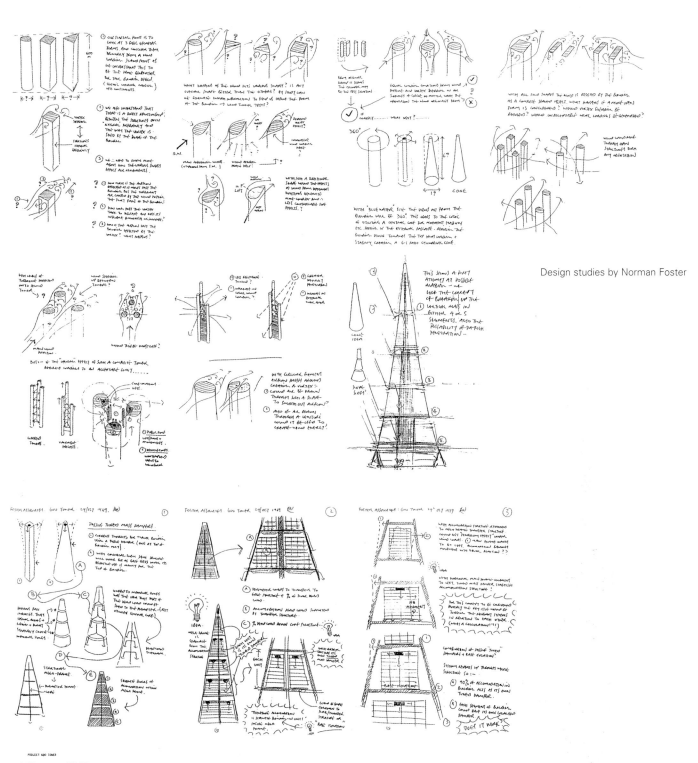

Design studies by Norman Foster

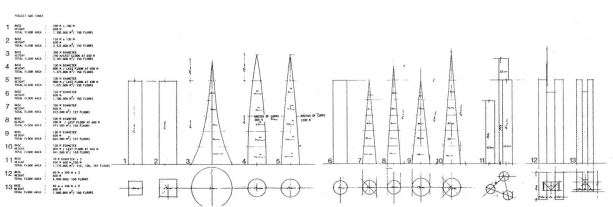

Chapter 6

Sustainable Development and Everyday Life

Phil Macnaghten

MISSING A CRITICAL DIMENSION

There is often an acute dislocation between the lofty rhetoric of sustainable development and the domain of everyday life concerns. This chapter outlines some key challenges for those seeking wider public involvement in the project of sustainability, and some specific implications for those involved in the world of construction.

There is a conventional understanding that sustainable development involves a process of integrating social, economic and environmental priorities. It entails focusing on the qualitative rather than quantitative aspects of people's lives. It attempts to meet people's current needs but not at the expense of future generations. And it seeks to promote human development that is not at the expense of other animals and eco-systems.[1]

These lofty aims are slowly yet systematically permeating institutional life in Britain and beyond. The mechanisms are numerous and include the development of indicators, the setting of standards, new rafts of regulation, 'green' taxes, the use of 'best practice', planning-policy guidance, new legal duties and so on. Yet, there can exist tension between the technocratic and often instrumental attempts to implement sustainability as opposed to the ideals and spirit in which the thinking was first developed.

For instance, there is currently a debate within the construction industry as to how best to come to terms with the new realities of sustainable development; indeed, this book is but one such response. Should the industry create new codes of conduct, attempting to improve energy efficiency and reduce resource use? Should the government promote more equitable housing policies, in the aspiration of developing a more socially sustainable society? And should such priorities be institutionalised through formal duties of care, or through more informal and non-binding mechanisms? These are difficult and far-reaching dilemmas. But, perhaps in important ways, this framing of the debate may be missing a critical dimension. The following sections set out a wider framework in which to situate this argument.

THE EMPHASIS ON EDUCATION

Worldwide environmental problems continue to escalate.[2] Governments, international institutions, industry and civic bodies, in different guises, have begun to recognise such realities, and have attempted to tackle such problems through formal programmes of sustainability. Indeed, across many countries, environmental sustainability requirements are reaching into more and more arenas of 'mainstream' policy, in such domains as energy, agriculture, industry, even fiscal policy. Following the Earth Summit in 1992 it has been commonly asserted that environmental problems extend beyond the traditional pariahs of 'dirty industry' and now include a wider array of economic and social actors and activities.

Responsibility also is seen as extending beyond that of governments and industry. The rhetoric of 'shared environmental responsibility' has reverberated throughout the 1990s, in Britain and Europe, across both local government and international initiatives.

In this model 'education' and 'information' are seen as logical and necessary steps in the move towards a more sustainable society. 'The public' needs to be educated so that people, as individuals and as part of communities, will act in more environmentally responsive ways. Just as governments and businesses need to develop environmental policies so too do ordinary people in their day-to-day lives. But what precisely does this imply?

In Britain, for instance, a number of government information campaigns have been launched designed to 'educate' people as to the environmental impacts of everyday activities such as driving a car, using public transport, recycling raw materials, throwing out waste, leaving the lights on, washing clothes and so on. The DETR asks us: 'Are you doing your bit?'[3] The Going for Green initiative asks whether we are following the 'Green Code'.[4] In a similar vein, environmental charities such as Global Action Plan have developed information packs aimed at helping people reduce their impacts on the environment at home, at work and at school.[5] Companies also seek to 'educate the public' to help reduce the overall 'ecological footprint' of consumer activities, both through purchasing activities and through forms of consumption. Unilever, for example, has an initiative called 'Washright', designed to 'educate' consumers in the ways in which they can reduce the environmental impact of domestic washing, both in reducing energy and the use of detergents.[6] Further and higher education establishments are also seen as playing a key role in the development of environmental responsibility. A recent British government report on this issue, the Toyne report, made a set of detailed recommendations, including the need for more specialist courses, for increasing access to such courses through more flexible methods of course delivery, and for the promotion of environmental education across the curriculum.

Across all the above initiatives one can detect a common narrative, relating not simply to how sustainability is understood, but how this itself is premised on a particular configuration of the environmental agenda. Put simply, the environmental agenda is seen as arising from a misplaced 'Enlightenment' faith in science and technology as though it was operating in a world without limits. The idea of 'limits' is now thoroughly spatialised. Environmental issues no longer operate in local or even national spheres, but are truly global, and include such issues as global warming, ozone depletion, the maintenance of biodiversity and the potential exhaustion of non-renewable resources, not least in processes of construction. As the Toyne report states, what has become increasing clear is 'our dependence on a global complex of environmental systems which are far more delicately balanced, and require far closer care and maintenance, than centuries of human activity had previously assumed'.[7]

The 'environmental agenda' can thus be characterised as consisting of a series of problems which are primarily physical in origin, and which arise from an ill-placed faith in (bad) science. What is also suggested is that such problems can be solved by (good) science, which more accurately learns to understand the ecological limits and constraints of particular forms of economic activity. The role for 'environmental education' not only conforms to such an agenda but actively places 'the individual' at its centre. Through education, the Toyne report states, we can better understand:

The idea of 'limits' is now thoroughly spatialised.

- the functioning of the planet's life-sustaining system (at least in outline);
- the need to maintain the delicate balance of these systems by living in harmony with them, and the skills this will require; and
- the reasons why non-sustainable activities come about, and the contribution which the individual makes to them.

Such a model for 'education for sustainability' is essentially 'top-down' in that it relies on experts – scientists, regulators, educators, architects and so on – determining ecological limits, presumably informed through science, and imparting such information to the public. Hence the appeal for information practices and new forms of consultation, aimed at encouraging sustainability and wider environmental awareness. In practice, many of the preferred techniques for dissemination are typically in the form of 'one-way' information provision. The model also can be seen as both moral and individualistic. Typically, a 'moral' code for environmental action is advocated to individuals, where moral responsibility is defined as to embrace wider, global ecological imperatives. In such ways education practices aimed at individuals are seen to be a key mechanism by which society can become more sustainable.

However, what tends to be insufficiently recognised is that individuals are also social beings, and that individual decisions always take place in social contexts that are both culturally and institutionally bounded. Indeed, it is the social context in which 'sustainability' takes place that tends to prove critical to the success, or otherwise, of such initiatives; if people are to genuinely participate in environmental sustainability initiatives, it is necessary that such initiatives connect with people, that is, that they reflect social trends in public values and sensibilities. What social trends are most relevant in this regard?

Perhaps most significantly, established forms of 'expert' knowledge, especially science, are being challenged across a diversity of domains. Such challenges reflect wider shifting public perceptions and values towards governments, industry, science, and indeed nature in its many guises. Understanding such dynamics may help inform the only limited success of official sustainability initiatives in harnessing sustained support and involvement.[8] This raises a number of questions: What is the impact of social and cultural trends on the ways in which people identify with the environment? Is the way in which people identify with the environment in concordance with the embedded understandings in official models of sustainability? How might 'the environment' be reconfigured such that it better resonates with how people are experiencing politics, environment and everyday life? And why does this matter?

In addition: How do people respond to different kinds of environmental information? How do people respond to those providing the information? How is this mediated by people's wider relationships to those providers? Under what conditions is 'information' trusted? What are the opportunities for the development of more two-way forms of interactive learning? And again, why does this matter?

A number of suggestions for how to approach 'sustainability' initiatives in the construction industry are outlined in the following pages.

LANGUAGES OF 'THE ENVIRONMENT'

Above it was suggested that the idea of 'the environment' in formal sustainability initiatives tends to be predominantly global in scale and physical in origin. In a recent research project on 'Languages of the

Environment', how people responded to a variety of global environmental issues was examined via a series of in-depth discussion groups.[9] The results were striking. The global environment was seen as somewhat 'distant' and 'abstract'. Threats such as global warming, ozone depletion, loss of biodiversity and resource depletion were perceived as a problem 'out there', detached from everyday life, making it easy for people to switch off. The following passages, involving two female participants, are illustrative of public responses to global environmental threats, in the form of key icons such as the rainforest, tiger, whale, smokestack, or blue globe.

In the following passages 'F' will refer to a female participant, 'M' to a male participant, and 'Mod' to the moderator.

F *...the 'Save the Whale' campaign and the 'Save the Tiger' and stuff like that; it all seems a long, long way away; so it's not my concern really...It feels a bit removed...We've all seen a pile of rubbish, but how many of us have actually seen a whale, or a rainforest, or been to an Amazonian forest or anything like that. You know about it and you're concerned about it, but it doesn't have the effect.*

Single women's group

F *When I'm confronted by it, I think yes, yes, I want to do something, and yes, it's impor-tant. And then you get back on the treadmill of your life...It's quite hard to reach that world.*

Mothers group

This does not imply that people were ignorant of global environmental problems. By and large people were aware of a wide variety of threats and of the need for collective action. Environmental responsibili-ty was seen as real, shared and increasingly global. As one man said:

M *We are custodians of the world, we are custodians at the moment, we've got to hand it on to the next generation, and so on and so on, in good condition. That's basically what it's all about.*

Anglers group

Even though the reality of global environmental issues has become almost commonplace, there was little sense that much could be achieved – either at the level of the individual or through existing avenues for col-lective action – to mitigate such threats. This perception of a fundamental lack of agency in the face of glob-al environmental threats permeated all the groups. Individual action was seen as largely ineffective, both due to the global scale of the problems and to the perception of powerful commercial interests intractably embedded in systems of self-interest antithetical to global sustainability. Indeed, this whole domain of think-ing about the environment was clouded in gloom and despondency, a finding that parallels previous research.[10] However, what appeared distinctive in these discussions were the strategies adopted. In differ-ent ways people were now *choosing not to choose* to dwell on global environmental threats, as a pragmat-ic response to apparently intractable problems, and in order to maintain a positive outlook on life:

M *Yes, it (life) is what you make of it; it's how you view things. I could be as miserable as sin, but there's no point in being miserable, so you make the best of what you've got, what-ever it is.*

Anglers group

F *I think when you are younger you think that your future is perhaps going to be far more worldwide, and that the whole of the bigger picture matters. But as you get older and you're just trying to survive through your humdrum lives, you realise that you don't matter to that huge world out there, unless something really exceptional happens out there.*

Mothers group

M *If you sat down and thought about that honestly, you'd be totally depressed all the time. You tend to close yourself off to it...You've got to get on with your own life.*
Mod *Is this true for other people?*
M *If we're honest, really we can only control our own domain, our own environment that we're for ourselves and our family. If you feel that strongly, if you want to get into the big-ger picture, then you've got to be focused...you've got to get into the right group that will allow you to influence a bigger picture.*

M   *You've got to be committed, haven't you?*
M   *Yes, it's got to be a heavy commitment…I'd have to be comfortably well off to do it.*
M   *Or be prepared to make sacrifices for the bigger picture.*
M   *The sacrifice could impact part of your family life*

Parents group

An added complexity was that people themselves felt implicated in global environmental problems. Although, on occasions, this led to a sense of the need for shared action, more commonly this led to feelings of resignation and detachment. For many people there were no easy answers; there was no longer a clear 'good guy' and 'bad guy', nobody to blame and no one beyond blame. Constrained by everyday pressures of work and parenting, people accepted their own partial guilt as consumers, as motorists, as employees of business, and so on. All people could do was their (little) bit, thinking more about (manageable) local issues than (unmanageable) global ones:

F   *All I do is try and do my bit, try and recycle things. I can't really see the whole thing because the whole thing looks fairly bleak…Things like global warming, I am aware of it, holes in the ozone layer and things like that, but I feel I'm powerless to do anything about it except the aerosol thing. Again I go back to the little things – unleaded petrol as opposed to diesel. You just try and do your bit.*

Parents group

F   *You're supposed to do your own bit but I think I'm selfish enough to think about my own bit.*
F   *Me too, what affects me.*
F   *I try to recycle things but I am only thinking of my own environment, or my own area as opposed to the world as such. I don't even think of the whole country, I think of my own area.*

Mothers group

So far we have suggested that the idea of a 'global environmental agenda' appears distant and abstract, and unlikely to engage people in their day-to-day activities. This does not imply that people are no longer engaged or interested in environmental issues but that the character of public concerns towards environmental issues has subtlety altered. There is a body of thinking that suggests that public engagement with environmental problems has shifted from distant threats 'out there' to more proximate threats 'in here'. Thus, issues such as Whales, the Amazon and Acid Rain, that were prevalent in the 1970s and 1980s, have migrated towards issues which impinge more directly and more immediately on 'me', my body, my family and my future – such as allergies, traffic, BSE and genetically modified foods. Jacobs suggests that this shift in orientation, directly associated with sociological trends towards individualisation, changes how the environment is experienced and how people are likely to collectively respond to environmental initiatives and campaigns.[11] Giddens, for example, interprets the growth of individualisation as a product of living in a world of high reflexivity, where 'an individual must achieve a certain degree of autonomy of action as a condition of being able to survive and forge a life'.[12] Beck, too, defines individualisation 'as a change of life situations and biographical patterns', arising out of 'removal from historically prescribed social forms', and the corresponding 'loss of traditional security'.[13]

In our research we found that the environment is experienced most intensely when it is part of the 'personal' realm of everyday life. The local and personal environment tends to 'hit home' and matter more. Indeed, it is often through personal rather than mediated encounters that people become involved in environmental matters:

F   *A lot of what we are involved in has come out of personal situations, hasn't it, more than anything. Whereas something like this, with it being such as global [thing], it's sort of how we get actually involved in it. I think it's something we all know it's something we should be aware of, but it's quite hard to reach this world.*
F   *I can't, I don't know who the leader is. There's no face to it.*

Mothers group

People do not think in terms of 'one big environment' that is the same for all people. Rather, there are many different 'environments', each connected to people's particular concerns, priorities, social relationships and responsibilities. For some, 'the environment' is a source of pleasure and escape from the burdens and stresses of everyday life. Activities of walking in the countryside, gardening, bee-keeping and fishing were discussed as ways of 'being in the environment', in proximity to nature, removed from modernity. Below is one such discussion of a young woman describing her passion for scuba-diving:

F   *It's the tranquillity kind of thing, you know, all you're concentrating on is breathing or not with snorkling. And what's around you. It's like taking your life right back to basics, you know, you're alive, you're breathing and you're floating around and then there's the sort of thing like you're other world...it just removes all the complications of modern life I suppose. For me that's why I go on holiday and spend most of the time under water. And it's so beautiful. The sort of crime and living in the city gets to me and that's one thing that is so completely the opposite that it's like, you know, some sort of therapy. It's like meditation, you're just concentrating on swimming or looking and just transported to another sort of level. It's so philosophical but you know what I mean.*

Single women's group

The environment becomes meaningful when it engages with life, inhibiting or facilitating the development of ongoing human relationships...

For other people the environment was seen as a set of problems, such as pollution, food safety and road safety, the putative effects of which had to be tackled as part of people's evolving responsibilities as mothers and parents. The environment was very much an issue in relation to its known or unknown effects on oneself or one's family. Health and food issues were particularly prominent and especially mothers were familiar and concerned over an apparently unending succession of food-health scares in recent years: from Salmonella in eggs and BSE, to pesticide residues and GM foods.

For others still, the environment was seen as providing an opportunity for maintaining important ties and bonds. Fathers, in particular, saw the environment as providing a context for the development of good parenting. This suggests that the environment is commonly experienced, not as a set of physical issues, but tangled up as part of social life. The 'human' and 'relational' aspects of the environment are often what are resonant. The environment becomes meaningful when it engages with life, inhibiting or facilitating the development of ongoing human relationships, whether in the context of the family, friends or communities of interest. Indeed, it was found that it is often the 'peopled' images of the environment, those with the human dimensions of environmental irresponsibility in the foreground that are most compelling. In contrast, those focusing solely on 'nature' and lacking clear and strong human reference points tend to be less compelling and lasting in their effects.

At certain stages of life, the environment appeared to grow in significance. For many women, the experience of motherhood was accompanied by a growing sense of care and responsibility, both towards other people and the broader environment. Below, some women talk about the relationship between motherhood and environmental responsibility, starting with one woman describing the development of more global forms of empathy and its origins in motherhood:

F   *I think very much when you give birth and you see your child, you become very much aware of that person as a person that lives and breathes and needs protecting, and feels the same as you do. And therefore you can project that to any other person round the globe and what they're experiencing.*

Mothers group

F   *Beforehand, I'd go down the pub, just me and my boyfriend. You don't give a toss about anything unless you're having a good time.*
F   *Changing since I became a mother, I suppose I did, my eldest son is very sort of into the environment. For me, he's the one who's really persuaded me. And really with the council supplying this green box, it's so much easier.*

Housewives group

Mod   *Can you think of where this (the environment) connects with your life?*
F   *I suppose in time having children*

Single women's group

A number of other social variables tended to be associated with a high level of environmental awareness. These included groups who lived in communities with strong local networks and social cohesion, those who lived a 'settled' life, those who were outward looking and generally reflective in outlook. While those groups who tended to be less environmentally aware included people who were high in mobility, who tended to adopt a consumer-oriented lifestyle, who were 'self'-regarding, and who were traditional and unreflective in outlook.

THE ROLE AND LIMITS OF INFORMATION-BASED LEARNING

Environmental information is often seen as the key to encouraging public involvement in sustainability. Yet little research has examined how people actually experience information. This section outlines key findings of a research project set up to examine the role of information provision by 'experts' and to derive lessons for industry, government and the media.[14]

Experts within industry and government whose role was to provide environmental information designed to inform and educate the public, tended to see themselves as enriching the body of fact available to the public at large. While at one level this seems uncontroversial, nevertheless it begged its own questions. The assumption that people reached judgements on the strength of the 'facts' deployed, and that this led to awareness, education, environmental responsibility and eventual shifts in behaviour, was encountered repeatedly during the interviews with information providers. Providing information was assumed to constitute a straightforward extension of the body of propositional fact on which people at large were then able to draw. However, the group discussions suggested that in practice a more complex reality prevailed. Particularly in areas where there was controversy (for example GM foods or global warming), people appeared to interpret information in the context of what they knew about its assumed source. What is more, they appeared frequently to have a shrewd sense of the motives and interests of the provider in question.

Information, provided by a government, a company, a non-governmental organisation (NGO), or the media, was assumed by the public not to be objective, impartial and unbiased, but to be framed so as to advance the organisation's self-interest. Indeed, it was taken for granted that any information on offer was framed with such interests in mind. Any previous experience, direct or indirect, of the particular provider was a crucial element in these judgements. Judgements of this kind were routine:

> M   *The words honest, government and debate just aren't synonymous*
>
> Singles group

> Mod *Would you believe what a company like Monsanto told you?*
> F   *Er, no. I think they would only tell you what they wanted you to know.*
>
> Empty Nester group

> F   *You always look to the bottom to see who sent you the information and if it's a supermarket who are in the business of selling food and want to make money – that's their line of thinking…It's just a marketing angle, because they want to sell you food.*
>
> Mothers group

> F   *Well, as far as newspapers are concerned, it's all about selling newspapers, isn't it? It doesn't really matter what the headline is.*
>
> Mothers group

> M   *As far as they're concerned (Greenpeace), they're looking at the bad side only.*
>
> Fathers group

> M   *What you really want is truly independent advice and that's so difficult to come by, because everyone's got an angle.*
>
> Internet group

This suggests that the process by which environmental information is understood tends not to be as simple as is commonly assumed. While providers appear to assume that information is pure, objective, factual, and that people accept such information in a simple, predictable, step-by-step manner, the focus groups confirmed that people do not act in such a simple, rationalistic fashion. Rather, they tend routinely to decode information for its provenances, and to triangulate particular 'packages' with data available from other sources. While this does not imply that all efforts at information provision are futile, it does point to a far more complex relationship between information and the institutions responsible for such provision.

Historically, those professionally preoccupied with information provision have failed to emphasise areas of scientific *uncertainties* or *ignorance* around 'expert' understandings of environmental processes. In the case of GM foods, for example, it was found that it was precisely the sensed dimensions of *uncertainty* or *ignorance* ('we don't know what we don't know' – that is, the sensed likelihood of anticipated conse-

Providing information was assumed to constitute a straightforward extension of the body of propositional fact...

quences) that have been giving rise to greatest concern. Reasonably so, it might be said. Yet it was revealed that information providers and educators had a wholly inadequate way of conceptualising the issue, let alone communicating it.

This suggests a wider problem. Overall, it is a reality of human experience that honesty about unknowns and areas of lack of control is intrinsic to all resilient social relations of trust. People need and expect to be able to make social preparations for unknowns, surprises and the uncontrolled as a routine feature of everyday life. It follows that institutions, which appear not to recognise such realities, are experienced as inherently suspect.

A WAY OF BEING IN THE WORLD

But how does this argument relate to the built environment? Heidegger argues that 'we attain to dwelling...only by means of building'. He makes a key distinction between a building and a dwelling. Dwelling does not merely relate to inhabiting a building; rather, it also means to 'cherish and protect, to preserve and care for, specifically to till the soil, to cultivate the vine'. Dwelling thus involves a particular mode of building, involving preserving, nurturing and cultivating as much as constructing. Furthermore, he argues that the process of dwelling is fundamental to our being connected to the world, arising from our mixture of labour with the soil. He also argues that the practice of dwelling facilitates a 'way of being in the world', enabling one to cherish and protect, to preserve and care for. Heidegger captures a crucial truth that has contemporary relevance for sustainability: '[t]he essence of building is letting dwell'.[15] He captures the sense of dislocation between people and their environments as exemplified in the distance between modern forms of building and their lack of dwelling.

So how can the building professions better connect with people in initiatives aimed at sustainability? Or rather, how can the profession of architecture facilitate 'dwelling'? Alongside more technical approaches, architects can help facilitate an ethic of care through initiatives aimed at enabling people to become more involved in the process of building. Britain, perhaps more than other countries, has lost its indigenous culture of building. Can the language and expressed commitments towards sustainability help restore this? One could foresee radical new possibilities for developing broad-based skills of building, for self-build initiatives aimed at enabling more widespread participation, all framed within a dynamic ethic of care and community.[16]

However, the practical challenges for such initiatives are far-reaching and would involve sizeable shifts in the culture of planning and building practice: if we are serious in understanding the conditions for a more sustainable society, we need to recognise that the more directly involved are people in the construction and preservation of their dwellings, the more likely they are to care for and cherish the planet we all inhabit.

People need and expect to be able to make social preparations for unknowns, surprises and the uncontrolled as a routine feature of everyday life.

Notes

1. World Commission for Environment and Development, *Our Common Future*, commonly known as the Brundtland Report (WCED, Oxford: Oxford University Press, 1987).
2. United Nations Environment Programme, *Global Environmental Outlook 2000* (Nairobi: UNEP, 1999).
3. Department of Environment, Transport and the Regions, *Every Little Bit Helps – Are You Doing Your Bit?* (London: DETR, 1999), www.doingyourbit.org.uk.
4. Department of the Environment, *What did you throw out this week? Going for Green*, DOE, 1996.
5. Global Action Plan, *Action at Home: A catalyst for change* (London: GAP, 1998).
6. Unilever (2000), www.washright.com/uk/index.
7. P. Toyne, *Environmental Responsibility – An Agenda for Further and Higher Education* (London: HMSO, 1993), p. 20.
8. J. Blake, 'Overcoming the "Value-Action Gap" in environmental policy – tensions between national policy and local experience', *Local Environment* 4(3), 1999, pp. 257–78; J. Burgess, C. Harrison and C. Harrison, 'Environmental communication and the cultural politics of environmental citizenship', *Environment and Planning*, A 30, 1998, pp. 1445–60; P. Macnaghten, R. Grove-White, M. Jacobs and B. Wynne, *Public Perceptions and Sustainability: Indicators, Institutions, Participation* (Preston: Lancashire County Council, 1995); J. Smith, J. Blake, A. Davies, R. Grove-White and E. Kashefi, 'Social learning and sustainable communities – an interim assessment of research into sustainable community projects in the UK', *Local Environment* 4(2), 1998.
9. P. Macnaghten and M. Yar, *Languages of the Environment* (Lancaster: Centre for the Study of Environmental Change, Lancaster University, 2000).
10. P. Macnaghten and M. Jacobs, 'Public identification with sustainable development – investigating public barriers to participation', *Global Environmental Change* 7(1), 1997, pp. 5–24; P. Macnaghten and J. Urry, *Contested Natures* (London: Sage, 1998).
11. M. Jacobs, *Environmental Modernisation – the New Labour Agenda* (London: The Fabian Society, 1999), p. 24.
12. A. Giddens, *Beyond Left and Right – The Future of Radical Politics* (Cambridge: Polity, 1994), p. 13.

13. U. Beck, *Risk Society – Towards a New Modernity* (London: Sage, 1992), p. 128.
14. R. Grove-White, P. Macnaghten and B. Wynne, *Wising Up – the Public and New Technologies* (Lancaster: Centre for the Study of Environmental Change, Lancaster University, 2001).
15. M. Heidegger, *Poetry, Language, Thought*, trans. A. Hofstadter (New York: Harper and Row, 1971), pp. 347, 349 and 361.
16. S. Fairlie, *Low Impact Development – Planning and People in a Sustainable Countryside* (Charlbury: Jon Carpenter, 1996).

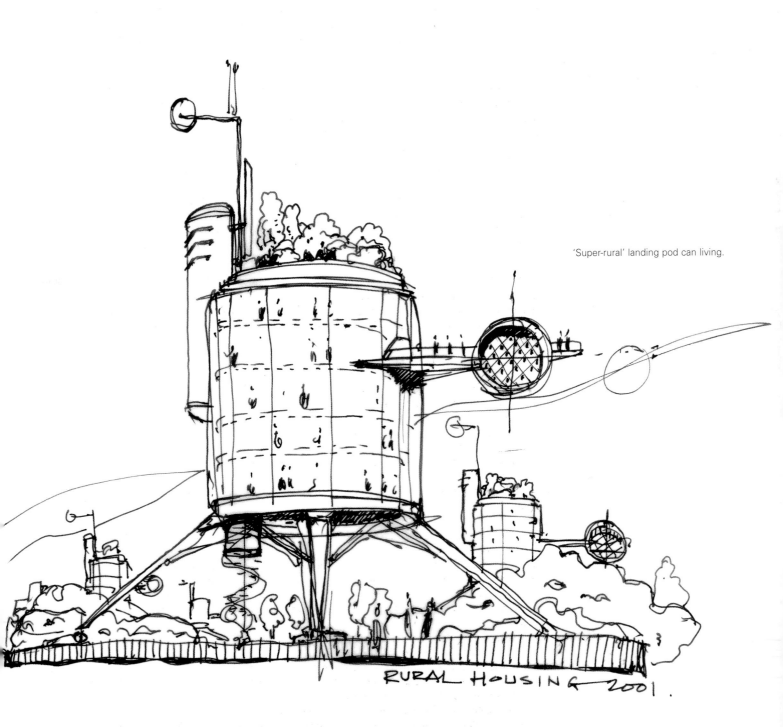

'Super-rural' landing pod can living.

Chapter 7

The Economics of Sustainable Development

James Heartfield

A PLASTIC CONCEPT

'By the late 1980s', wrote journalist and former aid worker Michael Maren, the aid industry 'had found a new mantra it could use: sustainable development. Everyone now talked about sustainable development. If you used the term, it sounded as if you knew what you were talking about.' 'The Beauty of the term', according to Maren, 'was that it could be manipulated for any purpose'.[1]

In 1992, at the Rio conference on the environment, US Vice-President Al Gore defined sustainable development as 'economic progress without environmental destruction', adding 'that's what sustainable development is all about'.

In her speech of November 1993, the Queen said that her government would 'promote sustainable development'. In its 1991 Annual Report the US Army boasts of 'expertise' in 'environmentally sustainable development'. Chairman of the Federal Reserve Alan Greenspan testified to the Senate Banking Committee on 26 February 1997 that recent stock-market gains had 'raised questions of sustainability'. Happily, the Dow Jones Sustainability Group keeps an Index, since 'the concept of corporate sustainability has long been very attractive to investors because of its aim to increase long-term shareholder value.[2]

The plasticity of the sustainability concept arises out of its dual character. On the one hand it implies development, and therefore material advance. On the other it implies that economic progress is properly limited, and can be pursued only insofar as it is sustainable. The concept of sustainable development emerged out of a debate over growth, and was consolidated through a number of international fora; the Club of Rome (1972), the Brandt Commission (1980) and the Brundtland Report (1987).

THE CLUB OF ROME AND LIMITS TO GROWTH

The first modern expression of the questioning of industrial expansion was the report commissioned by the Club of Rome, called *Limits to Growth*, in 1972. The Club of Rome was a 'non-partisan' think-tank under Fiat Chief Executive Officer Aurelio Peccei, and scientific advisor to the Organisation for Economic Co-operation and Development (OECD) Alexander King. It was founded in 1968 in the belief that 'the chief problems of the world today are not essentially problems of party politics and, being relevant to the survival of man, they even transcend current ideologies'.[3] These former industrialists hoped to leap over the depressing ideological clashes of the 1960s and 1970s by appealing to a larger 'problematique humaine'. For the Club, Massachusetts Institute of Technology (MIT) Professor Jay Forrester created a computer model of the global economy, 'World 2', and, with Dennis and Donella Meadows predicted that in the year 2100 'collapse occurs because of non-renewable resource depletion'.[4] Here was a challenge that would trump all of the worrisome clamour over the distribution of resources, by showing that these resources were on the verge of running out. With the oil-price hike being blamed for an economic slump, the belief that the impact of resource depletion was upon us took a hold on the public imagination.

However, the findings of *Limits to Growth* and the dire warnings based upon them did not go unchallenged. Forrester and the Meadows had taken the existing level of known resources as a constant, and simply projected the rate of consumption into the future, reaching their date of 2100 as depletion.

Perhaps surprisingly, reserves of mineral wealth are not a constant at all. On the contrary, with the passage of time, reserves tend to increase. Until 1999, when a small decline was reported, the world's oil reserves have been tabulated as increasing every year since 1992.[5] The reason is that reserves that were previously discounted as uneconomical to drill are reclassified as reserves when advances in productivity – or simply increases in price – bring them into reach. With new exploration and extraction techniques, new reserves of mineral wealth are discovered every year.

When *Limits to Growth* was published, Sussex University scientist William Page pointed out the error of assuming that reserves were a known or fixed quantity. Page referred to a 1944 review saying that had it 'been correct the Americans would by now have exhausted their reserves of about 21 of the 41 commodities examined'.[6] Page disputed the timescale of absolute resource depletion with a simple illustration of the untapped mineral wealth in the world's sea water:

- 1,000,000,000 years' supply of sodium chloride, magnesium and bromine
- 100,000,000 years' supply of sulphur, borax and potassium chloride

> *Perhaps surprisingly, reserves of mineral wealth are not a constant at all. On the contrary, with the passage of time, reserves tend to increase.*

- 1,000,000 years' supply of molybdenum, uranium, tin and cobalt
- 1,000 years' supply of nickel and copper
- 16,000 million tons of aluminium, iron and zinc

Furthermore, writes Page, with drilling going no further than 6 of the 40 to 65 kilometres of the earth's crust, reserves have as yet hardly been touched. Page's point is not that the resources of the earth are infinite, only that the *Limits to Growth* computer model massively understated them. He predicted, then, that in principle resources were sufficient for 'perhaps tens of thousands of years.[7] As Page says, 'the most pressing limits to growth are not geological: Mother Nature has put ample on the planet'. Rather, 'what limits there may be come from man's economic and technological ability to exploit these resources'.[8]

Page puts his finger on a recurrent problem in environmental economics. Limitations that are rooted in specific conditions of a given mode of social organisation are falsely attributed to nature itself. These limits are thereby rendered absolute and eternal, rather than being what they are – transient and specific. The mineral content of the oceans is a potential resource, but at the current level of technological development it is no resource at all. The error of the *Limits to Growth* model was that it abstracted from the very thing that it was seeking to demonstrate was problematic – increased productivity. Page's point is that that increased productivity, as the solution to scarcity, not its cause, is not only preferable but also necessary if resource depletion is to be avoided. Put another way, the oil-shock of the 1970s was evidence of relative scarcity, not absolute scarcity. It was scarcity relative to the ability to meet the cost of drilling the oil at the extant level of productivity.

However, strict proofs were hardly the point about the appeal of *Limits to Growth*. For the Club of Rome, Peccei and King cautioned: 'the conclusions of this first global research were generally taken to be a prophecy of doom'. As though absolute resource depletion in a century and a quarter could be anything but a prophecy of doom. 'While readily recognising the imperfections of the pioneering MIT effort, we regard it as a milestone'.[9] Indeed it was a milestone; not a milestone in the advance of geology, but in the transition of elite opinion from an emphasis upon growth to one upon limitation. 'Not the least significant result is that world attention has begun seriously to consider the basic issues raised by that report'.[10]

Commenting on this change in attitude in the Isaac Deutscher memorial lecture of 1971, the radical philosopher Istvan Meszaros said that '"the God that failed" in the image of technological omnipotence is now shown around again under the umbrella of universal "ecological concern"'.[11]

Compared to the activist and leftist agenda of environmentalists today, the 'limits to growth' debate was largely an elite and right-wing phenomenon. How can we account for this growing sentiment of limits among elites in the 1970s? The answer is to be found not in geology but in the social conditions of the day. The governing classes of the 1970s found themselves challenged at home and abroad by what the *Financial Times* called 'a revolt of rising expectations'.[12] Trade union militancy backed up 'excessive' wage demands, while in the less developed world radical nationalist movements accused the West of unfairly defending its monopoly on technological growth.[13] With the state 'overburdened' by demands, a 'crisis of governability' was the natural outcome of the revolt of rising expectations.[14] It was in that context that the attraction of a more austere emphasis upon the limits to growth recommended itself to an embattled elite.

The pertinent content of the world attention to the issues raised in the report was a growing emphasis on holding down consumption. Characteristic of the mood of middle-class fears was a pamphlet for the Conservation Society, *Towards the Creation of a Sustainable Economy*, by Margaret Laws Smith – a sort of literary equivalent of Felicity Kendal's performance as self-sufficient housewife in the TV comedy 'The Good Life'. Smith wrote of the need 'to stabilise the level of total incomes and total demand'.[15] Anticipating 'cuts in consumption', Laws Smith proffered 'we may hope that there will be some men in the most strongly organised unions who will recognise the necessity for the conservation of scarce resources'.[16]

'Political leaders may have their work cut out for them persuading labour union leaders to exercise restraint', wrote Lester Brown of the Worldwatch Institute, 'but at least they know what is needed'.[17] The Club of Rome saw the *problematique humaine* as being above political party. But on closer inspection it turned out to be an attempt at persuading people to 'accept sizeable cuts in their standard of living in order to meet the costs of "environmental rehabilitation"', said Istvan Meszaros. And all this with the 'additional bonus of making people at large pay, under the pretext of "human survival", for the survival of [the] social economic system' that favoured those elites.[18]

It seems contradictory that a social system whose central premise is growth would favour restraint. But these two souls always competed within the breast of the commercial elites. On the one hand growth was the condition for the reproduction of industrial society, and its justification. On the other, growth threatened to disturb the social order, jeopardising the privileges of the elite – especially when growth means the growth of a mass of discontented urban dwellers.

It seems contradictory that a social system whose central premise is growth would favour restraint. But these two souls always competed within the breast of the commercial elites.

Edward Goldsmith, brother to the financier Sir James and a key figure in the ecological movement, clarified the substance of the anxiety over growth. Urbanisation, he told the 'Alternatives to Growth' conference in 1975, 'is a particularly frightening prospect, since it is in the existing conurbations that the ills from which industrialised society is suffering are to be found in the most concentrated forms'.[19] Goldsmith added: 'it seems unnecessary to list these ills'. The misanthropic impulse of ecology is expressed in Paul Ehrlich's overpopulation thesis: 'Too many cars, too many factories, too much pesticide...too little water, too much carbon dioxide – all can easily be traced to too many people'.[20]

For Edward Goldsmith growth, such as urban sprawl, implies disturbance and change to the social order that is contrary to nature. 'It is a feature of a stable system that, in the face of change, it seeks to preserve not only its own structure, but also that of the environment to which it is committed', lectured Goldsmith, hopefully. But 'unfortunately, people refuse to face the evident fact that this principle must apply equally to man'.[21] The social stability that Goldsmith sees threatened by the burgeoning urban masses becomes, in his own mind, a law of nature. In this way Goldsmith wards off his own uncertainties about change by relocating his hostility to growth on to nature. Perhaps the natural order that Goldsmith has in mind is the one where the rich man is in his castle and the poor man at his gate.

In 1992 Donella and Dennis Meadows followed up *Limits to Growth* with *Beyond the Limits – Global Collapse or a Sustainable Future*.[22] This appealed to a similar natural law that they called a 'systems approach', where the economy and the environment are considered as *one system*. Consequently growth becomes a disturbance in the system, leading to overshoot and collapse. Plainly, the assumption of collapse is built into the model of systemic whole, for which all change is pathological.

In economics the method adopted by the Meadows and by Edward Goldsmith is known as the model of competitive general equilibrium. In equilibrium economics prices find their proper level as supply and demand meet. Artificial disturbances in the harmonious operation of the laws of the market are punished by counter-disturbances as the equilibrium reasserts itself.

The general theory of equilibrium enjoyed a degree of popularity in the 1980s. According to the theory, trade unions, in creating a monopoly price for labour, had disturbed the equilibrium, only to be punished by unemployment as the equilibrium reasserted itself. Equilibrium or harmonist economics provided a convenient explanation for rising unemployment and reduced wages. Furthermore, the conception of the economy as a zero-sum game, in which nobody gained except at somebody else's expense, corresponded to the era in which corporate raiders like Sir James Goldsmith made money by buying up firms and raiding their assets.

However, with the profound *dis*equilibrium of slump in the early nineties, faith in harmonist economics declined. The return of growth in the second half of the decade put paid to the idea that the economy could ever be a static state.[23] But though the general theory of equilibrium was discredited in economics, it was preserved in the ecological theory of a natural balance between man and nature. Though few today would have the self-assurance of a Margaret Thatcher or Milton Friedman to argue that unemployment is the unavoidable restoration of natural balances, the same explanation can readily be applied to famines, disasters and diseases.

'Growth', according to Lester Brown, 'has become the goal of every society, North and South. Indeed it has become a kind of religion or ideology that drives societies'.[24] But growth is only one of the ideologies at work in contemporary societies. The other, the predominant one, is the one that Brown advocates himself – the ideology of natural limits.

THE BRANDT REPORT AND APPROPRIATE TECHNOLOGY

In 1980, *North-South – A Programme for Survival*, the report of the Independent Commission on International Development Issues, dealt directly with the problem of the developed world's monopoly on technology. Under German Social Democrat and former premier Willy Brandt the report first popularised the case for 'appropriate technology' for the less developed world. The concept of appropriate technology anticipated the more developed idea of sustainable development. Like sustainable development, appropriate technology is a hybrid concept. It appeals both to the demand for better technology on the part of the people of the less developed world, and at the same time calls into question the generalisation of 'Western' technology.

Like the arguments for limits to growth, the Brandt Report regretted that 'industrialised countries stick to a guiding philosophy which is predominantly materialistic and based on a belief in the automatic growth of gross national product'.[25] The point of the intervention though was not in substance addressed to the developed world but the less so: 'We must not surrender to the idea that the whole world should copy the model of the highly industrialised countries'.[26]

The form of the argument seems to favour the underdog. The model of Western development is a negative one. But what is the consequence of the argument? The West's monopoly over new technologies is defended. It is cute to pose this defence of the status quo as a critical doctrine, but it does not change its substance. By an act of ventriloquism, Brandt's commission puts the words 'those technology grapes are sour' into the mouths of the less developed world.

If the model of industrial development and growth is inappropriate for the South, what is appropriate? Here Brandt's commission becomes remarkably coy. The section on appropriate technology – the principle reason for which the report is remembered – is hedged around with caveats. It suggests that it is not for us to say what is and what is not appropriate. Yet appropriate technology 'can include cheaper sources of energy; simpler farm equipment; techniques in building, services and manufacturing processes which save capital; smaller plants and scales of operation which can permit dispersal of activity'.[27]

What appropriate technology meant for the less developed world was the lowering of expectations; less capital input, less expenditure, less technology. Given the higher levels of consumption, life expectancy, natal survival, healthcare, air quality, nutrition, literacy and education in the West, one might have thought that far greater levels of capital investment were appropriate for the South. But at its core, the argument over appropriate technology rested on an assumption that people in the South were just not expected to handle industrial growth.

Arghiri Emmanuel, the University of Paris development economist, took issue with the appropriate technology thesis in *Appropriate or Underdeveloped Technology?*. Emmanuel struck at the conservative notion of preserving cultures, writing: 'cultural authenticity is also the tourist picturesqueness of underdevelopment', and adding: 'humanity is neither a zoo nor a museum of the anthropologically exotic'.[28] Striking at the faux-radical appeal of 'appropriate technology' Emmanuel charged that 'a certain addiction to the past' wrongly identifies 'less developed capitalist relations...as paradise lost, and slides from the criticism of capitalism in general to the denial of development within capitalism'.[29] Emmanuel appealed to the radicals not to forget 'that if capitalism is hell there exists a more frightful hell: that of less developed capitalism'.

According to Emmanuel, the implication that a 'technology would be compatible with a given culture presupposes that the "culture" exists *prior* to the technology'.[30] 'In the final analysis', argued the economist, 'one has the culture corresponding to one's technology and it is quite illusory to seek the technology corresponding to one's culture'.[31] In other words, making the technology appropriate to the culture would always mean arresting the technology at a low level of development.

THE BRANDT REPORT AND SAVING LABOUR

One argument put by the Brandt Commission is that 'it certainly makes no sense to impose methods of production in developing countries that leave their labour force largely unused'.[32] This is a reference to the well-known relationship between increased labour productivity and unemployment first noted by the economist David Ricardo in 1821, where 'the substitution of machinery for human labour is often very injurious to the interests of the class of labourers'.[33]

A more recent commentator, the German economist and environmentalist Elmar Altvater, put the point this way: 'Productivity of labour growing at a higher pace than output inevitably results in losses of jobs – unless working time is reduced.'[34] The correspondence is not quite as fixed as Altvater suggests, since capital released through increased productivity may be turned to new points of production, as can be seen by the twin growth in productivity and employment in the US over the last five years. The underlying tension between mechanisation and employment is undeniable, however its workings are moderated by other factors.

The implied coalescence between labour interests and those of ecological forbearance do not elude Altvater: 'the substitution of fossil energy consumption by living labour and the increase of employment would reduce the consumption of resources and emissions and reconcile policies of full employment and of ecological sustainability'.[35]

It is a perverse result of the ecological scale of values that the one resource that is to be squandered is human labour, by sustaining labour intensive production. This is perhaps the obvious consequence of a philosophy that subordinates humanity to nature – humanity can be wasted but 'the planet' must be saved. In the broadest scheme of things, the opposition between productivity and paid employment is not to be fixed by retreating from the application of labour-saving technology. As the sociologist Ulrich Beck rightly argues it would be defeatist to occupy the unemployed in pointlessly arduous activity.[36] As to relations between the less and more developed world, it would be a mistake to think that the former would gain by having labour-intensive production techniques imposed upon it. Rather this would merely increase the precarious dependence of the less affluent South upon the North.

Since the Brandt Commission sought to present itself in the guise of a friend of the peoples of the Third World and of labour, it seems pertinent to ask who these friends were. The European members of the commission, Brandt himself, Edward Heath and Pierre Mendes-France (who died before the commission

It is a perverse result of the ecological scale of values that the one resource that is to be squandered is human labour, by sustaining labour intensive production.

reported) were all associated with the introduction of austerity measures. Heath imposed compulsory wage restraint in the 1970s, while Mendes-France's attempts to retain Vichy levels of pay in post-liberation France provoked an explosion of strikes and protests.[37] In true colonial fashion, Heath also took the fatal step that triggered a quarter century of war in Northern Ireland: the introduction of internment of Irish nationalists without trial.[38] Nor were the Southern commissioners much more attractive. Abdlatif Al Hamad was the Director-General of the Kuwait Fund for Arab Economic Development. Indonesian Foreign Minister Adam Malik was 'a primary apologist for Indonesian atrocities in East Timor', according to Mark Curtis, who quotes him as saying: '50,000 or 80,000 people might have been killed...what is the big fuss?'.[39]

We have a good idea of what Malik thought was appropriate technology for the Indonesian government from the list of weapons he procured – eight Hawk jet aircraft, £200 million on the Rapier Air Defence System, £27 million worth of frigates.[40] We also know what Indonesia's armed forces considered appropriate technology for the East Timorese: 'almost every shred of personal wealth in East Timor was stolen or destroyed – cattle, chickens, motorbikes, phones, furniture and books'.[41]

THE BRUNDTLAND REPORT AND SUSTAINABLE DEVELOPMENT

The concept of sustainability was developed because of the declining credibility of the 'limits to growth' concept. Lester Brown explained in 1981:

> As sustainability becomes the goal of economic policy and planning, the debate that was launched in 1972 with the publication of the limits to growth will fade. The choice between no growth and growth will come to seem less relevant than that between one way of sustaining ourselves, and another.[42]

The concept of sustainability was developed to square the circle between the desire to limit growth and the empirical non-appearance of those limits. The static-state economy proposed by deep Greens like Edward Goldsmith, Herman Daly and the initial Club of Rome report was seen to be too extreme a proposal. The *Limits to Growth* had caught people's imagination in a period of social crisis. But the ecological movement in the early 1980s was seen to be asking too much of people. To fend off an unattractive image of ecology as unworldly back-to-nature types, the concept of sustainability was developed to reconcile the fact of development with the desire to see it restrained.

As a technical term, to describe management of specific resources, 'sustainability' has been around for years.[43] The broader philosophical concept of 'sustainable development' was developed at the 'Alternatives to Growth' conference in 1975 when it became apparent that the proposal of a static-state economy was unrealistic. It is the 1987 Brundtland Report that is generally credited with popularising the concept of sustainable development.

Under Norwegian Labour Party president Gro Harlem Brundtland, the World Commission on Environment and Development declared that: 'if needs are to be met on a sustainable basis the earth's natural resource base must be conserved and enhanced'.[44] As in Lester Brown's formulation, the Brundtland Report presents sustainable development as the more palatable alternative to absolutely limited growth. 'The concept of sustainable development does imply limits – not absolute limits but limitations imposed by the present state of technology and social organisations on environmental resources and by the ability of the biosphere to absorb the effects of human activities'.[45]

It could be said that sustainability is a fudge. It raises all the same presuppositions of the limits to growth thesis, that absolute resource limits are upon us, but avoids their implied conclusion, a moratorium on growth. What the concept of sustainability preserves of the ideology of limits is the sentiment of constraint and parsimony:

> Sustainable global development requires that those who are more affluent adopt lifestyles within the planet's ecological means.[46]

In the context of aid projects in the less developed world, sustainable development meant a lowering of expectations. Then an aid worker, the journalist Michael Maren recalls how 'sustainable development emerged as a reaction to criticism that most development projects for the last fifty years fell apart the moment the foreign money was pulled out'. The prefix 'sustainable' meant, in effect, modest in aspiration, 'so projects started referring to sustainable development'.[47]

In broader context of finance and economics, the appeals to sustainable growth made by central banker Alan Greenspan, or Britain's Chancellor Gordon Brown, express the desire to achieve growth without creating instability that could jeopardise the Dow Jones Sustainability Group's profitable investments. The cautious attitude of the elite towards growth is expressed in the prefix sustainable. The experience of inflation and social conflict in the 1970s and early 1980s lies behind the cautious approach. When the British Chancellor warns of the dangers of a 'boom and bust' economy, he is emphasising the need for stability, hence 'sustainable growth'.

The concept of sustainability was developed to square the circle between the desire to limit growth and the empirical non-appearance of those limits.

STEWARDSHIP OF NATURE'S CAPITAL

If the sentiment in general behind sustainable development is one of caution, the category does have a more specific meaning: 'It rests on the acknowledgement, long familiar in economic life, that maintaining income over time requires that the capital stock is not run down', writes Michael Jacob. He expands, tellingly, 'the natural environment performs the function of a capital stock for the human economy, providing essential resources and services, including the assimilation of wastes. Economic activity is presently running down this stock'.[48]

Translating ecology into economic categories is Michael Jacobs' way of rendering it commonsensical. This Fabian Society secretary is appealing to the established certainties of free market economics, ironically, as a way of criticising excessive growth. Certainly it was a definition that the champion of free enterprise Margaret Thatcher could readily understand. 'We do not have a freehold on the Earth', she told the Royal Society on 22 September 1988, 'only a full-repairing lease'. But the translation of ecology into economics does not just change the meaning of ecology. It also changes the meaning of economics. By reinterpreting natural goods as 'capital stock', Jacobs is also introducing a new (or in fact a very old) conception of property and ownership; the concept of *stewardship*.

Though the landed aristocracy is largely a thing of the past, the patrician concept of stewardship of the land is enjoying a revival as 'sustainable development'. So for example, David Pearce and his colleagues at the London Environmental Centre argue that the stock of natural capital must be taken into account alongside the stock of man-made capital.[49] Like the older concept of land stewardship, natural capital takes its justification from the idea that natural goods are held in trust for future generations. Lester Brown cited a comment in a United Nations (UN) report as the best definition of sustainability: 'we have not inherited the earth from our fathers; we are borrowing it from our children'.[50]

One quarter that readily appreciates the appeal of the argument for sustainability is the remnants of that landed aristocracy who originally framed them. Charles Secrett, Executive Director of Friends of the Earth, explained the appeal of environmentalism to the upper classes: Among the aristocrats there is a sense of noblesse oblige…a feeling of stewardship towards the land.[51]

Like the older concept of land stewardship, natural capital takes its justification from the idea that natural goods are held in trust for future generations.

In his Reith Lecture in May 2000, Prince Charles spoke of 'a sacred trust between mankind and our Creator, under which we accept stewardship of the earth'. The future King has accepted a considerable burden of stewardship: around 52,000 hectares with a rental value of £10 million a year, with a further income of £2 million from stocks values of £45 million, plus of course the proceeds from the organic beef and lamb produced by his Highgrove farm, along with its 'Duchy Original' biscuits.[52] On 16 August 1996, Norfolk farmer and Greenpeace director Lord Peter Melchett wrote to the Prime Minister appealing for restrictions on nature's bounty: 'So long as nature is available to be treated as a free good which can always be opened up, good stewardship elsewhere will be undermined'.

The historic role of the landed aristocracy was one of policing the boundaries of economic growth. The meaning of 'stewardship' in a nutshell was 'get orf my land!' – an injunction all the more compelling since the landlord was also the local Justice of the Peace. But today the role of policing the boundaries is done in the name of conserving the environment. The National Trust owns around 244,000 hectares of land (and recovered £19 million in rent from tenant farmers in 1996 to 1997). The National Trust for Scotland owns around 76,000 hectares, the Royal Society for the Protection of Birds controls some 99,000 hectares, the Woodlands Trust around 16,200 hectares, and between them English Nature, the Countryside Council for Wales and Scottish Natural Heritage control around 2.06 million acres. That is nearly one-tenth of Britain.[53]

The concept of stewardship sounds attractive, but it can also serve as a justification for setting limits to development that people need in the here and now. When the concept of sustainable development was first raised at the 1979 conference 'Faith, Science and the Future', one Indian delegate, Dr Kurien, pointed out the mystification involved in the appeal to future generations:

> If you claim to be concerned about the unborn humanity that you cannot see, but show no regard
> for the humanity that you can see all around you, you are a liar.[54]

The widespread perception that the forests and the countryside are in danger from rapacious agribusiness is not exactly true. In fact the amount of grain land under cultivation peaked in 1981 at 732 million hectares and has fallen since to 690 million hectares.[55] The major reason is the increase in yields due to modern farming methods, where land produces three times as much per acre today as it did in 1900. Environmentalism has also provided a rationale for the extensive retirement of land from agricultural production on conservationist grounds. With increased yields, less land produces more grain, so agribusiness needs land taken out of production to avoid a glut. Conservation provides a convenient justification for governments to exclude land from farm use.

The US government recently bought over 20,000 hectares of sugar cane land in the Everglades for conservation. Pressure is on developing countries to earmark land 'for conservation'. When Gabon declared

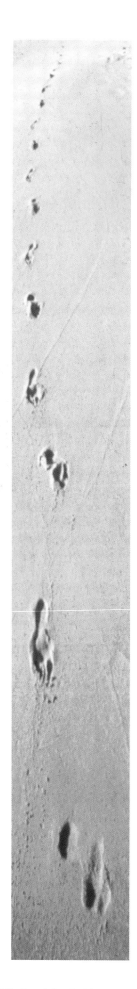

567,000 hectares of tropical forest at Minkebe a protected area for lowland Gorillas, the area of conserved land in Central Africa extended to around 26,000 square kilometres. With more land being turned to forest, world deforestation fell to just 0.3 per cent lost per year in the period 1990–95. Most of this was concentrated in the less developed world, as a result of the pressure of surplus populations on forestland. In the US, forestland is growing 5,886 square kilometres on average every year. In the European Union, forests are growing 486 million cubic metres every year.[56] Differential patterns of reforestation and deforestation have caused tension between North and South as American and European environmentalists have lambasted Southern countries for their destructive land use. Indigenous people in Brazil and Indonesia have affronted Western sensibilities by their adoption of slash-and-burn farming, which saves their labour at the expense of forestland.

The growth of national parks and wildlife reserves is the modern equivalent of the great estates. They are created to withhold productive land from labourers, and to limit the unchecked spread of land-squatting subsistence farmers. Professor Bernhard Grzimek, Hitler's curator of Frankfurt Zoo and the champion of the Serengeti nature reserve, claimed: 'A National Park must remain a primordial wilderness to be effective. No men, not even native ones, should live within its borders'.[57] Like the traditional stewardship of the land, the modern nature reserve serves to police the boundaries of economic growth.

RETURNS ON NATURAL CAPITAL?

The difficulty for the modern equivalent of natural capital is that, unlike more traditional property in land, it does not normally yield an income stream, like rent. Creative measures to derive value streams from natural capital, thereby rewarding sustainability, have been attempted, though with peculiar results.

Carbon-credits The best known scheme for making natural capital is that established at the Kyoto climate-change summit, where limited rights to produce carbon emissions can be traded. The scheme works to shore-up the developed world's monopoly on industrial growth, by rewarding less developed nations for fore-going such growth.

A research team led by William Laurance of the Smithsonian Tropical Research Institute deplored the incursions made into the Brazilian rainforest. The team's report in *Science* magazine suggests that the industrialisation is short-sighted because Brazil could lose up to £1.4 billion a year in selling carbon-credits. According to provisional figures, migration to the Brazilian Amazon has led to a big rise in its population over the last century to about 12 million. 'We cannot leave the local population living in a glass bowl just for the benefit of rainforest preservation,' said Jose Paulo Silveira of the Department of Planning and Strategic Investments. 'We need to keep on developing.'[58]

Nega-watts The Club of Rome's *Factor Four* report announced that business could double wealth and half resource use back in 1997. Its example of how to make money by saving the environment was the California electricity business. Instead of profiting by making megawatts, the California electricity companies were rewarded for making savings, or 'negawatts'.

'Around 1980, Pacific Gas and Electricity Company was planning to build some 10 to 20 power stations', said the report. 'But by 1992, P&GE was planning to build no more power stations, and in 1993, it permanently dissolved its engineering and construction division. Instead, as its 1992 Annual Report pronounced, it planned to get at least three quarters of its new power needs in the 1990s from more efficient use by its customers'.[59] In practice, the reduction in electricity generation simply increased the price – by as much as 900 per cent in December 2000. With electricity prices to customers capped, utility companies could not afford to buy electricity elsewhere and P&GE ran up losses of $12 billion before introducing the inevitable blackouts. Negawatts proved to be Negabucks.

Eco-tourism While innovative financial instruments like nega-watts and carbon-credits represent attempts to make natural goods behave like capital by artificial pricing mechanisms, a more conventional attempt to realise the returns on natural capital is eco-tourism. Through eco-tourism, it is hoped, Western sentiment can be turned into hard cash to reward developing states for preserving their undeveloped regions.

This is less innovative than at first appears. British colonialists created game reserves in Africa to clear the subsistence farmers from the land so that they would have to work on white estates. Once cleared, the land yielded an income as a playground for the 'great white hunter'. In post-independence Kenya, the keeper of the national parks, naturalist Richard Leakey, controlled more of the country's land area than any other individual, and even threatened at one point to overthrow president Kenyatta. Unlike the big game hunters, today's environmental tourists vow to leave a small footprint – though that remains to be seen. The money the European Parliament set aside to promote ecological tourism in 1992 seems mostly to have been plundered by officials in what euro-accountant Paul Van Buitenen describes as 'embezzlement, corruption and favouritism'.[60]

Eco-landlordism For the London Environmental Economics Centre, the distinction between modern ecological stewardship and old-fashioned land-owning matters little. They define the traditional ownership of forestland in Indonesia's outer islands as itself a form of sustainable development. Since the alternative preferred by indigenous people is to slash-and-burn the forests to farm them, the London Centre reckons that one kind of land stewardship is as good as another, and defends the rights of the landowners to their rent from forestry. It believes the landlords lost rents of $625–750 million as an unsustainable deduction from the natural capital.[61] The loggers-turned-farmers might disagree, seeing the rents as their surplus product, appropriated by the landlords on the spurious grounds of property in land.

THE CARRYING CAPACITY FOR THE EARTH

Allied to the concept of natural capital is that of 'carrying capacity'. Since earth's resources must be replenished, then it follows that only so many people can be sustained before the natural capital is reduced.

So productive capacity (p), divided by one person's basic needs (b), gives the carrying capacity of the earth (c), or $p/b = c$.

However, the numerator in the fraction p/b, p, or productive capacity is not static, as is assumed in the theory. For the planet as a whole productive capacity has tended to rise, due to agriculture, fossil fuels and fertilisers. As the numerator p increases in value, so does carrying capacity. 'These advances increased the human carrying capacity of the planet', writes Lester Brown, from 4 million 10,000 years ago, to 6 billion today.[62]

The concept that human societies have a 'critical carrying capacity' was first developed by anthropologists such as William Allan.[63] Allan mapped out the optimum population that a given area of land could sustain, assuming a given mode of production, in this case 'slash-and-burn' agriculture. From the perspective of the white settlers of Rhodesia it was of course a pressing issue whether African agriculturalists were 'excess to capacity', and they kept a close watch on their numbers. In principle the 'carrying capacity' theory echoes an old saw of political economy, the idea of the fixed wage fund. The prejudice that the sum of wealth available for the labourers' consumption provoked Karl Marx to protest that the 'attempt to represent the capitalistic limits of the labour fund as its natural and social limits' are a 'silly tautology'.[64]

Notes

1. Michael Maren, *The Road to Hell: the Ravaging Effects of Foreign Aid and International Charity* (New York: The Free Press, 1997), pp. 46–7.
2. www.sustainability-index.com.
3. Aurelio Peccei and Alexander King, 'Commentary', in Mihaljo Mesarovic and Eduard Pestel, *Mankind at the Turning Point* (London: Hutchinson, 1975).
4. Donella H. Meadows, Dennis L. Meadows, Jorgen Randers and William H. Behrens, *Limits to Growth – A Report for the Club of Rome's Project on the Predicament of Mankind* (New York: Universe Books, 1972), p. 125. Republished as *The Dynamics of Growth in a Finite World* (Cambridge, Mass.: Wright-Allen Press, 1974). (Commonly known as the 'Limits to Growth'.)
5. Martin Whittaker, 'Emerging "triple bottom line" model for industry weighs environmental, economic and social considerations', *Oil and Gas Journal*, December 20, 1999, Vol. 97, No. 51, pp. 23–26.
6. H. S. D. Cole, Christopher Freeman, Marie Jahoda and K. L. R. Pavitt (eds), *Thinking About the Future – A Critique of the Limits to Growth* (London: Chatto and Windus for Sussex University, 1973), p. 38.
7. Ibid., p. 37.
8. Ibid.
9. Aurelio Peccei and Alexander King, in Mihaljo Mesarovic and Eduard Pestel, *Mankind at the Turning Point* (London: Hutchinson, 1975), p. 202.
10. Ibid., p. 202.
11. Istvan Meszaros, *The Necessity of Social Control* (London: Merlin Press, 1971), p. 19.
12. Quoted in Gordon Brown (ed.), *The Red Paper on Scotland* (Edinburgh: EUSPB, 1975), p. 7.
13. See, for example, Walter Rodney, *How Europe Underdeveloped Africa* (Nairobi and London: East African Educational Publishers, 1995).
14. Claus Offe, 'Ungovernability, the renaissance of conservative theories of the crisis', in Claus Offe and John Keane, *Contradictions of the Welfare State* (London: Hutchinson, 1984).
15. Margaret Laws Smith, *Towards the Creation of a Sustainable Economy* (London: Conservation Society, 1975), p. 7.
16. Margaret Laws Smith, *Towards the Creation of a Sustainable Economy* (London: Conservation Society, 1975), p. 9.

17. Lester Brown, *Building a Sustainable Society* (New York: Worldwatch, 1981), p. 122.
18. Istvan Meszaros, *The Necessity of Social Control* (London: Merlin Press, 1971), p. 19.
19. Edward Goldsmith, in Dennis L. Meadows (ed.), *Alternatives to Growth: a Search for Sustainable Futures* (Cambridge, Mass.: Ballinger, 1977), p. 331.
20. Paul Ehrlich, *The Population Bomb* (London: Pan Books, 1971), p. 36.
21. Edward Goldsmith, in Dennis L. Meadows (ed.), *Alternatives to Growth: a Search for Sustainable Futures* (Cambridge, Mass.: Ballinger,1977), p. 325.
22. Donella H. Meadows, Dennis L. Meadows and Jorgan Randers, *Beyond the Limits – Confronting Global Collapse, Envisioning a Sustainable Future* (New York: Universe Books, 1992) and (London: Earthscan, 1992).
23. See Paul Ormerod, *The Death of Economics* (London: Faber and Faber, 1994).
24. Lester Brown and Christopher Flavin, World Watch Institute, *State of the World 1999* (London: Earthscan, 2000), p. 10.
25. Independent Commission on International Development Issues, *North-South: A Programme for Survival,* commonly known as the Brandt Report (London: Foreign and Commonwealth Office, 1980), p. 24.
26. Ibid., p. 23.
27. Ibid., p. 195.
28. Arghiri Emmanuel, *Appropriate or Underdeveloped Technology* (London: John Wiley, 1982), p. 106.
29. Ibid., p. 105.
30. Ibid., p. 102.
31. Ibid., p. 103.
32. The Brandt Report, p. 24.
33. David Ricardo, *Principles of Political Economy* (London: Everyman, 1984), p. 264.
34. Elmar Altvater, 'Growth, productivity employment, and ecological sustainability – a "globalization trilemma"', www.barkhof.uni-bremen.de/kua/memo/europe/tser/Altvater_24months.pdf. Paper builds on paper delivered at the TMR Workshop in Vienna 1998, and on a speech during the TMR Workshop in Brussels in October 1999.
35. 'Ecological Sustainability, Productivity, and Employment' Paper delivered for the Thematic Network: Full Employment in Europe, Vienna, 2–4 October 1998.
36. Ulrich Beck, *The Brave New World of Work* (Cambridge: Polity, 2000).
37. J. Campbell, *Edward Heath* (London: Pimlico, 1994), p. 531; F. Lynch, *France and the International Economy: From Vichy to the Treaty of Rome* (London: Routledge 1997), p. 75.
38. J. Campbell, *Edward Heath* (London: Pimlico, 1994), p. 427.
39. Mark Curtis, *The Ambiguities of Power: British Foreign Policy Since 1945* (London: Zed Books, 1995), p. 219.
40. Ibid., p.221.
41. James Traub, 'Inventing East Timor', *Foreign Affairs,* July/August 2000, p. 78.
42. Lester Brown, *Building a Sustainable Society* (New York: Worldwatch 1981), p. 365.
43. Douglas G. Chapman, *Utilization of Pacific Halibut Stocks: Estimation of Maximum Sustainable Yield 1960,* Report of the International Pacific Halibut Commission (Seattle: United Nations Press, 1962).
44. World Commission on Environment and Development, *Our Common Future,* commonly known as the Brundtland Report (WCED, Oxford, 1987), p. 57.
45. Ibid., p. 8.
46. Ibid., p. 8.
47. Michael Maren, *The Road to Hell: the Ravaging Effects of Foreign Aid and International Charity* (New York: The Free Press, 1997), p. 64.
48. The Real World Coalition, *Politics of the Real World* (London: Earthscan, 1996), p. 17.
49. David Pearce, *Sustainable Development, Economics and Environment in the Third World* (London: Earthscan, 1990).
50. *UN Environmental Programme, Annual Review 1978,* Nairobi, 1980, in Lester Brown, *Building a Sustainable Society* (New York: Worldwatch, 1981), p. 359.
51. John Vidal, 'Does your daddy know you're here?', *The Guardian,* 5 May 2000.
52. Dominic Hobson, *The National Wealth: Who Gets What in Britain* (London: HarperCollins, 1999), p. 29.
53. Ibid., p. 121.
54. Reverend Canon R. H. Preston, *The Question of a Just, Participatory and Sustainable Society* (Manchester: John Rylands University, 1980), p. 111.
55. Lester Brown and Christopher Flavin, World Watch Institute, *State of the World* (London: Earthscan, 2000), p. 120.
56. Office of National Statistics, *Britain 2000 – The Official Yearbook of the United Kingdom* (London: HMSO, 2001), p. 463.
57. Quoted in *The Guardian*, 6 August 1997.
58. *The Guardian,* 20 January 2001.
59. Ernst von Weizsäcker, Amory B. Lovins and L Hunter Lovins, *Factor Four: Doubling Wealth, Halving Resource Use – A New Report to the Club of Rome* (London: Earthscan, 1997), p. 160.

60. Paul Van Buiten, *Blowing the Whistle* (London: Politicos, 2000), p. 113.
61. David Pearce, *Sustainable Development, Economics and Environment in the Third World* (London: Earthscan, 1990), p. 98.
62. Lester Brown and Christopher Flavin, World Watch Institute, *State of the World* (London: Earthscan, 2000).
63. William Allan, *Studies in African Land Usage in Northern Rhodesia* (Manchester: Manchester University Press, 1949).
64. Karl Marx, *Capital: A Critique of Political Economy* (Moscow: Progress Publishers, 1974), p. 572, citing H. Fawcett, *The Economic Position of the British Labourer*, 1865.

Vertical container. Home stacking units with residents' social bar at the top.

Chapter 8

Engaging the Stakeholder in the Development Process

Miffa Salter, Office for Public Management

URBAN REVITALISATION

In 1998, 14 of the UK's leading urbanists were brought together by central government to set out a future for England's towns and cities.[1] Following a programme of in-depth research and intensive deliberation, the group published its final report in the summer of 1999. The document, entitled *Towards an Urban Renaissance*, set out a bold vision of what it termed 'sustainable development'. In so doing it convincingly demonstrated the need to challenge both the established cultures and the associated practices of architects, planners and developers alike.

> The process of urban revitalisation has to be owned by the people who it will affect most...We therefore need to promote consultation alongside more proactive mechanisms for active participation, linking people with the decision making processes which affect their own neighbourhood.[2]

While the report laid much of the blame for past mistakes at the doors of those professions most active in designing and managing the built environment, it also spoke of a shared responsibility for the future, which extends beyond the confines of a professional elite. In essence, it called for the public to take ownership of urban revitalisation, and highlighted the need to link people directly with the myriad associated decision-making processes that impact upon their neighbourhoods.

Of course the idea of placing citizens at the very heart of the development process is not new, and nor is its current profile purely the preserve of a government-appointed Urban Task Force. In fact, much of what was written in the group's final report echoes both the thinking and the practice that now guides everything from regeneration bids and comprehensive renewal schemes to individual newbuild projects. Engaging the public is not only desirable but also fundamental to an inclusive development process. Moreover, the enthusiasm that the professionals and the public have accorded to the host of consultative techniques suggests that 'participation' in all its various interpretations is here to stay.

The rationale for this approach can be seen from a number of different perspectives. At one level it recognises the benefits of drawing on local knowledge and expertise to guide the allocation of resources. In this context, involving people in urban development, it is fundamentally about encouraging individuals and groups to express their needs and aspirations based on 'real life' experience of the built environment. The community-visioning event, which invites local residents to describe idealised scenarios for the future of their neighbourhood, would be typical of this approach.

At another level, the renewed emphasis on public engagement is driven by a desire to share responsibility, empower communities and address what may be seen as an inequitable status quo. In this respect, much of the thinking expressed by the Urban Task Force echoes a wider agenda across government, which seeks to establish the community as the 'co-producer' of solutions, alongside the more conventional arms of state and commerce. Here, involvement is about a reallocation of the lines of either management or ownership, or both. In the most basic sense, it seeks through processes as varied as the independently appointed commission and the lay board member to establish an empowered community voice to sit alongside (or in the place of) more traditional power structures.

However, perhaps, most telling of all is the acknowledgement by the Urban Task Force that the approach it advocates in relation to urban development of the future is 'going to involve trade-offs'. These, it says, will inevitably 'encroach upon the desires and aspirations of individuals and existing urban communities'.[3] In this context it is clear that at least part of the reason to involve citizens in decision-making relates to the need to validate what may at least initially appear to be unpalatable options. Essentially, this means presenting choices and explaining the implications of these choices, with the hope that the 'informed public voice' will opt for the most socially responsible solution.

It is not surprising that the contradictions inherent in this new age of participation place both public and professionals on shaky ground. While the sentiment may be a worthy one, the terms of engagement are often far from explicit, and it is all too clear to see why apathy, distrust and participation-fatigue continue to dog so many of the well-meaning attempts at public involvement.

This chapter looks at some of the challenges presented by the heightened interest in stakeholder engagement and asks what impact, if any, this will have on the successful delivery of sustainable development in the future.

...it is clear that at least part of the reason to involve citizens in decision-making relates to the need to validate what may at least initially appear to be unpalatable options.

HEARING THE PUBLIC VOICE: CHALLENGES AND CONTRADICTIONS

Involving the public in all kinds of decision-making has become a national obsession. Words such as 'consultation', 'participation' and 'engagement' are liberally distributed throughout the government's policy guidance, while 'public', 'stakeholder' and 'community' have replaced the much-maligned 'consumer' of previous administrations. Whether one looks at the newly emerging Community Plans, the established Best Value Reviews, or the overhaul of political management structures, it is clear that hearing and responding to the public voice is seen as central to both improving service delivery and as a mechanism for addressing the accountability of government more generally.

The terminology is at times deceptively simple. Moreover, there is often an assumed understanding of what is meant by such a well-rehearsed vocabulary. This presents a particular problem for the range of professionals engaged in the design and development of the built environment, who often pride themselves on an established history of so-called community involvement.

For thousands of planners, architects and urban designers educated in the post-Skeffington era,[4] dialogue with the public is seen as a fundamental part of the professional process. No academic course is complete without its 'community' component. No design can stand up to scrutiny without reference to users, clients and stakeholders, and no decision is taken without the validation of the public voice. However, the reality is that the myriad of exchanges between technical expert and lay person that pass for public involvement are far more disparate in character, and far less comprehensive in nature than many would like to acknowledge.

One of the most fundamental mistakes is to assume consensus on what is meant by such terms as community and involvement. In so doing, we often fail to question both the 'why' and 'how' of what we are engaged in, let alone the 'who' we are engaging with.

Community can, of course, refer as much to the individual as it does to the collective. As importantly, it can include both those linked by place, that is the traditional concept of a geographically based community, and a more complex grouping joined by a whole range of different social, cultural and economic relationships. Similarly, involvement or participation can be defined in a number of different ways that cover everything from the most basic of information exchanges to more complex joint decision-making processes. Although developed over 30 years ago, Sherry Arnstein's Ladder of Participation,[5] which ranges from information dissemination at one end to devolved responsibility at the other, is still quoted as a gauge for assessing what is meant by such terms.[6]

No design can stand up to scrutiny without reference to users, clients and stakeholders, and no decision is taken without the validation of the public voice.

Table 8. 1: A ladder of citizen participation derived from Sherry Arnstein.[7]

Defining participation Ways to involve citizens	Rationale and/or outcome of participation
Citizen control	Citizen power
Delegated power	
Partnership	
Consultation	Tokenism
Informing	
Placation	
Therapy	Non-participation
Manipulation	

The problem is that such categorisation only takes us so far. While it allows us to distinguish between the different meanings associated with the terminology, it tells us very little about the relative merits of the various options. Nor does it say anything about what such mechanisms actually feel like on the ground and how any single 'level' may be interpreted for maximum results.

The reality is that from the professional perspective, involving the lay person in the design, the associated decision-making process or both, can mean absolutely anything from the constructive atmosphere of the most progressive of planning weekends right through to the more uncomfortable friction of the open meeting or the council committee. Best practice documents paint rosy pictures of the very best of community engagement techniques, be they focus groups, citizens' juries, or so-called visioning events, which show informed negotiations at their best.[8] By way of stark contrast, local papers and other media reports highlight fraught public debates, demonstrations, and 'sit-ins' which fuel distrust on both sides.

For the lay person, the experience can be equally varied in its nature. For many, participatory activities represent a tokenistic attempt to validate the decision-making process. Nowhere is this clearer than in the research carried out by the DETR into public participation in local government,[9] which confirms the negative views surrounding efforts to involve citizens. In particular, the work points to the following key issues in explaining low levels of involvement:

- The assumption that those in power will not respond to public concerns.
- The belief that certain groups will tend to dominate such processes.
- The lack of knowledge or awareness of opportunities to participate.
- An historical distrust of local government.

All too often, the ad hoc encounters between citizen, professional and state add up to little more than irritating reminders of a status quo in which power rests in the hands of a minority. Although it is important to explore what is meant by the language of involvement, such definitions may do little to ensure productive dialogue and even less with respect to delivering solutions on the ground. Rather, the requirement from both the public and professional perspective should be to work together to define the criteria for successful engagement, and to relate these directly to the achievement of key development objectives.

This stage is often overlooked in the consultation process as individuals steam ahead with a complex toolkit of surveys, focus groups and large group events, assuming a link between dialogue and outcome that is often at best nebulous and at worst non-existent.

Of course, it does not need to be like this. There are numerous examples where the mutual exchange of expertise between public and professional has led to a level of empowerment and a shifting of territories that would have been impossible without constructive involvement from all sides.

Some of the most well-known 'best practice' in the context of the built environment revolves around tenant participation in housing management.[10] However, there are also examples from a number of different policy areas such as Community Strategies and Local Agenda 21, as well as regeneration initiatives including Housing Action Trusts, City Challenge, Single Regeneration Budget bids and New Deal for Community partnerships. What has perhaps worked best in these instances is the narrowing of the gap between what could be termed professional capability – the ability of the trained individual to make an informed decision based on technical experience – and public expertise – the ability of the citizen to inform and guide the outcome based on a clear understanding of local needs and aspirations. The result in almost every case has been a shift in control and an associated reallocation of responsibility from professionals to the public.

The question this inevitably raises relates to the extent to which we should be looking to redraw lines of responsibility as an outcome of the consultation process. It would seem that the current emphasis on public involvement, which talks about the public as 'co-producer', suggests that to be truly successful participation needs to result in the kind of realignment of power associated with the top levels of Arnstein's ladder. Key documents, such as *Bringing Britain Together* by the Social Exclusion Unit, reinforce what is increasingly being described as the new agenda for public participation. In his introduction to the document, Tony Blair states that 'too much has been imposed from above, when experience shows that success depends on communities themselves having the power and taking responsibility to make things better'.[11]

The idea of tapping into the energies and imagination and talents of communities is not new. However, the emphasis on seeing them as a resource in their own right marks a departure from a more conventional – and perhaps paternalistic – approach to public engagement. The new agenda is about more than just ensuring people are aware of lines of responsibility and able to comment on what it is they do and do not like. The philosophy guiding current policy thinking sees the community, either collectively or individually, at the very centre of solution building. This is as true in relation to public involvement in decisions relating to the built environment as it is to participation in issues of governance more generally. But such an approach makes a number of rather dangerous assumptions.

Assumptions

Most importantly it assumes that the public wants to get involved in the first place. Yet research, such as that outlined above, shows that there is more often than not a well-justified set of reasons which explain why individuals and communities do not participate. This is particularly true for so-called 'hard to reach groups', including young people, elders, non-English-speakers, black and ethnic minorities, single parents, and the physically and mentally disabled. The DETR study highlights that in terms of public participation in local government, informal networks do still dominate, and that those who know how the system works are the ones who get most out of it. It is also true to say that certain groups are repeatedly excluded, and that complex issues are often oversimplified in an attempt to get a response, indeed *any* responses, from the public. This is as true with regard to the built environment as it is elsewhere.

The second assumption inherent in current thinking is that the public will, given enough time, speak and act as a collective. The reality is that often nothing could be further from the truth. Levels of participation may be high, but consensus as to the way forward may be totally lacking. The result is that indi-

...consensus as to the way forward may be totally lacking.

viduals and communities may well come together to pit their knowledge and talents *against* each other rather than operating in a more consensual manner. This is particularly common in cases where the trade-offs implicit in a given development proposal impact adversely upon one group of individuals. Taking the current call for higher urban densities as a classic example, it is easy to see how guidance that seeks to ensure above-average densities may have resonance with a local environmental lobby. However, this may be perceived as totally unacceptable by residents wedded to images of suburban England in all its sprawling glory. While both cohorts may sign up to the core principles enshrined in sustainable development, they will express their preferences very differently when a specific scheme challenges what they hold most dear.

A third, and perhaps more serious oversight is the belief that community engagement can occur in the absence of any significant investment in 'capacity building' – the host of complementary activities required to develop the ability of individuals and groups to take advantage of new opportunities. This oversight most often manifests itself as the failure by those in positions of power to give the public the necessary tools they need to make an informed comment. It also explains why the lay representative on regeneration boards, design panels and the like often represents little more than a token gesture at inclusion as opposed to a far more fundamental shift in power.

OBJECTIVES AND ASPIRATIONS

In the face of such criticism, we must begin to question why a more inclusive approach to any production process makes sense. If public and professional alike cannot see a superior outcome as a result of engaging with one another, it is clear that the tools and techniques so lauded by market researchers and policy pundits alike may well be redundant. Research undertaken by the Policy Studies Institute in the late 1990s showed that consultation has many positive and indirect benefits for the organisations involved, including an improved understanding of different perspectives and increased overall levels of job satisfaction. For consultees, involvement in consultation exercises, especially the most intense forms of interaction, was seen as both memorable and positive. However, the research also concluded that the 'current popularity of consultation appears to endow it with powers it does not possess. It is often not a suitable mechanism for resolving conflict or avoiding difficult choices...To address concerns successfully, consultation needs specific objectives as well as general aspirations'.[12]

In the case of decisions relating to the built environment, this recommendation calls for some difficult choices, because the 'general aspiration' to include and empower may run counter to a much more specific objective to get planning approval. Equally, a desire to involve everyone in the design of a solution which is better for society as a whole is totally different from engaging with a key group of end-users who may have their own ideas about what the 'superior product' might look like at the end of the day. In both cases the reason for engaging, the methods appropriated and the ultimate outcomes of consultation will vary significantly.

To move forward requires both professionals and the public to clarify what each is expecting from the consultation process and to acknowledge upfront that the drivers for dialogue may be totally different depending on which side of the line one sits. This will mean that almost inevitably one party will be disappointed by the outcome. For planners and architects as well as the other professions involved, the need to meet requirements or legitimise a process is often at the very root of participation practices. A desire to inform the public, to generate support for a proposed development, and to improve the decision-making process are also key in prompting dialogue with both key stakeholders (for example clients) and a wider audience. For the public, the rationale for involvement in the development process may be as much fuelled by a desire to protect the status quo (most obviously demonstrated by so called NIMBY-ism), as by a need to promote change. In order for both parties to move forward, there needs to be a rejection of the historic modus operandi that saw conflict negotiation at the very heart of the development process, and an acceptance of a more socially responsible way of collective decision-making.

However, in reality this has been associated with what can at best be described as consensus management, and at worst the abandonment of professional responsibility in favour of the collective decision-making process. More often than not the result is the dilution of design excellence. Essentially, the fundamental problem for planners, architects and others is that it is almost impossible to successfully 'co-produce' a solution in the holistic way which the government envisages. Moreover, efforts to progress down this path have left the public and professionals disillusioned and disenfranchised from the very product that both profess to caring so much about.

NO GOING BACK TO PATERNALISM

What this should not suggest is a return to a patriarchal system of an informed elite making judgements and committing resources on behalf of a receptive citizenship. However, it does mean looking at how

More often than not the result is the dilution of design excellence.

current guidance can best be interpreted in a context where, like it or not, responsibility for end-point delivery must rest with the professional concerned. Accepting professional responsibility and *at the same time* engaging with the public is much to ask of any individual. Historically, the training relating to participation has often focused on the former, requiring planners and architects to defend their position of 'expert' in the face of public criticism. Increasingly responding to the new agenda will require a more conciliatory approach to engagement, requiring the professionals involved to identify the fixed points in any debate and focus discussion around a collection of recognisable variables. Such an approach will by its very nature push more basic interpersonal skills to the fore of the professional toolkit.

To date, the ability to listen, communicate, facilitate and negotiate have too often been downplayed to the detriment of the engagement process. The time has come for professionals to think not only about the rationale and associated methods of engagement, but about the very ways in which such processes are best undertaken. Significant progress could be made in this respect by:

- *Exploring ways of making ideas accessible and understandable to the lay person*. This means revisiting the language and visual aids that have come to typify the development process, and which tend to relate more to other professionals than to a public audience. Significant efforts to address these issues have already been made by organisations such as the Architecture Foundation with its groundbreaking community road shows.[13]
- *Working wherever possible with independent intermediaries to develop ideas*. This could involve, for example, taking the model of the 'tenant's friend' used in housing transfers to help individuals and groups develop their own preferred options and to respond to proposals put before them by the professional.
- *Undertaking shared capacity building training with the public*. This could build on the models successfully adopted in the medical profession where the patient acts as 'teacher' to the professional and essentially advises on how best to engage with the lay person.
- *An outreach programme by the professional institutions concerned*. This would seek to dispel the myths surrounding the development process and invite public scrutiny and informed debate. It must be more than hosting exhibitions and seminar series that appeal to an interested minority, seeking instead to develop active engagement beyond the confines of the organisation concerned.

For many of these recommendations, information technology may hold the vital key. Computer games that allow players to explore the development process, and computer-aided designs that allow viewers a virtual experience of different environments have long been used to inform and engage professionals and the public. By the same token the rapid growth of interaction via the Internet presents all parties with a whole new medium for engagement. For example the interactive web site www.sheffield1.com, developed by Neighbourhood UK for Sheffield One (the newly formed urban development company), highlights what can be achieved by approaching public dialogue in a far more comprehensive and cohesive way.

What these suggestions do not do is relieve the professional of his or her own very specific responsibility to advise on what is technically practical and financially expedient.

What these suggestions do not do is relieve the professional of his or her own very specific responsibility to advise on what is technically practical and financially expedient. To be truly successful, engagement of any type must rely on the professional to bring it back to what is practicable in a given context. This means that dialogue must have an end as well as a beginning, and sustained indecision is not an option. The professional must have the confidence to influence public opinion as well as securing personal credibility as a good listener.

Inviting the lay person into the decision-making process is one thing – after all, eliciting comment and a level of informed critique can be both useful and constructive – but, asking the public to take on responsibility for solution-building is a very different type of 'consultation' altogether. At one level it requires the professionals at the centre of any dialogue to share, and at certain times even relinquish control. What it says in essence is that expertise is no longer the sole territory of the trained specialist and experience of life may be as valid a basis on which to form opinions. This is dangerous territory. As professionals steeped in the mysticism of their art, architects often find it harder than most to empower their clients, let alone a wider public audience. Delegating authority seems as much of an anathema as wearing trainers to work. But exploring what is meant by responsibility on both sides is critical to success. Where this has worked well it has provoked some startling revelations on both sides.

Professionals used to thinking 'inside their box' have been challenged to reach new levels of creativity, while members of the public have become informed orchestrators of their own environments. Difficult decisions which would previously have been the preserve of the board room or the committee process have been resolved by open and frank debate, and the product itself – the building, street or public park – has changed beyond recognition to more effectively address user requirements. While much work needs to be done to explore the parameters of professional responsibility here, as much effort needs to be addressed to develop the role of the citizen. Looking to the future, the DETR research recommends concentrating on practical concerns rather than abstract issues if both the level and the quality of participation is to be improved.

The study also points to the importance of community leaders as an avenue into public opinion, and highlights the need to actively invite or recruit participants rather than wait for parties to declare an interest. Clearly developing a range of different methods for different groups and different circumstances will be important in allowing individuals and communities to engage in the most productive ways possible. At the same time, it will be necessary to think beyond notions of 'representativeness' and to explore mechanisms for more effectively identifying and accessing those most likely to be excluded from conventional decision-making processes.

CITIZENSHIP

However, the reality remains that participation rates fall below half the national average among the poorest members of society. Arguably it is where engagement is most needed that it is seen as most irrelevant. So what can be done to mainstream a debate which is seen to have more relevance to a professional minority than to a majority of end-users who are neither qualified to participate at a technical level, nor rewarded financially for doing so on a sustained basis.

The first step must be to ensure the credibility of the process and at the same time ground it in the most practical concerns of real people. There also needs to be a growing recognition that the invitation to engage is much more than an opportunity to scrutinise a process. In this new world, the citizen takes on a new level of responsibility and to do this effectively he or she must be as informed as possible. From a public perspective, efforts devoted to both acquiring and using knowledge must be rewarded, and citizenship in its widest interpretation must be seen as superior to disenfranchisement. Such a debate strikes at the very heart of the value systems of a civilised society.

Unfortunately, the new-found enthusiasm for public engagement may often be doing more to undermine responsible citizenship than to promote it. In an era where both the public and private sector relentlessly chase public opinion, it is not surprising that participation-fatigue is rife. Moreover, as credibility in public engagement diminishes, the relevance of citizenship is inevitably eroded. As the public and professionals are pushed ever closer, is it in fact time to take a step back? We need to ask what is driving this new enthusiasm for consultation, and to question the degree to which engaging people as part of the construction process actually helps to achieve a more sustainable product at the end of the day.

At its very best, really successful stakeholder engagement can go a long way in helping all those involved to identify preferences, assess priorities and agree a way forward. It can also be crucial in the dissemination of information, the inclusion of communities and the empowerment of individuals and groups. However, to assume that community involvement will precipitate the most socially responsible solution is to have a misguided faith in the outcome of any consultation process. In terms of sustainable development there is every chance that left to their own devices individuals will reject those options needing the greatest private compromise, particularly in the short term. This may not be a reason to abandon involvement, but it calls for greater efforts to be made in demonstrating the inadequacies of the current context, and the superiority of the proposed options, as well as affording people real opportunities to experience the alternatives. Ultimately, such an approach requires that professionals maintain responsibility. In practice this means losing all the trappings of elitism, but retaining the technical credibility that sets the expert apart from the lay person.

THE PANDORA'S BOX OF PUBLIC OPINION

For the public, it can be argued that the future is more open to interpretation. Adopting the mantle of responsible citizen will have any number of manifestations. At one level it may translate as a concerted effort by individuals and communities to participate in decision making on a regular basis. At another it may be more a matter of holding others to account as opposed to holding the reins.

Irrespective of how this is interpreted it is clear that in opening the Pandora's box that is public opinion, we must ask ourselves how well equipped we are to deal with what comes flying towards us. Regarding the debate around sustainability, this inevitably focuses on one very significant dilemma – the degree to which engaging with the lay person can validate an approach – which places long-term collective good over and above the supremacy of short-term individualism. For the Urban Task Force vision to be realised we have no option but to make sure that this is in fact the case.

In an era where both the public and private sector relentlessly chase public opinion, it is not surprising that participation-fatigue is rife.

Notes

1. Terms of the establishment of the Urban Task Force under the chairmanship of Lord Rogers of Riverside, 1998.
2. Urban Task Force, *Towards an Urban Renaissance – Final Report of the Urban Task Force* (London: E&FN Spon, 1999), p. 46.
3. Ibid.
4. The Skeffington Report, *Report of the Committee on Public Participation in Planning – People and Planning* (London: HMSO, 1969).
5. S. Arnstein, 'A ladder of citizen participation in the USA', *Journal of the American Institute of Planners*, July 1969.
6. Audit Commission, *Listen Up! – Effective Community Consultation* (London: Audit Commission, 1999).
7. Miffa Salter after S. Arnstein, 'A ladder of citizen participation in the USA', *Journal of the American Institute of Planners*, July 1969.
8. J. Lewis and P. Walker (eds.), *Participation Works!* (London: New Economics Foundation in association with the UK Community Participation Network, 1998).
9. V. Lowndes, G. Stoker, L. Pratchett, D. Wilson, S. Leach and M. Wingfield, *Enhancing Public Participation in Local Government* (London: DETR, September 1998).
10. Video, 'Tenant Participation in Housing Management', Chartered Institute of Housing and Tenant Participation Advisory Service, April 1994, and *Tenant Participation in Housing Management* (London: Chartered Institute of Housing and Tenant Participation Advisory Service, 1989).
11. Tony Blair, introduction to *Bringing Britain Together – A National Strategy for Neighbourhood Renewal*, Report by the Social Exclusion Unit, TSO, September 1998, p. 7.
12. J. Steele and J. Sergeant, *Consulting the Public – Guidelines and Good Practice* (London: Policy Studies Institute, 1998).
13. Catherine Puthod, Paul Grover, Judy Hallgarten and Eleanor Jupp, *Creative Spaces – A Toolkit for Participatory Urban Design* (London: The Architecture Foundation, 2000).

LIGHTNESS AND SPAN

Stratford Market Depot, London

Wilkinson Eyre Architects

The 100-metre wide arched roof covers 11 maintenance bays where entire trains are cleaned, serviced and repaired. The parallelogram shape of the main shed is derived from a tight site and the track alignment constraints. The 30-degree 'diagrid' roof structure responds to this imposed form with 2.4-metre-deep arched lattice trusses at 9-metre centres crossing to form the space structure, and supported by an intermediate grid of 'tree-like' columns. Strip roof lights in the standing seam aluminium roof provide good natural lighting. Stratford Market Depot was completed in 1996 with John Laing Ltd, Hyder Consulting Ltd and the Hurley Palmer Partnership for London Underground Ltd.

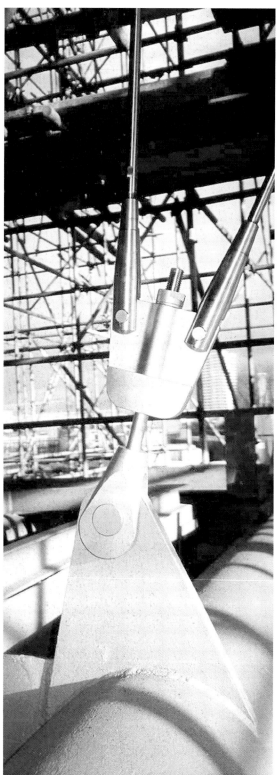

THE WELL TEMPERED ENVIRONMENT

Stratford Regional Station, London

Wilkinson Eyre Architects

Wilkinson Eyre Architects won the limited design competition for the new Stratford Station for Railtrack and the Jubilee Line Project Team in July 1994. The surface-level station replaced the dilapidated, sub-standard, below-ground station, providing an interchange and terminus for the Jubilee Line extension. The new station is easily accessible, with better passenger facilities.

Glazed lifts, escalators and stairs provide access over the North London rail line. A major element of the project was the construction of a new subway under the high-level platforms that remained operational while the subway was pushed through below in concrete box sections.

The form of the building is a curved roof springing from the upper-level walkway parallel with the main railway lines, which sweeps up to a high glazed wall facing the town centre and the Jubilee line. The lower part of the curved roof is exposed and glazed on the outside face to provide views through to the mainline platforms beyond. The ends of the building are also glazed for an open aspect.

The roof form allows natural lighting and provides solar energy assisted natural stack ventilation in the main space via the deep void in the double skin roof through which air is drawn by the 'stack effect', and exhausted at the highest point of the eaves. The natural ventilation maintains air movement and summer temperatures at comfortable levels, and also provides smoke ventilation should there be a fire on the concourse. Computer analysis was used to verify the concept and determine optimum thermal properties for the double-skin roof.

At night the profiled silver aluminium soffit is lit with high-energy, high-efficiency uplights and lower level walls are lit by wall wash downlights recessed around the perimeter. The building is bathed in light, providing a bright and welcoming space. The new railway station provides a strong identity and presence in the redevelopment of Stratford town centre.

Stratford Regional Station 1999 by
Wilkinson Eyre Architects with Kvaerner
Trollope & Colls, Hyder Consulting
Limited, Ove Arup & Partners and
Franklin & Andrews for London
Underground Limited.

Chapter 9

The Trouble with Planners

Alan Hudson

The trouble with planners is their assumption that once they get their act together, the latest jargon for which is 'joined up thinking', then all will be well.

PLANNER PREJUDICES

The title of this essay has been personalised and takes issue with planners and not planning for two reasons. The first is to take sides with people and against planners in a riposte to the pervasive and perverse idea that planners have solutions if only 'problem people' did not get in the way. The second reason is that I have no argument with planning.

The trouble with planners is their assumption that once they get their act together, the latest jargon for which is 'joined up thinking', then all will be well. This top-down approach, however well intentioned, is a species of social engineering. Without democratic participation it is not planning, and is not part of the solution but part of the problem.

These presumptions were neatly encapsulated in a Building Design article by Paul Hyett entitled 'The trouble with people', written before his election as President of the Royal Institute of British Architects (RIBA), but which gives an indication of things to come. This article is a reply to the planner prejudices therein.[1]

It could be argued that Hyett is an architect and not a planner as such. But Hyett does see himself, and I think correctly, as part of a wider network of architects, town planners and civil engineers conjoined as experts in environmental planning. As such they now have access to unprecedented power without direct accountability. All of these professionals are being given the force of legal influence in matters of design and management. Architects have their foot in the door of economic, social and environmental public policy, and policy-makers are very keen to talk about design. Hyett himself makes the point very well when he says: 'regeneration is about management, not just about design'.[2]

There is a happy association of regeneration, management and design but an absence of people in the process. This is now part of a wider argument for the privileging of technical and professional solutions over social engagement and the conflict of interests. At its baldest, a position that Hyett does not shirk, people become the problem, where 'so much that is unpalatable and criticised about life in our cities is directly consequent on social behaviour'.[3]

This is a black-and-white counter-position of the technical and the social, and seems to preclude a more mediated relationship between the two. Even as a matter of common sense, good design is better than bad design, but also certain social environments are more likely to produce and recognise good design.

This is why I want to adopt the opposite stance and privilege social engagement, participation and people. Thus this chapter is not about architecture or design at all. It is about the increasing distance between the elite and the people – a distance greater now than ever before, and one likely to increase in direct proportion to the adoption of the new models of regenerative planning that Hyett endorses and the Urban Task Force had wished to enforce.

CRITICAL UTOPIANS

To indicate how far I wish to stress this approach, I would emphasise that the limitations of the top-down approach apply as much to the great utopians of town planning as to the hustling profit makers of the 1980s and the managerialists of the present period. When contemplating the Garden City visions of an Ebenezer Howard and those like him, admiration is tempered by recollection of the homage by Frederick Engels to the great utopian socialists of the early years of the nineteenth century. Unstinting in his praise of their critical analysis of their own societies and their bold imaginative sweep, Engels points to the utopian character in their thought when they imagined blueprints plucked from thin air could eliminate the prevailing conflicts of social life.[4] In the *Communist Manifesto*, Marx and Engels noted the positive contribution of Henri Saint-Simon (1760–1825), Charles Fourier (1772–1837) and Robert Owen (1771–1858) as the 'critical utopian' tradition, where the critical is praised.

The work of Howard and other such utopians is full of a generous optimism and a concern for the expansion of the possibilities and potential of everyday life.[5] But it is already situated in an environment in which the fruitful relationship between expert knowledge and social dynamism is at the very least attenuated and often lost in its entirety.

The movement from their imaginings to the built environment is only negotiated through the association with bureaucracy, and ultimately failure. The possibility that it is within the compass of people to determine how we deal with our lived environment, rather than put up with a technical prescription issued by experts for both how we live our lives and the environment in which we do it, is lost. Planners should be told what to do by people, and this would be planning. Instead we have to negotiate the sterile antithesis between technical prescriptions and the lazy formulation that the development of lived environments, and particularly those of cities, is organic and by implication unknowable. This is an illegitimate adaptation of a category from the natural world to a set of circumstances that can only be predicated on human actions, interventions and decisions, whatever form they may take.

This is an easy mistake to make, especially when we consider what is enjoyable about the cities we like. In 1970 one of the major themes of the Venice Biennale was urban living. Part of the Italian exhibit was a series of maze-like white walls, which after many twists and turns led the visitor entirely out of the exhibition site on to a proper Venetian street replete with black-dressed widows, shouting kids and men playing cards. An environment convivial, attractive and unplanned said the subtext.

This piece of conceptual art in fact said nothing of contemporary Venice, a city that was already dying and had been for some time as it metamorphosed from the premier Mediterranean port to the tourist capital of Europe. In more recent years Barcelona would serve as a better example for the organic pleasures of the city. Square off the sun, sea and buildings and match tapas bars favourably against the attractions of Venice (I would take Titian and Tiepolo over Gaudi any day) and you would almost certainly prefer to live in Barcelona now. But for all that Venice speaks of a past and an energy that is incomparable to anything in Barcelona today.

PEOPLE ARE THE CITY

Cities are organic in the working out of change and continuity through human aspiration in specific economic and social circumstances. Great cities like Periclean Athens, the Rome of the late Republic and early Empire, Renaissance Florence and the New York of the first two-thirds of the twentieth century are just such cities:

> Manhattan is the product of an unformulated theory, *Manhattanism*, whose program (is) to exist in a world totally fabricated by man, to live *inside* fantasy…The entire city became a factory of man-made experience, where the real and natural ceased to exist.[6]

They were pregnant with social possibilities, however messy, to be engaged with, fought over and translated into the spirit of the place. Hannah Arendt put it very well in *The Human Condition*, as did *Freedom of the City*, an important contribution to correcting the overly technical emphasis of much contemporary discussion of public space.

> The *polis*, properly speaking, is not the city-state in its physical location; it is the organisation of people as it arises out of acting and speaking together, and its true space lies between people living together for this purpose, no matter where they happen to be. Wherever you go, you will be a *polis*.[7]

These cities speak of the teeming possibilities of human life, social conflict and even danger both to individuals and to the established order. Not surprising then that the elites who built and administered them wished to escape to the country and the suburbs, and to return at their convenience to keep the social order ticking over.[8] To live both in and beyond the city was the historical prerogative of elites. But from the end of the nineteenth century the masses began to approach their country retreats. First mass transit systems and then the automobile make this possible for a growing number of suburban dwellers. The possibility of a mass exodus from urban slums and the invasion of new space occasioned a new sense of fear and distaste in the elites who had to live in political proximity to the masses, through the extension of the suffrage, but now also in physical proximity.[9]

Were the new suburbanites running toward Arcadia or away from purgatory? The examination of their hopes and fears is a more fruitful study than the technical concern that suburbs produce isolation or even alienation. Much of the discussion about suburbia, with its emphasis on prescriptions for technical utopias, suggests that it is physical space that determines isolation.[10] However, in *The Fall of Public Man*, Richard Sennett suggests that it is the disruption of social networks and finally the collapse of social alternatives that determine the pre-eminence of the private sphere in both the city and the suburb.[11] The social takes on the technical form of privatised space. The suburb is not the cause of social alienation but is experienced as the phenomenal form of that alienation.

There is no intrinsic reason why having a back garden should cause alienation. Nor, as Paul Barker suggests in the *New Statesman*, that anyone should be denied this choice.[12] For this reason the debate between the superiority of brownfield development over greenfield development, or vice versa, is at best a spurious one. At worst it hides an overwhelming hypocrisy that denies opportunities for many either to live in pleasant rural surroundings or in the increasingly ghettoised inner-city developments of the new rich.

For the majority of people, for most of the postwar period, the housing question was having a dwelling and not particularly where it was or of what type. What else could account for the popularity of the post-

war prefab?[13] High-rise, suburban cottage, town terrace or new town semi-detached – none of these types of housing are the issue. Having a home of one's own while living in a society in which you think you have the possibility of getting a better one, and a chance to participate in the decision-making that effects those choices are important issues.

MANAGERS PREFER PARTNERSHIPS

Postwar Britain did not get Howard's network of Garden Cities but instead a pot-pourri of New Towns and council estates often modelled as if in homage to Nye Bevan's misty-eyed conception of the traditional country cottage. The problem was not in out-of-town living but in the limited resourcing. The market was the essential problem in the late 1940s, in the form of scarce materials, meaning that housing production was inadequate. The problem was tackled differently in the 1970s in that shoddy materials were used to produce more units.

The modernist planners of the 1960s and the 1970s have a lot to answer for, but the high-rise or tower block form is not one of them. A well-situated reasonably built tower block is an attractive proposition, not least for the views. The Barbican is sufficient evidence of this. Many more may have worked if sufficient money had been put into making the lifts operable. The degradation of the urban landscape is not a function of people. Their exclusion from decision-making makes planning impossible. We are now asked to believe that more management and more regulation are the way forward. The Urban Task Force report *Towards an Urban Renaissance* contains 105 recommendations, not all of which were acted upon by the government, whilst claiming that its approach to achieving the anticipated 'urban renaissance' 'is not a question of regulation'.[14] The annex summarising the numerous recommendations, *Sharing the Vision*, called for strengthened planning guidance.

> Devolve detailed planning policies for neighbourhood regeneration, including urban priority areas into more flexible and targeted area plans, based upon the production of a spatial master plan and the full participation of local people. The resulting policies and guidelines should take the form of strengthened supplementary planning guidance where necessary.[15]

The supplementary planning guidance reinforces Hyett's presumption that people are the problem and planning can rectify their misdemeanours. As New Labour rejected his renewed call for an urban regeneration bill to enact the raft of Urban Task Force recommendations, Lord Rogers of Riverside said: 'I am disappointed'. He explained why.

> The fact that 90% of us live in the cities has got to be recognised. All the government's vision on schools, health and crime can't possibly come to fruition otherwise. Educational improvements depend on people not fleeing our cities.[16]

The object of his city is more important than the freedom of movement for people animating them. For Rogers the city is the built form, and not the people. The insistence that people stay around to bring policy to fruition is more revealing, in that the subjective rejection of 'the government's vision' is not tolerable. The fact that the government itself is reticent to regulate beyond the twin policy statements of the Urban and Rural White Papers shows its lack of confidence.[17] But equally that same nervousness about its own regenerative projects means that sooner or later it will regulate further to appease the master-planners like Rogers who constitute the New Labour elite. After all, they agree with each other in principle.

They believe that people should make policy work and be grateful for the environment being carefully planned and designed, in consultation with themselves, for their own good. This is the elitist assumption – that most people are incapable of organising their own lives – at the heart of the New Labour project. Of course this is not to suggest that individual managers or professionals do not have a high degree of expertise in engineering, architecture and allied skills. It is also not to argue that their power to exercise their talent creatively should be curtailed. It is only to suggest that their skill is precisely that – a technical accomplishment, and nothing more. There are elite designers and planners. There are no elite people.

Being good at design or planning is not a convincing or even a plausible argument for running people's lives to fit the economic, social or environmental blueprint. It doesn't matter whether this is expressed as a professional responsibility, a mission statement or a vision thing. The vocabulary changes but the misconception remains the same.

Hyett poses his misanthropic analysis of how people constitute the danger to the regeneration of society in the context of a three-stage overview. He effectively adopts the following schematic periodisation of postwar Britain:

- 'New Jerusalem' in which beneficent state legislators and planners hoped to construct a new Britain, rising phoenix like from the ashes of the Great Depression and the Second World War. The resultant welfare state failed.

- 'Mammon' or the free market red in tooth and claw replaced 'New Jerusalem' in the late 1970s and the 1980s, and for the zealots of this approach the market was no less a utopian vision than that which preceded it. For the majority who remained to be convinced dystopia would be a better word. For Hyett, both approaches failed but the only reason given or blame attached is that people wanted to appropriate too much space. People stand condemned for aspiring to flexibility and mobility through car ownership and suburban life.

I too agree that there has been a fundamental failure of postwar redevelopment, but we need to go a little further and make some attempt to discover wherein the failure lies. In line with my defence of people against planners, and the primacy of the social over the technical, this is where we need to look. All the more so given the presumption that a new alliance between the two failures, a recast bureaucratic planning system and the operation of the market is mooted as the new solution of the Third Way. This is not the answer to the problem but the problem writ large.

- 'Partnership' as epitomised in the Urban Task Force report envisages a level of state intervention beyond the wildest dreams of civil servants operating under the 1947 Town and Country Planning Act. Not only is the scope of intervention much wider and more prescriptive but state authority is wielded through the private sector to encourage the profit margins of entrepreneurs who are now graced with the adjective 'social'.

This Third Way mechanism goes by the name of partnership, which is a euphemism John Poulson or T. Dan Smith might well have been proud of. To round off the new package the intensive government initiatives to aid private profit are wrapped up in the syntax of sustainable development with the grammar of management theory. Identify something environmental to measure, make it a target, and then deliver, on a rolling programme of profitable collaboration. The language of empowerment and sustainable development is employed to describe a policy-making framework with less to do with the active participation of citizens, or a concern for their environmental needs, than at any time during the postwar period.

This is the Third Way that privileges a technical project over social engagement. It speaks not to the citizen but to the bureaucrat in either the public or private sectors. Its propensity for regulation is in inverse proportion to its relationship with people. The top-down planning mechanisms so beloved of Blairite technocrats might provide 'joined up thinking' for bureaucrats, but are fundamentally alienating for the majority of the British population.

The original Third Way was a description of the attempt in Swedish social democracy to find a socially just and equitable reconciliation between the First Way of market capitalism and the Second Way of the centrally planned economies of the Soviet bloc. The Third Way of Blair is a very different beast. It is the third attempt in the postwar period to define a strategy to solve the twin problems of economic decline and social fragmentation. The characteristic features of the Third Way are the unreserved embrace of the Second Way Thatcherite injunction that there is no alternative to the market, additional to the shedding of state socialist and redistributionist prescriptions of the First Way welfare state. The peculiarity of the Third Way is the assertion that we now live in a win-win society in which our interconnectedness allows technical solutions to overcome all social problems. If only we do what we are told. This implies a very different message and understanding of society than the First and Second Way.

THIRD ATTEMPT

The welfare state of the First Way was indeed a consensus embracing both Old Labour and Conservative over the need for state intervention, presupposing the need for this consensus as a weapon in the battle to overcome and eliminate social evils that blighted society. The substance of the consensus was the presumption, derived from the experience of the Depression, that capitalism left to its own devices did not work.[18] It argued that the people who had fought, suffered and died in a war had social rights which it was the duty of the state to satisfy if it was to command their allegiance. In this vision, best exemplified by the Festival of Britain in 1951, there was a measure of congruence between the elite and the people, or between politicians, policy-makers, bureaucrats and planners and the voting population.

The new idea of the role of government and the nation's own conception of itself embodied in the Festival of Britain survived and prospered for a generation. But from the late 1960s onwards this mode of social organisation was examined much more critically. The outlook and institutions once held to be the solutions to Britain's problems stood accused as being the cause of those problems. The relative decline of Britain as a world power in both the economic and political spheres was the evidence that the welfare model did not work, and also led to its identification as the cause of decline. Alongside economic decline, social conflict and social fragmentation were laid at the door of the 'Nanny State'.

The erosion of certainty and the observed failures of state intervention, both in terms of industrial efficiency and the provision of welfare services, led to growing disenchantment among the political elite and within the general population, whose expectations became more privatised. In retrospect it becomes easier to see the genesis of social disengagement in a much earlier period, but at the time the unbroken continuity of such institutions as the trade unions leant credibility to the assumption that little had or was changing in Britain. In this sense the ideological attack launched in the Thatcher years against the outlook and institutions of postwar consensus was beating on an open door, occupying territory that had already been vacated by important sections of both the establishment and the people.

The Second Way of Thatcherism, which rained fire and brimstone on the iniquities of state socialism and the Nanny State, served to wipe away the remnants of collectivist Britain. But in the process of doing so it removed the last remaining social networks and civil institutions that not only stood between the individual and the cold blast of the market but also mediated between the elite and the people. The result was a far more fragile sense of community and a sense that the institutions of government were far more divorced and unconcerned with people's hopes, fears and aspirations.

It is the absence of social engagement that is the characteristic feature of our lives, not the technical activity of planning and building in geographical space. As such it is the social relations between people and not technical relations between administrators and things that must be grasped and grappled with in the argument about policy-making. Only through the results of social interaction and social contestation, not technical prescription, will policy solutions arise.

BASILDON NEW TOWERS

The history of Basildon New Town illustrates this point.[19] The New Towers were in the forefront of the hopes and challenges involved in the reconstruction of Britain in the immediate postwar period. When a measure of prosperity arrived at the end of the 1950s much appeared to be unchanged. But the formal continuation of the limited collectivism of traditional Labourism disguised its limited appeal to ambitious Basildonians.

In the 1980s the old collectivist enterprise was swept aside by Thatcherite individualism and Basildon Man came to the attention of the nation. There are two problems with the sweeping generalisation of Basildon Man. First, individual aspiration had been a significant aspect of Basildon life for much longer than the Thatcher era. Second, there was no historic conversion to Thatcherism. A temporary allegiance to popular conservatism was only the manner through which Basildonians made a final break from the constraints of the postwar model.

Basildon New Town is an appropriate story of British planning, but even more representative of social change. The new towns express the consensual arrangements of the postwar period envisaged by Bevan as Labour Housing Minister, and executed under Macmillan, the first postwar Tory Housing Minister.

There was little money available for anything except the houses themselves. This was a factor that initiated a seemingly continuous concern with education, health and facilities among Basildonians, and must be an important contributory factor to the disenchantment with what was on offer that became very clear from the late 1970s onwards.

The plan specified 15 neighbourhoods of various sizes with their own community centres and shops. These would be self-contained communities separated from industrial areas. Work would be only a 10- or 15-minute cycle or bus ride away, but Basildonians came to define distances through the private car rather than the bicycle or public transport because they valued their independence.

Over the years prosperity in Basildon began to be measured through increased car ownership and vehicular arrivals at the town shopping centre. Council figures emphasise that 3,000 households have three or more cars. Road access is good by British standards even though the early planners underestimated the number of private cars in use. Concerns about maintaining good roads, transport and garaging have remained high on the agenda for Basildonians despite recent environmental arguments about private car use.

Basildonians do not see the use of private cars as either a cause for environmental concern or a cause of social and community breakdown. They are more likely to report a fear of unemployment as a cause for concern, because unlike car use it is a direct threat to their autonomy. The recession of the late 1980s had a sharp effect in Basildon, and although unemployment is now much lower, a fear of its return remains close to the surface in the collective memory. It is important to remember that there are still core social issues pertinent to everyday life for Yorkshire miners, Welsh steelworkers, Coventry car workers as well as many inner-city dwellers, alongside the reputedly more prosperous southern working-class.

Basildon was the seventh, the largest, and the last of the first wave of postwar new towns. The first wave of new towners may have been moved to Basildon as part of a pragmatic wave of slum clearance, but mostly it was the new residents who made the decision to relocate there. They saw themselves as

It is the absence of social engagement that is the characteristic feature of our lives, not the technical activity of planning and building in geographical space.

pioneers, and made a covered wagon the emblem of the first tenants' association. As early resident and later Basildon Councillor Alf Dove commented:

> Suddenly, the chance of starting a new life...The concept of the new town was, you came here from the smoke and you got a house. People like me just back from the war I was pleased just to have a house to rent. So our ambition was if only we could get a place to rent! And it came along. If you worked in a factory you rented a house. Marvellous. A garden. Flowers. Everyone was happy![20]

It was a simple vision, embedded in a social environment that had a more utopian view of what Basildon should represent. In a speech given in Basildon in 1948, Lewis Silkin, then the minister of town and country planning, explained that:

> Basildon will become a city which people from all over the world will want to visit, where all classes of the community can meet freely together on equal terms and enjoy common cultural and recreational facilities. Basildon will not be a place that is ugly, grimy and full of paving stones like many large modern towns. It will be something which the people deserve; the best possible town that modern knowledge, commerce, science and civilisation can produce.[21]

However, these were a difficult set of aspirations to meet, and Basildon fell a long way short of them. In the early decades of Basildon the congruence between the planning vision and the aspirations of Basildonians was eroded. There were numerous campaigns to improve health and educational provision that were central to the community life of the area but without producing a real change in the quality of service. This was not the golden age of socialism, as many old Labourites, including Alf Dove, believe. It attached grace and favour such as food parcels and trips to Southend for the OAPs to a system of state bureaucracy and services standardised in every way to guarantee mediocrity.[22]

In the course of the generation following on from 1948, the Labour Party became associated with poverty and welfare, or a party for losers that would not give Basildonians what they wanted. In response, Basildonians sought out and defined a reformulation of their original dream – a home of their own – and if possible an opportunity to sort out their own lives. As a vote-seeking councillor, Alf Dove recognised home ownership as the reason for the shift to the Tories.[23] There was, however, no ideological conversion. Thatcherism was rather the attempt of the elite to recast its relationship to society through the market. But the market failed to provide legitimacy for the government.

For a short time there was an expectation that the Conservatives could deliver the material improvements and opportunities that Basildonians had always sought. When the Tories did not come up with the goods, what little enthusiasm there was vanished. Even in 1992, the flagship policies of popular conservatism, such as privatisation and share ownership, had little impact. The exception was home ownership; 36 per cent said it was the best thing the Conservatives had done, yet in the same survey 39 per cent of respondents thought that the government had done nothing they considered good.[24]

The experience of the Thatcher period did not create a new set of allegiances. It has left nothing behind in the way of substantive institutions. But the Thatcher era did deal a final blow to the tattered forms of collectivism, which had long-since passed their sell-by date. The Thatcher regime successfully, at least temporarily, spoke over the heads of the collective organisations of postwar Britain, but only by destroying the traditional ways in which the elite negotiated and decided priorities with the majority of the population.

It is in this context that we must understand the New Labour desire for 'joined up thinking', to restate priorities, and gain the approval of the population. What emerged from the Thatcher period is a political landscape in which individuals stand isolated, without much reference to each other and with only the most minimal relationship to institutions and organisations. This means that the policy-making elite is further away from the general population than at any time in the postwar period because it has no means to gauge, engage and respond to hopes and aspirations.

Paradoxically it also means that it can present its own agenda almost without opposition. It is the final irony that the elite is so lacking in confidence that it feels it necessary to clothe its managerial agenda in a language supposed to privilege the people. The experience of local government in Basildon, as elsewhere, is that it has no mechanism to discuss priorities. Yet central government requires it do so.[25] In accordance with and in order to meet central government targets, to obtain funding local government is expected to establish partnerships and run participatory focus groups. Such exercises do not overcome but tend to exacerbate the distrust of official organisations and institutions, as the partnerships often find a set of priorities conforming to their own agenda.

This agenda is the deliberation of experts at the centre of regeneration and sustainable development projects. The planners may well be able to solve their interdisciplinary conflicts through 'joined up thinking', but in a language not listened to by citizens. The regulatory impulse of the planners is not perceived as the guarantor of more opportunity and security, but as an imposition on individual lifestyle and identity.[26] For example, if Basildonians think about government at all, they think it is a waste of money.

The planners may well be able to solve their interdisciplinary conflicts through 'joined up thinking', but in a language not listened to by citizens.

THE MANAGERIAL MISCONCEPTION

New Labour will be faced with either indifference or cynicism, for the Third Way has no measure of participation and no democratic core.

In the old political arrangements of the First and Second Ways, policy-making came out of contested interests and priorities. The Third Way assumes that there is no conflict of interest so policy need only be the dovetailing of administrative options, made possible through technical expertise.

Policy-making is so much easier when people are not involved. However, Third Way initiatives will be appreciated in the same spirit as previous attempts to define a strategy to solve the twin problems of economic decline and social fragmentation. New Labour will be faced with either indifference or cynicism, for the Third Way has no measure of participation and no democratic core. The trouble with planners is that they will interpret this response as apathy and as 'the trouble with people', for which they will suggest regulation and more planning.

Notes

1. Paul Hyett, 'The trouble with people', *Building Design*, 19 January 2001, p. 13.
2. Paul Hyett quoted in David Littlefield, 'Blair's speech divides profession', *Architects' Journal*, 26 April 2001, p. 4.
3. Paul Hyett, 'The trouble with people', *Building Design*, 19 January 2001, p. 13.
4. F. Engels, *Socialism – Utopian and Scientific,* foreword Alan Hudson (London: Junius, 1995), pp. xxiii–xxiv.
5. E. Howard, *To-morrow! A peaceful Path to Real Reform* (London: Swan Sonnenschein, 1898); E. Howard, *Garden Cities of To-Morrow* (London: Swan Sonnenschein, 1902).
6. Rem Koolhaas, *Delirious New York*, quoted in Marshall Berman, *All That Is Solid Melts Into Air* (London: Verso, 1995), p. 287.
7. Hannah Arendt, *The Human Condition,* quoted in Ken Worpole and Liz Greenhalgh, *Freedom of the City* (London: Demos, 1996), p. 6.
8. Lewis Mumford, *The City in History* (London: Harcourt, Brace and World, 1961), ch. 16, 'Suburbia and Beyond', pp. 482–524.
9. John Carey, *The Intellectuals and the Masses* (London: Faber, 1992), ch. 3, 'The Suburbs and the Clerks', pp. 46–70.
10. Kenneth T. Jackson, *Crabgrass Frontier – the Suburbanization of the United States* (Oxford: Oxford University Press, 1985).
11. Richard Sennett, *The Fall of Public Man* (London: Faber, 1986), ch. 7, pp. 130–49.
12. Paul Barker, 'You can't plan a good city', *New Statesman*, 12 February 1999, and 'The future belongs to the suburbs', *New Statesman*, 21 June 1999.
13. Peter Hennessy, *Never Again Britain 1945–1951* (London: Vintage, 1993), p. 173.
14. Urban Task Force, *Towards an Urban Renaissance – Final Report of the Urban Task Force* (London: E&F Spon, 1999), p. 40.
15. Urban Task Force, 'Sharing the vision', annex to *Towards an Urban Renaissance – Final Report of the Urban Task Force* (London: E&F Spon, 1999).
16. Richard Rogers quoted in Neil Bowdler, 'Labour angers Rogers', *Building Design*, 29 June 2001, p. 1.
17. Department of the Environment, Transport and the Regions, *Our Towns and Cities – the Future, Delivering an Urban Renaissance* (London: HMSO, November 2000); Department of the Environment, Transport and the Regions and the Ministry of Agriculture, Fisheries and Food, *Our Countryside – the Future, A Fair Deal for Rural England* (London: HMSO, November 2000).
18. Noel Annan, *Our Age* (London: Fontana, 1991), pp. 3–4.
19. D. Hayes and A. Hudson, *Basildon – the Mood of the Nation* (London: Demos, 2001); D. Hayes and A. Hudson, *Who are the C2s? Basildon Revisited – Change and Continuity* (Whitstable, Kent: E&WRG, 2001).
20. D. Hayes and A. Hudson, *Basildon – The Mood of the Nation* (London: Demos, 2001), p. 16.
21. Ibid., p. 20.
22. Ibid., p. 17.
23. Ibid., p. 17.
24. Ibid., p. 39.
25. Lawrence Pratchett (ed.), *Renewing Local Democracy – the Modernisation Agenda in British Local Government* (London: Frank Cass, 2000).
26. D. Hayes and A. Hudson, *Basildon – the Mood of the Nation* (London: Demos, 2001), p. 45.

A FLY-BY-LIGHT ARCHITECTURE

Airlander 1999
Jonathan Schwinge

Airlander is situated on the north bank of the River Thames, London, at Charing Cross station. The building absorbs the dense urban fabric at ground level and then accelerates it to form a systematic, vertical urbanism. In doing so, the mixed-use 400-metre skyscraper investigates new programmatic approaches to urban existence and connectivity.

The history of the site is preserved in a series of 'reinvented' arcades at ground level. Briefing desks and check-in counters line an enclosed 'street' from the old Charing Cross frontage to a new Bridge Station, where incoming trains and boats are greeted by Airlander. The angled façade of the building houses a series of vertical streets, branching off into ' side-pocket' activity pods. This 'free activity zone' is linked throughout by vertical 'sky gardens'. To the rear, four 15-storey containers support the offices and research centres of urban industry, while the 'town centre' of this vertical city is located at the building's midriff, a nerve centre of overlapping and compact activity. This vertical intersection extends on a horizontal axis, where a detached 'Saturn-ring', 200 metres in diameter, houses the sky gardens and introduces the concept of city overlayering. This concept is repeated at the top of the building, where a vertical take-off and landing (VTOL) Airdeck extends into the urban fabric. Thus the horizontality of the existing city is absorbed, digested and finally expelled in the form of sightseeing airships and tilt-rotor aircraft. In this way, Airlander pushes the concept of vertical cities within the urban fabric – live/work/play skyscrapers that are linked (both to each other and to more distant cities) by the overhead connections of a new dynamic Airbus transportation system.

New aviation technology is also applied within the building itself. Transfer technology allows a modified version of the 'fly-by-light' system to 'trigger' the building's adaptive glazing system and internal environmental systems in response to climatic changes.

(Extract from Mark Rappolt (ed.), AA News, Architectural Association, Winter 1999–2000).

View from Trafalgar Square.
Site plan.

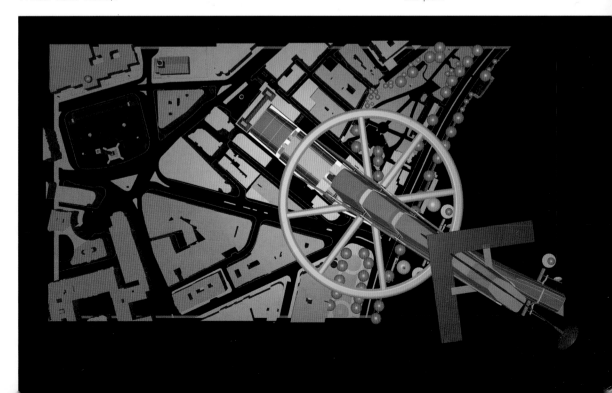

Key technological features

- Modified aircraft 'fly-by-light' system utilising control signals via fibre-optics rather than electrical cables as part of an integral sensory or nervous system. Fly-by-light relays information of environmental stimuli through a processor to generate a feedback response, adapting building environmental and monitoring systems.
- Active self-diagnostic and fault-diagnostic technology for constant sensory health and structural monitoring.
- Shape memory alloy actuators for ventilation systems.
- Solar energy reflecting 'windshielding' with photochromatic light responsive coatings.
- Contratherm syntactic phenolic foam fire protection.
- Friction stir welded steel and aluminium components.
- Anti-sway tuned mass damper connected to the 'nervous system' located at the top of Airlander.
- Various building elements, utilising semi-monocoque construction comprising transversals and longitudinals with integrated skin.
- Potential for future 'memory recall' and artificial intelligence integration, enabling the building to become 'instinctive' and communicative. (Future bio-architecture with 'conversational' diagnostics.)

Overcoming the false separation of town and country by air

The Airlander building provides a platform for a rural commuter service of VTOL aircraft at an urban transport interchange. More than just a physical link between town and a developed countryside, Airlander has an economic interrelationship with agriculture.

The contemporary discussion of the high-density urban renaissance has encouraged the idea that urban development must stand alone, reducing carbon emissions as an architectural exercise in energy demand management. This has led to the mistaken belief that the development of existing cities has no relation to the countryside other than in minimising the uptake of greenfield land. There is a preoccupation where architects try to minimise the environmental impact of buildings which, at the same time, are meant to have architectural impact. Architects have so far thought of sustainability as using less land and creating less carbon pollution over the life cycle of their designs; the green reinterpretation of the aesthetic formulation that 'less is more'. This is technologically obsolete thinking.

While the engineering formulation that 'doing more with less' holds the prospect of greater functionality from the efficient use of resources, there still comes a point where a supply-side solution is required to meet increasing demand for advanced buildings. In the twenty-first century it has become possible to overcome the false separation of town and country, to design to make an environmental impact using the synergy of a range of advanced energy technologies that require architectural integration. More than an exercise in carbon reduction we face a hydrogen-fuelled future, dependent on the integration of urban and rural development, where energy supply is assured, cleanly and indefinitely.

Future-proofing investment

All the international energy suppliers are developing a range of hydrogen fuel cell applications that vary in their chemistry and the niche markets they are aiming at. But all of them generate electrical power at the point of use. In a process best thought of as reverse electrolysis, the combination of hydrogen gas fuel with oxygen, preferably from fresh air, silently produces electricity with an exhaust product of water and heat. Fuel cells vary in scale in addition to their composition, but are modular. It is possible within the next few years that the first large-scale whole building applications will move beyond their research and development phases into commercial use.

Airlander verticality and overlayering.

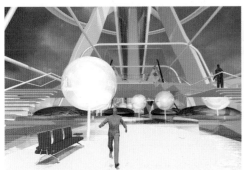

TOP: Giselle watches the tiltrotor commuter shuttles carrying the air-networkers, while in the distance airships circle Airlander with London sightseers.

FROM LEFT TO RIGHT:

Arcade and check-in.

Ground condition of the reinvented Arcade and Airlander check-in.

Horizontal to vertical interception.

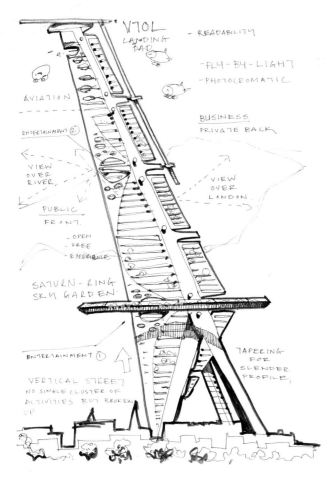

TOP: Side elevation

BOTTOM: Model showing relationship to the river photographed by E Woodman of the Architectural Association.

Initially installations will be expensive, but the point of developing a high-rise and high-density development around a fuel cell hub is that the development will be able to assimilate the emerging renewable energy technologies awaiting changes in the energy market.

Hydrogen infrastructure

The prospect of generating electricity from hydrogen on-site has a number of opportunities. There is an immediate saving in the transmission inefficiencies of centrally generated electricity. The low efficiency of the national grid can be avoided by shipping a source of hydrogen gas direct to the fuel cell. At present the best source of hydrogen is natural gas, which can be re-formed on the premises. As the market for hydrogen develops the gas will become deliverable by a main supplier, but in the interim on-site gas re-formation will be viable. The government is addressing the infrastructural problem of hydrogen supply, but the advantage of hydrogen being investigated by energy suppliers is the range of renewable energy sources it makes practicable. The problem with solar, wind and tidal power is their intermittency. The ability to use these technologies to electrolyse hydrogen from water while the sun is shining, the wind blows, or the tide is strong means that renewable energy is stored in the form of hydrogen gas for the time it is needed by the building users.

The ability to generate solar or wind energy on-site is limited by the urban microclimate, the orientation and scale of the building, and the cost penalty of sacrificing useable floor area to additional plant. The advantage of hydrogen as a storage medium is that the renewable energy can be generated remote from the urban centre in a dedicated rural installation. This also makes maintenance and replacement of equipment easier in spacious surroundings.

While banks of photovoltaic panels, wind or tidal turbines are possible for hydrogen electrolysis in a rural setting, another source of renewable energy generation might be the prospect of 'electrofarming'. This is where crops, genetically modified for the purpose, are grown and burnt in a carbon neutral cycle of cultivation and combustion to generate electricity for hydrogen electrolysis. In the absence of a national hydrogen supplier it would be possible to develop a hydrogen production facility in the countryside, dedicated to a pioneering project until that facility were absorbed into a wider hydrogen economy. Investment in high-rise urban development could be accompanied with investment in a source of hydrogen that, as time goes by, can be purchased more conventionally. In the short term the creation of a function for agricultural land being retired will enable the building development to support its own energy needs through an economically interdependent relationship between town and country. Airlander can be refuelled by lighter than air transportation technologies in the absence of mains hydrogen utilities.

Part L and the climate change levy

The saving of transmission inefficiencies will immediately and substantially allow the building to meet the requirements for the conservation of fuel and power in the anticipated revisions to the Building Regulations. This allows the calculation of carbon emission reductions that 'Part L' of the regulations requires to optimise the building envelope, reducing the need for carbon emissions reductions technology in the construction itself. The reliance on renewable energy sources will also take full advantage of the climate change levy.

TOP: View up spine to VTOL urban overlayer.
BOTTOM: Airlander concept tower model.

ABOVE: Airlander concept tower model.

OPPOSITE: View of the 'urban overlayer' airdeck with the V22 Osprey tiltrotor. CAD aircraft model kindly supplied by Viewpoint.

Building integrated systems

That said, and if worthwhile, additional building integrated photovoltaic-cladding systems can be assimilated into the overall servicing system, as BIPV becomes more effective and efficient. This may turn the building into a net supplier of electrical power to the locality. The subsequent cladding refits will be the opportunity to reappraise the advantage of emerging and improving renewable energy systems for the envelope. Similarly wind turbines or solar chimneys could be incorporated at the highest storeys of the building, but such approaches will always be secondary and less elegant than using these technologies off-site in the commercial activity of large-scale and cheaper hydrogen production. As the technology and market improves the modular upgrading of the fuel cell hub will also be available.

Together, the potential to incorporate other technologies and the improving economies of hydrogen-fuelled power generation will allow a sophisticated integration of energy systems to cope with peak loads and respond to the changing patterns of local demand.

Cooling and solar gain

An advantage of not having to conserve energy through an insulated cladding system to achieve 'Part L' compliance because efficiencies have been obtained from the fuel cell, is that fabric heat losses can be designed in, provided that occupant comfort is not adversely affected. Most buildings need cooling, so the conservation of heat at the envelope is counterproductive because cooling is still required. Heat from increasing levels of small power information technology, from the occupants, and from solar gain needs to be controlled either naturally or mechanically, or by solar energy-reflecting photochromatic light responsive coatings to the glazing. The aim should be to avoid a plethora of shading devices that only serve to increase maintenance costs and clutter the building with complex access equipment.

For the envelope to be capable of retrofitting, and for general maintenance, a system of external access vehicles will need to be developed to integrate with the cladding support structure. These systems are often inconvenient and dangerous for the operatives, and it is here that the savings made on simplifying the external construction should be directed. There will be substantial budgetary and aesthetic advantage in avoiding the need for a complex building fabric by expenditure on the fuel cell and the hydrogen supply.

Structural diagram.

Adaptability and scale

Just as the fuel cell hub is the centre of the servicing strategy, the building is conceived as a form that has to support changing function over time. The structural core is the long-life element that supports the serviced space. The ability to refit the accommodation several times during the life of the core, and to upgrade the building fabric systems connected to the fuel cell hub, requires the building elements to be designed for renewal and technological advance. The scale of the building is the key to achieving the efficiencies and productivities of prefabricated and co-ordinated construction products.

This approach not only suggests a hierarchy of elements in the building fabric and the systems integrated into them, but also informs the architectural treatment as an assembly of pods, panels and components co-ordinated on a structural core that contains the vertical circulation. Airlander needs to be manufactured, not completely built on site, to provide all the benefits of labour productivity and resource efficiencies unprecedented in Britain.

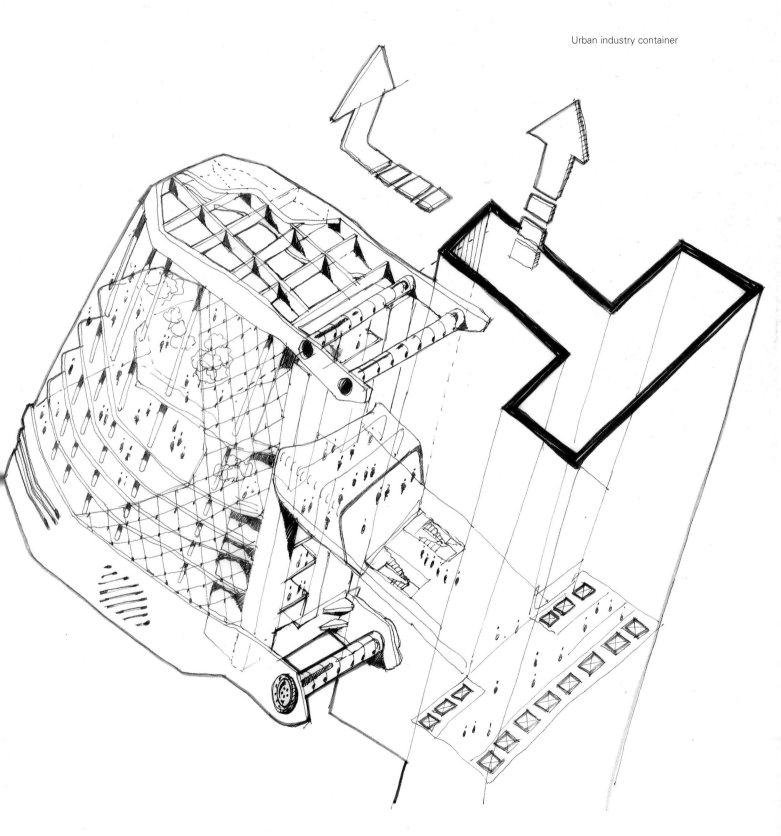

Urban industry container

Chapter 10

Why it is No Longer Appropriate to Underestimate the Opposition

Margaret Casely-Hayford

A NEW VICTIM?

The 'self help' industry has always advocated that the best way to help oneself is to 'take control'. Understanding where your weakness is, working towards avoiding being made a victim, and fully regaining control helps one to realise the full opportunity and potential of many situations. Understanding and acknowledging that there is a problem is said to be the greatest part of the battle.

The development industry is now beginning to realise that towards the end of the twentieth century it was inappropriately treating itself as the subject of a new 'victimhood'. However, at the start of the twenty-first century it has begun to re-evaluate, to reassert itself and to regain control in order to re-establish its own well being and to continue the substantial contribution to the economic growth of the country that it has made in the past. Importantly, it has realised that development is more than ever a question of balance.

Invidious comparisons are made with planning systems that operate within countries that have a far greater land mass per head of population, where development mistakes are likely to be seen as less environmentally catastrophic. Developers trying to work in Britain complain of how hard it is to work with a system that is increasingly over-regulated, unpredictable and slow. What should these new 'victims' be doing instead? How should they recognise their problem? How do they seek to gain greater control? Admittedly, they are not legislators, and neither are they the decision-makers in planning terms. But as applicants for planning consent they are increasingly recognised by central governments as having much to give to the new policy objectives. Does this mean they retain a degree of power?

Government puts far greater emphasis on developmental responsibilities being borne by various stakeholders, representative of different elements within the community. Recent enactments of legislation have served to create an interesting shift in the power base towards what is arguably a more balanced system – one in which the environmental protectionist lobby, those wishing to preserve their own local amenity and those wishing to extract cost from the developer to counter-balance any perceived harm from the development, has been secured.

HUMAN RIGHTS AND PLANNING

One fundamental alteration to the domestic legislation came with the incorporation of the European Convention on Human Rights. This was introduced in England by the Human Rights Act 1998 and came into effect on 2 October 2000 (having already been introduced in Scotland upon devolution). A number of its provisions have a bearing on planning law, but the cases that have so far been debated in the English and Scottish Courts have primarily involved rights arising out of Article 6 of the Convention. Article 6 states:

> In the determination of his civil rights…every person is entitled to a fair and public hearing within a reasonable time by an independent and impartial tribunal.

The Courts have decided that this provision does not prevent the Secretary of State (when he acts as planning authority) from having the dual functions of planning policy-maker and decision taker (on appeals or call-in inquiries). The House of Lords said that the Secretary of State does not have to worry about being independent or impartial, as his role is one of a principal administrator and not that of a judge. It is likely that by analogy local authorities will also be able to continue making local policy for planning purposes and also taking planning decisions based on their own policy.

However, no case has yet been brought to test the question of whether the planning system as it currently stands is fair to third parties. Under the current system third parties have no legal right to challenge the grant of a planning permission. Article 6 of the Convention is likely to open up this debate. In the meantime those who feel aggrieved by the grant of a planning consent try increasingly frequently to challenge grants by attempting to establish that the decision was arrived at without adherence to the necessary procedural requirements.

A SENSE OF PROPORTION

Where developments are in line with the development plan, and can therefore be shown to serve a greater planning purpose in complying with the local authority's planning objectives, it is arguable that on balance, a decision to grant the scheme consent is defensible if a degree of proportionality is applied. The

Developers trying to work in Britain complain of how hard it is to work with a system that is increasingly over-regulated, unpredictable and slow.

European courts have recognised the appropriateness of compromising certain of the rights. Those promoting schemes under the modern Human Rights regime would be well advised to refer in their planning-application support material to the contribution that the proposal would make to:

- public safety
- the economic well-being of the country
- protection of health
- protection of the rights and freedoms of others

These are defensible grounds upon which certain of the civil rights enshrined in the Convention might otherwise be compromised. However, these days it is not just the planning application support material that needs to be more carefully drawn up.

It was formerly the case that if a developer gained a planning permission any third parties would sit back feeling themselves defeated, because the relevant Town and Country Planning legislation does not incorporate any right of appeal for third parties in such a situation. Lately, those who feel themselves 'wronged' by the grant of a consent to a developer have become increasingly knowledgeable about the basis upon which they could challenge a decision in the courts through the process of judicial review.

Third parties are now all too aware that if the decision-maker has possibly arrived at 'the right' decision but through a procedurally inappropriate channel, the decision may be challenged in the courts. As a consequence, third parties are more vigilant in trying to ascertain whether the procedures of regulations such as Environmental Impact Assessment requirements have been properly followed. Many major schemes have been stopped in their tracks or delayed through such successful challenge, and the strength of third parties in this regard must not be underestimated. An analysis of some of the recent cases that have been brought by third parties by this procedure demonstrates that the way forward is to work with them, understand the extent to which they have concerns, and seek to incorporate compromise solutions within the application process.

There is an obvious tension between the EC directive on assessment of environmental effects and the desire on the part of developers for an easy and simplified method of obtaining 'in principle' acknowledgement of the appropriateness of the scheme of development for a particular location. To get this 'in principle' approval should only technically require submission to the planning authority of a purely outline planning consent. However, the proper assessment of the effects of a development scheme, which might be required to satisfy the Environmental Impact Assessment regulations, could be so detailed as to obviate the possibility of an outline planning application at all. This has been demonstrated to cause difficulties with major schemes where developers obviously do not want to incur the vast expense of making a full application where the principle might otherwise not be accepted.

ENVIRONMENTAL IMPACT ASSESSMENT AS AN OBJECTOR'S TOOL

Everyone involved in the development business knows that major projects such as oil refineries, power stations and motorways cannot even be considered for planning consent unless an environmental impact assessment has first been carried out. The result of the assessment must be properly recorded, a statement made of any proposed mitigatory measures that might be necessary to counteract any adverse effects, and any required monitoring process noted to enable continuing assessment to be properly set up and arranged. For over a decade there has been a list of such major projects incorporated in Schedule 1 to the Town and Country Planning (Environmental Impact Assessment) Regulations 1988, updated in 1999.

However, the grey area in environmental assessment arises because there is a second schedule of types of projects for which it is not 'cut and dried' as to whether or not there is going to be a need for an environmental impact assessment. While it is clear that a major project, as listed for the purposes of Schedule 1, will require an environmental impact assessment, it is within the decision-maker's discretion whether or not other types of development alluded to in Schedule 2 of the regulations will require one. For this category of projects the local authority must decide whether there is likely to be significant impact on the environment by virtue of the nature, size or location of the development proposed.

A third-party objector well known in the courts as a formidable opponent is Lady Berkeley, who brought an action against the Fulham Football Club in connection with its proposal to develop the Craven Cottage football ground. No formal environmental impact assessment had been carried out or formal statement submitted, the view being taken that this was a Schedule 2 scheme for which an assessment was not strictly required. However, there were sensitive environmental issues involved concerning the likely effect on bird habitats on the Thames abutting the ground from the proposed enlargement and intensity of activity. Having given that issue full consideration, the council resolved to grant consent. It had taken into consideration the fact that the National Rivers Authority (which was then the statutory consultee on conservation issues) had withdrawn its initial objection on condition that Fulham FC built a wetland shelf planted with reeds on the foreshore.

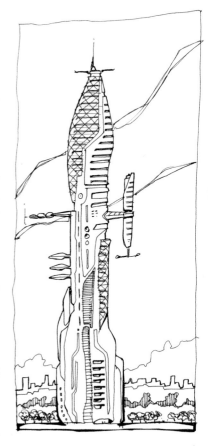

400 metre super development, live, work, play vertical existence.

Lady Berkeley lobbied for the Secretary of State to call-in the application and a public inquiry followed. The applicants had prepared a good deal of environmental information as part of their planning application, and in statements of evidence to the public inquiry. These were duly considered, and the Secretary of State granted planning permission following the close of the public inquiry.

It was this decision that was challenged in the High Court on the grounds that it was unlawful in the absence of an environmental assessment and statement.[1] The courts decided that the information had been available and had been taken into account. Not to be thwarted, Lady Berkeley brought the matter to the House of Lords and eventually won.[2] Their Lordships considered the Environmental Impact Assessment regulations to be procedural in nature. The procedure had to be followed. The planning authority should have shown itself to have regard for whether or not an environmental impact assessment was necessary before the granting of planning permission. It was also decided that it was insufficient for the relevant information to be found in disparate documents rather than in a formal assessment with a non-technical summary to assist lay people.

HOW DOES THE DEVELOPER REGAIN CONTROL?

As the applicant, the developer should request a local authority to carry out a 'scoping' exercise, so that the need for an environmental assessment is clear. This is not the same as inviting the council actually to assess an environmental impact assessment submission, but just a question of playing safe and providing an opportunity for the council to consider the appropriateness of environmental assessment in the circumstances and if so, the parameters of such an assessment.

Again, taking control would require the applicant to suggest the areas for the 'scoping' exercise that would seem to be appropriate in the circumstances so that there is no open-ended invitation for every single environmental aspect to be thoroughly investigated. In this regard there is no reason why there cannot be early agreement on the issues that should form the subject matter of the assessment.

Taking control of the 'scoping' exercise is not the only area over which the developer needs again to reassert his or her position. Even the basic preparation of a planning application is something on which there is now a new relationship between the developer and other interested parties as stakeholders in the protection of the environment.

A development company wished to develop a business park in Rochdale. It made an outline application in order to establish the principles for development. The application constituted a 'redline' plan, illustrative master plan and an environmental statement. Local residents challenged the outline on the basis that it incorporated little information. The High Court decided that as the outline consent is the planning application it has to contain sufficient information to enable a local authority to decide whether or not to grant consent, and what conditions they can sensibly impose. In this case, the court decided that there had been insufficient description of what the development was intended to be to help the planning authority decide the basis on which it could assess any impact. The council claimed that they had all the necessary information, and that the imposition of planning conditions set up the mechanism whereby they[o] could control the siting, design and scale of the development. The court decided that there was no way in which one could guarantee that the scheme would be developed as depicted in the illustrative material and that the grant of planning permission should be quashed.[3]

The applicant amended the business park outline application in a subsequent submission. It then included a schedule of proposed land uses and floor spaces – a masterplan for the site layout showing physical forms and land uses. The access and highway proposals were separate, full applications and landscaping and open spaces were shown fixed where this would not compromise future design flexibility. A development framework was drawn up, setting out the physical parameters to be adhered to in creating a high-quality and cohesive development. The assessment could be seen to be part of the process of design evolution. There was a clear assessment of the likely effects and investigation of possible areas of and solutions for mitigation and feedback into the design. A number of important principles were established on a worst case basis with regard to certain fixed parameters. The court accepted the position that the provision of environmental information was not a once-and-for-all event, and that parameters could be set to enable a formal impact assessment to be carried out at an initial stage in a project's lifetime.

The same group of local residents again challenged the grant of planning permission. This time their appeal was dismissed (ironically by the same High Court judge before whom they had succeeded when they brought their first challenge).[4] The judge recognised the desire of the development industry to maintain the flexibility that exists in the ability to make a purely outline application, but he then carefully reconsidered the need for compliance with the assessment regulations. He made it clear that the assessment must contain certain specified information whether or not the application is in outline.

The practical implications of this decision are clear. Apart from the pointers in the judge's decision it also seems that, in so far as it is possible, the developer should seek to limit the likelihood of third-party interference. This should be done by agreeing and putting on record a formal 'scoping' with the council, and by preparing an environmental statement if there is any doubt in a given situation. To avoid doing this is a false economy. The preparation of such a statement will be likely to be more cost effective than the ensuing delay or cost of a court battle if consent is granted without one and third-party objectors decide to test the matter in court.

It is increasingly the case that where third parties see a strong likelihood of a scheme for development being granted consent, they will try to influence the number and type of conditions and obligations that will be imposed in order to restrict or limit the development proposal.

For this reason it is often the position that third parties will stand to benefit from an obligation included in an agreement entered into under Section 106 of the Town and Country Planning Act 1990. For example, if money is to be contributed for the provision of an open space by a housing developer, or contribution to public transport provisions is to be made by a retail developer, the third-party 'beneficiaries' could well be the whole 'class' of local residents – the people on whom the benefit would be conferred by virtue of the obligation enshrined within the planning or Section 106 Agreement.

The recent enactment of the Contracts (Rights of Third Parties) Act 1999 has changed the law of contract. Even though the third parties have not actually been signatories to or party to the agreement between the developer and the planning authority, third parties can sue on the contract to get it enforced in their favour if for any reason the developer fails to perform.

Furthermore, once the main agreement has been entered into, if the actual parties to the agreement wished to vary the document, they would have to consult with and obtain the consent of the third party. The third-party rights as expressed in a Section 106 Agreement can be limited by, for example, clearly stating in the introductory recitals in the agreement what the limited purpose of the agreement actually is. Another way is to specifically limit certain rights by, for example, only allowing an action to enforce the rights under the contract to be brought by way of arbitration and not by litigation. This helps the developer reassert some control.

The Contracts (Rights of Third Parties) Act 1999 has been described as 'a busybody's charter' but the fact is that third parties are now seen as important stakeholders acting in the interest of the environment.

The Contracts (Rights of Third Parties) Act 1999 has been described as 'a busybody's charter' but the fact is that third parties are now seen as important stakeholders acting in the interest of the environment.

The developer becomes a 'victim' of the recent sea change in legislation to the extent that he or she might forget the need to have regard to third parties. There is a need to balance their objectives and interests as environmental stakeholders with the developer's ambitions and those of government. This is a sea change that leads to something rich and strange. As we are all probable beneficiaries from general economic growth, and ultimate beneficiaries of environmental good practice, these are riches of which we all need to partake.

So the dialogue should continue.

Notes

1. *Berkeley v. Secretary of State for the Environment, Transport and the Regions*, 12 February 1998 (1998) 3 PLR 39; (1998) PLCR 97.
2. *Berkeley v. Secretary of State for the Environment, Transport and the Regions* (No. 1), 6 July 2000 (2000) 3 WLR 420; (2000) 3 All ER 897; (2001) JPL 58.
3. *R. v. Rochdale MBC Ex p. Tew (No. 1)*, 7 May 1999 (1999) 3 PLR 74; (2000) JPL 54.
4. *R. v. Rochdale MBC Ex p. Milne (No. 2)*, 31 July 2000 (2001) 81 P&CR 27; (2001) JPL 470.

Chapter 11

Reinvigorating the English Tradition of Architectural Polemic

Miles Glendinning and Stefan Muthesius

THE ARCHAEOLOGY OF ARCHITECTURAL POLEMIC

In the course of research some ten to fifteen years ago on the history of modern mass housing and the 'tower block', we were particularly struck by the extreme vehemence and volatility of debates about the built form of housing in England. That applied not only during the years that were the subject of our research, roughly 1940 to 1970, but also during the 1980s and 1990s. This was a time when modern housing and tower blocks were still the subject of general and bitter public condemnation. It led us, seeking as we were a more balanced historical evaluation of modern housing in *Tower Block – Modern Public Housing in England, Scotland, Wales and Northern Ireland*, to argue against the 'destructive influence' of 'simplistic architectural polemicists', and 'the empty cut and thrust of "debate"'.[1]

Since then, of course, the balance of debate and esteem has swung back decisively towards a positive reappraisal of modernist urbanism, and we have seen a sudden re-emergence of several of the key urban controversies and concepts of the 1950s and 1960s modernist period. These urban controversies and concepts, such as high density, high building and mixed development, are all foregrounded in the Urban Task Force report and in PPG3, for example. In this context we felt that it might be of use to present-day practitioners to sketch out a historical overview of this uniquely English tradition of polarised debate on housing, and to put it into the wider context of the history of architectural polemic in England.

What we are dealing with here is not a fleeting phenomenon of the later twentieth century but a movement stretching back to the early nineteenth century, and even beyond; an enduring and widely accepted convention that architectural criticism in England should take the form of a rapidly shifting succession of mutually antagonistic utopian visions or recipes, each integrating the architectural forms of housing with forceful social and ethical values, and each supported by a coalition of architects and allied lay people. We say 'uniquely English', although other countries have, of course, also been familiar with architectural polemic and utopian visions, and with the underlying contrast in most utopias between organic community and modern alienation.[2] This is nevertheless a uniquely English tradition in that the popular pervasiveness and deep roots of the approach, almost analogous to adversarial politics in its debating conventions, have been uniquely marked in England.

Nothing was more typical of English architecture of the nineteenth and twentieth centuries than the constant quickfire of polemic, with its violent alternation of utopianist, and sometimes professedly anti-utopianist rhetoric.

Nothing was more typical of English architecture of the nineteenth and twentieth centuries than the constant quickfire of polemic, with its violent alternation of utopianist, and sometimes professedly anti-utopianist rhetoric. From a non-English perspective, what also seems striking is disparity between this emphasis on extreme and passionately held positions, and the stereotypical picture of 'English pragmatism' or 'moderation' famously presented by Nikolaus Pevsner.[3]

The purpose of this chapter is not only to present an overview of this tradition of architectural criticism, but also to pose the question of its future. In the twenty-first century, is it still 'sustainable' to discuss architecture and the city in this combative way? Our conclusions are that this tradition, with its close affinity to adversarial politics and public debate, has played a highly constructive role in the past in helping to 're-embed' society at times of disconcerting change in the built environment. There is no reason why polemic should not continue to play a similar, if perhaps more modest, role in the future.

PUGINIAN POLEMICS

The special polemical English approach to architectural debate first started to emerge in the mid-eighteenth century, when architecture began to take its place in the growing public sphere between civil society and the state. This was an area occupied by a new, engaged citizen body, able to discuss and criticise matters of policy. It was only natural that architecture, with its mixture of aesthetics and the practical, should launch itself into this new arena, but this came about differently in different countries. In France, the main vehicles for its intervention were grand projects and proposals based on the reality or the potential of state patronage. In England, the emphasis was on private debate and patronage, a process lubricated by growing exchanges between informed lay people and professional designers, rooted in the intense debates in London's coffee houses and liberalised press. It was in this climate, in the England of the mid-eighteenth century, that modern architectural criticism began to emerge. Early controversies, such as that surrounding George Dance the Elder's Mansion House in the early 1740s, or the writings of James Ralph in 1733 to 1734, focused fairly narrowly on issues of corruption or aesthetics.[4] But the potential also existed for those debates to take on a social reformist character.

That potential was first realised in the early nineteenth century, in the coincidence of two new factors: first the emergence of competing 'historic styles', and second, the stressful growth of urban class-based society. Reformist critiques of national social regeneration could coalesce around particular styles, and appropriately this first happened, once again, in England, the first country to experience the traumas of large-scale industrialisation and urbanisation. In the polemical writings of A. W. N. Pugin, the universal applicability of the gothic style was argued for, not in narrowly visual terms, although Pugin's designs were rooted in a kind of English picturesque, but as a means of moral and religious salvation for England. This was clearly an integrated 'utopia', but one radically opposed to the previous utilitarian modern utopias of Owen or Fourrier. Pugin idealised the supposed lost golden age of the Middle Ages and reviled utilitarian modernity as 'everything new and everything beastly'.[5]

In the wake of Pugin, polemical debates began to become embedded in English architectural culture, supported by an interaction between practice, books and journalism. They were highly variegated. On the one hand there were those, led by John Ruskin and William Morris, who emphasised an 'artistic' anti-modernity and ethical passion, and concerned themselves especially with old buildings and the issue of 'restoration'.[6] There was also a constant fluctuation of debates and factions within the 'gothic revival' camp.[7] But this approach also penetrated the more practical 'modern' or 'professional' elements in mid-nineteenth century English architecture represented by such practitioners as Sir G. G. Scott, and by commentators such as *Builder* editor George Godwin. The 'battle of the styles' between gothic and classical reached a symbolic climax in debates about the new Foreign Office buildings, 1857 to 1858.[8]

At first, these debates were an elite affair, concerned mainly with public and religious buildings, and putting forward highly individualistic ethical positions. They initially ignored more mundane urban building types, especially housing and the question of its reform. There was still a wide gulf between emotional or religious condemnations of the slums and the urban problem, and the technical language of sanitary engineering and medical officers. But in housing, a kind of parallel process of exaggerated fluctuations in fashion was already establishing itself in the nineteenth century, without the explicit articulation of the architecture debates. For example, the previously prestigious terrace fell sharply in status in favour of detached and semi-detached villas. This gulf between 'elevated national discourse' and 'everyday local practice' began to be filled by the late nineteenth century, when William Morris and the Arts and Crafts Movement integrated housing with the Pugin tradition by developing a full-blown utopian discourse of the 'ordinary home', or the 'English House'.

UTOPIANISM AND THE MODERN MOVEMENT

In the mid-twentieth century, the general context of all English debates about the built environment was revolutionised, and it was a mark of the flexibility of the polemical tradition of polarised utopias that it was able to adapt to the new circumstances with striking success. In reaction to the divisive class and national conflicts of the twentieth century, politics and public affairs became simplified into polarised collective blocs of opinion, with the state, served by powerful bureaucracies, occupying a central role. The state's main duty in the built environment was to try to provide modern 'services' for the lower strata through disciplined collective means. A new breed of public-authority professional architect-planner became dominant. During the 1940s and 1950s, the planning of housing was the almost exclusive preserve of the demiurges of the Welfare State. They constantly devised dynamic, collectivist slogans like 'the war on bad housing', 'the battle against the slums', or 'fighting suburban sprawl'. The political and architectural arms of that campaign were united about the fundamental procedure that should be followed. First, experts would define a solution, on the basis of scientific research. Then the state would build to the standards they had defined, and on a huge scale. This degree of state interventionism could have astonishing results: for example, in allowing an impecunious family from the housing waiting list to be given the permanent enjoyment of a view over central London from a brand new council flat on the top floor of a tall tower block.[9]

In England, the Pugin tradition, with its powerful adversarial character, was well able to adapt to this climate, and forged new alliances between key opinion-forming public authorities, such as the London County Council (LCC), the new town development corporations, architectural journalists and the wider intelligentsia.[10] In their new concern with the design of mass housing and other social building types, public architects were able to combine their input into the new vast command-production forces with, if anything, an increased scope for design individuality, and an increased fluctuation of opinions and factions. One of the most renowned LCC housing designers in the 1950s, Colin Lucas, 'group leader' in charge of the famous Roehampton Lane project from 1955, would 'crumple up memos about money and throw them out of the window, if he didn't like them!'[11] Social-democratic housing architecture and urban theory of the

1940s to 1960s, in its sheer diversity and passion, was like Christian gothic church architecture and debate of a century earlier, only extended to embrace potentially the entire built fabric of the country.

It was in this fevered atmosphere that the vigorous modernist debates about density and housing began to coalesce. At one level, 'density' was used as a factual word that could embrace most aspects of the visual or spatial surroundings of homes. But it also now became a polemical jargon term, a term that incited and excited the professional designer and planner then as now. Already, around 1900, when the housing reform debate intensified, or, more precisely, when the layout of small types of dwellings became a more contentious matter, the term density had become more prominent, as a kind of statistical explanatory word. The main initial message was clear: density is a bad thing. High-density housing first came to the fore in England in the 1930s, but it did not really become a live issue then, as it was essentially seen as a mere necessity, as an unavoidable substitute for low density. High-density development was for use only in circumscribed and inner urban areas in the form of utilitarian 'block dwellings' – that is, massive four- or five-storey tenement buildings with external access balconies.

The density debate became particularly energised and complicated, however, by the 1940s and 1950s with the acceptance and advocacy of fully fledged Continental Modernism. No longer was 'high density' a bogeyman. On the contrary, it could become a positive value itself. There began a succession of visions of high-density public housing, each in turn to be rejected as crude and utilitarian once they became adopted and implemented by the municipal and state agencies of mass production. In all this, the 'providers' were speeding far ahead of English public opinion, which still viewed all flats with great suspicion.

The first utopia of modern housing took the form of high blocks of flats, freestanding in landscaped open space, as exemplified by the slender towers and Corbusian slabs of the LCC's Roehampton project. The utopian ideal was now one of building a new community of egalitarian freedom, where 'the view belongs to everybody'.[12] This was to be achieved through 'mixed developments' of different types of blocks and dwellings, catering for a precisely determined mix of households, determined by 'experts', where 'the idea of community life is the big human factor which the planners have detected and which underlies all their planning'.[13] The polemical demand for a bogeyman was satisfied not only by garden suburb 'sprawl' but by the older, prewar and early postwar utilitarian slum-clearance municipal 'block dwellings'. The *Architects' Journal* attacked these as 'inhuman' in 1949.[14]

In reflection of the new and positive view of density, the way in which even 'factual' density calculations were devised became much more complex. The early twentieth-century's simple engineering-style of 'dwellings per acre' was replaced by 'persons per acre', or 'bedspaces per acre', a much more sophisticated measurement which also brought in the additional variable of the 'occupancy' of dwellings. In the best known of all postwar local-authority housing zoning policies, that of the LCC, based on the 1943 County of London Plan, the maximum net density for new housing in Inner London was set at 200 persons per acre. The average occupancy was set at 3.6 persons per dwelling, which meant about 55 dwellings per acre. For the suburbs, the corresponding zoned levels were 136 and 100 persons per acre, or about 38 and 28 dwellings per acre.[15] An acre is about 0.4 hectares, so it should be emphasised that these levels were far higher than today's PPG3 demand for 30 to 50 dwellings per hectare.

- 55 dwellings per acre for LCC urban centres equates to 137 dwellings per hectare.
- 38 dwellings per acre for LCC inner suburbia equates to 95 dwellings per hectare.
- 28 dwellings per acre for LCC outer suburbia equates to 70 dwellings per hectare.
- 20 dwellings per acre equates to 50 dwellings per hectare for PPG3.
- 12 dwellings per acre equates to 30 dwellings per hectare for PPG3.
- 10 dwellings per acre equates to the national average of 25 dwellings per hectare.[16]

But as the successive postwar utopias of density rolled onwards, high-density, although initially associated with modernist 'high rise', began to steadily distance itself from strict or doctrinaire International Modernism. From the 1940s and 1950s, it became bound up with another expression which was not a dry statistical term but a concept which seemed to be directly and intimately related to people's lives, that of 'urbanity'. Up to that time town planners would have considered it tautological to talk of 'urban' town planning. Now 'urbanity' became the key value, and a strong catchword for all plans for housing. Other associated words such as 'townscape' were of more restricted or partisan currency. Although many planners demanded high-density housing in order to protect the countryside from overbuilding, the advocacy of 'urbanity' was above all a polemical utopian conviction in the Pugin tradition, concerned with fostering lively spaces and 'communities'. For example, Clifford Culpin argued in 1954 that 'subconsciously we need space enclosure'.[17] It was this that led avant-garde designers to condemn so violently the look and feel of any back-to-the-land concepts, or any liking for the ordinary suburban, as the dreaded 'Subtopia'. The editor of the *Architectural Review*, J. M. Richards, argued that 'the gregarious Englishman…of the old English or Georgian market town…has been turned into a misogynous suburban'.[18]

There began a succession of visions of high-density public housing, each in turn to be rejected as crude and utilitarian once they became adopted and implemented by the municipal and state agencies of mass production.

The immediately preceding 1940s phase of modern architecture-planning, focused on the New Towns, was now scornfully dismissed, although the first of the New Towns were barely under construction. The July 1953 *Architectural Review* blasted the 'failure of the New Towns', with their 'prairie planning'.[19] Chamberlin Powell and Bon were the architects of that ultimate English dense city scheme of high towers and slabs, the 45-storey Barbican, which was planned from 1955 and built from 1962. In 1955 they invoked the reproach from D. H. Lawrence that 'the English do not know how to build a city, how to think of one, how to live in one', suggesting that we need 'that instinct of community which makes us unite in pride and dignity in the bigger gesture of the citizen, not the cottager', where 'the great city means beauty, dignity and a certain splendour'.[20]

One of the towers at the Barbican, London.

Soon, however, a clear gap started to emerge between 'urbanity' and modern high-rise, and there was a growing indirect reassertion of elements of the English picturesque, which were used as an anti-utilitarian reference point just as Pugin had done before. There were factions within English postwar modernism, such as that associated with Reyner Banham, which reacted against the early modern movement by advocating an even more technological emphasis.[21] But within housing the trend was emphatically away from any kind of machine-age utopianism, and towards more and more complex and socially 'organic' formulations.

The 'crude' bogeyman category of polemic began to be extended to include the open housing layouts of the 1940s and 1950s, along with their density calculations and the whole of the older town-planning aura that had underpinned them. Such housing schemes were now damned as mechanistic and 'diagrammatic'. This was tied to an increasingly forthright architectural and social rejection of tower blocks, even while the vast majority of them were under construction, and while the more daring heights were still on the drawing boards. Alison and Peter Smithson argued that separate point blocks work against communication, and that planning a high-density development necessitated the utmost effort to facilitate communication between flats. In line with this thinking, the second phase of English high-density public housing particularly stressed horizontal communication, beginning with Sheffield's Park Hill from 1955. Added to this, from the late 1950s, was a new picturesque tendency which repudiated standard modernist regimentation, whether in point blocks or slab blocks, or any kind of uninterrupted verticality or horizontality.

Overall, building contours became increasingly jagged, with highly complex spaces between buildings. Designers also aimed at an ever-greater variety of dwelling units and their surroundings. They argued that the equivalent of a small house with a small back or front garden could be provided even on an upper storey of a development in the highest LCC density band of 200 persons per acre. Perhaps the best known example of this philosophy was Darbourne & Darke's Lillington Street development in Westminster, from 1960, while probably the most intricate estates ever were built by the Borough of Camberwell, later to become Southwark, such as Bonamy-Delaford and North Peckham, with a maximum height of five to six storeys. The utopian character of this new phase in modern housing theory was emphasised in the range of catchwords coined by the Smithsons and others, all combining architectural and social 'community' meanings. For example, the talk was of 'aggregation', 'vitality', 'street decks', 'habitat', 'nodes', 'foci', 'cluster blocks', all of which made up the 'Cluster City – a New Shape for the Community'.[22]

The early 1960s left these projects behind as the polemical debate took its next turn, and many architects and critics began to condemn a major ingredient of high-density, namely the inclusion of any multi-storey element at all. The new slogan was 'low-rise, high-density'. This was to be achieved by closely packing a layer of dwellings above a vehicular access level, as can be seen in various permutations built at Harlow New Town, some of an immense complexity. As might by now be expected, complexity as an ideal also enjoyed only a short life. In the 1970s it was replaced, again, by its opposite, by decomplication. This was a return to the street of terraced houses, lower in density than the complex projects but much higher than the still reviled outer-suburban individual houses. A new attitude to cars and movement required a rejection of any segregation of different modes of transport, and an integration of pedestrian and car traffic together in the 'ordinary' street again. The small-scale and the 'vernacular' became polarised against anything big or massive. Alison Ravetz claimed in 1980 that 'the appropriate architecture for domestic life is the vernacular and not the monumental'.[23] Community now meant not something new, but something old, to be protected from the new. With the rise of the conservation movement, old buildings, ever since Pugin only the supporting actors in utopias of new architecture, began to assume a more autonomous role.

One of the most articulate late 1960s and 1970s advocates of the turn to the 'ordinary', that is the older English inner-suburban street, was Nicholas Taylor. Taylor denounced as vastly exaggerated the warnings from the modernist planners and the 'urbanists' about the danger of 'swamping' the countryside with housing. He attacked the 'Gaullist rhetoric' of tower blocks as an imposition on the freedoms of their occupants, in opposition to the English character, and poked fun at previous modernist density concepts, criticising 'the great god Urbanity, and his cosmetic soul-sister Townscape'. For Taylor it was no longer just a matter of the failure of the New Towns or the failure of high rise, but of *The Failure of 'Housing'* as a

There were factions within English postwar modernism, such as that associated with Reyner Banham, which reacted against the early modern movement by advocating an even more technological emphasis. But within housing the trend was emphatically away from any kind of machine-age utopianism...

whole.[24] He concluded that 'almost all the most renowned high-density housing schemes were in fact dangerous rubbish, precisely because they were conceived of merely as "housing" and not as part of the fabric of a total living community'.[25]

Up until this point, it had seemed that the polemic was between factions within an overall 'left' consensus, even when, eventually, social democratic provision and the love of the 'new' and 'progress' was rejected. It is sometimes forgotten nowadays that radical leftists vociferously attacked state paternalism in the 1960s, culminating in the 1968 riots across Europe. The 1970s saw more strident attacks on tower blocks from the left by 'community architecture' activists, such as the indefatigable Sam Webb, mastermind of the ultimately successful campaign to demolish Ronan Point. With the rise in demands for freedom of the 'user', and the continuing suspicion of flats among many ordinary English people, there were growing claims that the entire modern mass-housing movement was a betrayal of socialism and the working classes.[26]

But from the 1980s, with the emergence of Prince Charles and his coterie of architectural advisers, it became clear that the utopian attacks on mass housing sat more logically with a right-wing political agenda, linked generally to the assault on welfare socialism.[27] Now all modern housing was tarred with a pathological brush.[28] Rod Hackney attacked tower blocks as symbols of the 'state dependency support system', and Alice Coleman claimed that their occupants were vandals and criminals. In the words of Roderick Gradidge, 'blocks of flats are very similar to prisons'.[29] These attacks were couched in what seemed to be anti-utopianist terms, with Coleman's book entitled *Utopia on Trial*,[30] but in reality they represented a fresh phase of polemical utopianism. For example, while commenting on 'the desolation that is felt at the realisation of the maddest of all Utopian schemes, the open-planned housing complex', Roger Scruton argued that 'it is surely absurd to think of the popular outrage at these things as no more than a "matter of taste", rather than a reaffirmation of injured moral feeling'.[31]

UTOPIANISM TODAY AND TOMORROW

This new, anti-modernist phase, no less than its modernist predecessors, seemed to participate enthusiastically in the twentieth century's violent class politics of housing. But in the event it marked an important turning point. From now on, the association between state building power and passionate design ideologies was broken for good. At first, 'high-density' was totally rejected by these fundamentalist critics as being indelibly associated with the state's supposedly minimum-standard mass developments of flats. But this did not mean a return to the low-density of the old garden suburb. It was now old districts of Victorian and Georgian terraces of a middling density that were praised as 'urban'. The enclosure-planning principles of showpiece new developments such as Leon Krier's Poundbury masterplan for the Prince of Wales had a lot in common with the postwar 'townscape' school, or with the ideas of Nicholas Taylor. But at any rate, 'density' could no longer be a watchword, a panacea. It returned for a time to the obscure domain of technical figures.

That situation endured until the very end of the 1990s, which saw the start of a swing back towards modernist advocacy and architectural form. A sudden spread of modernist popular chic and a decline in the old-fashioned English prejudice against flats coincided with a new international architecture-planning advocacy of ultra high-rise high-density as a 'sustainable' way of developing scarce urban land. The results included a sudden and almost total reversal in the status of the tower block from bogeyman to icon in England. At any rate that was the case in inner London. The ever-expanding heritage movement was another constraint. From 1994, the first 1950s tower blocks were 'listed'. A further element was a growing 'practical' reappraisal of the merits of high flats by housing managers, underway since the mid-1980s.[32] By May 1999 a Museum of London symposium, 'Tower Blocks – love them or loathe them?', produced an unexpected situation. The anti-tower block veteran Sam Webb was disconcerted to find himself in a minority of one on the symposium discussion panel, otherwise dominated by the new breed of tower enthusiasts.[33]

Was this a full circle, back to the debates and policies of the mid-twentieth-century modernist era? Hardly – for with the continuing contraction in the role of the state and the depoliticisation of housing, the gulf between architectural form and mundane private-sector building production was, and still is, widening. The combative ideological confrontations of the twentieth century are becoming ever more remote and even alien to us today. Housing 'causes' have become less emotive and shocking. 'Homelessness' and demographic change are quite different to the 'battle against the slums'. Today's 'retro-modernism', in its disconnection of image and function, is quite different from the passionately integrated utopianisms of the 'real' modernist era. Public and commercial buildings are now once again the most prestigious architectural projects and the focus of elevated debate. It would have been unheard of in the 1950s to argue, as did Peabody Trust director Dickon Robinson recently, that new tower blocks should be designed with

With the rise in demands for freedom of the 'user', and the continuing suspicion of flats among many ordinary English people, there were growing claims that the entire modern mass-housing movement was a betrayal of socialism and the working classes.

'wit and fun', and should be inspired by commercial towers such as Foster & Partners' 'erotic gherkin'.[34]

While image-led plans for commercial skyscrapers are surging higher and higher, especially in the wake of London Mayor Ken Livingstone's proposals to relax constraints on their construction, the likely scale of new urban housing will be far smaller than that of the mid-twentieth-century mass-housing towers. The twenty-first-century 'beacons of good modern housing' can only be like statues of renaissance princelings, dwarfed by the ruins, or the memory of ancient Rome itself.

A further significant factor diminishing the potential for further rip-roaring confrontations in the Pugin manner is the seemingly irreversible rise of heritage, with its fundamentally neutral, inclusive, cumulative method of spread. Even the emotional criticism of utopianism has been absorbed and subtly neutralised by the conservation movement, as has the controversial force of tower blocks themselves. For example, the pioneering modernist 'lister' Andrew Saint described Sheffield's massive Park Hill deck-access project at a conference in 1996 as 'this vast and strange and by no means unromantic Englishman's castle'.[35]

Yet it is possible for vigorous debate to thrive within a consensus, as did the gothic revival debates in the mid-nineteenth century and the different factions of socialist-housing design in the twentieth. The same should be possible under globalisation in the twenty-first century. The need is to 're-embed' society and the built environment in the face of the disorientating influences of capitalist commodification. To be truly sustainable, urban development must be rooted in place and culture, rather than assembled out of collages of image-buildings and signature designs.

Each place must, by definition, confront this challenge in its own way, though England has a head start in its polemical tradition of architectural discourse, through its ability to dramatise and communicate specific choices and solutions. However, today its task is no longer to inspire diverse patterns of mass public housing, but instead to animate and guide the work of the private sector. Increasingly architects are engaging collaboratively with private developers in individual housing projects, and are participating in wide-ranging planning research studies aimed at establishing new frameworks for urban development, whether greenfield or brownfield. As the Netherlands has demonstrated, the most effective combination is a mixture of practical demographic/land-use reports of the VINEX Plan type, and more visionary, even utopian studies such as MVRDV's *Metacity/Datatown* report of 1999.[36] In England, the first approach is being pursued competently in studies such as the Urban Task Force report, or the *Cambridge Futures* report into the management of population growth in Cambridge. But in today's climate such semi-official statistical reports, unlike the mid-twentieth century Beveridge Report, County of London Plan or Parker Morris Report, stand little chance of stirring the popular imagination. What is needed now is a dash of verve and controversy.

It is precisely in energising these debates and linking them to public or political issues that we can best learn from the impassioned postwar density polemics. They can serve as reminders or evocations of the energy of the 'real' modern movement in England. In the quest for a sustainable sense of place, it is not the specific machine-age rhetoric of modernism that is relevant today, but its more general ethos, its combination of fervour and rationality, and its ability to mobilise the architectural culture of each place in its own way. Now, perhaps, in debates over density and the housing land crisis, the robust modernist spirit of England can be reinvigorated and brought to bear on the new urban problems of the twenty-first century.

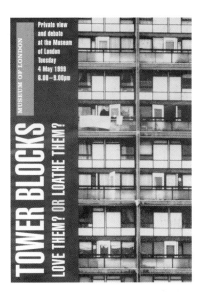

Museum of London

What is needed now is a dash of verve and controversy.

Notes

1. Miles Glendinning and Stefan Muthesius, *Tower Block – Modern Public Housing in England, Scotland, Wales and Northern Ireland* (New Haven: Yale University Press, 1994), p. 327.
2. F. Toennies, *Gemeinschaft und Gesellschaft*, 1889, W. J. Cahnman, editor, *In Memoriam F. Toennies* (Cambridge: Leiden, 1973; M. Stein, *The Eclipse of Community* (Princeton: Princeton University Press, 1960), pp. 334–7.
3. Nikolaus Pevsner, *The Englishness of English Art* (London: Architectural Press, 1956), pp. 188–92.
4. B. Bergdoll, *European Architecture 1750-1890* (Oxford: Oxford University Press, 2000), p. 44.
5. A. W. N. Pugin, *Contrasts* (London: Polman, 1836), and *The True Principles of Pointed or Christian Architecture* (London: John Weale, 1853); T. A. Markus, *Order in Space and Society* (Edinburgh: Mainstream, 1982), and *Buildings and Power* (London: Routledge, 1993); J. Carey (ed.), *The Faber Book of Utopias* (London: Faber, 1999), pp. 184–219.
6. John Ruskin, *The Seven Lamps of Architecture* (London: Smith, Elder and Co., 1849).
7. Stefan Muthesius, *The High Victorian Movement in Architecture* (London: Routledge & Kegan Paul, 1972).
8. A. Saint, *The Image of the Architect* (London: Yale University Press, 1983), pp. 59–71.
9. A. Ravetz, *Council Housing and Culture* (London: Routledge, 2001); N. Bullock, *Building the Postwar World* (London: E&FN Spon, 2001).
10. Noel Annan, *Our Age* (London: Fontana, 1990), pp. 280–93; M. Garlake, *New Art, New World* (London: Yale University Press, 1998); R. Hewison, *Culture and Consensus* (London: Methuen, 1995).

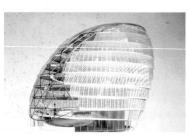

Greater London Authority Headquarters.

Model view of the building.

Various views of the study models.

Panoramic photomontage.

11. A. Saint, lecture at a Twentieth Century Society conference, London, September 1992, and A. Saint, *The Image of the Architect* (London: Yale University Press, 1983), pp. 68–71 and 146–9.

12. F. R. S. Yorke and F. Gibberd, *The Modern Flat* (London: Architectural Press, 1937), pp. 13 and 40; R. Jensen, *High Density Living* (London: L. Hill, 1966), pp. 29 and 36.

13. E. J. Carter and E. Goldfinger, *The County of London Plan Explained* (London: Penguin, 1945), p. 29.

14. 'LCC housing', *The Architects' Journal*, 17 March 1949, p. 251.

15. J. Forshaw and P. Abercrombie, *The County of London Plan* (London: Macmillan, 1943); Miles Glendinning and Stefan Muthesius, *Tower Block – Modern Public Housing in England, Scotland, Wales and Northern Ireland* (New Haven: Yale University Press, 1994), p. 41.

16. Urban Task Force, *Towards and Urban Renaissance – Final Report of the Urban Task Force* (London: E&FN Spon, 1999), figure 7.11, p. 187.

17. Clifford Culpin, *Housing Review*, July to August 1954, p. 28.

18. J. M. Richards, *Architectural Review*, July 1952, p. 34.

19. J. M. Richards, 'Failure of the new towns', *Architectural Review*, July 1953, p. 29; Miles Glendinning and Stefan Muthesius, *Tower Block – Modern Public Housing in England, Scotland, Wales and Northern Ireland* (New Haven: Yale University Press, 1994), p. 117.

20. National Housing and Town Planning Council, *Yearbook 1955 of the National Housing and Town Planning Council* (London: NHTPC, 1956), pp. 106–9.

21. Peter Reyner Banham, *Theory and Design in the First Machine Age*, first published by Reed Educational and Professional Publishing, 1960, ninth reprint of paperback edition (Oxford: Architectural Press, 1997).

22. *Architectural Design*, September 1955; *Architectural Review*, November 1957; *Architectural Design*, September 1967; *Architectural Design*, May 1963.
23. A. Ravetz, *Remaking Cities* (London: Routledge, 1980), p. 181.
24. N. Taylor, 'The failure of "housing"', *Architectural Review*, November 1967, p. 341.
25. N. Taylor, *The Village in the City* (London: Temple Smith, 1973), pp. 11 and 79.
26. P. Dunleavy, *The Politics of Mass Housing in Britain* (London: Clarenden, 1981); S. Merrett, *State Housing in Britain* (London: Routledge & Kegan Paul, 1979).
27. C. Jencks, *The Prince, the Architects and New Wave Monarchy* (London: Academy Editions, 1988); A. Papadakis (ed.), *Prince Charles and the Architectural Debate* (London: Architectural Design, 1989), pp. 46–55.
28. L. Esher, *A Broken Wave*, London, 1981.
29. R. Gradidge, broadcast on BBC Radio 4, 9 December 1991.
30. A. Coleman, *Utopia on Trial* (London: Shipman, 1985), pp. 12, 103, 158, 161 and 171.
31. R. Scruton, *The Aesthetics of Architecture* (London: Methuen, 1979), p. 250; C. Booker, articles in *Spectator*, 2 April 1977 and 17 February 1979.
32. R. Anderson, M. Bulos and S. Walker, *Tower Blocks* (London: Polytechnic of the South Bank, 1985).
33. Museum of London conference, 'Tower Blocks – Love Them or Loathe Them?', 4 May 1999, and accompanying exhibition, 30 April to 27 June.
34. Dickon Robinson quoted in *Building Design*, 25 May 2001, p. 2.
35. 'Park Hill Symposium', London, 1996.
36. Winy Maas, *Metacity/Datatown* (Rotterdam: 010 Publishers, 1999).

Town and Country in Perspective

James Heartfield

THE OPPOSITION OF TOWN AND COUNTRY IS THE ORIGIN OF THE MACHINE AGE

'Am I allowed to go to the country?',[1] wonders Tony Blair in a cartoon in *Private Eye*, a joke on the combined restrictions on access to the countryside and the decision to delay the general election as a response to the foot-and-mouth epidemic. Throughout Prime Minister Blair's first term in office, conflict and anguish informed relations between town and country and will continue into his second. The Countryside Alliance, principally in opposition to a proposed ban on the upper-class sport of foxhunting, called the largest popular demonstration in decades. Farmers and hauliers joined forces to paralyse the country with protests against petrol taxes, blocking refineries. Booing and slow-hand-clapping humiliated the prime minister during a speech to the Women's' Institute. Then in March 2001 the foot-and-mouth outbreak saw the administration grind to a halt in panic.

The government has clashed with Lord Rogers, the Urban Task Force and the Council for the Protection of Rural England (CPRE) over continuing plans to build what they say are too many new homes on greenfield sites in the countryside. Similarly, plans to build new roads after a long moratorium have provoked protest from environmentalists. The objection of the Countryside Alliance that New Labour is an urban elite that does not understand Middle England exposes a profound anxiety on the part of Millbank about how government should handle the relationship of town and country.

They would do well to read Jane Jacobs in *The Economy of Cities*, where she convincingly argues that 'the town created the country',[2] wittily inverting the ideology of modernisation that sees the town emerging from the countryside as a more highly developed social form. The truth of this proposition is that the countryside is not an original state out of which towns developed. Town and country were and are mutually determining in their opposition. The countryside does not become the countryside until the town separates from it, shaping it into a distinctive realm, just as the town is that part of the nation that is not the country.

In developmental terms the mutual opposition is more compelling. The transformation of farming from a labour-intensive activity to a capital-intensive one creates the surplus population that makes up the city-dwellers. The ensuing increase in farming productivity is the precondition of the division of labour that allows the specialisation of towns as centres devoted to the production of goods other than food. Part of the capital generated in towns as centres trading in agricultural surpluses was reinvested in the countryside, transforming communal land into capital. The politico-legal transformation of property rights in land from common ownership to private is the mechanism for clearing the 'surplus population' from the land. The agricultural revolution that drew a close to medieval property is the precondition of the industrial revolution that inaugurated modernisation and the machine age, now held in low esteem. The opposition of town and country is based upon the social division of labour wherein the country feeds the town, and the town mechanises the country.

This model of modern opposition of town and country is in its basic form the developmental model that all advanced societies have followed, albeit with local variations. In the US the surplus populations were recruited from a geographically distant European countryside in England and Germany, then Ireland, Italy and eastern Europe.

At the core of the transformation of land into private property are some pointedly artificial titles of ownership. The Acts of Enclosure in England from the fifteenth century onwards broke up the commons and distributed them among those whose legal claims were recognised by the courts. Far from enjoying legitimacy, such claims were openly resisted and ridiculed.

> The law doth punish man or woman
> That steals the goose from off the common,
> But lets the greater felon loose
> That steals the common from the goose.[3]

Aristocratic lineages were invented to justify the wholly modern seizures by reference to fictitious ancient rights. Only two noble families survived the Norman Conquest, now both long since passed away, and all subsequent titles are the creations of kings from Henry VII onwards. Enclosure did not just suit the elite in the countryside – it was also a necessary condition of the reduction of England's yeomanry to a landless proletariat. Arnold Toynbee observed that 'a person ignorant of our history…might surmise that a great exterminatory war had taken place'.[4] For that reason the enclosures were wholly endorsed by the new industrial ruling classes as well. Once robbed of their ability to subsist on the land, the 'surplus populations' had no choice but to take employment in the mill. To keep the hands from escaping the factory to live on the land, the landlords punished poaching and squatting.

So successful was the system of invented nobility as a rationale for dispossession of peasants that it was reproduced in Scotland and Ireland. In the US both the French and English courts went so far as to recognise the land claims of native Americans, who had no conception of land ownership, rather than permit the colonists to flee from their indentured servitude within the stockades and estates.

The 'historic compromise' between aristocracy and industrial plutocracy left the business of warfare, maintaining order, the arts and the decorative part of government in the hands of the former, while the latter organised the creation of wealth and commerce. The pretensions of the landed aristocracy were tolerated while useful in their role as local magistrates, soldiers and churchmen. As the elegant decoration upon wealth they were even imitated by industrialists who, recoiling from the slums they had made, bought up country houses and titles to boot.

Interestingly, the full celebration of the English countryside in the romantic movement is possible only at the point that industrial society has separated the individual from nature, such that he or she can turn back and contemplate it in the abstract. The romantic poets first turned nature into an ideal, in fact the screen on to which their own inner selves were projected, and more prosaically, into a tourist attraction. Wordsworth's cottage is still the stop-off point for charabancs to the Lake District. The attraction of the countryside for the romantics was in direct proportion to their revulsion at the city. 'Hell is a city, much like London – a populous and smoky city', wrote Shelley.[5] While romanticism began as an intense exploration of the individual psyche, it settled into the rural idyll of English pastoral.

By the end of the nineteenth century, the historic compromise between landed aristocracy and urban capitalist was exhausted. In Britain, ancient rules that barred the sale of land more than once within a generation were lifted in the Settled Land Act of 1882, ostensibly to remove the burden on the indebted aristocracy, allowing them to raise funds by sales. Within a century aristocratic land ownership had fallen from four-fifths to just a quarter of the country.[6] Farmer William Hampson complained to J. W. Robertson Scott, editor of the *Countryman*, that: 'the owner of the land's always been poor and living away…there's never been none here to take an interest in the place, never none here but the labouring people and the farmers'.[7]

In the greatest shift in land ownership since William the Conqueror, most of the land was sold to the tenants who were farming it. In October 1918 the *Estates Gazette* took the view that the sales marked 'not so much the foundations of a new aristocracy as the foundations of a new yeomanry'.[8] It is this agricultural class, landowners for less than a hundred years, that is the foundation of the modern countryside, and perhaps the last countrymen.

The character of the modern countryside owes remarkably little to ancient tradition, except in the imitation of country houses. The current class of farmers owes more to the great growth of the middle classes that began under Prime Minister Stanley Baldwin's first term in office in the early 1920s. Their numbers were swelled by the 'back-to-the-landers', who were mostly people of independent means investing small bequests in farm businesses. Robertson Scott complained that 'they have no relationship to the hamlet' and 'go neither to church nor the parish'.[9] This burgeoning rural middle-class is the human material of the rural idyll that came to stand for the essence of Englishness, just as it also became the social basis of the Tory shires. It is also a pattern that is repeated across the developed world. As the urban proletariat grew in numbers and social weight, the counterweight of the rural population became ever more important to the powers-that-be. Rural districts, large and relatively sparsely populated, could be counted upon to vote for the Christian Democratic and Conservative parties all across Europe. Theirs was a moderating influence upon the social democratic movements based in the cities.

AGRICULTURE IN CRISIS

The last economic crisis in agriculture took place in the 1920s, preceding and pre-empting the wider crisis that followed the Wall Street Crash of 1929. Agriculture worldwide was ruined by overproduction, leading to falling prices before governments took control of the process and rationalised production by consolidating small farms into larger ones, forcing more bankrupt farmers off the land. The social ramifications were international.

In the mid-western US, farmers responded to falling prices by over-farming their land, creating the ruinous 'dust-bowl'. In the South, former slaves who had survived a generation working the land as truck farmers, being paid in goods rather than by wages, were also ruined. The dispossession of the black truck-farmers inaugurated the single greatest internal migration since the push West, as three million moved north between 1930 and 1960, swelling the depressed inner cities. In Germany farm prices fell while other

The character of the modern countryside owes remarkably little to ancient tradition, except in the imitation of country houses. The current class of farmers owes more to the great growth of the middle classes that began under Prime Minister Stanley Baldwin's first term in office in the early 1920s.

Agriculture worldwide was ruined by overproduction, leading to falling prices before governments took control of the process and rationalised production by consolidating small farms into larger ones, forcing more bankrupt farmers off the land. The social ramifications were international.

prices rose. Inflation ate up the small farmers' savings and drove them, ruined and embittered, into the hands of Adolf Hitler's National Social Democratic and Workers' Party, the NSDAP, or the Nazis. Hitler's appeal to blood and soil was framed to appeal to the farmers who were flattered in right-wing ideology as the backbone of the nation. Hitler solved the farming problem by effectively nationalising land ownership and reducing the once-independent peasants to state employees, working to feed the nation.[10] In Soviet Russia, Stalin imposed a brutal policy of forced collectivisation on the Kulak peasantry.

The agricultural crisis of the 1920s arose out of a reconfiguration of the balance between town and country. With investment directed largely at heavy machinery and incomes depressed, the market for foodstuffs was held down. The agricultural crisis led to a consolidation of many smaller farms into fewer larger ones, often with the state taking a key role in organising agriculture, and a development even more pronounced with the outbreak of war. Larger farms meant more mechanisation and a divergence between farm labourers and farm-owners. The countryside was becoming more like the town with the emergence of modern agribusiness.

SIMULTANEOUS POSTWAR EXTENSIVE AND INTENSIVE GROWTH

At times it appeared as if the town and country divide would assume global dimensions, as an international division of labour emerged. The metropolitan core countries became overwhelmingly industrial, while the periphery, southern and eastern Europe, Russia and the colonies were pushed into agriculture and raw materials. World war raised the importance of food security for European nations, and self-sufficiency informed the war effort as allotments were dug and in Britain a 'land army' of women recruited to farm the countryside. Robertson Scott in a happy 1947 postscript to his 1925 jeremiad *England's Green and Pleasant Land*, proclaims: 'I could not have believed that between 1924 and 1947 the countryside would have got more than three-quarters of a million new cottages'.[11]

Anxiety over food security informed the exponential rise in farm subsidies across the developed world after the Second World War. That experience of food rationing was still informing policy throughout the 1970s in an attempt to achieve self-sufficiency in food production by restricting the development of agricultural land through planning and introducing mechanisms for economic support. The European Union's (EU's) Common Agricultural Policy (CAP) is only the best-known example. CAP subsidised prices by empowering governments to sustain a premium price by intervening in the markets to buy whenever market prices fell below the nominal price. The effect was to boost farm incomes while accruing vast surpluses in European stores, known euphemistically as the Beef and Butter Mountains, and the Wine Lake. The public support for rural populations that had started for reasons of national security had mutated into a social policy to maintain a conservative population as a counterweight to the more radical towns. The blanket subsidies to farming led to extensive growth, with more land being farmed by more people creating more food. Robin Page describes this process in *Town and Country*, where after the Second World War and shortages, increased yields made the policy of increasing farmed area through loss of landscape diversity unnecessary. There was a case for increased production, but massive injections of public funding had contradictory consequences for the countryside.

> But how did the politicians see that increase being achieved? Apparently by increasing the area of land in production; consequently attractive grants were offered for ripping out hedges, draining wetland and ploughing grassland. Even then the urbanisation of Parliament was producing politicians who did not understand the land and who did not understand farming. With more knowledge they would have understood that farming itself is in a constant state of change, development and improvement. Advances in animal and crop husbandry; breakthroughs in botany, biology, chemistry and technology have for years meant higher yields. Consequently just as more land was being brought into production, agricultural sciences were rapidly increasing yields and making self-sufficiency attainable in any case. As a result, by the time we joined Europe – to face quotas actually reducing our own, national self-sufficiency – we quickly drifted from a situation of food deficiency to one of food surplus.[12]

On the one hand farmers prospered across the board, as small farmers were shielded from the judgement of the free market by artificially boosted prices. Farmers became voluble as a force in Western societies and an important constituency of support for the RPR in France, the German Christian Democrats, the Liberal Democratic Party in Japan, the British Conservative Party and the American Republican Party. In Britain the cultural paradigm of the countryside embodied in the present-day Countryside Alliance was taking shape, centred on the Womens' Institute and the Church, with jam making, village fetes, and a sense of Merry England.

On the other hand something quite distinctive was also taking shape economically. With a determination to banish the politics of hunger that had dominated the inter-war years, both US and European gov-

The countryside was becoming more like the town with the emergence of modern agribusiness.

...after the Second World War and shortages, increased yields made the policy of increasing farmed area through loss of landscape diversity unnecessary.

ernments put resources into the application of science to agriculture. Without too rudely disturbing the conservative social framework of rural life, the modern agribusinesses were taking shape. In time a 'Green Revolution' of increased yields through fertilisers and selective breeding would transform output. While small-scale agriculture was growing extensively, the Green Revolution would lead to intensive growth, with more produce from less land and less farmers.

In 1955 Jacob Roisin of the Montrose Chemical Company and *Readers Digest* editor Max Eastman published the classic exposition of the green revolution, titled *The Road to Abundance*. 'The time has come to recognise that our dependence for food on the dilatory and inefficient plant is a cruel bondage. We have given the plant almost the entire floor space of our planet and devoted to it by far the largest part of our energies. And in return we have not got enough food to go round.' The authors complained that 'our social and political scientists often deal astutely with problems concerning distribution of resources, but the thought of creating new resources such that these problems may be made obsolete is alien to their minds.' Citing the application of pesticides and fertilisers to increase yields they trumpet that 'chemistry has already rescued agriculture', and its potential 'is to replace agriculture altogether, except as a pastime.'[13]

The ambition to abolish want was not realised in full, but the transformation was indeed remarkable. Lester Brown of the Worldwatch Institute had been among those warning of the impending food disaster, but his most recent survey explains that the world grain harvest has increased from less than 400 million tons in 1900 to nearly 1.9 billion tons in 1998. Combined mechanisation, high-yield crops, chemical fertilisers and irrigation have increased the yield per hectare from 1.06 tons in 1950 to 2.73 tons in 1998.[14] These new techniques of the 'Green Revolution' are the basis of modern agribusiness in big exporting countries like the US. Brown estimates that a farmer in 1900 produced enough food for seven people when today his great-grandson feeds 96 people.

The Green Revolution implied a shift in the division of labour between town and country. As agriculture became more productive, fewer people at less cost produced more food. Farming fell as a proportion of the workforce. The consequence was cheaper food for the growing urban population. According to the British Household Survey, spending on food and clothing fell from around a third of income in 1950 to a tenth in 1998. That cheapening of basics released income to spend on cultural goods and services, which make up a correspondingly greater proportion of spending. Chris Haskins, Chief Executive of Northern Foods, reminded us of this productive triumph in *The Guardian*.

> If this remarkable increase in productivity had not taken place, and consumers had to pay for the inflation of the past 40 years, the price of wheat would be more than £1,000 a ton instead of £70, and the farmer would be receiving more than £2 per litre for milk compared with the admittedly untenable existing price of about 18p. Consumers would be paying more than £2 for a loaf of bread, against less than 50p today, and a pint of milk would cost about £2 compared with less than 35p in a supermarket now…If we wanted to recreate the countryside of 40 years ago, either the consumer or the taxpayer would have to pay at least twice as much (an extra £50 billion) for food.[15]

Ironically, the greater the volume of goods that are produced their total value falls, due to the cheaper methods of production. Not only did farm labour fall as a percentage of the workforce, but so did the new value added by the agricultural sector fall as a proportion of the country's output. As the Countryside Agency noted: 'agriculture's direct contribution to the national economy declined to less than one per cent Gross Value Added (GVA) for the first time in 1999 and farming income fell to its lowest level in 25 years in 2000', at 'just £7,800 per capita'.[16] Productive and wider social success was a commercial failure.

The revolution in productive technique ought to have led to a transformation of social conditions in the countryside too, but for many years those consequences were masked by the public policy of subsidising a rural lifestyle. By subsidising agricultural prices, the small family farmer and the agribusiness cartel alike were rewarded. The competitive pressure of the market was muted. But underneath the surface something quite remarkable had already been achieved. In the US in 1994, fully 50 per cent of farm products came from just 2 per cent of the farms. Conversely smaller, family farms, which make up 73 per cent of farms, produced just 9 per cent of US farm products. Concentration and centralisation of agricultural production has changed the character of the farming sector in the West. Smaller family-farms are in economic terms all but redundant. Larger agribusinesses like Cargill and Phillip Morris produce the lion's share of consumer goods. In the US 80 per cent of beef was slaughtered by just three firms – Iowa Beef Production, Cargill and ConAgra.

However, in the 1990s the defences protecting the small farmer were beginning to be dismantled. With the expansion of the EU in the 1970s to include the more agricultural southern European countries such as Greece, Spain and Portugal, the Common Agricultural Policy (CAP) surpluses spiralled out of control. The political will for reforming the CAP was a long time in coming but come it did. In 1992 the CAP

While small-scale agriculture was growing extensively, the Green Revolution would lead to intensive growth, with more produce from less land and less farmers.

shifted from subsidising prices after the event to subsidising production before it happened, as Robert Ackrill explained in *The Common Agricultural Policy*:

> Large farmers do not have to set aside land. If they do not, however, they will not receive the direct payments. This raises the question of whether farmers have sufficient incentive to comply. Roberts[17] indicates that in England during the first year of the scheme, about 95% of land that could be set aside was removed from production. By determining the 'indifference price', where producer profits were the same in and out of the scheme, it was found that these were high relative to market prices. That is, market prices would have to rise by several ECU per tonne before most farmers could afford to opt out of the scheme, not receive compensation and still generate higher profit by being able to plant on their whole area.[18]

This was the case for arable farming but similar policies were established for the headage of livestock, where an 'extensification programme' had to be implemented to qualify for the subsidy. Farmers could no longer expect a cheque for everything they produced. Output had to be justified according to the goals of the EU, which now included reducing surpluses. As the earlier regime of price subsidies was taken away, incomes tumbled for smaller farmers, while big farms that used cheaper production methods weathered the storm and prospered. CAP payments were £4.1 billion from 1996 to 1997 and fell to £2.5 billion from 2000 to 2001.[19] The US additionally demanded that countries lift the subsidies on farming and get farm produce included in the international General Agreement on Tariffs and Trade (GATT) free trade talks. The need to lift farm subsidies was pressing given that the US Agriculture Department was warning that net farm income was falling so low that it could be overtaken by government subsidy. US farm income in 2000 was a total of $45.4 billion, and is expected to fall to $35.6 billion in 2002. Meanwhile, the US agriculture subsidy in 2001 is estimated at $32 billion and expected to rise.[20]

With rural subsidy equating to 50 per cent of output, and fixed capital valued at less than the construction industry builds yearly, farmers have land they are not free to develop.

Under the pressure of falling prices, small farmers are trying to hang on to their farms and livelihoods. Government and European policy is to ease these small farmers out of farming altogether. Subsidies were given to farmers not for producing but for foregoing production by paying farmers enough for 'set aside'. Also for foregoing production indefinitely under the various schemes for returning land to its wild state, for example the recreation and management of environmentally sensitive areas, countryside stewardship or habitat schemes. The government Rural White Paper *Our Countryside – the Future* promises cash-strapped small farmers that: 'we will support new opportunities to diversify', which means get out of farming if you can.[21] The assistance available through the *Rural Development Programme*,[22] likely to increase, aims to further the objectives of the Ministry of Agriculture, Fisheries and Food (MAFF), now the Department of the Environment, Food and Rural Affairs (DEFRA), in establishing a *New Direction for Agriculture*.[23] That means try to do anything other than efficiently produce food.

The total European and British support schemes for rural areas give a subsidy of between £3 billion and £3.5 billion before the effects of foot-and-mouth have been accounted for.[24] Though agriculture contributes just under £7 billion to the British economy, and has only £33.5 billion in fixed capital stock excluding the value of land and livestock, it provides 70 per cent of all domestic food requirements with a workforce of only 600,000, or 2.1 per cent of the total employed.[25] With rural subsidy equating to 50 per cent of output, and fixed capital valued at less than the construction industry builds yearly, farmers have land they are not free to develop. Nevertheless, within the constraints of PPG7, the planning policy guidance on development,[26] farmers have diversified into tourism, with guesthouses, rural sports and activities, others into non-food crops, while a few have sought business by shifting into organic farming – a high-value niche market.

Organic farming has lower yields, and in the very best of conditions it produces 20 per cent less than mainstream farming at a far higher cost, currently accounting for less than 1 per cent of farm produce in the developed countries. Since the Organic Farming scheme was launched in 1999 with parallel schemes in Wales, Scotland and Northern Ireland, a total of 218,470 hectares have been assisted into organic farming, 60 per cent of which are in Scotland. The annual expenditure for this loss of productivity is £15.7 million, disproportionately directed at converting English farms to organic with only £1.8 million going to Scotland, and less than £2.2 million being directed at research and development initiatives.[27] New institutions are being funded to further the exercise, such as the Organic Conversion Information Service and the UK Register of Organic Food Standards, all devoted to making agriculture more labour intensive.

Nevertheless, 60,000, or 10 per cent of total farm jobs have disappeared in the last decade. As a distinctive social group the small farmer is looking over the abyss, and, as in the 1930s, can be expected to protest at his or her lot. In Britain the Countryside Alliance is one expression of the protests of the small farmer. Another is the Organic farming lobby, and organisations such as the Soil Association. Gentleman farmers like Lord Peter Melchett and the Prince of Wales have given the complaints of small farmers an environmentalist twist. The CREE recoils at 'the notion of surplus farmland as a dangerous oversimplification'. Against the evidence that taking land out of production is the intention of government policy it considers that 'less intensive forms of food production are likely, in the long term, to put a new premium on farmland as output per hectare stabilises or decreases'.[28] In France the small farmers' leader José Bové led protests against US mass-production of food, as represented by MacDonalds, that saw him imprisoned. Noticeably, Bové's small farmers' association is outside the main Farmers' Union in France, which is rather more influenced by agribusiness.

THE END OF TOWN AND COUNTRY

The real meaning of the small farmers' movements is that anticipated by Roisin and Eastman so many years ago: agribusiness aims to 'replace agriculture altogether, except as a pastime'[29] The diversification strategies adopted by small farmers are indeed turning agriculture into a pastime. They bear the same relation to farming that the industrial museum does to industry.

More broadly, the transformation of agriculture into agribusiness is abolishing that distinction between town and country. First, agribusiness is making farming into one more industry. Big corporations employ workers to manufacture primary products for food. With the involvement of supermarket chains, farming is just one stage in the food processing industry worth about £57 billion a year to the economy and providing 3.3 million jobs.[30] The uniquely distinctive geographical division between town and country makes less and less sense. There is no need for a spatial opposition between one part of the production cycle and another.

Furthermore, the concentration and consolidation of farming into large businesses is having a revolutionary impact upon land usage. Increased grain production can be achieved in two ways, either by taking more land into cultivation or by increasing the yield per hectare. In the 30 years between 1950 and 1981 the grain-harvested area globally increased from 587 million hectares to 732 million hectares. Since then, however, the grain area has shrunk to 690 million hectares with a rising population that is increasingly better fed. That has been made possible by more intensive farming methods. These new methods mean that less and less land is needed, freeing it for other uses. Consequently there is an imperative felt by governments to retire land from farm use to reduce surplus production.

Both Europe and the US have seen deforestation reversed in the last decade with the initiation of reforestation. More and more land is being set aside as nature reserves and parks, and more golf courses are being built. Most importantly, though, more land is being freed up for housing development. Martin Pawley understood this in the *Architects' Journal*:

> Nowhere is there any acknowledgement that the predicted need for more building land is more than matched by a tremendous superfluity of agricultural produce, which has left a huge surplus of unused agricultural land. So striking and so irreversible is this situation that – were they allowed to – impoverished farmers, land-strapped greenfield house builders and would-be home owners could solve one another's problems at a stroke.[31]

The distinctive trends at work in the agricultural economy presage the end of the historic divide between town and country. Big farms have become businesses, much like any other. Small farms are being diversified, mostly into recreational and tourist areas. Most pointedly the pressure on land use from cultivators is easing off, just as more and more city-dwellers long for abundant living space. The only thing that keeps the countryside distinct today is not the special role that farming plays in the division of labour, but planning restraints on development.

Postwar planning policy sought to remove development rights from farmers to protect all agricultural land for food production. The denial of development rights remains, but the policy on protecting all farmland lasted until the late 1980s. Then the protection of the 'Best and Most Versatile' land was instituted, and this is the conception that pertains today. The 1995 White Paper *Rural England – A Nation Committed*

The uniquely distinctive geographical division between town and country makes less and less sense.

to a Living Countryside[32] accepted greater flexibility in the development of the lower grades of best most valuable (BMV) land, but the current position is contained in PPG7, *The Countryside – Environmental Quality and Economic and Social Development*.[33] As the CPRE recognises of PPG7: 'despite the watering down of policy for the protection of agricultural land since 1987, there still remains a tight overall policy on development on BMV land. There are policy exceptions to the general rule, but these are not easily satisfied'.[34] This is now further bolstered by PPG3 on *Housing*, published in 2000, with a presumption against developing greenfield land,[35] and the entire thrust of the first term of New Labour policy.

THE REACTION AGAINST AGRIBUSINESS

Urban populations distrust food manufacturers. Since working people first left the countryside to swell the urban working class, their experience of losing sight of the cycle of food production has been disorienting. Where country people could see the food grown, harvested and prepared before their eyes, city-dwellers must cope with prepared foodstuffs. More than that, the mutual distrust of market exchanges assumes a peculiarly exaggerated form where nourishment is concerned. The motto *Caveat Emptor*, or 'Let the buyer beware', carries a special meaning where poor goods will do more than let you down, but may make you ill or even kill you. City-dwellers have always been susceptible to panics over food quality because they distrust food manufacturers.

In nineteenth-century London a rumour spread that the titled chairman of the milk marketing board bathed in milk before bottling it, leading to a collapse in sales. The panic was fantastic but summarised all of the attitudes of the working-class consumers. They objected to the poor quality of the product, deeply distrusted the new capitalistic food production, and where the process of getting milk from cow to bottle was veiled they projected their most lurid fears into the darkness. Finally, the image of Lord Milk's extravagant luxury served as counterpoint to their straitened circumstances. Subsequent food panics repeat the basic structure of the milk panic. During the Second World War the urban legend that a live tumour had been discovered pulsating in a cut of whale meat expressed an inchoate dissatisfaction with the effects and uncertainties of rationing. In 1985 an injudicious comment about salmonella in eggs by health minister Edwina Currie led to a collapse in sales. But it was the BSE (bovine spongiform encephalitis) crisis of the late 1980s that really lost public confidence in agribusiness.

Leeds-based scientist Richard Lacey first proposed that BSE caused Creutzfeld Jacob disease (CJD). Lacey was reported in *Nature* as saying that virtually a whole generation of people might die.[36] On the basis of Lacey's reports, *One World* reported that: 'recently, it was estimated that 34 million people could be infected by 1997'.[37] In fact the number of confirmed cases of CJD by March 2001 was just 85, giving an annualised rate of 17. This makes dying from CJD in Britain about as likely as being killed by lightning in the larger population of the US. The National Weather Service publication *Storm Data* recorded 3,239 deaths from lightning between 1959 and 1994, or 95 deaths per year. Furthermore, the link between CJD and BSE remains entirely speculative.

Though CJD cases are one for every three million of the population, the fear of CJD, and its association with BSE, was firmly established in the public imagination. Agribusiness was widely distrusted by the public, and the revelation that feed contained remnants of slaughtered cows became emblematic of a determination to make profits at any cost to the health of animals or people. The fact that the government defended British beef probably did more damage, since the Conservative government's standing was by that time at an all-time low. Agriculture minister John Selwyn Gummer's public show of confidence in beef, by feeding his daughter a burger on national television, only tended to excite suspicion. Beef sales collapsed, along with public confidence in British agribusiness. In *Contested Natures*, Phil Macnaghten and John Urry describe the changing attitude to the countryside as one that transformed the issue of Conservation over the 1980s:

> Largely through the innovation of such groups as the Ramblers, Friends of the Earth, the Council for the Protection of Rural England and the World Wildlife Fund, a new discourse of the countryside began to permeate public consciousness. Farmers were no longer identified as the self-evident guardians of the countryside, but were now seen to pose a threat to nature just as with any other industry. No longer were 'people' perceived as the main threat to the conservation of the countryside.[38]

The contemporary environmental movement is marked by its hostility to modern agribusiness in the way environmentalists attack factory farming in general and practices such as genetic modification or live calf exports in particular. This range of interests is a shift from the original outlook of the Victorian preservation societies, like the National Trust and the Royal Society for the Protection of Birds. Those earlier conservationist movements were 'established during the latter stages of the [nineteenth] century, largely because of perceived concerns about the negative impact of industrialism and urban growth'.[39] Where those earlier campaigns identified with the countryside against the towns, the modern environmental movement draws its support from the towns to protest about the actions of country people. The distinction was thrown into relief by the debate over foxhunting. Responding to the pressure from anti-foxhunting campaigners, who were mostly townsfolk, the New Labour government entertained a ban, provoking a mass reaction from the Countryside Alliance. Environmentalists were profoundly uneasy about the Countryside Alliance demonstrations, feeling that their right to speak for the countryside was being taken away.

The current government is more susceptible to influence from environmentalist critics, who are often supporters, or at least critical supporters of New Labour, than it is to the ideas of the Countryside Alliance, which is much closer to the demographics of the Tory shires. The New Labour instinct is to try to appease all. The confusion of influences was evident in the government's reaction to the foot-and-mouth crisis. Within the first few weeks of the epidemic the prime minister gave a speech at an agricultural college, where he repeated the environmentalist criticisms of the impact of business on farming. In particular, Blair bemoaned the 'stranglehold' of supermarkets on farmers. In that the prime minister was influenced by the intellectual milieu of urban, left-of-centre thinking, that is sympathetic to environmentalist ideas. Superficially, Blair repeats a lot of green ideas, but in the end it is agribusiness that is likely to have the decisive influence given the obvious government commitment to the competitiveness of British business, including farming, food processing and retailing.

This can be seen in the way that the MAFF is using the foot-and-mouth epidemic, as it used the BSE crisis, to force the pace of consolidating farming in the hands of larger producers. The green rhetoric serves in the end to justify the closure of smaller farms, as the BSE alert served to close down small abattoirs. Rather than being anti-capitalist, environmentalists serve the same process of the domination of the market by agribusinesses able to compete at a scale and with a greater degree of fixed capital investment.

DEVELOPMENT RETREAT AND ADVANCE

In 1996 the environment minister John Selwyn Gummer announced the need for 4.4 million new homes by 2016. As a measure of the contentious nature of the proposal, Gummer recalls for Barnett and Scruton in *Town and Country*: 'I chose the lowest number I could truthfully support.'[40] The book gives 2006, but that is an error, and the correct figure is in the report *Household Growth – Where Shall We Live?*, presided over by Gummer to condition government policy before the election.[41] The New Labour government subsequently revised the household growth figure down to 3.8 million by 2021, but this does not overcome the wide expectation that Gummer's figure was an underestimate.

Rapid development caused social upheaval, and an alliance of shire Tories with the grungy eco-warriors combined to oppose the developments and motorway extensions, such as those at Oxleas Wood or the Newbury bypass. This kind of activism drew on a purposeful minority, but rarely won the support of all locals, since many were themselves users of the transport facilities and developments that were being protested against. In Newbury, polls supported the bypass, and the Liberal Democrat MP who championed it increased his vote despite a challenge from a Green candidate in the 1997 election. However, beyond the residents of the local countryside, such road protesters articulated an inchoate but popular disappointment with modern living, the misery of congested roads and box-like developments. The Major government responded by suspending new road building, and transport minister Stephen Norris declared retrospectively that the protestors 'were right'. The incoming administration followed suit under Tony Blair and John Prescott, creating a super-ministry supposedly for 'joined-up-thinking' between environment, transport and regional development, but which maintained the town and country distinction. The Urban Task Force established by Prescott under Richard Rogers reflected the ill-defined hostility to greenfield development, as well as an attempt to encourage neighbourhood pride in ideas like 'urban villages':

> We need a vision that will drive the urban renaissance. We believe that cities should be well designed, be more compact and connected, and support a range of diverse uses – allowing people to live, work and enjoy themselves at close quarters – within a sustainable urban environment which is well integrated with public transport and adaptable to change.[42]

The proposals to eschew greenfield sites in favour of brownfield development sounded like good sense, and corresponded to the protests of the eco-warriors as well as New Labour's café society. Gentrification also appealed to the urban intelligentsia's long-held distaste for 'Essex man', that nasty little upstart who had betrayed them for Mrs Thatcher in the 1980s. Even the shire Tories reviled Essex man, whose votes they were grateful for, but they despaired of his presumptuous move to spoil their countryside.

The case for brownfield development of under-used, derelict or contaminated land in urban areas made excellent sense, except of course in economic terms. Brownfield sites are awkward to prepare for redevelopment, involve developers in nightmare planning-application tussles, and demand bespoke developments to fit the largely predetermined conditions with their attendant problems of servicing and access.

Furthermore, land values were spiralling in city centres, while they were falling in the countryside, as a consequence of excess demand in the first instance and planning-restricted supply in the second. The growth in unsatisfied demand is driven by rising expectations, with more people wanting to move out of the inner-cities into the suburbs, and changing lifestyle patterns that suggested to Gummer that 'more than half the new units that are required are for single person households'.[43] Yet as Essex man knew, motor-mobility has contracted distances, so that even though the average distance travelled by people has increased from 8 kilometres per day in 1950 to 40 kilometres today, the amount of time spent travelling has barely changed.[44] The demand for living space nearer to the countryside is not necessarily so related to having children as might be imagined. And, by smashing the utilitarian space standards that had served postwar public-sector house building as a minimum, the Conservative party had both allowed meaner space standards and raised the expectations of home owners for better accommodation:

> We have traditionally demanded more living space and we continue to do so. It was one of the distinguishing features of the old Parker Morris standards for council housing, unparalleled in other European countries.[45]

If the country is no longer reserved for agriculture, then there is no need to be denied the choice to live there.

Gummer preposterously chooses to forget that the Tories attempted to solve the profitability problems of house builders by scrapping minimum space standards, making an ideological virtue out of doing so. Today there is an even clearer crisis in house building. The brownfield planning presumption heightens the problems of development profitability when living space standards have been reduced about as far as they can physically go. This is why increasing density is such an obsession, as developers try to use up every available external space for more units. Push factors of rising aspirations to space and clean air, and pull factors of cheap land vacated by farmers, along with growing mobility, now combine to create an unavoidable case for developing more of the countryside. Historically, the division between town and country is effectively redundant. If the country is no longer reserved for agriculture, then there is no need to be denied the choice to live there.

New Labour has caught itself in a clash between a lofty ideal of urban villages and untouched countryside on the one hand, and the reality of people's actual choices about where they wanted to live on the other. It has commissioned the Urban Task Force report, but the economic and social pressure to build on greenfield sites has proved too difficult to face down in a housing market that only likes the idea of sustainability. With the benefit of hindsight, it was perhaps inevitable that the commitments to refrain from new road-building and greenfield developments would not last. Growing congestion on roads and the pressure on housing stock, especially the growing demand for single-person dwellings, meant that no serious government could persist with the existing policies. New Labour's u-turn on road building and greenfield development was an adaptation to market forces that it simply did not understand.

The chairman of the government's Sustainability Panel, Sir Crispin Tickell, can urge Blair to relinquish the plan to build 4.4 million new homes, arguing that there is no need, because 'if you build more houses, more people will live alone rather than live in couples with granny upstairs'.[46] But he lives in a country farmhouse in Wiltshire. New Labour is getting used to believing one thing and doing another. The pale green tinge to its policies is entirely at odds with the practical case for developing countryside for the majority to enjoy. After all, it isn't the countryside anymore. At least it's not a special place marked out by any distinctive role or responsibility. It is just prime land, waiting to be developed.

Notes

1. *Private Eye*, No. 1024, 23 March to 5 April 2001, p. 5.
2. Jane Jacobs, *The Economy of Cities* (New York: Random House, 1969).
3. Traditional.
4. Arnold Toynbee, 'England in 1760 – the decay of the Yeomanry', in *The Industrial Revolution,* a reprint of lectures on the Industrial Revolution in England, popular addresses, notes and other fragments (Newton Abbot: David and Charles reprints, 1969), p. 59.
5. Percy Bysshe Shelley, 1792–1822, *Peter Bell the Third*, Part 3, 'Hell', 1819, quoted in *The Oxford Dictionary of Quotations*, third edition (Oxford: Book Club Associates for the Oxford University Press, 1979), p. 502.
6. *Estates Gazette*, quoted in Dominic Hobson, *The National Wealth – Who Gets What in Britain* (London: HarperCollins, 1999), p. 79.
7. William Hampson writing to J. W. Robertson Scott, editor of the *Countryman*, quoted in *England's Green and Pleasant Land* (Harmondsworth, Middx.: Penguin, 1947), p. 23.
8. Dominic Hobson, *The National Wealth – Who Gets What in Britain* (London: HarperCollins, 1999), p. 79.
9. J. W. Robertson Scott, *England's Green and Pleasant Land* (Harmondsworth, Middx.: Penguin, 1947), p. 38.
10. Alfred Sohn Rethel, 'The Reich food estate', *The Economy and Structure of German Fascism* (London: Free Association Books, 1987).
11. J. W. Robertson Scott, *England's Green and Pleasant Land* (Harmondsworth, Middlesex: Penguin, 1947), p. 168.

12. Robin Page, 'Restoring the countryside', in Anthony Barnett and Roger Scruton (eds), *Town and Country* (London: Jonathan Cape, 1998), pp. 100–101.

13. Jacob Roisin and Max Eastman, *The Road to Abundance* (London: Rider and Company, 1955), pp. 23, 144 and 122.

14. Lester Brown, Christopher Flavin, 'Feeding nine billion', in World Watch Institute, *State of the World 1999* (London: Earthscan, 2000).

15. Chris Haskins, Chief Executive of Northern Foods, 'Down on the farm', *The Guardian*, 7 March 2001, p. 21.

16. Press release, *State of the Countryside – 2001*, The Countryside Agency, 3 April 2001.

17. D. Roberts, J. Froud and R.W. Fraser, 'Participation in set aside – what determines the opting in price?', *Journal of Agricultural Economics* 47(1), 1996, pp. 89–98.

18. Robert Ackrill, *The Common Agricultural Policy* (Sheffield: Sheffield Academic Press, 2000), p. 68.

19. Department of the Environment, Transport and the Regions with the Ministry of Agriculture, Fisheries and Food, *Our Countryside – the Future* (London: DETR, HMSO, November 2000), p. 100.

20. Nancy Dunne, 'US subsidy bill for farms nearly as high as net income', *Financial Times*, 15 March 2001.

21. Department of the Environment, Transport and the Regions with the Ministry of Agriculture, Fisheries and Food, *Our Countryside – the Future* (London: DETR, HMSO, November 2000), p. 91.

22. Ministry of Agriculture, Fisheries and Food, *England Rural Development Programme* (London: MAFF, November 2000).

23. Ministry of Agriculture, Fisheries and Food, *A New Direction for Agriculture* (London: MAFF, December 1999).

24. Department of the Environment, Transport and the Regions with the Ministry of Agriculture, Fisheries and Food, *Our Countryside – the Future* (London: DETR, HMSO, November 2000), p. 91.

25. Ministry of Agriculture, Fisheries and Food, *Agriculture in the United Kingdom – 1999* (London: The Stationery Office, 2000), pp. 1.5 and 2.2.

26. Department of the Environment, Transport and the Regions, *The Countryside – Environmental Quality and Economic and Social Development*, Planning Policy Guidance 7 (London: The Stationery Office, February 1997).

27. Ministry of Agriculture, Fisheries and Food, *Agriculture in the United Kingdom – 1999* (London: The Stationery Office, 2000), p. 3.43.

28. Fiona Reynolds, foreword to Geoffrey Sinclair, Environment Information Services, *The Lost Land – Land Use Change in England 1945-1990* (London: Council for the Protection of Rural England, 1992), p. 8.

29. Jacob Roisin and Max Eastman, *The Road to Abundance* (London: Rider and Company, 1955), p. 122.

30. Department of the Environment, Transport and the Regions with the Ministry of Agriculture, Fisheries and Food, *Our Countryside – the Future* (London: DETR, HMSO, November 2000), p. 90.

31. Martin Pawley, 'So, Lord Rogers, why shouldn't we build on surplus rural land?', *Architects' Journal*, 24 February 2000, p. 20.

32. Department of the Environment, *Rural England – A Nation Committed to a Living Countryside* (London: HMSO, 1995).

33. Department of the Environment, Transport and the Regions, *The Countryside – Environmental Quality and Economic and Social Development*, Planning Policy Guidance 7 (London: The Stationery Office, February 1997).

34. Green Balance, *Valuing the Land – Planning for the Best and Most Versatile Agricultural Land* (London: CPRE, September 2000), p. 15.

35. Department of the Environment, Transport and the Regions, *Housing*, Planning Policy Guidance note 3 (London: The Stationery Office, 2000).

36. *Nature*, no. 345, 1990, p. 648.

37. 'Mad cows and Englishmen: a scientific report', OneWorld News Service, April 1996. http://www.oneworld.org/news/reports/apr96_bse3.html

38. Phil Macnaghten and John Urry, *Contested Natures* (London: Sage Publications, 1998), p. 55.

39. Ibid., p. 35.

40. John Selwyn Gummer, 'Those four million houses', in Anthony Barnett and Roger Scruton (eds), *Town and Country* (London: Jonathan Cape, 1998), p. 180.

41. Department of the Environment, *Household Growth – Where Shall We Live?* (London: Department of the Environment, November 1996), p. 5.

42. Richard Rogers, chairman's foreword to Urban Task Force, *Towards an Urban Renaissance – Final Report of the Urban Task Force* (London: E&FN Spon, 1999), p. 8.

43. John Selwyn Gummer, 'Those four million houses', in Anthony Barnett and Roger Scruton (eds), *Town and Country* (London: Jonathan Cape, 1998), p. 180.

44. John Adams, 'Carmageddon', in Anthony Barnett and Roger Scruton (eds), *Town and Country* (London: Jonathan Cape, 1998), p. 225.

45. John Selwyn Gummer, 'Those four million houses', in Anthony Barnett and Roger Scruton (eds), *Town and Country* (London: Jonathan Cape, 1998), p. 177.

46. 'Advisers urge Blair to drop plan for 4.4m new homes', *Telegraph*, 6 February 1998.

Chapter 13

The Sand-Heap Urbanism of the Twenty-First Century

Martin Pawley

THE COST OF THE PAST AND THE BILL FOR THE FUTURE

There are several possible starting points for an argument in favour of non-urban settlements, but the most pressing can be seen in the baleful consequences that flow from the preservation of historic street patterns and old and undersized buildings – a process seen as a heroic cause by the exponents of tourist-heritage culture, instead of the self-damaging built-environment pathology that it really is. The more we shoehorn, pinch and blandish new uses into old spaces instead of clearing their sites for new development or building from scratch in green fields, the more chaotic and unmanageable our towns and cities are becoming. This situation is an offence to good sense and nature. It leads directly to the huge wastage of effort that goes into patching up out-of-date transport systems, and invites the burden of pollution, poverty, crime, public disorder and unemployment. All this should be obvious, and so it is, but it is only when we give due weight to the obvious that we can see the absurdity of the orthodox – that all new building should take place in cities while the countryside should be preserved untouched. In response this chapter poses the question: if all the problems are urban problems, why should we expect the answers to be urban answers?

THE EVENTS OF 18 JUNE 1999 IN LONDON

At midday on Friday, 18 June 1999, the City of London was taken by surprise when a squadron of cyclists 300-strong brought traffic to a halt. This demonstration of pedal power was put on by a militant group called 'Reclaim the Streets', but their presence soon revealed itself as a cover for a large number of other demonstrators intent on holding a so-called 'Carnival against Capitalism'. By early afternoon the event had mushroomed into the biggest London riot since the Poll Tax disturbances of 1990. The 'Carnival' became a pitched battle between 5,000 rioters and the police that saw 28 people arrested, 38 people taken to hospital, and thousands of lives disrupted.[1] The demonstrators smashed windows, set fire to buildings and caused £2 million of property damage. More significantly they blocked London's east–west traffic routes north of the Thames and led to the closure of five underground stations, so for several hours it was impossible to travel between the City and Docklands.

There was worse to come in the same month when London's Underground, the 393-kilometre core of the city's public transport system, capable of carrying more than 3 million passengers a day, came close to complete breakdown. The underlying cause was years of inadequate investment and long-overdue maintenance, made worse by the recent plundering of parts and equipment from other lines in order to speed up the delayed opening of the £3 billion Jubilee line extension. As a result the older parts of the underground system were slowly but surely ceasing to function. So much so that by June, with the tourist season in full swing, every aspect of its operations was at the point of overload. The incidence of stoppages was increasing daily. Vitally needed investment totalled an impossible £1.5 billion. Train drivers were threatening to strike over pay, and 80 years of public ownership seemed to be about to end in a privatisation deal that would break up the network, sell different lines to different operating companies, and place regulatory powers in the hands of an as yet unelected mayor.

What this state of demoralising confusion meant for the users of the network was already known. At the end of May an electrical fault had stranded 100,000 passengers on the Circle, Metropolitan and Hammersmith and City lines, trapping them in their trains in sweltering heat for three hours. Two weeks later the Circle line was scheduled for closure for two months for urgent repairs. The Circle line is the key to the underground system, a 32-kilometre orbital railway that intercepts all the cross-London lines and connects the termini of all the mainline stations.

The closure took place four days before the City riot, and trains ceased to be able to orbit the central area. Within hours plans for the diversion of traffic to other lines had broken down and by midday the entire Circle line was at a standstill. Two days later London Underground announced that the line would have to remain closed for two months, as would sections of the Northern and the Hammersmith and City lines, due to urgent repairs. By 18 June, at the beginning of Wimbledon fortnight, 90 kilometres of track were out of action and the system was operating at its lowest efficiency since the Second World War.[2]

The more we shoehorn, pinch and blandish new uses into old spaces instead of clearing their sites for new development or building from scratch in green fields, the more chaotic and unmanageable our towns and cities are becoming.

IS YOUR JOURNEY REALLY NECESSARY?

From this 1999 picture of the nadir of urban civilisation, London staggered forth only to meet the same intractable ingredients again and again, in the shape of the autumn petrol crisis, the knock-on effects of the Paddington, Hatfield and Doncaster rail crashes, the Northern urban riots of 2001, and further problems on the underground. Each time the official response was the same, a dogged emphasis on the need for more patience, more buses, more railway investment and more paint-on-the-road traffic engineering.

More buses

No-one ever asks why this knee-jerk obsession with throwing bad nineteenth-century technology after good is continually allowed to divert attention from the enormous organisational potential of twenty-first century electronic communications. If the country were under threat of a Kosovo-style bombing attack no-one would question the need to keep physical travel to a minimum. As it is no-one even appears to acknowledge the scale of network disruption that is already accepted as normal in old systems like road and rail; 80 per cent efficiency on the national rail network is thought to be a good performance, whereas its information technology equivalent – no dial tone on the telephone for 12 minutes in every hour, no electric power for 4.8 hours a day – would be wholly unacceptable.

There is a kind of anti-synergy in these matters whereby new networks are not allowed to develop to their own fullest potential, but are used to prop up old systems instead. Thus for example the mass-produced plastic rubbish bag does nothing new, it merely facilitates the refuse-collection strike, which would otherwise be a public health crisis of the first order. Stationary or crawling traffic is made acceptable through the use of mobile phones. Perhaps the unique horror of being trapped in a deep tunnel in a stalled underground train stems from its failure, so far, to attract similar relief.

LONG-WAVE VERSUS SHORT-WAVE TECHNOLOGIES

To see beyond this unresolved mixture of past and future technologies it is necessary to skip a generation and try to visualise a new urban reality, beyond traffic or administrative boundaries.

The identity of this possible reality is defined by, rather than shored up by 'short-wave' technologies instead of the old-fashioned 'long-wave' street patterns, railways, motorways and bus lanes that are our present channels of communication. These long-wave technologies are all heavy, slow and expensive, while short-wave electronic technologies are lighter, cheaper and more efficient in their use of resources. Yet their different wavelengths still have a common denominator in their efficiency of use.

For example, to have created the pre-electronic equivalent to a mobile telephone network 140 years ago, when the first tube tunnels were being built, may have been possible. However, it would have required an army of runners, signallers and controllers, far too massive an enterprise for even the greatest tyrant to organise. Yet today we can achieve the same result easily via entirely different means and without a penny of public money. Telecommunications corporations can create not just one mobile telephone network but as many as we want – not just national networks but international too.

What we cannot do either easily or cheaply is replicate or repair labour-intensive nineteenth-century infrastructure. There is a cycle of progress in these matters. We have been there, and we have done that. We cannot go back and do it again. What we can do now is something else.

MEDITATION ON A TRAFFIC JAM

Ever since the dotcom boom it has been common knowledge that developments in communications and information technology have annihilated distance, if not absolutely today, then nearly enough to promise the simulation of close proximity tomorrow. It is now already part of business routine to teleconference around the world, with the participants meeting nowhere in reality but everywhere in cyberspace. But to know this, and what it portends, and to act upon it appropriately appear to be two different things. As a result we seem reluctant to follow the conquest of distance to its logical conclusion in the abandonment of movement, even though – as the car phone and the mobile phone demonstrate – it is movement as well as distance that is under technological attack, and will be so increasingly in future.

Today mobility is prized but increasingly redundant, if only insofar as instantaneous communication alone makes great tranches of human movement potentially unnecessary, for example commuting into crowded cities. Indeed it is already clear that uninterrupted personal communication by mobile phone is the reason why traffic congestion, which threatens mobility, has so little apparent effect on the operations of the economy. This is because, unlike overcrowded trains delayed for one reason or another, cars locked in a stationary traffic stream are still unalienable destinations in themselves – spacious, comfortable air-conditioned recliners in a vast linear chatroom that can shrink and grow by the hour or the day of the week. The spread of crawling traffic, with its tidal flow of metal capsules carried plankton-like from exit to exit on the motorways, is still treated as though it were an anomaly rather than as a direct intimation of the

More railway spending

All that is required of us now is to decide whether to insist upon mobility, or to relinquish it in favour of a solution to the greatest urban problem of all – density.

shape of non-travel to come. Otherwise it would have been criminalised for reasons of pollution or starved of petroleum long ago. In fact it is one of the key indicators of the new age of immobility.

Notwithstanding many such indicators, immobility in our culture is still deplored. Because of our historically unprecedented capacity for movement and communication we live in Venn diagrams of overlapping circles, moving physically in cars and trains and planes, but also communicating from locations that lack any meaningful materiality. Here is a paradox. We guard our atavistic, energy-guzzling and disease-spreading privilege of physical mobility, a tradition barely 200 years old in a world that measures its history in millions. We do so while it is being eroded away by the increasing ease with which we can communicate with one another without moving from our chairs whenever we need to. The present circumstance makes clear the promise that we have the potential to choose, having become a species that can live either as a plant, rooted to the spot, or as an animal with nomadic propensities. All that is required of us now is to decide whether to insist upon mobility, or to relinquish it in favour of a solution to the greatest urban problem of all – density.

THIRTY HOUSES ON A FOOTBALL PITCH

A football pitch is approximately 0.4 hectares in area. A proposed development envisaged 1,100 houses on a 12-hectare greenbelt site, at a density of 90 dwellings per hectare:

> Imagine more than 30 houses on a football pitch. Then imagine 30 football pitches full of houses side by side. Sooner or later the authorities will have to admit that this is detrimental to the area. Who wants these houses?[3]

Who indeed? Certainly not the people who attend protest meetings to oppose the building of high-density 'Millennium village' housing on greenbelt land. These people understand that the urban development crisis is not founded upon an objection to building in the countryside in principle, but a rooted objection to the urbanisation of the countryside by building in it at urban densities. Such sentiments are not confined to the residents of the shire counties, but are expressed everywhere that a share of the four million new households coming onstream in the next 20 years is remorselessly making its way from planning policy guideline to local planning permission to building site.

IS THERE AN INFLUX OR AN EXODUS?

High rural densities are the 'medicine' that is programmed to go down with the spoonful of sugar of the 'urban renaissance' that has been so aggressively promoted by the Urban Task Force chaired by Lord Rogers of Riverside. The theory of the urban renaissance is based upon centric urbanisation. Major cities must be allowed to increase their density of occupation to an economic and practical maximum. At the same time rural towns and villages must increase their populations too, sufficiently to conserve farming land for recreational and agricultural purposes, and sufficiently to obtain a critical mass of population to make public transport viable.

Already by 2000 this 'invasion of the countryside' driven by an alleged 'exodus from the cities' had the leader of the Urban Task Force calling for more funds to spend on improvement of the street environment and public transport. Unhappily this call for extra funds coincided with the annual conference of the Police Federation. Its spokesman garnered more headlines by announcing that because of inadequate funding, under-manning, the closure of 90 police stations and curtailment of foot patrols, many parts of London, Liverpool, Leeds and Manchester were now descending into 'disorder and anarchy' at night.[4] The Urban Task Force, shadowed by the 'Design Watchdog', the Commission for Architecture and the Built Environment (CABE), took a different approach to crime in the city asserting that it can be 'designed out' by investment, good design and the creation of integrated communities in salubrious new high-density neighbourhoods.

Clearly, without a fresh look at the basics the deadly cocktail that has now been mixed out of equal doses of 'urban flight', 'the rape of the countryside', 'improving the street environment' and 'disorder and anarchy at night', has no antidote, only an endless parade of symptoms. At one and the same time Urban Task Force supporters not only insist that there is no such thing as an 'urban exodus', but also demand 'swift action' from the government to halt it by way of tax breaks and other sweeteners for developers prepared to build on brownfield sites. The position of the Urban Task Force on 'urban flight' has always been contradictory. In *The Times* of November 1997, Lord Rogers announced that 'nine out of ten Britons now live in cities, most of them communities of more than 100,000 people. This startling statistic reveals us to be predominantly urbanised'.[5] However, despite his 'startling statistic', by February 1999 the picture had changed dramatically. Again in *The Times*, Rogers bemoaned 'the potential loss of green land in the face of demographic change and the flight of the middle classes from the cities'. He confessed: 'my Urban Task Force has no easy answers on how to solve the urban exodus which is leaving towns and neighbourhoods desolate'.[6] Alternative sources such as the statisticians Martin Mogridge and John Hollis have another view, suggesting that on average 90,000 people a year leave Greater London, while as many as 100,000 a year may come in.[7]

WHY IS THERE NO DUNKIRK SPIRIT?

Meanwhile, the related worlds of planning, transportation, education and law enforcement seem set into an irreversible decline that no political party appears capable of arresting. At the heart of this muddle lie major misconceptions that appear to be shared by all parties:

- that the issue of mobility, defined above, has nothing to do with population density;
- that 'community spirit' is created by density of population, where the higher the density the more intense the 'community spirit'; and
- that while there is plenty of room to build dwellings in the cities, there is no room at all to build them in the countryside.

First, we are mistaken if we try to relate mobility to density without interposing technology between them. Without the railway system and the century of new roads and road-widening that followed the invention of the motor car, there would have never been the tidal flow of commuting in and out of the cities that we know today. Nor, without later developments in communications technology, would there have been any prospect of reducing the phenomenon in the future.

Second, we must briefly consider the ingredients of the 'community spirit', or the 'Dunkirk spirit' that is so often invoked in connection with urban life. For example the fact that restaurateurs, shopkeepers and property owners had taken the 'threat' of the May Day demonstrations of 2001 too seriously, and not kept their premises open while demonstrations continued, was seen as a lack of 'Blitz spirit' by the *Evening Standard*.[8] Solidarity of this kind cannot be drawn into existence by exhortation. Broadly speaking it comes from group exposure to scarcity, anxiety or danger, hence the repeated references to the Second World War, Dunkirk and the Blitz. In consumer societies not much scarcity, anxiety and danger exists. But where security cameras check the faces of passers by against the features of known criminals, and where the entire trend of consumer technology is in the direction of yet more social fragmentation and domestic self-sufficiency, 'community spirit' is being 'designed out' far more effectively than crime.

Third, as for the wrong-headed argument that there is space aplenty to build in the cities but not a spare corner of a field in the countryside, this obsession defies all logic. It is clearly not based upon any knowledge of land use outside London, or any knowledge of the impact upon British agriculture of cheap food imports and European Union (EU) subsidies. Instead it is backed by the claim that because 11 per cent of the land area of England and Wales consists of buildings, roads, car parks, shopping centres and so on, the countryside must henceforth be regarded as more sacrosanct than it was during the era of the 'Dunkirk spirit' – a period of crisis when it was entirely given over to the needs of food production.

This conclusion is illogical for both absolute and relative reasons. It is absolutely illogical because while 11 per cent of the land area of England and Wales may be occupied by development, 70 per cent of that 11 per cent is concentrated in the southeast quarter of the country, leaving the remaining quarters comparatively lightly developed. It is relatively illogical because, compared to our nearest European neighbours, the percentage of built up land in the British Isles is very low; Belgium rates 22 per cent and the Netherlands 38 per cent. In any case the urban development crisis is not about how much development is permitted, but the way this development is deployed – in short its density. After all the protests had died down the government's 2000 figure for the 900,000 new houses needed by 2016 in the southeast of England was only marginally below the house-building industry's initial 'predict and provide' estimate of 1.2 million, proposed in the Crow Report of 1998.[9]

In any case, Lord Rogers has no anxiety about this. He is on record as calling for the planting of a million urban trees, and urging the creation of a corps of 'Urban Pioneers' to recolonise the cities.[10] But as far as the countryside is concerned he favours '50 or even 100 per cent increases' in rural development densities. To support this position he makes dubious comparisons between the present density of the population in southeast England and the density of occupation in the Australian outback or the US mid-Western prairies.[11] Setting aside the propensity for using global and local figures interchangeably, it is telling that, despite his often-stated ambition to be 'a man of the twenty-first century', Rogers was once ordered to leave a courtroom because he was unable to switch off his mobile telephone.[12] The Rogers-led Urban Task Force has a vision of the city, but it is essentially a pre-electronic, nineteenth-century vision spurning modern communications technology, and apparently laying heavier emphasis on chance meetings in 'public spaces' like pavement cafés. What he and his Task Force do not see is that there is a very positive aspect to the pattern of dispersed and low-density development that grew up in rural areas – pos-

...the urban development crisis is not about how much development is permitted, but the way this development is deployed – in short its density.

The Rogers-led Urban Task Force has a vision of the city, but it is essentially a pre-electronic, nineteenth-century vision spurning modern communications technology, and apparently laying heavier emphasis on chance meetings in 'public spaces' like pavement cafés.

itive despite the passage of the 1947 Town and Country Planning Act, notably in the shape of the Greater London Council's 'decanting' and 'overspill' policies that helped reduce the population of inner London from its five million peak in 1911 to half that by 1981.[13]

Today, because of motorways, electronic communications, scientific agriculture and the globalisation of the food industry, the old Ebenezer Howard diagram of the relationship of town and country as radial and concentric no longer describes reality. The corrected version would be a distributed network in which the 11 per cent of the land surface already urbanised is shown as becoming progressively less densely developed, by means of selective demolitions, while the 89 per cent of non-built-up countryside is shown as becoming more densely developed, by means of dispersed new housing and related services. The whole would be programmed to reach an Arcadian mean in which the arbitrary distinction between agricultural and building land is removed, and a uniform network of low-density settlements served by appropriately sized distribution centres is growing up to replace it.

INTERSECTIONS IN AN OPTICAL CITY

Twelve years ago, when I wrote my book *Theory and Design in the Second Machine Age*, I was eagerly anticipating the assembly of a global electronic network that would trigger a massive redundancy of traditional urban elements and bring about the kind of disurbanised alternative outlined above.[14] At that time I believed that the world economic recession that had begun with the stock exchange crash of October 1987 marked the beginning of an urban collapse in which the historic 'treasure house' conception of the city would lose its value.

Cities themselves would become no more than salvage dumps. Vast accumulations of wreckage left over after a process of accelerating urban decay following the end of urban investment. Confronted with economic failure, which seemed to be overtaking them as the 1987 crash expanded into the international recession of the early 1990s, all cities, it seemed to me, were already beginning to consist of no more than the detritus of consumption, their supposed wealth revealed as a confidence trick propped up by a 'culture' that was no more than the consumption and reconsumption of obsolete forms, so as to preserve all that was extravagant, wasteful and outworn. As a result all cities, I was sure, were ultimately headed for a fate of abandonment comparable to the evacuations that characterised the urban policies of Europe's cities under aerial bombardment half a century before.

In the course of this massive process of urban bankruptcy, I believed, one of the first casualties would be art historical urban thinking, the perpetuated, pre-revolutionary art of the pursuit of axes and vistas that epitomised all that was old and outworn, mad and meretricious about the 'treasure house' urbanism. That urbanism had overtaken the 1980s so that every old building was considered to be of priceless value, even if derelict and unusable except as a museum for itself. This kind of planning, along with the old static arts such as literature, sculpture and architecture itself that had for so long derived sustenance from it, would have no place in the decentralised networks of the future. All of them would be swept away by the electronic simulations of proximity achieved by space, sound, image and sensation in a virtual world, of which much has already been said, written and demonstrated. As far as the urban world was concerned a transformation would take place comparable to the defeat and diminution suffered by painting at the hands of photography, or cinema at the hands of television and video. And part of this rupture with the past would be a sudden demonstration of how easily the simulation of presence could supplant the actuality of proximity. A good example of this would be provided by electronic solutions to traffic problems.

URBAN TIME VERSUS URBAN SPACE

As Einstein taught, the connection between space and time is not remote. In fact it can be illustrated in the operation of a camera, where time values are inversely proportional to aperture values.[15] The faster the shutter moves the larger the aperture required to correctly expose the film, and vice versa. Applying this demonstration of the relativity of time and space to one of the simplest of traffic problems produced a hypothesis in which urban space equated with aperture size, and urban time with shutter speed. According to this piece of algebra the more space a city possessed, the less time it would require, and the more time it had, the less space it would need.

Time in the city can be measured in different ways. If it were to become instantaneous, as it might if continuous online communications encompassed the world, then the whole world's population might require no more space than an urban 'aperture' 300 atoms in diameter. This is a measurement that helpfully corresponded to the width of the light beam in an optical computer system. This substitution of optical computer beams for conventional traffic streams provided a practical means of looking at the space-time continuum in cities through the example of the street-level four-way intersection. This is a feature of urban structuring since the dawn of time and one that still survives in virtually every world city. As traffic speed and density have increased it has become a controlled intersection, then, by means of robot coloured lights, an automatically controlled intersection. But even in its ultimate form, with filter lights and computer-phased sequencing, its traffic capacity is still tiny because its 'aperture' is fixed and only four vehicle directions can be accepted at one time – as opposed to the theoretical twelve. By contrast an optical traffic intersection – if such a thing existed – would have no problem with 'vehicles' passing through one another in all directions, simply by varying time, in the form of the optical wavelength of its light beams.

In the real world the traffic density of a conventional urban street system is limited by its intersections. But the 'traffic density' of an optical road network would be unaffected by any number of intersections. That advantage, multiplied by the number of four-way intersections in a city, is a measure of the potential of switching from aperture to time – from the urban past to the post-urban future.

URBAN MINISTRUCTURES VERSUS INFINITE SPACE

In his 1991 essay *Three Times*, the Czechoslovakian media philosopher Vilem Flusser identified the sequential evolution of three different conceptions of time.[16] The first of these he called 'wheel time', a cyclical notion of time that found its origins in the repeating seasonal and generational patterns of the agrarian pre-industrial world. Next came linear or 'stream time', which flowed from the past to the future by way of progress and mastery of the earth.

This idea of time governed the age of exploration and discovery, the era of science and industrial production: modern time, in fact. But Flusser was a post-modern thinker who had lived beyond the modern age. His last conception of time, the time of the planar present, was what he called 'sand-heap time'.

Sand-heap time is a time of uniformly distributed particles, the events of which are neither cyclical as in 'wheel time', nor linear as in 'stream time'. The events of sand-heap time are random and accidental contacts made on the way to inertness. Sand-heap time does not rotate or progress. Its only activity is its own limited inertia. External forces distribute and redistribute it continually from the kinetic gradient to the inert, uniform layer.

A good parallel for the transition from stream time to sand-heap time might be the production process that involves breaking a treated silicon wafer, only 0.25 mm thick, into hundreds of microchips. Once the wafer is broken the chips have no further connection with one another except the uniformity of their destination, which is a random location somewhere in the exponentially increasing global distribution of processing power. After the wafer has been broken, each chip, like a grain of sand, is an event on the way to 'eventlessness'.

The imagery of Flusser's sand-heap time, realised through such analogies as the camera, or the traffic intersection and the breaking of a silicon wafer, enabled me to see that the sudden collapse of urbanism that I had expected was less likely to occur than I had thought. Instead, a new entropic, non-cataclysmic urban future, which had been gaining strength over a long period of time, had already half-replaced the 'treasure house' city before its economic collapse began. Translated into urban space, sand-heap time is the key to a redefinition of urbanism as an instantaneously timed, infinitely apertured, omnidirectional phenomenon.

Interestingly, the architect Paolo Soleri had already indicated, though rejected, this possibility. In a magazine interview he was quoted as having said:

Urban megastructures used to be considered the worst thing possible because they were confused with suburbia, which is not a structure at all, not an organism, not even a system. Suburbia doesn't work because it is endless matter which is flat, amorphous and tenuous. It promises so much but it gives so little.[17]

Clearly Soleri sees the significance of suburbia, but he cannot accept it. Similarly, it must be said, Vilem Flusser seemed unwilling to follow the logic of his own final definition of time. Yet suburbia and sand-heap time are part of the same phenomenon. In their different ways they are factual evidence of the existence of an omnidirectional distribution of particles that is the entropic destination of the post-modern world. When Soleri dismisses suburbia and Flusser rejects entropy, each of them does less than justice to their own insights.

URBAN SPACE AS STRUCTURAL FAILURE

As stated at the beginning of this chapter, the predilection of today's architects and planners for a corrosive sentimentality in urban matters is shown by their addiction to the past. Sentimentality is what prevents architects and planners from contemplating the existence of a non-specific urbanism based upon an entropic pattern of in themselves meaningless events. But it cannot prevent us from looking through ecological or macroscopic eyes at the urban phenomena over which they appear to preside, and perhaps drawing less sentimental conclusions than do architects and planners.

Sand-heap time does not rotate or progress. Its only activity is its own limited inertia. External forces distribute and redistribute it continually from the kinetic gradient to the inert, uniform layer.

...suburbia and sand-heap time are part of the same phenomenon. In their different ways they are factual evidence of the existence of an omnidirectional distribution of particles that is the entropic destination of the post-modern world.

In *Environment, Power and Society*, his important study of the importance of energy flows in man-made and natural ecologies, Howard Odum drew parallels between modern cities and 'concentrations of consumers' among seabed creatures such as oysters, clams and barnacles. All of these creatures rely upon strong power inflows to bring energy and oxygen, and strong outflows to dispose of heat and waste. From his studies of renewal and decay in the habitat of these 'concentrations of consumers', Odum concluded that monolithic rigid structures akin to cities only emerged where power flows were highly concentrated, and that in all cases the power needed was in direct proportion to the amount of structure to be maintained. Examples of connected associations dependent upon strong power flows were reefs of oysters, heavy root networks in tropical rainforests, and contiguous urban structuring in human cities. Examples of unconnected associations, or entropies, without strong power flows were the organisms in plankton in the sea, the scattered plants in a newly sown field, or suburban housing. Odum's analysis concluded:

> Only connected associations develop senescence at the group level as well as within individuals. We are used to the idea in urban renewal that some continuous building structures are more cheaply replaced than repaired. An example of this in a simple ecosystem is the ageing of barnacle associations. When old and top-heavy they break off or are broken off and new growth and succession refills the gaps.[18]

The important thing about Odum's research is that it explains the economics of urbanism in a way that is neither 'art-historical sentimental' nor 'real-estate commercial', but instead is more closely related to the depersonalised spatial implications of sand-heap time. Odum's ecological perspective shows us that space in a natural 'city' is no more than a gap – it has no survival function. In the natural associations that he has studied, gaps occur by accident and are repaired by accretion into the surrounding mass, because accretive construction achieves synergetic strength advantages. If the gaps outweigh the mass of structure, repair grows proportionally more expensive, time consuming and problematic. Too many gaps and a natural megastructure will break down and be lost.

Thus it is possible to argue that urban space in human cities is 'gap' space and, in reality, no more than evidence of ageing and decay. As far as we can judge, the medieval cities were 'concentrations of consumers' virtually without gaps. Large open spaces appeared in these cities only centuries after when later fortifications were demolished, fires destroyed whole districts, or natural disasters befell them. In effect their urban spaces were all gaps that could not be filled. After the Renaissance, the buildings and vistas, parks and gardens that were laid out across these gaps were soon rationalised into principles of urban planning, but only after the collapse of the gap-filling capability of the original megastructural urban idea.

From this we might speculate that the whole concept of an art-historical-derived urban planning appears only in the natural and man-made world when regimes or structures are in decline. The megastructure is the original and perfect form of the natural and the human concentration of consumers. Urban planning only rationalises its disappearance. Applying this same Darwinian analysis to the world of human cities we are immediately confronted with a clear spectacle of urban breakdown and decay. Given the scale of the failure of gap repair we must conclude that our cities are dying or, if they are not, then clearly some more productive form of gap repair must be taking place on a much larger and more diffuse scale.

This is something the immense urban implications of which the conventional urbanists do not recognise because it is heading towards them on a non-culturally acceptable path – something that Soleri missed when he argued that:

> In nature as the organism evolves, it increases in complexity and also becomes more compact and miniaturised. The city too must become a more compact and miniaturised container for social, cultural and spiritual evolution. Nobody has ever understood that the megastructures we proposed at Arcosanti are in fact ministructures: that putting things together is a miniaturization, not a 'mega-turization'. My solution is an urban implosion, rather than an explosion.[19]

The something that is evident only on different wavelengths from those that are received by the art-historical, urban planning, commercial redevelopment coalition is the disurbanised urbanism of sand-heap time. This is the new urban structure of instantaneous time in which urban space is continuous, not miniaturised.

THE URBANISM OF THE SAND HEAP

During the 1980s a new city network was built in non-historic Europe, however it was not called a city network. While forests were being cut down to provide paper to debate the architectural merits of single buildings, all over the continent millions of square metres of business park and distribution centre floorspace were being constructed at breakneck speed. Outside the old towns and cities, at thousands of exits on nearly 50,000 kilometres of AutoRoute, a million new commercial complexes were springing up with no reference to urban context or the supremacy of history at all. In England more than a hundred out-of-town shopping centres were projected, 39 of them more than 10,000 hectares in covered area and no less than 9 of them planned for locations on the M25 London orbital motorway.

This new 'abstract urbanism of the trade routes' – its locations are often designated only by numbered road exits – was ignored by critics of architecture and urban planners. Yet in economic terms it soon became far more important than the sum of all the art-historical architecture built in our ancient towns and cities over the last half century. It has taken warehousing, distribution and retailing out of the cities altogether. According to the London property research organisation Applied Property Research there were at the end of the 1990s no less than 690,000 hectares, or 6.9 billion square metres of land, currently effected by 'abstract urbanism' in England and Wales alone. In and out of recession, out-of-town superstores and their associated distribution centres are still the biggest growth areas in development. In Britain, while architecture critics agonised about what should happen on a 0.4-hectare site in the City of London, hundreds of thousands of hectares were developed along our motorways and major roads on sites that are already becoming the nuclei of disurbanised 'towns' – places where a direct and adequate local road network leads to and from service areas with ten car parking spaces for every square metre of floor space, instead of one for every 500 square metres as in London or Bristol.

Today, after two decades of frenzied construction, these new out-of-town office, manufacturing and distribution and shopping parks in England boast nearly 80 million square metres of high-tech serviced floorspace – an enclosed area three times larger than the area of London's Docklands, equal to 30 separate Canary Wharfs, and all built on greenfield sites without reference to ancient towns or city centres.

This new pattern of construction is not art-historically recognised architecture. It is the 'something bigger than urban planning' that is the unsentimental face of the sand-heap urbanism of the era of sand-heap time – a manifestation of an abstract, digital, commercial network that links the EC countries and beyond into a seamless web of consumption, the distribution nodes of which are ports and airports, freezer stores, warehouses, vast truck parks, railheads and ferry terminals.

Today all that this network of infrastructure requires to absorb the overspill from overcrowded cities is a permanent population of its own in the shape of a network of low-density settlements liberated from the rural planning restrictions that began with the 1947 Town and Country Planning Act. These restrictions were originally intended to protect land required for food production from sporadic and inappropriate development, but in recent years they have increasingly been interpreted as an almost biblical injunction to 'save' the whole of the countryside from development of any kind.

Under present circumstances the repeal of the 1947 Act might seem an almost unimaginable step, were it not for the recent series of crises in agriculture resulting from falling produce prices, the BSE and foot-and-mouth epidemics of 2000 and 2001. These have illuminated the non-competitive status of subsidised food production at the latitude of Hudson Bay, which is where Britain is. Then there was the recent legal challenge to the 1947 Act under the Human Rights Act. The spin-off from these events has revealed that the 'industry' responsible for the retailing of lunchtime sandwiches is more profitable than farming, and that there are large areas of so-called farming land without useful purpose. Furthermore, under pressure of these events, the principles of the 1947 Act have to some extent been breached by diversification of land use permitted to farmers faced with cheap food imports and falling subsidies.

Taken to its logical conclusion, in the way that the 'Enterprise Zone' scheme was in the 1980s, drawing the teeth of the 1947 Act could permit farmers and other landowners to sell off house-building plots in selected locations. This could happen on condition that they took advantage of attractive landscape features such as copses, woods, valleys and views, to permit the ensuing dwellings to be invisibly sewn into the landscape with minimal visual intrusion. Preliminary investigations into such a measure suggest that between 1.5 and 2 million house-building sites within range of existing distribution nodes, A-road and motorway routes would be put on the market within a year of the launch of such a scheme. This would immediately release much of the pressure for more building land in the southeast of England without venturing into more 'Millennium density' football pitches. Indeed, the preliminary investigations in north Oxfordshire and south Northamptonshire agricultural land, distributive nodes and road networks suggest the ultimate housing 'land bank' made possible by such a scheme would probably top 10 million units within a decade, thus resolving the problem of the 'urban exodus' for half a century or more. If only for this reason it is worth examining in outline how such a policy change might be managed.

A PROTOTYPE SPECIAL RURAL DWELLINGS PROGRAMME

Given that these 'special rural dwelling' sites, or SRDs, will have been made available under uniquely advantageous circumstances, it will be appropriate for entitlement to them to be subject to certain enlightened conditions. These might be developed along the following lines:

In Britain, while architecture critics agonised about what should happen on a 0.4-hectare site in the City of London, hundreds of thousands of hectares were developed along our motorways and major roads on sites that are already becoming the nuclei of disurbanised 'towns'...

...drawing the teeth of the 1947 Act could permit farmers and other landowners to sell off house-building plots in selected locations. This could happen on condition that they took advantage of attractive landscape features such as copses, woods, valleys and views, to permit the ensuing dwellings to be invisibly sewn into the landscape with minimal visual intrusion.

- Plot size to relate to size of house. Minimum distance between houses to be 100 metres. Minimum plot size to be 0.404 hectares. No maximum plot size.
- Required thermal performance to be specified for a small number of standard modular designs but the means to achieve it must remain open to innovation.
- Maximum energy consumption to be specified for a small number of standard modular designs but the means to achieve it must remain open to innovation.
- Each household to be equipped with state-of-the-art electronic communications equipment sufficient to make home-working employment feasible. Each household to have the use of at least two small energy-efficient non-polluting motor cars, suitable for round-trip journeys of up to 75 kilometres. The importance of the motor car in all projects for rural revival cannot be underestimated. Suffice to say that that the present rural 'densification' policy, designed to achieve critical mass for the efficient operation of public transport, is designed to fail. More than any other instrument of modern life it is the motor car that has made year-round rural living possible. To try to step back into the pre-supermarket era of horse riding and country buses is, thoughtlessly or deliberately, to refuse to understand that the key dichotomy is between time-tabled public and freelance private transport, not between the diesel bus and the petrol motor car. Setting aside political policy, the technical problems of pollution and energy consumption have all been resolutely addressed by the motor industry, and will continue to be so.
- All purchasers of SRD sites and houses to relinquish their right to public passenger transport except for long journeys commencing at the extreme range of their cars.
- The modular standard designs referred to will have been commissioned earlier by Government departments from competing teams of motor, aerospace, ship and railway rolling-stock manufacturers. This is a conscious reprise of the 1944 Emergency Factory Made programme, which led to the manufacture of 150,000 prefabricated dwellings within three years. Without an industrialised modular building service of some sort the required economies of scale will be difficult to attain and prices will rise. The invitation to the motor industry to produce prototypes for the SRD programme is an acknowledgement of its tremendous production capability, in terms of speed, precision and performance, far in advance of that of the construction industry. Until such invitations are issued the motor industry will remain one of the most seriously neglected sources of high-speed construction expertise.

Clearly under these circumstances the SRD sites available would be most numerous in the least populated parts of the country, and least numerous in the densely populated southeast, thus applying an immediate counterbalance to the 'town cramming' favoured by urban enthusiasts today. In a similar vein government advertising campaigns, commercials and TV documentaries of the progress of the SRD programme and a feature film would be commissioned to quicken interest in the scheme as it progresses. The estimated cost of the entire SRD programme is £90 billion. This is exactly half the government's estimate for the creation of an integrated transport system. If the SRD initiative succeeds in consumerising the entire congestion problem by reducing it to the level of domestic technology, an integrated transport system will no longer be necessary.

What the SRD programme promises to create is a new disurbanised city-living process, a process that through copses and woods, valleys, views and electronic communications expands the identity of the city to encompass global associations, simultaneously to reduce it to the dimensions of a pattern of dots on a computer screen, anywhere and everywhere that roads, electric power and information exist. The SRD project will create a post-agricultural and dispersed electronic simulation of a city – a dematerialised metropolis, ephemeralised, entropic, evenly distributed, and without gradient at last.

WE ARE THE PLANKTON OF THE LAND MASS

What the entropic urbanism of sand-heap time demands of us is a different conception of the significance of urban design from any that we have held before. This is a conception that is contrary to the whole tradition of permanent architecture that continues to rule our old 'treasure house' cities. In this new order of significance the act of building will become not more and more ponderous and fraught with significance – as it has appeared to become in the post-modern heritage city – but more and more abstract, impermanent and dispersed.

This form of settlement is the true urban signifier of the third time of which Vilem Flusser wrote; the coming of an urbanism of insignificant, undifferentiated, uniformly distributed particles without urban space, without urban identity, without heritage, without history. In conformity with our ascent into sand-heap time we have already seen the public urban spaces of our cities leak away into instantaneous electronic communications and transportation networks that can never stop. With the advent of a special rural dwellings programme the flexibility of our built and mobile environment would spread like a net over the whole country, offering ease and freedom in place of urban strife.

Such has been the impact of instantaneous time upon historic urban space that soon our closest urban ecological model will become the entropic deployment of organisms in the plankton of the ocean. A fate that we will experience as a low-low-density pattern of settlement based on undifferentiated land use for the first time in 53 years.

Notes

1. 'Internet message sets off a rampage', *The Times*, 19 June 1999; 'Protesters "paid" to riot in City', *The Sunday Times*, 20 June 1999; 'Police examine videos in hunt for riot leaders', *The Times*, 21 June 1999; 'PCs thought they were "losing control" of City riot', *Evening Standard*, 24 June 1999.
2. 'The service no one in power cares about', *Evening Standard*, 14 January 1999; '100,000 in Tube chaos as signal fails in peak', *The Times*, 20 May 1999; 'Fiasco on the Circle Line', 'Tube chaos beyond belief' and 'Prescott's plans will topple trains', *Evening Standard*, 18 June 1999; 'How Labour has let down the Tube', *Evening Standard*, 22 June 1999; 'The realities of Prescott's vision for the Underground', *Evening Standard*, 23 June 1999; 'We need a new Tube policy – and quick', *Evening Standard*, 25 June 1999; '56 Tube miles out of action as branch of Northern line shuts', *Evening Standard*, 2 July 1999.
3. Tony Baldry, North Oxfordshire MP, quoted in local newspaper *The Banbury Cake*, 11 May 2000.
4. Summary of Police Federation conference keynote speech, 'Funding forces police to abandon cities to anarchy', *The Times*, 16 May 2000; Martin Pawley, 'The countryside can be developed but not at urban density levels', *Architects' Journal*, 25 May 2000, p. 24.
5. Lord Rogers, 'You, too, can help to save London', *The Times*, 24 November 1997.
6. Lord Rogers, 'Richard Rogers explains his brave vision for a new Britain', *The Times*, 6 February 1999.
7. Martin Mogridge and John Hollis, 'London's population set to soar by 2016', *Evening Standard*, 26 January 1999.
8. 'Where was the Blitz spirit?', *Evening Standard*, 2 May 2001.
9. 'Prescott opens the way to 900,000 homes', *The Times*, 5 March 2000.
10. Rowan Moore, 'Return of the Taste Police', *Evening Standard*, 29 June 1999.
11. Lord Rogers, 'Richard Rogers explains his brave vision for a new Britain', *The Times*, 6 February 1999.
12. *Evening Standard*, 20 February 1999; *The Times*, 31 March 1999.
13. Martin Mogridge and John Hollis, 'London's population set to soar by 2016', *The Times*, 26 January 1999.
14. Martin Pawley, *Theory and Design in the Second Machine Age* (Oxford: Basil Blackwell, 1990).
15. James Bernstein, *Einstein* (New York: McGraw Hill, 1973), pp. 206–13.
16. Vilem Flusser, 'Three Times', *Art Forum*, New York, February 1991.
17. Paolo Soleri, 'Soleri's Laboratory', *World Architecture*, No. 21, January 1993, pp. 58–63.
18. Howard Odum, 'Power for Order and Evolution', *Environment, Power and Society* (New York: Wiley-Interscience, 1971), ch. 5, p. 139.
19. Paolo Soleri, 'Soleri's Laboratory', *World Architecture*, No. 21, January 1993, pp. 58–63.

ADVANCED TECHNOLOGY BEYOND MERE STYLING

Chapter 14

Revolutionary Energy

Shane Slater, Ben Madden and Duncan Price, Whitby Bird and Partners

CAN YOU STEP OUT OF THE CAR PLEASE?

Should you ever find yourself in the unfortunate position of being stopped by the police and asked to exhaust the contents of your lungs into the dreaded breathalyser, take my advice. Politely ask the officer if you can keep the breathalyser as a memento: bring it home and take it apart. For at the heart of the lowly breathalyser is a piece of technology known as a fuel cell, and the fuel cell is at the heart of a revolution that will transform our cities and our society in the twenty-first century.

The aspiration of 'sustainability' – particularly applied to a city – is sufficiently complex and multi-faceted that it has resisted attempts at definition at all but the most generalised levels. In recognition of this and of our position as scientists and engineers this chapter will, in the main, address one aspect of sustainability that is more likely to yield to scientific analysis – namely the production, distribution and consumption of energy in cities, and the implication these issues have upon the quality of life of the city's occupants.

The coal-blackened bricks of Victorian buildings have now become a familiar and respected element of the urban tapestry of Britain. The urban smog, which for decades passed beneath them as breathable air, has tainted the most majestic cathedral spires towering above the surrounding rooftops as they strain towards the heavens and God. The juxtaposition of the sacred and the profane has manifested itself as the blackened and decaying stone from which these structures were built.

The urban smog of this era imprinted upon society the notion that energy is inextricably bound up with pollution: how certain Victorian city-dwellers must have been that this oppressive environment was the price to pay for wage and warmth. This legacy exists to the present day, where the leaders of some western countries are convinced that a reduction in emissions levels (particularly carbon dioxide – CO_2) will harm economic growth, and instead they choose to follow a 'business as usual' approach.

Aerial view of London.

As the industrial revolution progressed, fewer industries were located in urban areas, and the passing of the first UK clean air act in 1956 ensured that cities would never return to the levels of pollution witnessed in the nineteenth century. While industrial processes have, on the whole, become cleaner, nevertheless the main impetus for pushing large industry out of urban areas was not to reduce pollution per se, rather it was to displace it to where its effects were less noticeable. This movement reinforced the delineation between a city that consumes and a countryside from which the citizens derive their sustenance. Far more worryingly, it reinforced a linear system of consumption, without any feedback mechanism, which would ensure that the effects of our actions are made clear to us. Such a linear system promotes waste and redundancy, thus requiring excessive consumption of resources. The size of our planet in comparison to our homes, cities, and even our countries has led many to presume this linear system is acceptable, but it is now clear that the task of supporting our way of life has become too onerous for our planet. Our greatest long-term concern is the excessive release of CO_2 to the atmosphere, certain to result in some degree of planetary warming. However, the effects of our excessive levels of consumption are already obvious, particularly in urban areas.

In half of the cities of the developed world, the air is unsafe to breathe due, in the main, to automotive emissions.[1] The incidence of breathing difficulties in children rose substantially over the latter half of the twentieth century. As a consequence of our insatiable desire for personal transportation, cities have become less attractive places to live. Heavily trafficked roads present near impenetrable barriers between conjoined sections of the cityscape. The noise and airborne pollution from vehicles makes many footpaths, cafés and public gardens unpleasant, unsafe and, as a source of refuge from the boiling city, futile. Buildings that might have been designed to avail of natural ventilation are forced to seal themselves off from their unpleasant surroundings. In consequence, these buildings consume more energy in the provision of heavily serviced and highly artificial environments. For many of their citizens, large cities have become necessary places to work, but undesirable places to live. This dichotomy is responsible for a vicious circle: the desire to live in a cleaner environment but requiring to work in cities increases the urbanisation of the countryside and commuting distances, contributing to the urban pollution which provoked the commuting in the first place.

Instead, we have a vision for a more sustainable city, one that is centred on the production, distribution and use of energy. While we recognise that this can only contribute one of the many elements required of a sustainable solution, nevertheless we believe that issues pertinent to this are so pervasive that any sustainable solution must have them at its core.

SUSTAINABLE ENERGY PRODUCTION

Imagine a future where paths bounding busy city streets are reborn as sites for reflection and contemplation, or discussion over languid cups of coffee. A future where cities are no longer seen as a place where one 'does time', earning enough money to finance a move to the countryside. The lungs of city dwellers are free from sulphurous and nitrous oxides, and particulates; their ears can pick out birdsong once more. Buildings no longer reach skyward to free themselves from the pollution below: because there is none. The vehicles on the roads, if not propelled by the city dwellers themselves, are truly clean and quiet, emitting nothing more menacing than water vapour. Not only are these vehicles free of emissions at point of use, the fuel they consume is produced from renewable sources, such as solar and wind; hence there are no greenhouse gas emissions. Buildings will be less reliant upon the conventional energy infrastructure, instead providing much of their own energy requirements using the same renewable fuel as the vehicles below.

The machines in which this fuel is consumed in the provision of electricity and heat are compact, simple to mass produce, and have no moving parts. In this vision, buildings will be free to embrace rather than ignore this more benign environment, permitting it inside their boundaries in largely untempered form. Many buildings will make full use of the natural synergies between daylight provision, passive solar heating, and photovoltaic electricity generation. Some will be capable of storing excess renewably generated energy for distribution to other buildings locally, or for use in these clean quiet vehicles. Widespread architectural integration of renewable energy technologies will act, then, as a more direct and visible link between energy use and the effort required for its generation. The clarity of cause and effect will help to close our current, linear system of consumption, perhaps promoting a degree of voluntary energy rationalisation.

One may even be bold enough to envisage the gradual dismantling of the vicious circle described above, to be replaced with one where clean transportation and buildings, fuelled from sustainable sources, catalyse a revitalisation of urban centres and reverse the urbanisation of the countryside. It will be nothing short of a revolution.

THE HYDROGEN-BASED ENERGY ECONOMY

The key to using renewable energy for transportation, unlocking a future of clean and pleasant urban environments, is both simple and elemental, for it takes the form of the simplest element of all: hydrogen. The main elements of the future hydrogen-based energy economy will be summarised in this chapter.

A significant portion of the electricity generated from renewable energy sources will be passed through devices known as electrolysers. The essence of this device is that if an electric current of sufficient energy is passed through water, then the H_2O is split into its constituent elements hydrogen (H_2) and oxygen (O_2), which bubble out of the liquid. In this process, the original electrical energy is in effect stored as hydrogen gas; it may release its energy at any time in the future by recombination with oxygen. The hydrogen can then be stored and compressed for transportation, if required. Preferably, if the hydrogen-generation system is linked to a local renewable-energy supply, then hydrogen fuel can be generated locally, removing the need for the intricate and expensive supply infrastructure associated with today's fossil fuel supply. This highly decentralised model of energy production takes power out of the hands of a select few and promotes a more equitable distribution of resources – a key element of sustainability.

The potential energy of hydrogen, released when it recombines with oxygen to form water, can be harnessed in many ways. The most obvious method is to make use of the familiar combustion engine, where the hydrocarbon fuel, such as diesel or gasoline, is replaced with pure hydrogen. However, combustion is a relatively inefficient method for the production of mechanical energy. The point of combustion is to produce heat, and this heat must then be made to work in order to produce motion. Instead, an unprecedented worldwide research and development effort is currently underway aimed at bringing to market a technology that has languished on the shelf for over a century. The 'fuel cell' will revolutionise our society by opening the door to a 100 per cent renewable and clean energy supply. It is based on a process that is effectively the reverse of electrolysis. A thin membrane separates the hydrogen and oxygen gases: a catalyst impregnated into the membrane promotes recombination and in doing so they form water. This electrochemical reaction releases electrical energy and a smaller quantity of heat. The fuel cell is substantially more efficient than a combustion engine, is compact and practically silent, has no moving parts and is more versatile.[2]

An increasingly rapid rate of technological development has brought fuel cells to the point where they are a viable option for almost all of our energy needs. There are a number of different technologies within the field of fuel cells, suited to different applications. The size of the application ranges from the very small (laptops and mobile phones), through medium sized (domestic energy supplies and automobiles) to very large (community heat and power generation and large-scale power production). The crucial feature of fuel cells is that if hydrogen is the fuel, the only emission is water. If that hydrogen is generated from renewables, there are no harmful emissions in the system. The replacement of fossil fuels with hydrogen is a revolution because it can deliver, for the first time, an abundant and secure source of energy that will be entirely carbon-free, not just at the point of use (electricity is an example of this) but right through production, distribution and consumption.

The use of fuel cells in transport is worthy of particular note. A long-standing technical challenge has been the integration of renewable energy sources and transport. Experiments with all-electric battery-powered vehicles have betrayed the fact that battery technology still has a long way to go. However, fuel cells are light and compact, and lend themselves to all aspects of transport, from electrical-assist bicycles to articulated trucks. The concerns that many proactive city authorities have regarding the poor quality of urban air (Los Angeles is a case in point) have required automotive companies to invest huge sums into fuel cell research. An example of this is the Californian fuel-cell partnership, which involves a spectrum of automotive and petroleum or energy companies. This is likely to deliver workable solutions to the technical difficulties automotive fuel-cell technologies still face. In 2002, Londoners will participate in a pan-European research and demonstration project by playing host to two fuel-cell buses available for public transport. General Motors has projected that by 2010, 10 per cent of their new cars sold in Europe will use fuel cells.[3] An annual report on the status of automotive fuel cell markets predicts fuel cells will have 4 per cent market share (US), with 608,000 vehicles by 2010.[4]

INTERMITTENCY

Harnessing energy from renewable sources is a vital element of any sustainable agenda where the goal must be 100 per cent of our energy supplied by renewables. Laudable as it is, severe technical difficulties retard us. Perhaps the most severe is security of supply – to match our patterns of energy consumption with the availability of energy from natural, random sources.

The sun does not always shine, nor does the wind always blow. We live in a world where energy is expected to be available as and when necessary and not at the whim of nature. Even with today's energy mix, based on steady output from fossil fuel and nuclear power stations, substantial efforts are required to cope with irregular demand – at half time in a World Cup final when everyone wants a cup of tea, for example. The energy storage facility at Dinorwig in Wales has been built at great expense to pump water up to a reservoir at times of low electricity demand only to regenerate that power to satisfy peak demand. With an intermittent power supply such as renewables, this issue is made many times worse. The electrical grid can cope with only a limited amount of penetration by renewables, and this is of the order of just 20 to 30 per cent. The problems of intermittency have already manifested themselves on a number of islands (particularly in Scandinavia) where there have been substantial efforts to move towards a 100 per cent renewable-energy electricity supply, based on wind turbines. On windy days, particularly at weekends, the power supply exceeds demand and electrical energy is either wasted or the turbines have to be isolated from the grid to avoid potentially destructive power surges.

Therefore, even if we rationalise our use of energy, some form of energy storage medium is required if we are to make full use of intermittent renewable sources. In our vision of the future hydrogen-based energy economy, inherently temperamental renewably generated electricity will be consumed in efficient electrolysers, producing hydrogen and oxygen. In so doing, energy is stored in the form of hydrogen and this store can feed fuel cells to provide energy as and when required, spanning the time when the renewable energy source is either insufficient or unavailable to meet demand.

THE DAUNTING SCALE OF THE TRANSITION

The path to hydrogen is also the one that will lead to 100 per cent sustainable renewable energy supply. The move towards a hydrogen-based rather than a fossilised hydrocarbon economy is daunting, though not entirely without precedent.

The technological development of western societies has always required them to look to more concentrated sources of power. The move from wood to lignite and brown coal, to black coal, petrochemicals and most recently natural gas, was not only motivated by technical development, but was also facilitated by it. As fuels become outdated, their replacement typically requires a more significant and sophisticated infrastructure to extract, refine and distribute the fuel. Western societies have made transitions between fuels before; there is no basis for assuming they will never do so again, even if the next transition will be on a greater scale.

The crucial feature of fuel cells is that if hydrogen is the fuel, the only emission is water. If that hydrogen is generated from renewables, there are no harmful emissions in the system.

The sun does not always shine, nor does the wind always blow. We live in a world where energy is expected to be available as and when necessary and not at the whim of nature.

It is perhaps more telling if we look at the molecular structure of the fossil fuels we have and continue to make use of. Each fuel is a hydrocarbon, in that its molecular structure contains atoms of hydrogen and carbon (among others) in varying ratios. If we look at the molecular hydrogen to carbon (HC) ratio of each of these fuels, an amazing trend is apparent when in each case, when a fuel is replaced, the HC ratio increases.

The HC ratio of wood is 1:10, coal is 7:10, while petroleum has a HC ratio between 2:1 and 2.5:1. Natural gas has the highest HC ratio of fossil fuels (4:1), which is why it has replaced coal as the fuel of choice in electricity production. With each transition to a new fuel, the quantity of CO_2 released per unit of energy generated becomes less. The natural extrapolation of this process is the complete elimination of the carbon atoms in the fuel, while retaining the only element we really wanted in the first place: hydrogen.

Even hydrogen-powered buses are not novel. The scarcity of petrol during the Second World War led to the use of coal, via gasification, to produce town gas. Apart from significant levels of impurities, and being coal-derived it certainly wasn't clean, the main constituent of town gas and its variants is hydrogen. Many vehicles were to be seen with inflatable-bladder tanks filled with the gas. Its return in alliance with fuel cell buses will help us fight our battle with another menacing enemy – urban pollution and climate change.

We recognise that we are proposing a highly technological path to a sustainable society, and that this must take its place near one end of a spectrum of opinion. Others may argue a return to a time when mechanisation was limited, our lives were simpler and slower and relations with one another more straightforward. Our current search for such pastoral idylls mirrors, and perhaps has been informed by the utopian societies constructed in the nineteenth century in response to the brutality of the industrial revolution. Their failure points to the fact that obscurantism cannot succeed in delivering sustainable societies that not only protect the environment, but also ensure more equitable distribution of resources and the proper valuation of cultural heritage.

Nevertheless we, as engineers and technologists, must be aware of the mistakes our predecessors have made in selling to their generations the benefits of emerging technologies, without presenting some of the inevitable reservations. It would be rash to assume that hydrogen and the technologies required to bring it to maturity will emerge solely as a force for the greater good. There are real concerns.

SAFETY

Safety is of paramount importance, but we are certain that the technical issues regarding the safe generation, transportation and use of hydrogen will be resolved. What is less clear is whether future societies will accept hydrogen as elemental, vital and pervasive in their lives.

The Hindenburg Zeppelin disaster seems to have burned its way on to our collective consciousness, even though hydrogen was neither the cause of, nor did it exacerbate the Hindenburg accident. The Zeppelin's surface finish was a varnish of powdered aluminium, in a mixture that resembles modern solid rocket booster-fuel. It was this which ignited (probably from an electrostatic discharge) and which burned furiously. As hydrogen is so light, upon its release it took much of the heat and combustible materials upward and away from the passengers and crew, thus helping to minimise the death toll.

In its favour, hydrogen rises and dissipates very quickly, and in instances of accidental release it is generally not as dangerous as petrol. Acceptance of hydrogen will not arise spontaneously from the development of the technology; public consultation, education and involvement will be required to overcome resistance.

Transitional technologies

Of great concern is that, given hydrogen's inherent merits as an energy carrier, many energy providers are touting the use of nuclear electricity, or large-scale reformation of fossil fuels as paths to the production of hydrogen, and ignoring the renewable option.[5] If the limited use of cleaner hydrocarbons acts as a transitional path then it is to be guardedly welcomed.

Nevertheless, significant uptake of hydrogen may only be accomplished if the political will is founded in environmental concerns regarding greenhouse gas emissions and global warming. The large-scale transition to a hydrogen-based energy infrastructure will be costly, and will require no less important a motivation than the safeguarding of this planet for future generations.

Infrastructural investment

Another significant unknown is the amount of energy embodied in the machines and systems of a hydrogen infrastructure, in which we will need to invest if we are to realise its true potential. A solution to this would be to ensure that the increased levels of energy that may be usefully harvested by conversion of renewable sources to hydrogen would then be reinvested in hydrogen technologies.

Cities have already made a significant investment in energy supply infrastructure, and this is likely to retard their large-scale uptake of hydrogen. In energy terms, it is likely that the first truly sustainable soci-

With each transition to a new fuel, the quantity of CO_2 released per unit of energy generated becomes less. The natural extrapolation of this process is the complete elimination of the carbon atoms in the fuel, while retaining the only element we really wanted in the first place: hydrogen.

eties will be the inhabitants of islands and remote villages, many of them in the developing world. Energy supply to these areas comes at a premium and this facilitates an accelerated uptake of renewable energy technologies. The European Community has identified a hundred islands that will be supported in their efforts to become truly sustainable communities by 2010.[6] Already the issues of energy storage and the provision of sustainable transport have been identified as central to unlocking the potential of renewable-energy technologies. Hydrogen, created from excess renewable energy and powering transportation requirements, is seen as the most promising solution for the future. In a welcome and perhaps apposite reversal of the trends of the industrial revolution, cities will import energy technologies and techniques developed in more rural areas of the world.

Implementation

Cities will also benefit from social lessons being learned in rural areas regarding some of the wider implications of sustainability. The siting of wind turbines on land is always controversial, often meeting with significant local resistance. A successful approach that has been pioneered by the Danish inhabitants of Samsoe island is community ownership, where there is significant local consultation, education and, crucially, local investment in new wind turbines. When this approach has been taken, the results have been very positive indeed: not anger and resentment in the face of 'progress', but co-operation, a renewed sense of rural identity made tangible, and pride in the many layers of value evident in an investment that safeguards future generations. Through these turbines, the community on Samsoe has identified itself on the world stage as being singular, significant and successful.

We hope that the technical and social lessons learned in the above projects will serve to inform how cities of the future may produce, distribute and consume energy. Large conurbations may never be able to produce all of their power from renewable sources within their own boundaries, but they could contribute quite a significant fraction. The use of fuel cells will permeate right through society, and buildings will be no exception.

SOCIALLY INTEGRATED APPLICATIONS

The buildings of the future will play a central role in the production, storage and delivery of energy. Functionally, these buildings will be an optimal synthesis of traditional architectural principles, bringing with them all of the lessons of low-energy passive environmental design combined with the opportunities facilitated by fuel cells. Widespread use of building-integrated solar panels will produce significant quantities of hydrogen from sunlight. This hydrogen will be consumed in fuel cells to provide electricity, while the heat generated by this process will be used in the provision of space heating and hot water.

This highly decentralised and localised model of energy production and provision has the potential to deliver more to cities than clean streets. As already identified, the localisation of the production and use of energy will strengthen the link between the consumption of energy and the effort required in providing it. This can only help to increase respect for the environment and lend weight to arguments for energy rationalisation. Larger buildings, with the capacity to produce excess hydrogen, could then contribute to their local environment by distributing that energy to the community through district heating schemes and by supplying fuel-cell vehicles.

Following the example of the inhabitants of Samsoe, local communities would be offered the opportunity to invest in the solar arrays in their region. Buildings acting as a renewable, highly decentralised source of clean energy for clean cities would be provided with another mechanism to contribute to a sense of community – one that is self-sufficient in the main, with an enhanced level of local responsibility and interaction through community ownership. Like the city cathedrals of the past, by looking towards the heavens these buildings will draw to them the citizens they serve – not for spiritual replenishment, but for the sustainable fuel that will benignly power their lives.

THE CHALLENGE OF SUSTAINABILITY

No doubt many in the architectural profession will be concerned that such an energy-centric vision of the future will be overly prescriptive with regard to the functional requirements of building design. The realisation of a sustainable future comes at the price of a stronger and more urgent functional aesthetic, but this should not be interpreted as being more restrictive.

Like many of our colleagues in the engineering profession, we look to the future with excitement, for the requirements of sustainability present new challenges to our creativity and will require us to deliver not just incremental changes but whole new paradigms. If the ultimate goal of science is reduction and simplicity, then hydrogen and the fuel cell are surely the most articulate manifestation of the purpose of science that has yet been engineered into technology. Simple, silent, compact, benign, almost 100 per

If the ultimate goal of science is reduction and simplicity, then hydrogen and the fuel cell are surely the most articulate manifestation of the purpose of science that has yet been engineered into technology. Simple, silent, compact, benign, almost 100 per cent efficient, and with no moving parts, the use of this technology will release, not restrict, the design of buildings and urban spaces.

cent efficient, and with no moving parts, the use of this technology will release, not restrict, the design of buildings and urban spaces.

As with every revolution, some of us will choose to embrace change, while others will decide to maintain the status quo. Yet, where the status quo is inherently destructive, standing still is unacceptable. Many professionals in the building industry will find themselves either incapable or ill-prepared to meet the challenge of sustainability. Well, so be it. Someone has got to go up against the wall – after all, it's a revolution, right?

Notes

1. The World Health Report, *Conquering Suffering, Enriching Humanity* (Geneva: World Health Organization, 1997).
2. J. Larminie and A. Dicks, *Fuel Cell Systems Explained* (Chichester: John Wiley & Sons Ltd, 2000).
3. Jeffrey All, 'Automakers Race to Sell Cars Powered by Fuel Cells', *The Wall Street Journal*, 15 March 1998,
4. Allied Business Intelligence, *Automotive Fuel Cell Markets – the Future is Here*, Report code: AFC00, ABI, May 2000.
5. Cesare Marchetti, 'Nuclear plants and nuclear niches – on the generation of nuclear energy during the last twenty years', *Nuclear Science and Engineering*, No. 90, 1985, pp. 521–26.
6. International Scientific Council for Island Development, *Island 2010 – Towards 100% Renewable Energy Sources Supply for Island Sustainable Development* (Paris: INSULA, UNESCO, 2001).

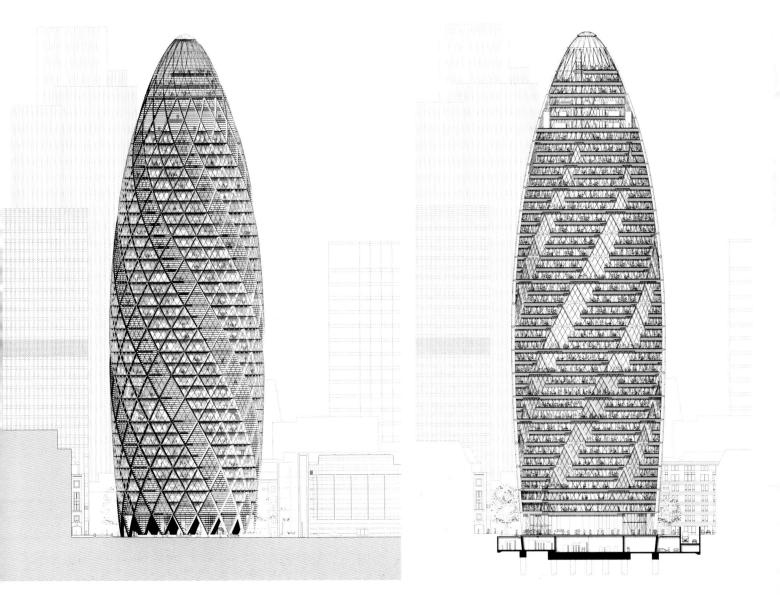

Swiss Re Headquarters, City of London, Foster and Partners
Bury Street elevation.
Cross section.

Chapter 15

Smalltowne

Sean Stanwick

A NOSTALGIC ARCHITECTURAL VERNACULAR

A curious phenomenon is sweeping the North American suburban landscape. With increasing frequency, the quintessential American small town, immortalised in the paintings of Norman Rockwell, is being dusted off and rising anew. At the heart of this nostalgic resurgence is a planning and architectural paradigm known as the new urbanism, or neo-traditional design.

By utilising the traditional small town as a model for suburban development the new urbanism is gaining widespread national and international popularity. Promoting a user-friendly neighbourhood the ultimate goal is a pedestrian-based, sustainable suburban community. This is achieved primarily through the restoration of traditional planning techniques and by adopting a nostalgic architectural vernacular reminiscent of pre-war America. As several examples are now sufficiently established, a pragmatic and theoretical review is thus possible.

This chapter examines the physical results, and reviews implications of using architecture to fabricate community. In seeking to match theory with reality, the philosophy and goals of the movement are summarised and possible sources of popularity are examined. Conclusions reached indicate that the new urbanism does not produce the authentic town its proponents claim. While the mandate of the movement draws on legitimate urban-planning strategies, this chapter further suggests that the new urbanism is simply a by-product of North America's propensity for theming and entertainment.

AN EDENIC RENAISSANCE

Repetitive and dictated largely by the wants of the motor car, the cottage in the country has been replaced by an unsustainable field of garages and banal uniformity.

A recent census revealed that nearly 50 per cent of North Americans now live outside of the metropolitan areas in what is traditionally known as the suburbs.[1] Originally promoted as a pastoral garden community, the suburbs were symbolic of the search for the mythical Garden of Eden. The new Eden, however, would take a form that was slightly more in line with the twentieth century and would satisfy few of the original promises. Repetitive and dictated largely by the wants of the motor car, the cottage in the country has been replaced by an unsustainable field of garages and banal uniformity.

Essential to the making of a great city is the provision of a network of liveable, useable spaces that foster meaningful exchange – a framework clearly absent in current suburban planning efforts. Founded on the desire to effect positive change in the built environment the new urbanism is looking for answers in the lessons of the past. By restoring traditional planning principles and historic architectural designs, it has risen from an isolated urban anomaly to a mainstream architectural and social paradigm in just a few short years, and with good reason. As outlined in the *Charter of the New Urbanism*, the movement proposes measurable alternatives, including:

- the restoration of the compact neighbourhood form;
- a reduction of motor car dependency while increasing pedestrian activity; and
- the promotion of a more sustainable pattern of growth.[2]

Ultimately these efforts combine to forge the social keystone of the movement, the restoration of a sense of community in a context devoid of humanism. A passage from the charter reads:

> We stand for the restoration of existing urban centres and towns within coherent metropolitan regions, the reconfiguration of sprawling suburbs into communities of real neighbourhoods and diverse districts, the conservation of natural environments, and the preservation of our built legacy.[3]

The vehicle for implementing this restoration is the traditional neighbourhood development model, or TND. Modelled after the traditional American small town, the basic premise of the TND is both simplistic and logical. By persuading builders to abandon typical suburban patterns in favour of compact sustainable neighbourhoods it is hoped that the framework will provide a network of quality public spaces. Here a healthy mix of residential and commercial types is promoted, density is increased, narrow tree-lined streets and rear lanes replace wide arterial roads, and a restored town-centre within a five-minute walk will act as a catalyst for social and economic activity. The goal of course is to provide an environment where diversity prevails over uniformity, character over banality, and ultimately sustainability over sprawl.

For the new urbanists, the original small town represents the historical pinnacle of social and planning practices. As the apparent manifestation of 'the good life', the small town symbolises a sustainable method of planning characterised by limited size, increased density, pedestrian access and a distinct sense of place. Socially it is an embodiment of the human graces that suburbia has squelched, being social interaction at a variety of locations and levels within the town framework. With these credentials, using the nineteenth-century small town in the modern context seems a logical alternative.

Urban design issues aside, the new urbanism is best known for restoring an architectural vernacular largely ignored since the 1930s. While it does not adhere to any specific architectural style, its developments thus far indicate a wide-sweeping preference for the classical vernacular. Mandated by a strict set of design codes and standards, developers have skilfully reproduced a colourful mix of Colonial revival to Georgian town homes and Victorian mansions. Add rows of shady porches, white picket fencing and the romance of a stroll by a babbling brook, and the pre-war small town is complete. Refusing to accept the soul-deadening banality of typical suburban architecture, it is hoped the reintroduction of historical architectural vernacular will breathe life into a relatively young, yet dying body.

Promoting itself as an embodiment of the fundamental traditions of community, family and town, the results of the new urbanism are hard to dislike. Numbed by the effects of life behind the windshield, it is as much a state of mind – a psychological paradigm – as it is about planning or architectural expression. The new urbanism is a place where human scale replaces industrial proportions, and where proximity to work, shopping and homes replaces motor car dependency. It is a place where community presides over placelessness and where homes replace houses.

Many new urbanist communities now dot the North American landscape, and popular examples include Kentlands in Maryland, Seaside in Florida, and Celebration in Florida, widely considered the flagship of the movement. Canadian examples include McKenzie Towne in Calgary, and Cornell in Toronto. The most notable European counterpart to the new urbanism is Poundbury in Dorchester, England.

Cornell Community, Markham, Ontario.

URBAN MISFITS

As support for the new urbanist small town grows, and numerous examples are now up and running, the results raise dangerous practical and theoretical concerns. Conclusions indicate that the model does not support the physical claims made by its proponents and in fact falls short of its primary social objectives.

While the new urbanism actively promotes its communities as fully operational, authentic towns, at issue is the legitimacy of the town itself. Historically, towns developed as a locus of commercial activities around shared values, geographic location or employment. The new urbanist town indiscriminately dispenses with many of these essential forces and retains only superficial geographic and social relationships. At McKenzie Towne it appears the only determinant for location was the availability of land and direct access to a major thoroughfare. Conveniently ignoring physical location, social or economic factors as development considerations, the town lacks a bona fide sense of urban purpose.

Further, in generically reconstructing a new town entirely from scratch, the new urbanism either fails to address or has conveniently chosen to ignore many basic principles of rural and urban growth. Rather than evolving slowly and incrementally, the town rises to fully functioning status in a matter of a year or two. A residential sales brochure proudly boasts that at Cornell 'they are making history...It's surprising how long it has been since anyone thought of creating an old fashioned town'.[4] Here, history is relevant only insofar as it can be used to generate an appealing lineage; when tradition is non-existent, it is fabricated, when community is required, it is scripted. With no historical path we can surmise that there was no legitimate 'there' from which the town came. Without a clear point of origin, its validity as a town becomes highly suspect.

Nevertheless, the new urbanists hold fast to the notion that people, if given the choice, would still prefer to live in a traditional community. Heidi Landecker writes that Americans 'like the iconography of porches and picket fences because it signals...a return to an era when everything was certain and the same.'[5] A recent Gallup poll supports this notion. When Americans were asked where they would like to live, 34 per cent chose a small town, as compared with 24 per cent who chose a suburb, 22 per cent a farm and 19 per cent a city.[6]

It is in these statistics that the new urbanism finds justification for the recreation of a nineteenth-century small town in the twentieth century. By imposing a physical infrastructure on the landscape, it seeks to change the patterns of suburban social behaviour. Heidi Landecker optimistically suggests that 'if you give Americans a traditional neighbourhood to live in...they will behave like neighbours...give home owners front porches, and they will eschew the television, the air conditioning and the Internet and talk to each other'.[7] This notion is potentially flawed, as community cannot simply be fabricated into existence. Simply, porches and back alleys do not make a community. To plan and design communities around a predetermined framework belies their true nature. Advocating social engineering through built form, the 'community' that the new urbanism promotes, is for the most part

Kentlands, Gaithersburg, Maryland.
Cornell Community, Markham, Ontario.

little more than a developer's construct and a marketer's sales strategy designed to sell houses in a field as homes in a community.

In marketing the notion of community, the new urbanism also creates the expectation of a specific lifestyle. Residents are flocking to these towns, their heads replete with notions of community, a restoration of family values and increased neighbourly interaction. The inherent problem is that the values and attitudes of post-modern society are not commensurate with those of the time when the traditional small town flourished. Acting only as signs symbolising community, neighbourhood and a value standard, the new urbanism only signifies a certain lifestyle – it does not embody it. In his latest work *The Celebration Chronicles*,[8] Andrew Ross tracks his year-in-the-life of Celebration. His socially centred review casts an interesting light as he exposes a community ripe with class friction, threats to property values, and generally fading visions of a utopian lifestyle. What is ironic is that for all its attempts at verisimilitude the community he found unified itself not by way of the small town model, but by its shortcomings.

Still, we willingly subscribe to the notion that the new urbanist framework can foster community interaction, regardless of the fact that demographics and social attitudes are entirely different. We are reminded of Alberti's poignant dictum 'the house is a small town, the town is a large house'.[9] Nostalgia for the simple life makes the recreated town acceptable, as consumers are ready and willing to buy into the idea. Residents of these towns quoted in a marketing brochure claim that first they bought the small-town concept, and then they bought the home.[10] Nowhere is this more obvious than in the architecture. Enhancing the curb appeal of Smalltowne is a vernacular ripe with American pride. The traditional detailing not only perpetuates nostalgia for the traditional small town, but it is largely responsible for its overall allure. In the vast suburban landscape of garages and sterilised landscaping, it is safe to assume that the decorated porches and gables will be the preferred aesthetic of potential residential buyers.

At issue, however, is that the porches, gables and overt Colonialism only pretend to be authentic versions of the traditional home. In most cases, to meet the nostalgic needs of the consumer the developers need only apply the 'authentic detailing' to the street side of the house; a visit to the rear alley reveals typical construction techniques, vinyl eaves and plastic pickets. Further, when the veneer of extruded-foam detailing bears little relation to geographic context, historical era or construction techniques the aesthetic remains a mere image of the original referent. In much the same way as a soundtrack enhances a movie, the façade serves only to graphically support the small-town theme. While the use of decoration in residential design is certainly not a new phenomenon, what separates the new urbanism is that it represents a strategic attempt at thematic coherence. Remove the nostalgic façade and you remove the theme of the small town; remove the theme and the new urbanism simply becomes another suburban development.

Witold Rybczynski writes: 'historical revivals...faithfully imitate the appearance of a particular style. They were based on scholarly study of the past and usually reflected an admiration not only for the furnishings, but for the mores of the period'.[11] However, research indicates that residents are not interested in the finer points of the period being revived by the new urbanism. A case in point is the floor patterns of the houses. The literal translation of exterior form to interior plan produces houses that simply don't sell. Residents are nostalgic only for houses that *look* like a Colonial style house, not ones that *function* like one.[12] The fundamental homogeneity among the house plans is cloaked in simulated diversity, because residents desire picture-perfect homes that incorporate the 'traditional style' with all the conveniences of modern living:

The fact that people will be out strolling on the street is wonderful. And since we drive all day,
it's great to know you don't have to drive to the store when you get home![13]

Holding fast to the notion that its model can reduce motor car dependency, the new urbanist solution is simply to redesign cities to reduce the need to drive. The premise is that you should not have to drive a kilometre to buy a litre of milk. However, to believe that a fabricated town-centre within walking distance will alter mobility patterns is a wide sweeping assumption. In a Buyers Preference Survey on new urbanist communities, John Schleimer concluded that there is a 'lack of a discernible impact on resident's behaviour patterns as there exists little external incentive to change'.[14] He notes that 95 per cent of residents occasionally or always commute, 91 per cent by private motor car, and that there is significantly lower transit usage than non-new urbanist towns. As these statistics indicate, the notion that if given the opportunity people would prefer to walk rather than drive is simply not true.

If one should choose to walk to the centre, there is however little to be found. Less function and more fiction, the centre is largely a token urban element, a pre-programmed space that only imitates the real thing. At McKenzie Towne, the potential for external life is limited, as the entire square is framed not by cafés and retail amenities, but by Georgian town homes and a token one-stop-shop. These mute edges serve not to enliven the space but act only as ornamental framing devices.[15] Tour Kentlands, and one will

Cornell Community, Markham, Ontario.

find the commercial centre is nothing more than a strip mall situated on the outer edges of the town, decorated with nostalgic add-ons.

Hardly the urban panacea as promised, we are left with sugar-coated versions of suburbia, no more sustainable than the typical sprawl found immediately across the street. Unfortunately, after the superficial façade and the revivalist rhetoric are peeled away, the new urbanism is perhaps nothing more than colourful icing on a poorly baked modernist cake. Unless the larger patterns of daily mobility are altered, and the internal economic questions addressed, the new urbanist town will forever remain a turnkey operation, fully equipped with happy streets, friendly architecture and a polished aesthetic. One wonders when creative-minded developers will realise that they could probably sell the franchise rights for the town to the town.

THE CITY THAT IS A SHOW

The architectural results of the new urbanism, while hard to dislike visually, are a contradiction in terms. 'Neo-traditionalism' is an oxymoron. Apparent victims of 'topophilia', the love of place, we either miss the point, or simply do not care that these places are not authentic towns.[16] However, when it is considered that the prevailing currents of urban design are undergoing a significant paradigmatic shift, the new urbanism seems very much at home.

North American urbanism is having a mid-life crisis and the results would likely give Walt Disney an orgasm. In *Amusing Ourselves to Death*, Neil Postman writes that (North) Americans are perhaps the best entertained culture in the world.[17] It seems we have taken these words to heart. Co-opted by the cult of entertainment, virtually every object, place or event is now subject to redefinition as a themed rendition of something or somewhere else. In much the same way as a cigarette is a device designed to deliver nicotine, architecture is now simply another means of delivering entertainment.

Offering an exciting mix of physical space with entertainment imagery, the themed spectacle is rapidly becoming the accepted measure of reality and the benchmark for appropriate urban architecture. Even Venturi's once-seminal 'decorated shed',[18] born of the Las Vegas spectacular, is now rendered passé. Shopping mall corridors are being replaced with yellow brick roads; at the newly renovated Motel-6, the honeymoon suite is converted to La Parisian suite d'amour; and it is not uncommon to see a giant illuminated UFO doubling as the local movie house. Clearly the propensity for theming has become a cultural obsession, as only in the themed environment would a public library curiously mimic the Coliseum, the Sphinx reappear as a casino, and a suburban housing development imitate a small town.

Vancouver Public Library, Vancouver, British Columbia.

Colossus Theatre, Toronto, Canada.

At Kentlands the entire process of house shopping is delightfully entertaining. Prospective buyers are treated to a free audio driving tour. Narrated by a future 'neighbour', you experience the town's rich history and tradition entirely from the comfort of your car. However, it should be remembered that this is a town designed to be experienced on foot. Just like the movies, you consume what you want, when you want it, being able to put the experience on pause when required. If history can be made, it can certainly be paused. When you leave for work you are in effect changing channels. When you return you can pick up the programme exactly where you left off. If the existence of an ersatz history and tradition is the cassette tape, then new urbanism is the VCR, pausing the experience until you are ready to press play. Illustrating the uneasy links with the entertainment genre we are compelled to ask, will the ride stop when the last house is sold?

North Americans are willing accessories to a great hoax, played out by themselves, on themselves. Daniel Boorstin hit his mark when he wrote: 'we risk being the first people in history to have been able to make their illusions so vivid, so persuasive, so realistic, that we can live in them'.[19] Intentional or not, the new urbanists have transformed suburban living into a theatrical event, a continuous performance piece, scripted from beginning to end. There is a fully decorated set, a producer, extras – played by visitors from other towns – a script and plenty of investors. Of course, the episode of history the new urbanism produces gets a 'G' rating for 12-year olds.

The Jim Carrey picture *The Truman Show* could not illustrate this situation more poignantly. Shot in a popular new urbanist community, Seaside Florida, the film finds a young man discovering that his idealised life in the bucolic small town has been the subject of a popular and long-running televised performance. In addition, the town itself is nothing more than a collection of stage sets populated by a community of actors. In the spirit of the writings of Baudrillard, this clearly illustrates the power of the entertainment media to reduce legitimate experience, space and place to those associated with the theme park spectacle.[20]

If, as Ada Louise Huxtable suggests, the use of an entertaining narrative is an integral component in the creation of the themed environment,[21] by what means has the small-town story entered our collective consciousness?

One need only take a cursory glance at the prevalent American culture to see the roots of the small-town mindset. Awash in homespun sentimentality and nostalgic nomenclature, it permeates every aspect of society. Martha Stewart has turned the simple lifestyle into a billion-dollar empire. Norman Rockwell immortalised it through his paintings of the simple life. Forrest Gump has become a national hero, a fictional spokesman promoting the American Dream. Electing Ronald Reagan, not just any movie actor, but a champion of the western frontier to the office of President clearly indicates the nation's willingness to believe that old movie heroes can indeed be real-life heroes. Even the small town itself has been dusted clean and given the exalted position of a suburban panacea.

America holds fast to its memories and the original picturesque town is as much a part of the American collective consciousness as apple pie and the 'Star Spangled Banner'. Maintaining a longstanding 'anti-city' disposition, the image of independent rural living has sustained a prominent position in our cultural memory. Sociologist Thorstein Veblen wrote: 'country towns had a greater part than any other American institution in shaping public sentiment and giving character to American culture'.[22] Its roots are lodged firmly in the American Dream, and can be traced as far back as Thomas Jefferson, who when promoting the pastoral aesthetic suggested 'piling ourselves up into high-density cities is not only unhealthy, but essentially un-American'.[23] In fact, the notion of the American Dream, the classical vernacular and the small town are, in the American mindset, one and the same. The new urbanists were wise to restore the traditional vernacular, as this critical association justifies its use in the modern context, and more importantly is imperative for the believability of the overall theme.

While the modern context may be virtually devoid of the pleasing country town, its *myth* persists stronger than ever. From the Bible we learn that the paradise of the Garden of Eden represented all that was pleasing, a state of bliss existed between man and beast, and that God would fulfil all the needs of its inhabitants. In *The Longing for Paradise*, Mario Jacoby suggests that nostalgia is based primarily on the notion of separation, where 'the yearning begins after the loss of Paradise'.[24] If we apply Jacoby's definition, a search for paradise-lost has taken us directly into the outstretched porch-fronts of the new urbanism, only now paradise-found is the new urbanism, with the buyers acting as a collective Adam and Eve.

A major promulgator of small-town myth as paradise-found is the film and television industry. Hollywood movies and television re-runs bombard us with references to a bucolic past. The images these films promote go directly to the heart of America's consciousness and secure the new urbanism squarely in the company of the small-town theme. In the minds of many Americans, movie and television dramas are a clear representation of what America really is. It's no surprise then that the mythical small town is raised to hero status as an entire *genre* is dedicated to it. In the Frank Capra films of the 1930s and 1940s we are shown that the small town is the best place to be. Classics such as *It's a Wonderful Life* immortalise a town taken straight out of the works of Norman Rockwell, and promote a safe, conflict-free existence where homespun values prevail.

Without question, however, Disneyland is the apogee of the nostalgic spectacle. The levels of simulation to support the themed entertainment mandate are staggering. Yet, the implications of such a perfected illusion on the built environment are enormous. As the process of Disneyfication spills out past the gates, the surrounding context is beginning to look curiously less like itself and more like the park that imitates it. In a somewhat expected merging between Disney and the new urbanism, the latest progeny is a discomforting extension of Main Street, USA, situated coincidentally just outside the Disney gates. Aptly named Celebration, the resemblance to its theme park parent is unmistakable. If Main Street, USA is seen as a perfected facsimile of the ideal town in which to live, Celebration, then, is believed to be the physical realisation of that facsimile.

In an episode of *Star Trek – The Next Generation*, a computer-generated, holographic image of Professor Moriarty leaves the holodeck to join the other crewmembers. The only reason for his ability to exist in the real world was that he believed he could. In a similarly bold effort, Main Street, USA has left the park grounds unnoticed and developed into a fully functioning holographic-like image of a town. The only reason for its success is that we believe it can succeed.

Perhaps this is precisely the context in which the new urbanism can thrive. While it may not be an authentic town by the pragmatic definition, it is very much in keeping with the context in which it resides. Ours is a visual society where 'what we see is what we get' and we like what the new urbanism shows us – the sleepy small-town theme. Replete with an inherent Americanism, it is perceived as the tangible realisation of nostalgic images already made popular through the entertainment media and theme park experience. In *Brave New World*, Aldous Huxley feared a society that was numbed by the effects of that which they loved.[25] In North America it is precisely what we love – the entertainment spectacle – which threatens us.

In the world of the simulated, monuments to fiction, whose only desire is to entertain and recreate the mood of an imagined past, become reality. As our incessant desire to be perpetually entertained increases, it would come as no surprise if someday there would be an *Edge City Theme Park*[26] – a scaled-down version of sprawling suburbia fully equipped with cul-de-sacs, animatronic neighbours, and simulated auto-mobiles to take you on the ride of your life because this time the pedestrian is *not* welcome.

HOW FAR ARE YOU WILLING TO GO?

Inherent to the themed environment is the potential for the framework to determine our behaviour. This is precisely what the new urbanists have in mind as it is hoped that the framework will affect our normal patterns. For the model to be successful and maintain its (perceived) authenticity, we must become the modern *flaneur*, or sit on the porch and wave as other neighbours walk by. When buying into a new urbanist town you are buying into the concept of small-town life, but are also potentially subscribing to the social expectations as well. Yet, if we voluntarily adhere to the behaviour patterns implied by the framework, are we not potentially pretending to be something we are not? While this chapter does not offer answers, and is cognisant of the fact that these issues warrant further research, it nevertheless poses the following situations:

- If you choose not to participate in the small-town ideology, will you be considered a social outcast?
- If you do choose to play along simply because it is fun to participate in the act of waving, are you then just playing the role of the happy communitarian?
- If no one waves, is the town a failure?

The new urbanism promotes and sells a controlled environment that dictates a mediated experience, and as such has the potential to determine our daily patterns. In much the same way as a trip to the mall activates our *consumer* selves,[27] it is hoped that the small-town framework will activate our *community* selves. However, social engineering cannot be achieved through land planning alone. Nevertheless, will we self-actualise ourselves simply because the mechanism is present, or will we do it because it is fun to play along? It is in fact a combination of both.

Acting in the roles of our lives and taking direction from the new urbanists, we willingly accept by what means, and under what circumstances we will live. Oscar Newman writes that the new urbanists are 'creationists, who, with one grand gesture that fashions perfect beautiful places, believe they are god'.[28] The model implies that joining the community is as easy as moving in, and for this the new urbanism makes sense. Flush with utopian promises, it is a fresh start in a nation gone wrong. We like the playful imagery, that Muzac is piped into the streets, and that the sidewalks are vacuum-cleaned each morning. Even if mandated by a strict set of design codes and overseen by a pseudo-Orwellian town council, we voluntarily embrace that which the model can provide: the closest thing to an authentic community our generation will ever see. Even knowing that deviations from the established codes of neighbourly behaviour might well result in banishment from paradise, we nevertheless accept this as the price to pay for inclusion in our own Edenic renaissance.

Michael Sorkin, author of the appropriately titled collection of urban essays *Variations on a Theme Park*, writes that the new urbanism has sinister underpinnings. Its generic existence presents a cheerful version of reality geared towards entertainment by 'stripping urbanity of its sting, of the presence of the poor, of crime, of dirt, of work'.[29] Underlying the overtly polished visuals, an uneasy sense prevails. What is not right is that everything is too right.

Conspicuously missing is the unpainted stoop, the sagging porch, or Otis the town drunk, the friendly down-and-outer, for his authenticity would taint the simulated bucolic scenery. While it is these elements of conflict that allow a community to grow and develop its authentic character, it is these very same incidents that will shatter the perfect image. Unfortunately, the new urbanism can never take credit for its advances in verisimilitude for fear of unmasking its perceived authenticity. The success of the movement depends on its ability to deliver an authentic and pleasing small-town experience.

It is important to note that not all developments subscribe to this generic approach to town building. Poundbury in Dorchester, England, is a notable example, and does support a legitimate *raison d'être*. With the presence of a significant industrial base, key connections to neighbouring towns and a local economy, all of which are of its cultural and geographical context, Poundbury approaches a state of sustainable existence. Unfortunately it too utilises a caricature-like vernacular, and relies on verisimilitude to help establish the behavioural patterns of its residents. The inherent problem is that regardless of its contextual associations, it runs the risk of reducing a legitimate planning vehicle to a stage-set, an imitation consisting of a sham of decorative do-dads hung on the facade like a theatrical scrim.

Like it or not, the new urbanism will undoubtedly have a profound impact on the appearance and perception of our built environment. Cognisant of the significant planning efforts required to bring this model to fruition, architects, planners and consumers alike must support a duty of care in understanding what it *is* and, more importantly, what it is *not* if the built environment is to be preserved as a healthy and sustainable entity. The familiar maxim 'if it looks like a shoe, it must be a shoe' has significant bearing on this

When buying into a new urbanist town you are buying into the concept of small-town life, but are also potentially subscribing to the social expectations as well.

In the landscape of simulation, it seems that we are more than willing to play the game. Walt must be laughing in his grave.

discussion, for in the case of the new urbanism, if it looks like a town, it must be a town. However, looks can be deceiving, as the only difference between the new urbanism and a typical suburban development is the level of verisimilitude. While it may indeed offer a better visual alternative to the current suburban situation, the new urbanist small-town exists largely as a generic copy of only the positive elements of the stereotypical town. Playing a hand stacked with simulated cards, the new urbanism has bluffed us out of the money. In the landscape of simulation, it seems that we are more than willing to play the game. Walt must be laughing in his grave.

Notes

1. K. Jackson, 'The suburban house', in L. Taylor (ed.), *Housing – Symbol, Structure, Site* (New York: Viking, 1995), p. 72.
2. 'Charter of the New Urbanism', *Third Congress for the New Urbanism*, San Francisco, 1997.
3. 'Charter of the New Urbanism', *Third Congress for the New Urbanism*, San Francisco, 1997.
4. Promotional material, Cornell, Law Developments, Markham, 1998.
5. H. Landecker, 'Is new urbanism good for America', *Architecture*, New York, April 1996, p. 70.
6. P. Langdon, *A Better Place to Live – Reshaping the American Suburb* (Amherst: The University of Massachusetts Press, 1994), p. 119.
7. H. Landecker, 'Is new urbanism good for America', *Architecture*, New York, April 1996, p. 68.
8. A. Ross, *The Celebration Chronicles – Life Liberty and Pursuit of Property Values in Disney's New Town* (New York: Ballantine Books, 2000).
9. L. Lerup, *After the City* (Cambridge, Mass.: MIT Press, 2000).
10. Residential sales advertisement, *The Toronto Star*, Toronto, November 1997, p. K15.
11. W. Rybczynski, *Home – A Short History of an Idea* (New York: Viking, 1984), p. 175.
12. L. Dearstyne-Fowlow, *Nostalgia as Marketing Tool* (Calgary: Faculty of Environmental Design, University of Calgary, 1997).
13. Residential sales advertisement, *The Toronto Star*, Toronto, November 1997, p. K15.
14. J. Schleimer, *Neo-Traditional Buyers Preference Survey*, based on Sample Survey of owners in Kentlands, Harbourtown, Seaside and Laguna West (Sacramento: Market Perspectives, 1996).
15. L. Dearstyne-Fowlow, *Nostalgia as Marketing Tool* (Calgary: Faculty of Environmental Design, University of Calgary, 1997).
16. L. Lerup, *After the City* (Cambridge, Mass.: MIT Press, 2000), p. 78.
17. N. Postman, *Amusing Ourselves to Death – Public Discourse in the Age of Show Business* (New York: Alfred A. Knopf, 1984), p. 106.
18. R. Venturi, *Learning from Las Vegas – The Forgotten Symbols of Architectural Form* (Cambridge, Mass.: MIT Press, 1972).
19. D. Boorstin, *The Image – A Guide to Pseudo Events in America* (New York: Vintage Books, 1992), p. 240.
20. R. Barton, *Jim Carrey Goes to Seaside – Constructing Reality,* 86th ACSA Annual Meeting and Technology Conference, Portland, 1998, pp. 605–9.
21. A. Huxtable, *The Unreal America – Architecture and Illusion* (New York: The New Press, 1998).
22. R. Louv (ed.), *America II* (Los Angeles: Jeremy P. Tarcher Inc., 1983), p. 135.
23. Ibid., p. 38.
24. M. Jacoby, *The Longing For Paradise* (Boston: Sigo Press, 1980), p. 9.
25. A. Huxley, *Brave New World* (New York: Harper and Row, 1932).
26. Adapted from J. Garreau, *Edge City – Life on the New Frontier* (New York: Doubleday, 1991).
27. M. Gottdiener, *The Theming of America – Dreams Visions and Commercial Spaces* (Boulder, CO: Westview Press, 1997), p. 7.
28. O. Newman, quoted in H. Landecker, 'Is new urbanism good for America', *Architecture*, New York, April 1996, p. 70.
29. M. Sorkin (ed.), *Variations on a Theme Park – the New American City and the End of Public Space* (New York: Hill and Wang, 1992), p. xv.

OPPOSITE:

Lost Exchange, Liverpool and Birkenhead

Plan showing detached routes connecting to the urban.

Lost Exchange model.

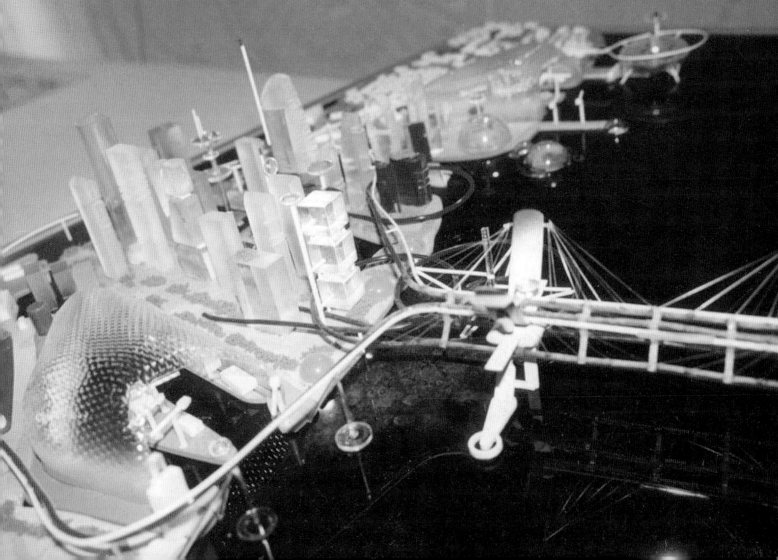

LOST EXCHANGE

Liverpool and Birkenhead 2000
Jonathan Schwinge

Baggy City
At present Liverpool is known as the 'Baggy City', with a current population of approximately 460,000, but with a total possible capacity for 2 million people. The area has received an 'Objective 1' status from the European Union (EU) and been granted £1 billion of regeneration renewal funding. Liverpool is the poorest city in Europe.

The brief is the introduction of a bridge from Liverpool leading to a new development on the redundant industrial site on the 'Landing' Birkenhead side. The proposal is to stimulate new economic growth in a declining area desperately needing attention by introducing the idea that a bridge is an 'icon-economy-reactivator' – a symbol of old, present and new Liverpool, driven by a new confidence of social and technical reinvention. The essence of the project is one of 'hope and optimism', looking forward in time with an understanding of the past – an element of inhabited infrastructure.

There are three programmatic bridge hangers representing past, present and future Liverpool as an economic sequence leading into a new cityscape at Birkenhead; a representation of design-led technological innovation and an eagerness to regain lost industrial markets – or 'lost-exchange'. This strategy is bold and is based on the manufacturing principle 'innovate or die'. The prime objective is to build a 'job accelerator', not in the new superficial service sector of employment, which has replaced industrial activity, but to regain lost industrial markets and secure new markets of technological exchange.

Beginning of the end
During the 1980s the Liverpool area, like most 'Northern towns', was politically engaged in the conflict between Margaret Thatcher and the unionised reluctance to change industrial working conditions. An ideological battle was fought between competing interests; those arguing for the preservation of working conditions and those arguing against 'restrictive practices'. This 'beginning of the end' to industrial output resulted in Margaret Thatcher signing a ten-year agreement with the EU for England not to construct ships; £45 million was given to 'flatten' shipyard sites, therefore crushing the strong rebellious unions. This subsequently eradicated people's livelihoods and ended the most modern shipyards in the world based on 600 years of highly skilled shipbuilding and engineering labour.

At that time, Japan and Korea 'reverse engineered' all that English shipbuilding had to offer, taking the valuable know-how, production plant methods and advanced machinery overseas. Today, Japan and Korea are the world leaders in ship manufacturing, utilising greenfield sites based on automotive 'assembly-line' production methods. Shipping demand is now higher than ever with increasing populations and 'Super Liners' being designed, combined with increased ocean-going freight markets. Shipyards abroad are government supported with new and prospering yards in Finland, Germany, France, Spain, Holland and Italy. Yet in England, London's financial square mile and the government have ignored support for traditional productive industries like shipbuilding and engineering. This has ruined cities and towns across northern Britain.

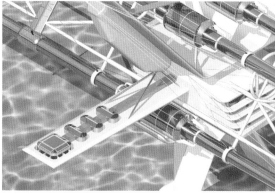

ABOVE: View from 'public attractor'.

FAR LEFT: Aerial street.

LEFT: Bridge 'plugs' into urban fabric on a series of detached routes.

ABOVE: Three programmatic Bridge
Hangers and detached 'routes', Past,
Present and Future.

RIGHT: Concept model of bridge hanger.

OPPOSITE: Models of bridge hanger and
x-wing.

Key market features

- 98 per cent of world trade is carried by sea, representing a major market.
- Presently Japan holds 80 per cent of the shipbuilding market.
- New opportunities in smart cargo vessel design for corporate identity.
- Demand for Super Liners with new destinations that include the Antarctic and Alaska.
- Leaders in naval architecture are Italy, and Finland's Kvaerner Masa yards.
- 1998 electricity generation capacity in the US was 779,000 MW, and in the UK 70,000 MW, while the power demand on the worlds' seas was about 800,000 MW. The market for ocean-going fuel-cell motive power technologies is commercially the equivalent of that for static fuel cells in the US.

Lost exchange into new exchange

The project proposal was to include Camel Laird Shipbuilders, which would receive the commission to construct the bridge as the first major step to economic recovery in pursuit of these new markets. Once complete the infrastructure will be inhabited as public space, and will contain activities demanded by the working people of Liverpool. These will be engineering workers' social clubs, chapels, information technology economy-pods, public-attractors as a 135-metre-high viewing platform, a job centre, comedy clubs, bars, port authorities, energy utilities or super bingo. The function follows the new and old aspirations of the area as an economic catalyst: a form of 'oceanic-urbanism' rich in the cultural activity of a productive city, attracting more people to new employment.

The bridge becomes 'destination to sub-destination to destination', plugging into the urban environment via a series of routes. This becomes a network or matrix of interconnecting nodes by foot, cycle, monorail or car, entering a new programmatic cityscape at Birkenhead. Knowledge, research, training, marketing and productive output is integrated as a technological mixed-use environment of old and new industries. 'Innovate or die' is paramount to the success of such a proposal, and programming the cityscape would be crucial to the economic turn-around. This would encourage confident investment in radical design studios, research and development, bio-technology and engineering, material science, nano-tech-

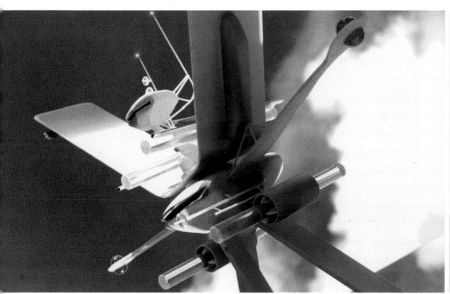

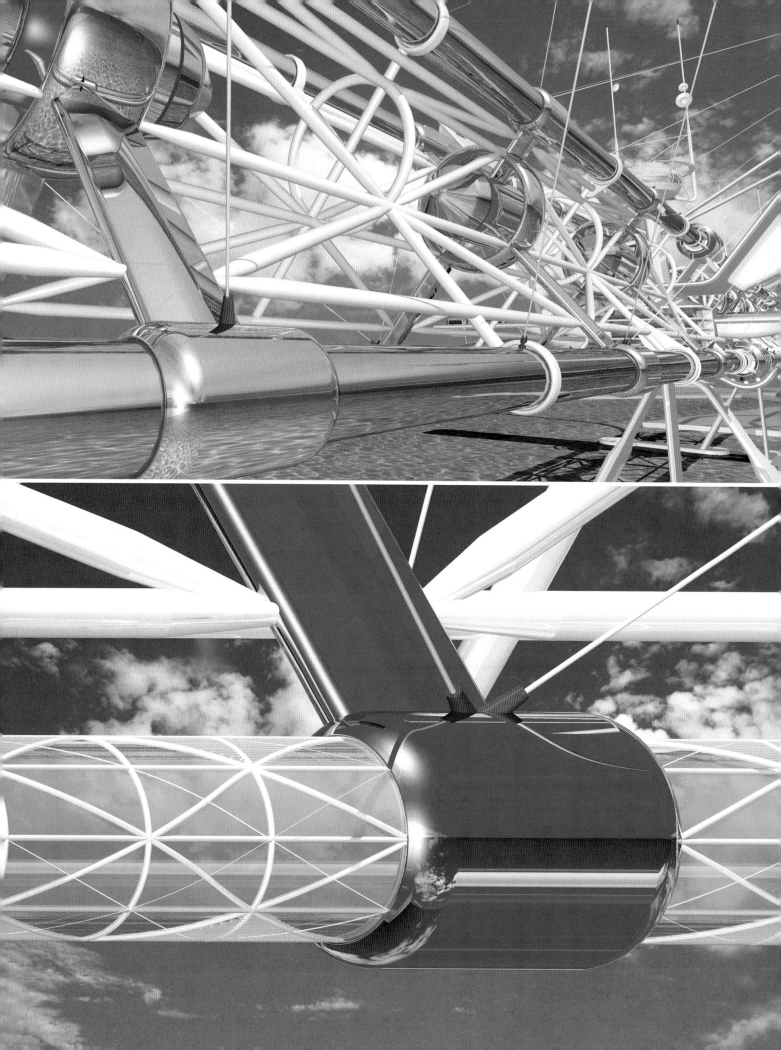

nology (the multibillion-pound industry anticipated by the DTI Future Unit), mechanical engineering, a naval university, enclosed all-weather shipyards, robotics, electronics, market research, oceanic study, computer programming, ecology, personnel and accountancy. The project takes a long-term and powerful view of the social, cultural, technical and economic regeneration of Liverpool and Birkenhead.

Key bridge features

- 200-metre-high bridge hangers giving 65 metres of shipping clearance.
- 135-metre-high public-viewing attractors.
- Bridge span of approximately a mile.
- Cable stay structure for economical construction.
- Four steel lattice tunnel urban connections.
- River Mersey has a tidal range of 10 metres, making tidal power generators integrated into the x-wing structural frame a possibility.

Thanks
Liverpool Architecture and Design
Liverpool Vision
Liverpool Planning Department
Wallasey Regeneration
Hamilton Quarter
Architectural Association 'Open-Jury' critique panel - Feb 2000.
Department of Trade and Industry
The Metropolitan Borough of Wirral Council Planning and Economic Development Department
The Royal Institution of Naval Architects, London
Patrick Turnbull, of Turnbull Shipbuilding Engineering, Sunderland.

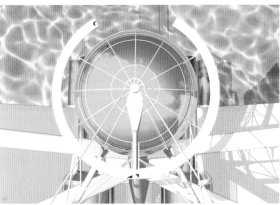

OPPOSITE TOP TO BOTTOM:

A collective community of shared objectives, the new pod economy of the individual.

Detail of transportational node with preferredexpressed steel lattice tunnel and photochromatic 'windshielding'.

ABOVE TOP TO BOTTOM:

Node with steel lattice tunnel.

Bridge hanger plan.

Public Attractor plan.

LEFT: Internal view of steel lattice structure.

IF ONLY HOUSES WERE DESIGNED AND MADE TO THIS STANDARD

Nic Bailey Design

Proposal for a 36m Catamaran.

A new 17.5-metre-long cata-maran design for a paraplegic client who requires access to all areas. This means a level deck area with two external lifts to enable him to embark/disembark from either hull, and two internal lifts to enable him to access the accommodation in each hull. In addition, all the sail controls are fully automated using hydraulic systems, so that he can sail the boat single-handed if necessary. The hulls and superstructure are entirely built of carbon fibre, as is the mast, and advanced aramid fibres will be used for the rigging, instead of traditional stainless, to save weight wherever possible. For the power required to drive the hydraulic systems the boat will utilise solar panels, as well as a near-silent diesel-powered Stirling (external combustion) engine that provides heat as well as constant DC power.

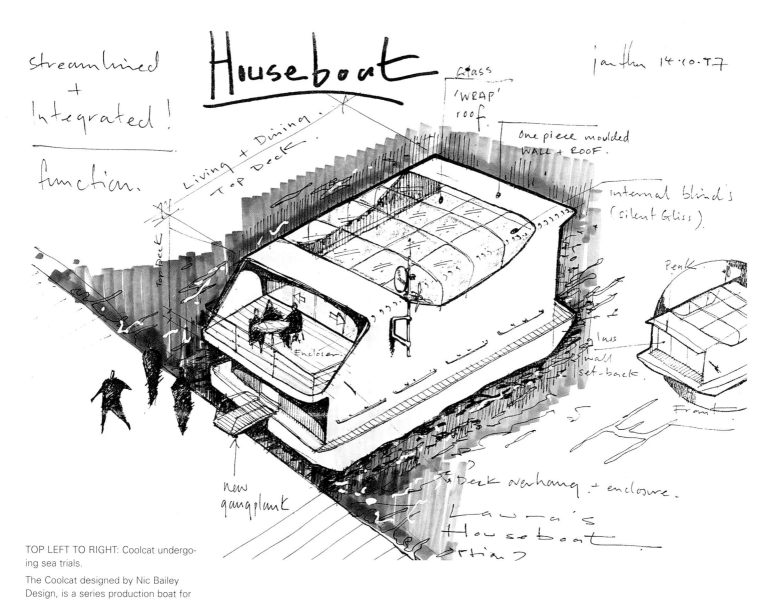

streamlined
+
Integrated!

function.

Houseboat

jonthn 14·10·97

Glass 'WRAP' roof.

One piece moulded WALL + ROOF.

Living + Dining. Top Deck.

Top Deck.

Internal blind's (silent Gliss).

Enclosure.

Peak.

wall set-back.

Front.

new gangplank

Deck overhang + enclosure.

Laura's Houseboat option?

TOP LEFT TO RIGHT: Coolcat undergoing sea trials.

The Coolcat designed by Nic Bailey Design, is a series production boat for which the builder now has a complete set of some 20 different component mould tools that ensure dimensional consistency as well as quality control on the final product. There is no automotive style production line, as boats are built to order on about two months.

ABOVE: Single houseboat by Jonathan Schwinge.

Architecture or Clerkitecture?

Chapter 16

Daniel Lloyd and Deborah Brown

NEW AREAS FOR ARCHITECTS' DUTIES

There have been a number of recent changes in the legal environment in which architects operate. These changes combined with recent developments in the practice of architecture now operate to place architects in an invidious position. On the one hand architects may now have less design responsibility in major construction projects than they have had in the past. For example, it is now quite usual for architects or clients to subcontract the detail design of major parts of buildings to specialist sub-consultants. On the other hand the legal environment in which architects operate has become less certain. Recent legislation and developments in case law when taken together have expanded the scope of architects' liability and placed new duties and responsibilities upon them. This has happened at a time when they have less responsibility for the whole of the design for a project, although they generally remain responsible for the co-ordination and integration of the designs of others. More worryingly, perhaps, as this chapter will show, these new duties are often ill-defined, thus robbing architects of the relatively certain legal environment in which they have operated until now.

...new duties are often ill-defined, thus robbing architects of the relatively certain legal environment in which they have operated until now.

The chapter is divided into sections. In the first section, Daniel Lloyd analyses some recent changes in the law as to their potential impact on architects' duties and responsibilities. In the second section Deborah Brown looks at 'partnering agreements' and what they may mean for architects in practice. The effects of these changes combined are outlined at the end of the chapter in 'Responsibilities Beyond Definition'.

PART 1: CHANGES TO BASIC DUTIES FOR ARCHITECTS IN THE LAW
Daniel Lloyd

Reasonable skill and care

Architecture is the art and science of designing and building structures. Once law is added to the mix, the standards expected of architects expand even further. Just as it is no defence for a criminal to plead ignorance of the law that makes his or her conduct a crime, architects are expected to have knowledge of the laws governing the performance of their services. What follows is not intended to be an exhaustive account or list of the legal obligations to which architects are subject, but aims to highlight how some recent legislative developments have impacted upon the practice of modern architecture.

What are the basic duties expected of an architect? Leaving aside questions of aesthetics or art (which the courts are not overly concerned with), an architect's obligations will differ according to the role in which he or she is employed. The Royal Institute of British Architects (RIBA) Standard Form of Appointment SFA/99[1] asks the client to select the architectural services required from the following list:

- Perform the services of design only.
- Perform the services of design leader.
- Perform the services of lead consultant during pre-construction work stages.
- Perform the services of lead consultant during construction work stages.
- Perform the services necessary for completion of the work stages indicated in accordance with the services supplement.
- Make visits to the works as the architect at the date of the appointment reasonably expected to be necessary.
- Perform any other services identified in SFA/99.

Whether an architect is appointed under a bespoke form of contract (SFA/99), an exchange of correspondence or orally, and whatever the services, he or she is (at the very least) required to exercise 'reasonable skill and care' in the performance of those services both under Section 13 of the Supply of Goods and Services Act 1982 and as a result of numerous cases.

But what does 'reasonable skill and care' mean? At first glance, if a roof leaks due to a design error a client might say that his or her architect has failed to exercise the required standard of care. But this is not necessarily so. If the architect has used the skill and care that would be expected of a competent professional in the field, the failure to design a weather-tight structure is not necessarily the architect's fault

– particularly if there is a genuine difference of opinion within the profession in relation to the particular design. This was the case in *Bolam v. Friern Hospital Management Committee*.[2]

If reasonable skill and care can be defined, to what does it apply? The most obvious area is in the production of designs, but there are also administrative or 'clerkitecture' services such as inspection and certification under building contracts, and possibly project management services.

However, architects are also expected to have a positive regard for the health and safety of any person at work carrying out construction work under Regulation 13 of the Construction (Design & Management) Regulations 1994. As might be expected, the RIBA standard form attempts to reduce this ostensibly very wide obligation. Under SFA/99 the references to CDM place the onus entirely on the client to supply information to the architect and comply with its obligations as a client under the regulations. But this is not to say that an architect who failed to comply with obligations as a designer under the regulations would not be negligent or in breach of SFA/99, since the architect would not have exercised the required standard of skill and care under clause 2.1:

> The Architect shall in performing the Services and discharging all the obligations under this Part 2 of these Conditions, exercise reasonable skill and care in conformity with the normal standards of the Architect's profession.[3]

The Building Regulations provide another instance where failure to comply with statutory requirements is linked to a failure to exercise the required standard of skill and care. In *Turner Page v. Torres* the architect's failure to design proper means of escape in case of fire resulted in a refusal of Building Regulations approval. What is significant is that the court was unwilling to divorce the obtaining of statutory consents from the standard of skill and care expected of a designer. It rejected the proposition that to agree that 'refusal of Building Regulation approval is a routine experience which does not reflect in any way upon the designer'.[4] This should be borne in mind when having to obtain consents on the revised 'Part L' of the Building Regulations,[5] and the new requirement to calculate carbon emissions consequent on designs that, for reasons of project programming or cost control, may be revised during the course of the works. This may be particularly awkward if the building control officer is having difficulty assessing the more complex submissions, as will be likely in the absence of staff familiar with the methodologies behind the 2001 'Part L' revision.

Obtaining planning permission or providing information to allow it to be obtained has generally always been part of an architect's services, and this adds new obligations of skill and care in respect of design. A reasonable architect is expected to have a sufficiently detailed knowledge of planning law to advise the client, either directly on the planning application, or, where the architect is not able to do so, to advise the client to consult an expert in planning law. There are a number of recent statutes that have introduced important legal changes that may impact on the practice of architecture, including the Contracts (Rights of Third Parties) Act 1999.

An end to the privity of contract

The Rights of Third Parties Act, which received royal assent in November 1999, effectively abolishes the common law doctrine of privity of contract. Under this doctrine only parties to a contract can sue upon it. Third parties to the contract had no right to sue upon the contract even where their interests were directly affected. The Act allows third parties to a contract to sue upon it in accordance with the Act. In doing so it potentially extends the liability of architects to third parties. Let us see how the Act works.

- Section 1 (1) provides that 'a person who is not a party to a contract (a "third party") may in his own right enforce a term of the contract if (a) the contract expressly provides that he may, or (b) subject to subsection (2), the term purports to confer a benefit on him'.
- Section 1 (2) provides that a third party does not have the right to enforce a term 'if on a proper construction of the contract it appears that the parties did not intend the term to be enforceable by the third party'.
- Section 1 (3) provides that 'the third party must be expressly identified in the contract by name, as a member of a class or as answering a particular description but need not be in existence when the contract is entered into'.
- Section 1 (5) provides for the third party to have available 'any remedy that would have been available to him in an action for breach of contract if he had been a party to the contract'.
- Section 1 (6) provides that the third party avails himself to any 'exclusion or limitation' contained within any term of the contract.

This Act creates two potential areas for concern regarding the enforceability of third-party rights and the identification of third parties upon whom benefits are conferred.

Muddy water

The enforceability of third-party rights

Party autonomy is preserved for the most part in that third-party rights can be created only by express contractual terms to that effect. However, the enforcement of such terms by a third party is subject to a two-limb test. The first limb is relatively uncontroversial – where the contract expressly states that a third party may enforce the terms of the contract. This cannot be a cause for concern as it merely gives effect to the intentions of the contracting parties.

The second limb holds that a third party may have enforceable rights where a term of the contract purports to confer a benefit on the third party (unless, on a proper construction, the parties did not intend the term to be enforceable by the third party). So in effect there must be implied into the contract term an intention to create third-party enforcement rights.

Furthermore, in the event of dispute, the burden of proving that no such intention was present will fall upon the contracting parties, where they have conferred a benefit upon a third party. It is in this second limb that there may be cause for concern. It will create a degree of uncertainty in practice as to whether the parties really intended to create third-party rights and what amounts to a term of the contract for this purpose.

The identification of third parties

There is also the question of who or what is a third party? Section 1 (3) provides that 'the third party must be expressly identified in the contract by name, as a member of a class or as answering a particular description but need not be in existence when the contract is entered into'. The scope of identifying a class of individuals with third-party enforcement rights cannot be underestimated, and particularly with regard to environmental matters.

Any creative lawyer would have a field day with the expression 'answering a particular description'. This again leads the way potentially to uncertainty and difficulty in balancing third-party rights against the intentions of the contracting parties. In fact it would seem that the intentions of the parties to the contract are trumped by this expression.

The prospect of creating third-party rights for 'third parties not yet in existence' also has frightening implications. Where benefits are conferred upon companies or people yet to exist there can be no certainty at the time of making the contract as to the actual liability that either contracting party may be exposing themselves to. This may relate directly to the idea of sustainability, which explicitly concerns itself with the interests of future generations.

What does all this mean for architects? Most importantly, no third-party rights are created if the contract contains a term or terms that expressly state no third-party rights are created by the contract. Contracts need to contain *terms that explicitly deny the creation of third-party rights*. Problems may occur where contracts come into existence between architects and clients or sub-consultants without such express terms denying third-party rights being incorporated. In this scenario architects may be in for a shock. The Rights of Third Parties Act could operate in such a way as to undermine the restricted liability to third parties that architects currently enjoy under *Murphy v. Brentwood District Council*.[6]

Murphy v. Brentwood is authority for the proposition that architects should not owe a duty of care in tort to the occupiers of property they have designed beyond the first occupier of that property, save for in the most limited of circumstances. The judges had very sound policy reasons for reaching this decision. The decision has protected architects from claims made by third parties in the distant future for work that architects may have done in the distant past.

The decision reinforced the primacy of contract over tort in the determination of liability for negligent building construction. *Murphy v. Brentwood* seriously restricts the liability of architects to third parties in the tort of negligence. It has created a legally certain environment that has given architects a greater freedom to be audacious in the buildings they design. The scope of the duty architects owe to third parties was recently extended to a limited extent in *Baxall v. Sheard Walshaw*.[7] The architects Sheard Walshaw were found to owe a duty of care to Baxall Securities, a subsequent occupier of a building designed by Sheard Walshaw, but only in respect of latent defects of which there was no reasonable possibility of inspection. *Baxall v. Sheard Walshaw* would appear to be authority for the proposition that an architect may remain liable and may owe a duty of care to subsequent purchasers and tenants by failing to adequately specify design parameters, or negligently approving subcontractors' designs. The case is consistent with the principles outlined in *Murphy v. Brentwood*, under which architects do not have to worry about liability to third parties in the future. On the face of it *Baxall v. Sheard Walshaw* represents only a very limited extension of architects' liability to third parties.

The Rights of Third Parties Act on the other hand could effectively recreate that liability in contract where it no longer exists in the tort of negligence. To many lawyers this at first sight appears strange. But it is strange and true. The Act explicitly states that the third parties that benefit from a contract need not

Where benefits are conferred upon companies or people yet to exist there can be no certainty at the time of making the contract as to the actual liability that either contracting party may be exposing themselves to. This may relate directly to the idea of sustainability, which explicitly concerns itself with the interests of future generations.

exist at the time the contract is made. It also states that third parties may acquire a benefit under the contract if on a proper construction the contract 'purports to confer a benefit on him'.

Architects must be very careful to avoid this 'Alice in Wonderland' world. It is very important that 'denial of third-party rights' clauses are inserted into contracts. Otherwise architects could find themselves liable to classes of persons unknown, for indeterminate amounts of money, into an indefinite future.

The contradiction of teamwork and adjudication

The Housing Grants and Regeneration Act 1996 (Construction Act) has served to make architectural practice more difficult. Under this Act all construction disputes must first go to adjudication, either agreed to in advance by the parties in the contract, or otherwise by reference to the statutory alternative provided for in the Act. Under the fast-track adjudication procedure applied to construction contracts under the Act, adjudication must take place within seven days of a notice of intention to refer a dispute to adjudication. With some exceptions the adjudication decision must be reached within 28 days. There is no obligation on the adjudicator to give reasons for a decision unless the adjudicator is explicitly asked to do so, and a court must enforce an adjudicator's decision without allowing a reference to arbitration or the resolution of any counterclaim.

An aggrieved party could argue that this procedure conflicts with Article 6 of the Human Rights Act. For example, the timetable for adjudication runs from the time when only one of the parties gives notice of its intention to refer a dispute to arbitration. However, it has been recently held in *Austin Hall Building Ltd v. Buckland Securities Ltd*[8] that an adjudicator exercising functions of the sort required by the Housing Grants and Regeneration Act was not a public authority. Thus an adjudicator is not bound by the Human Rights Act 1998 to avoid acting in a way incompatible with a convention right. However, this is not to say that adjudicators are not bound by the rules of natural justice. In *Discain Project Services Ltd v. Opecprime Development Ltd*[9] it was held that an adjudicator had to conduct proceedings in accordance with the rules of natural justice, or as fairly as the limitations imposed by Parliament permitted.

The enforceability of an adjudicator's decisions and the statutory regime that governs the timetable of adjudication ensure that architects have to stay on their toes. If facing adjudication under the Act, either by reference to the contract or the statutory alternative, then architects have little choice but to make addressing the matter their priority. Failure to do so can be costly. The prospect of adjudication at short notice requires the contracting parties and the contract administrator to maintain adjudication files on each other in anticipation of claims being made. This is an immense amount of work in anticipation of disputes, and completely against the spirit of partnering or teamwork. Parties to the construction contract are simultaneously expected to trust and suspect each other.

This brings us to the promotion of partnering in construction. This section has sought to highlight how some recent changes in the law may make architects' lives more difficult. The following section turns specifically to the question of partnering agreements and discusses some of the issues these raise for architects in practice.

PART 2: PARTNERING AGREEMENTS
Deborah Brown, CMS Cameron McKenna

The expansion of professional duty

In common with consultants of other disciplines, indeed all those who work within the construction industry, architects have long understood the need for teamwork. As a means to achieve faster completion of projects or savings in the cost of materials and design, clients embrace partnering and it is now almost a prerequisite for an architect wishing to win a tender to stress that he or she is co-operative and responsive. However, clients' use of partnering agreements or charters (even if not written into architects' contracts) has brought about its own problems.

Increasingly, architects may find that their duties have been expanded by obligations to act proactively, to comment on other consultants' designs and to reduce costs – obligations over and above their existing duties to perform their services with reasonable skill and care and to co-ordinate and integrate the designs of others.

This section does not propose to define a partnering agreement, partly because there is no accepted definition. Partnering agreements can, like contracts, be oral or written, bespoke or standard form, such as PPC2000, published by the Association of Consultant Architects. They can be binding or non-binding, project specific or cover an ongoing relationship between client and consultant, include the whole project team or just the architect and the client. But various principles are common to all types of agreement. An

---

It is very important that 'denial of third-party rights' clauses are inserted into contracts. Otherwise architects could find themselves liable to classes of persons unknown, for indeterminate amounts of money, into an indefinite future.

The prospect of adjudication at short notice requires the contracting parties and the contract administrator to maintain adjudication files on each other in anticipation of claims being made. This is an immense amount of work in anticipation of disputes, and completely against the spirit of partnering or teamwork.

obligation to act in a spirit of mutual trust and co-operation, attend project team meetings and act proactively to reduce costs, time and conflict within the team form the core of most partnering agreements. However, these are obligations that do not necessarily sit well with the tried and tested obligations of an architect. For example, would an architect under a partnering agreement have to use reasonable skill and care to reduce the client's costs? This would considerably expand the architect's existing duties, and some possible further expansions are discussed below.

The only judicial opinion on partnering comes from the first instance decision in *Birse Construction Ltd v. St David Ltd*, where the court used the provisions of a non-binding partnering agreement to interpret the conduct required of the parties under the substantive contract:

> The terms of that document (the partnering charter), though clearly not legally binding, are important for they were clearly intended to provide the standards by which the parties were to conduct themselves and against which their conduct and attitudes were to be measured.[10]

Although the parties had not intended their partnering agreement to be anything more than an expression of their common goals, the result of *Birse v. St David Ltd* is that the courts (or, more likely, an adjudicator) can now expand the parties' duties and standards of care from those stated in the contract to include new principles of co-operation. If, for example, an architect or a client agrees (even in a non-binding charter) to act reasonably, he or she must act reasonably under the subsequent contract. If the architect or client has agreed to co-operate, he or she must not do anything inconsistent with the obligation to co-operate.

The obligation to inform

What might this mean in the practical context of an architectural appointment? One of the greatest dangers for the client is that reasonable conduct might prevent him or her from activating provisions for damages when external circumstances make performance within the contractual deadlines difficult as opposed to impossible (contrast the rules on frustration where only impossibility discharges a contract). For architects, the danger may lie in the inter-relationship with the work of other consultants, irrespective of whether the architect is acting as lead consultant. Architects already have a duty to report on the performance of other professionals during the works. In *Chesham v. Bucknall Austin* it was noted that the architect had a contractual duty to 'provide management from inception to completion...appoint and co-ordinate consultants, construction managers, agents and contractors; monitor time cost and agreed targets; monitor progress of the works'.[11] It was held that this meant the architect owed the client a continuing duty of care to warn of the structural engineer's and quantity surveyor's actual or potential deficiencies. This was so despite the architect's appointment containing an equivalent to clause 3.11.1 of SFA/99, which requires the client to hold the other consultants and not the architect responsible for the performance of that consultant's services. Clause 3.11 provides:

> The Client, in respect of any work or services in connection with the Project performed or to be performed by any person other than the Architect, shall:
> 1. hold such person responsible for the competence and performance of his services and for visits to the site in connection with the work undertaken by him;
> 2. ensure that such person shall co-operate with the Architect and provide to the Architect drawings and information reasonably needed for the proper and timely performance of the Services;
> 3. ensure that such person shall, when requested by the Architect, consider and comment on work of the Architect in relation to their own work so that the Architect may consider making necessary change to his work.[12]

Use of a partnering agreement and its obligations to co-operate and act in a spirit of trust can only strengthen this existing duty.

The obligation to co-operate

Arguably, clauses 3.11.1 and 3.12 of SFA/99 are exclusion clauses, as they attempt to exclude the principles of *Chesham v. Bucknall Austin*. Clause 3.12 provides:

> The Client shall hold the Principal Contractor and/or other contractors appointed to undertake construction works and not the Architect responsible for their management and operational methods, for the proper carrying out and completion of the Works in compliance with the building contract and for health and safety provisions on the site.[13]

Whether an exclusion clause is enforceable depends on what it attempts to exclude. Some clauses are automatically unenforceable, such as those excluding liability for negligently caused death or personal injury. Others may be enforced if the clause is fair and reasonable under Section 3 of the Unfair Contract Terms Act 1977 (which applies to written standard terms of business – including SFA/99). The circumstances to be taken into account when determining whether the clause is reasonable are those which

An obligation to act in a spirit of mutual trust and co-operation, attend project team meetings and act proactively to reduce costs, time and conflict within the team form the core of most partnering agreements. However, these are obligations that do not necessarily sit well with the tried and tested obligations of an architect.

were known, or should reasonably have been known by the parties at the time when the contract was made (Section 11(1)). And at this time both the architect and the client will know that they have agreed to a partnering arrangement. If it subsequently falls to the courts to consider whether clauses such as these are reasonable, in addition to the factors normally taken into account, if they are found to be inconsistent with partnering the clauses may be more likely to be held to be unreasonable and therefore unenforceable.

This is not such a contentious proposition as might first appear. Courts have found that events and conduct preceding the contract determine the question of reasonableness. In *St Albans City & District Council v. International Computers Ltd*,[14] the fact that one party was pressured by the other and by circumstances into expediting its agreement to the contractual terms made it unreasonable to allow the other party to rely on those terms. An analogy can be drawn between the pressure to expedite the contract's execution for economic reasons in *St Albans* and the pressure inferred by the implication that the party who did not agree the contract containing the exclusion clause would not be acting in accordance with its partnering obligations. A pre-contractual expression of co-operation might therefore impose a similar 'pressure' to agree to the exclusion clause, as not to do so may not be co-operative.

However, before architects cry foul on the basis that partnering agreements are inherently biased towards the client, they should consider that increased duties might also fall on the client as well as the architect. This is so, not only under clause 3.11.3 of SFA/99 which requires the client to ensure that other consultants comment on the architect's work in relation to their own work, but also under the common law, for example in the area of variation of contract. The law requires co-operation between parties in the sense that they perform the contract according to its strict terms. But co-operation between business contractors often implies a degree of flexibility, that they will not insist on strict contractual rights, that they will make concessions in times of difficulty. Minor variations to the contract may go unchallenged.

But what is the position if a variation in the terms of the contract is agreed informally or simply arises out of performance of the contract in a different way, where the client accepts this difference in performance without protest? Where consideration is given for the variation clearly it is binding even if the consideration in question is tenuous, as in *Williams v. Roffey Bros. & Nicholls (Contractors) Ltd*.[15] In the absence of consideration the variation is not normally enforceable unless it can be implied that the client has agreed to it because it is reasonable and necessary to do so.

Suppose, for example, that market conditions make the architect's performance more difficult or less profitable than envisaged at the time of the contract. An insistence by the client on strict compliance with all contractual terms effectively destroys co-operation in such circumstances. Does it follow that a prior expression of co-operation requires the client to share the risk or to agree to changes that relieve the architect from some of the burdens (including liquidated damages if applicable) brought about by changes in market condition, such as a labour dispute? Clearly a client would not wish to commit him- or herself in this way, but the law may be moving towards a position where co-operation between the contracting parties imposes other obligations, one of which is to agree to alterations that are commercially necessary given the prevailing market conditions.

...before architects cry foul on the basis that partnering agreements are inherently biased towards the client, they should consider that increased duties might also fall on the client as well as the architect.

A false sense of security

This brings us on to another possible expansion of duties when partnering – namely the implication of duties of good faith. Courts do not rewrite contracts, but they imply terms in order to preserve the reasonable expectations of the parties, assuming that to do so gives effect to the true but unexpressed intentions of the parties, that is, when it is reasonable and necessary to give business efficacy to the contract. As in *Trollope & Colls Ltd v. North West Metropolitan Regional Hospital Board*,[16] English law does not normally imply a duty of good faith in the absence of a special relationship between contracting parties (such as between employer and employee or between insurer and insured). However, the use of a partnering agreement may be one area where new duties of good faith could be implied. For example, courts have implied terms that parties will conduct themselves in such a way as to allow the contract to be carried out in a reasonable manner, as in *Davy Offshore Ltd. v. Emerald Field Contracting Ltd*.[17] In the context of an architect's appointment, business efficacy might justify the imposition of certain obligations consistent with the spirit of the partnering agreement – namely that both parties will act reasonably and in good faith.

What would be the position if the architect's traditional appointment were replaced by a partnering agreement? For example, the standard form partnering agreement produced by the Association of Consultant Architects (PPC2000) is contractually binding and intended to replace all of the traditional two-party contracts used in a construction project.

PPC2000 includes clauses covering design liability, time for completion, provision of warranties, intellectual property, insurance, etc. – in fact, everything a client could wish for together with additional duties not found in any of the traditional professional appointments. These include the dangerous obligation that

Apparent calm

partnering team members contributing to a partnering document (which is defined as including design documents, the project timetable and the brief, and which therefore would involve an architect) are responsible for the consequences of any error or omission in the document except to the extent of its reliance on information provided by another member of the partnering team. So, the architect who provides information to a structural engineer, even informally at a team meeting or over drinks, could potentially be held responsible for the engineer's design documents. Architects, and not least their professional indemnity insurers, would quite rightly balk at this expansion of duties if it were included in a traditional appointment. The use of the more 'warm and fuzzy' PPC2000 should not lull either into a false sense of security.

Responsibilities beyond definition

Architects are today in a difficult position. In terms of modern practice more and more responsibility for the actual design of buildings is moving away from them. For example, architects may increasingly seek to transfer the detail design of components of buildings to specialist sub-consultants. This can give rise to considerable difficulty both in resolving questions of design responsibility for defects in design and also in the process for information flow necessary to allow the builder to construct and complete the works. Often the parameters within which the design must be carried out will be left to the sub-consultant with the unsurprising result that the sub-consultant will choose the cheap solution in order to win the contract and maximise profits. Responsibility for the integration of the sub-consultant's design will often be largely borne by the architect under the general co-ordination and integration duty.

While their responsibility for the actual design of buildings may have diminished, architects are at the same time assuming more responsibility in other areas. It is not unusual today to see architects being involved much more in the project management (which encompasses more than simply contract-administration duties) than they ever have been in the past.

It is in this scenario that architects must learn to cope with the new duties and liabilities that they are subject to, often in circumstances where those duties and responsibilities are ill-defined, and in some cases incapable even of definition.

As has been demonstrated, the vista of liability to which architects are now subject is opening up. The relatively certain legal environment in which architects have practised for the last ten years is now being undermined. It is being undermined from without by the introduction of legislation that creates new liabilities and responsibilities that architects need to be aware of. It is also being undermined from within by changes in the way business is conducted in the construction industry through the introduction of partnering agreements, in which the actual rights and responsibilities of architects are often ill-defined. The relative certainty of the past may be lost.

Architects must now be careful in negotiating the legal minefield that lies ahead.

Notes

1. Royal Institute of British Architects, *Standard Form of Agreement for the Appointment of an Architect*, SFA/99 (London: RIBA, updated April 2000).
2. *Bolam v. Friern Hospital Management Committee* (1957) 1WLR 582.
3. RIBA, *Standard Form of Agreement for the Appointment of an Architect*, SFA/99, RIBA, updated April 2000, clause 2.1.
4. *Turner Page v. Torres* (1997) CILL 1263.
5. Department of the Environment, Transport and the Regions, *The Building Regulations Approved Document Part L – Conservation of Fuel and Power*, Interim Draft (London: DETR, March 2001).
6. *Murphy v. Brentwood District Council* (1991) 1 AC 398.
7. *Baxall v. Sheard Walshaw* (2001) CLC 188.
8. *Austin Hall Building Ltd v. Buckland Securities Ltd* (2001) All ER (D) 137.
9. *Discain Project Services Ltd v. Opecprime Development Ltd* (2001) All ER (D) 138 (Apr).
10. *Birse Construction Ltd v. St David Ltd* (1999) BLR 194.
11. *Chesham v. Bucknall Austin* (1996) CILL 1189.
12. Royal Institute of British Architects, *Standard Form of Agreement for the Appointment of an Architect*, SFA/99 (London: RIBA, updated April 2000), clause 3.11.
13. Ibid., clause 3.12.
14. *St Albans City & District Council v. International Computers Ltd*, TLR 11.11.94.
15. *Williams v. Roffey Bros & Nicholls (Contractors) Ltd* (1991) 1 QB 1.
16. *Trollope & Colls Ltd v. North West Metropolitan Regional Hospital Board* (1973) 2 All ER 260.
17. *Davy Offshore Ltd v. Emerald Field Contracting Ltd* (1991) 55 BLR 1.

...architects may increasingly seek to transfer the detail design of components of buildings to specialist sub-consultants. This can give rise to considerable difficulty both in resolving questions of design responsibility for defects in design and also in the process for information flow necessary to allow the builder to construct and complete the works.

The relatively certain legal environment in which architects have practised for the last ten years is now being undermined.

Chapter 17

From Strategic Adviser to Design Subcontractor and Back Again

Peter Walker

THE WAY WE WERE

In the process of creating buildings, architects traditionally occupied a fulcrum position between the demand side – the client or building promoter – and the supply side – the construction industry. The role was well established and was broadly to translate the promoter's brief into a finished building. In this arrangement architects enjoyed a frontline intimate relationship with their clients. He (and it was almost exclusively a he) was engaged and paid by the promoter. In return he took the brief, advised and guided his client through the procurement process and prepared the drawings and specifications used by the building contractor to construct the building. On the voyage from idea to building, the architect embarked at the port of origin. This was the traditional model. It was for many years, with one or two very minor variations, the only game in town, and it was of course carried out with varying degrees of thoroughness and competence.

The process rarely followed a neat or linear progression. The early appointment of the architect brought to the fore all the questions arising from the physical examination of the development: was the site big enough?, would planning permission be forthcoming, could the building be built for the budget?, and so on. This then became an iterative process where earlier assumptions were revisited. After several trips around the houses the development would gradually settle down and take on its physical form – a process rather like adjusting the horizontal and vertical hold until a clear picture emerges.

The important point, however, was that the architect was intimately involved in this process more or less from the outset. The architect was the gatekeeper to the construction industry and an influential adviser to building promoters on all sorts of development matters. The architect had the ear of the client, and his advice was sought and acted upon. No one came between client and architect.

The system of course contained much inefficiency. Clients complained that buildings were not being delivered on time or to budget, that the risky business of putting up a building seemed to be made more, rather than less risky by the architect, and that many of the values and aspirations set by the brief were not fulfilled by the finished building. The construction side complained that the architect's designs and specifications were not readily buildable and added time and cost to the process of construction to no useful effect.

...the ability to effectively address sustainability issues by design diminishes the further downstream the architect becomes involved.

So a process of change began – changes which over the past 20 or so years have served to move architects increasingly from the position of upstream strategic advisor to building promoters, to the position of suppliers of design services, often directly engaged by construction or project management companies. Architects have as a result lost much of the considerable influence they once had as gatekeepers, introducing and guiding promoters of buildings through the construction process. In *The Strategic Management of Architectural Practice*, Winch and Schneider describe how the architect's position 'has changed from being the client's representative located between the client and all the other members of the project coalition, to reporting to a project manager in that position. In some cases architecture is little more than just another works package'.[1]

The loss of this privileged role has not only changed the timing of the advice from early in the project cycle to a point much further downstream, but has also changed the type of advice from being both *strategic* and *detail* advice, to often no more than *detail* advice. In extreme cases architects have become little more than suppliers of design services rather than full-blown professional advisors.

There are, however, wider and more important implications arising from this drift downstream which go beyond the commercial well being of the architectural profession and impact on the quality of buildings and the built environment. In particular the ability to effectively address sustainability issues by design diminishes the further downstream the architect becomes involved.

EMBARKING ON THE VOYAGE FROM IDEA TO BUILDING

At the outset of a building project the promoter must make fundamental, strategic decisions regarding the proposed development. These will include deciding on the site for the building, the budget, operational or functional requirements, the business case for the development and the procurement method. Conscious or informal consideration will be given to the opportunity costs associated with the development, the commercial risks, how these are to be allocated, and the projected value and market for the completed development.

This project strategy is developed in consultation with internal and external advisors. Many of the early decisions will cast the die, or at the very least reduce the building design options. But although many of the decisions will have an architectural or design component, increasingly no architect will be appointed at this stage to advise on or to be an advocate for these design matters. Reed and Gordon describe the situation in the US in the particular context of 'building green:

> Significant steps often occur before the architect is brought on as a consultant. Typically the owner identifies the building concept, the site is selected and analysed by non-design professionals and the building form is laid out by a civil engineer or is significantly impacted by a municipal zoning ordinance. As a result, sustainable objectives such as build/no-build decisions, alternative transit options and building orientation are predetermined. Ecological design objectives are not identified, developed and incorporated early enough in the planning process.[2]

What Reed and Gordon describe is with one or two changes of title pretty much the situation in the UK. But how did this come about and why does it matter?

THE DRIFT DOWNSTREAM TO THE WAY WE ARE

How did architects come to drift away from the upstream position and the intimate client-architect relationship? Many factors have no doubt contributed to this:

- architectural education;
- culture and institutions of architecture; and
- the commercial organisation of architectural practice.

These aspects of our own profession have all played a part in the drift downstream. In addition the context in which we practise has altered because the construction industry is experiencing a period of fundamental change, which has in many respects served to accelerate this drift:

- the influence of Latham and Egan;
- contractors as developers and clients bringing changes in contractual relationships with the rise of design and build and 'partnering' alliances;
- changes in building procurement and the Private Finance Initiative; and
- shifting professional boundaries with the rise of the quantity surveyor as project manager.

These factors are also combined with a changing attitude to professional authority by society at large:

- the decline of professional status.

They have all served to blur and in many cases, from the architect's perspective, to undermine the way we used to practise. These will be considered in turn.

ARCHITECTURAL EDUCATION

Architectural school studio design centres on the individual and is characterised by the absence of a real-life collaborative design approach. Teaching focuses on the high-profile grand scheme. Low-cost, modest commercial buildings with realistic construction budgets and technology – the staple diet of most practising architects – are generally not the stuff of architectural school projects. The pedagogic justification for this is along the lines that if you can do the big hard stuff, you can also do the small easy stuff. The evidence that it requires the same skills, simply throttled back, is not patently obvious, or in practice demonstrated.

The absence of a client, or even of the kinds of concerns a client might have – the cost of the building, its value, the return on investment or the commercial risk – is another key characteristic of school studio projects. This education sets the tone for a profession little concerned with issues perceived as being outside their realm of influence and beyond its own horizons. The paucity of teaching in the economics of property and the economics of building means that architects are not prepared in such a way as to be capable of engaging in an articulate and meaningful way with the property and construction industries. The lack of a knowledge base in the upstream property process – issues to do with the valuation, return on investment or appraisal – combined with a very limited understanding of the determinants of building costs and of cost management processes, excludes architects from contributing meaningfully at a strategic level.

Perhaps more significant than the absence of 'hard' management skill, however, is the lack of soft management skills – people, leadership and team-building issues. Collaborative working skills, in particular with those involved in building cost and value matters, are with very few exceptions generally not developed. The relationship of the architect to the quantity surveyor on a building project is analogous to that of the company director to the management accountant of a firm. In the same way that the director of a company requires a working knowledge of financial issues, architects require a similar type and level of knowledge of building cost issues. It is not so much that architects need to have the applied skills to carry out, for example, life-cycle cost analysis; more that they have the strategic knowledge to know when and how life-cycle cost information should be used. If architects are to provide objective validation for their

How did architects come to drift away from the upstream position and the intimate client–architect relationship?

The absence of a client, or even of the kinds of concerns a client might have – the cost of the building, its value, the return on investment or the commercial risk – is another key characteristic of school studio projects. This education sets the tone for a profession little concerned with issues perceived as being outside their realm of influence and beyond its own horizons.

designs they require an understanding of the basic concepts of discount rates, sensitivity analysis, obsolescence and deterioration – in particular how these can be used to inform and (importantly) to support a design strategy. Discussions about sustainability without a supporting commercial case are of little use in determining, or selling to clients, a particular design strategy.

Architects see cost as a construction matter, value as a property matter. There is indeed often an apparent inability to distinguish between *cost* and *value*. By the time the architect is employed the development appraisal is complete or the business case is made with the budget for the building defined and set. From then on the task is to design a building that can be built for that budget or better still for less. By this stage it is generally too late to explore the possibility of spending more capital to reduce long-term costs – a perfectly sound commercial proposition for a building promoter. Even among speculative developers spending more to attract tenants more quickly or to attract tenants on better terms is a good and profitable idea.

An architect's training, by and large, does not adequately equip him or her to be able to demonstrate, both by design and importantly by hard numbers, that spending more on a building can be a good commercial decision. Although the emerging Royal Institute of British Architects (RIBA) Part 3 professional studies syllabus makes reference to the requirement for 'an understanding of the social and economic context for investment in the built environment', the bulk of the syllabus remains concerned with either the management of architects or the management of the building process. At the research level, architecture (and therefore its research forum and agenda) is established as architecture, engineering and construction (AEC), which also tends to exclude upstream property matters.

The case for the British system of architectural education is perpetuated by a widely held view, at least among British architects, that Britain produces some of the best architects in the world. That they are often appreciated and patronised more abroad than at home is seen as proving the point. The argument goes that tampering with the established system will risk destroying this. This view seems to be based on all sorts of presumptions including the fear that teaching pragmatic skills will lead to prosaic designs, or that burdening students with practical skills and knowledge will somehow inhibit their 'design' work. Although great attention is lavished on the physical context, the social, commercial or economic context – in particular the commercial motivation to build – is frequently either ignored or reduced to a meaningless and unrealistic model. Economists joke that they build models, compare them to the real world and if the model doesn't work they then change the world. So it seems to be in schools of architecture.

Culture and institutions

Architects have a strong tradition of peer approval as an important measure of success. This centres on the quality of the product – the completed building – with 'soft' qualitative measures of success. Promoters, owners and users of buildings increasingly focus on the process of creating the building and on the function or the output of the finished product. These are measured with 'hard' quantitative methods – acceptable returns on investment, high operating profit, low maintenance costs, and so on.

Many architects and others see architecture as a unique occupation, separate and aloof from the property and construction industries. Indeed, in as much as architecture is a creative profession, and one with a belief in responsibilities beyond the immediate project, it is at least to that extent unique. In Britain the separation of the property design professional body, the RIBA, from the property marketing, finance and management professional body, the Royal Institution of Chartered Surveyors (RICS), perpetuates this split. This situation is mirrored in the fragmentation of professional firms, with companies that span design and property consultancy being almost unheard of.

One important implication of this split is the loss of feedback on the long-term performance of buildings. The feedback loop from the property side as marketing and management agents for the finished product, such as data on energy consumption and patterns of use, is not readily accessible to architects. It has to be said that it is also not particularly vigorously pursued. It is interesting to reflect on why the architects' 'plan of work', as set down in the *Architect's Job Book*, sensibly refers to Stage M 'Feedback',[3] while the *Architects Appointment* stops at Stage L 'Practical Completion'.[4] There seems to be a deliberate desire to avoid contracting for feedback on the performance of the completed building, presumably lest this should give rise to unwanted criticism or worse still to litigation. Indeed, the *Architect's Job Book* warns that 'investigations for feedback' should not be attempted 'if there is a risk of inviting acrimony or dispute' – precisely the circumstances where feedback would be most informative![5]

Integration of the two bodies is unlikely in the foreseeable future and in any case would probably only go a small way to breaking down this barrier. A greater integration of firms involved in managing and marketing property (surveyors) and those designing (architects) would be likely to, at the very least, encourage some consideration of the impact of each on the other.

By the time the architect is employed the development appraisal is complete or the business case is made with the budget for the building defined and set...By this stage it is generally too late to explore the possibility of spending more capital to reduce long-term costs – a perfectly sound commercial proposition for a building promoter.

The nature of architectural practice

The way in which architects contract for their services, generally based on the construction cost of the finished building, differs from the property sector. Much of the early work in commercial property development is traditionally carried out at risk with the participants sharing in some way in the financial returns if the development goes ahead and is successful.

Where this is not the case the participants share equally in the loss – that is the risk in property development. While the architectural profession has reluctantly been forced to adopt some of these practices, issues to do with the link between cost, value, risk and fee levels are frequently confused. There is seen to be a large investment of time and added value at the time of greatest risk, which is not usually reflected by way of reward in the commercial arrangement of the architect's engagement. This is a commercial disincentive to architects becoming involved in the early stages of a development. Paradoxically, it is particularly at this early stage that architects can add most value.

For architects a further upstream complication is the difficulty of accessing, or even identifying the key development stakeholders – the user or the occupier of the building. An obvious added complication is that the concerns and preferences of the various stakeholders may not be mutually compatible. There may also be deliberate or unconscious distortion of the briefing information to suit one party. Significantly it is often those who will own and maintain the building that set the brief rather than those who will use it.

At the other extreme is the difficulty of capturing at an early stage the supply chain expertise of subcontractors and specialist suppliers, many of whom can make significant contributions during the early design work. This is largely due to the difficulty of crossing contractual transaction barriers in the construction industry. Mechanical and electrical elements of the building may be designed on the basis of a performance specification and then shoehorned into the finished building. Such an approach fails to support or encourage a holistic view of building design, particularly in the pursuit of sustainability.

...the link between cost, value, risk and fee levels are frequently confused...This is a commercial disincentive to architects becoming involved in the early stages of a development.

The influence of Latham and Egan

Sir Michael Latham was commissioned to carry out a wide review of the construction industry, an industry that was seen to be inefficient, fragmented and unnecessarily and unproductively adversarial. His report, *Constructing the Team*, in 1994 was to prove hugely influential. It encouraged, among many other things, the use of partnering (one-off or long-term project alliances), and a more influential role for project managers, greater involvement upstream of subcontractors and suppliers, and a general rethink of the briefing process.

While Latham argues for 'patronage and good design' and advocates 'good design [that] will provide value for money in terms both of total cost and cost in use',[6] little interest has been shown in this aspect of the report. Certainly little has been done by way of tangible change in pursuit of this. Instead the agenda has been almost exclusively concerned with the process of making buildings and has given little or no attention to the effect this might have on the buildings produced. It was of course implicit in the report that a more efficient process would lead to better buildings, although quite how this was to be achieved was not articulated.

The later report in 1998 of Sir John Egan's Construction Task Force, *Rethinking Construction* shared many of the Latham themes and perpetuated the process-based agenda.[7] Viewed from an architectural point of view it strikes a more aggressive tone and in doing so avoids even a passing mention of architects.

Both reports encouraged a culture of change and questioning – not before time and not an unhealthy exercise for any industry, particularly construction. However, not only did they promote a debate that centred almost exclusively on how you make buildings, as opposed to where or why you make them, but they often promoted ephemeral untested solutions based apparently on instinct and unsupported by any credible research. This has not diminished the enthusiasm with which the construction industry has taken up many of the recommendations. In this brave new process-centred drive what has become important is not the emperor's new clothes but rather his new way of putting them on.

Caught in the tide of this debate, the RIBA responded, at least in thought if not in deed, to this supply-side agenda. The publication *Architects and the Changing Construction Industry* is very much a response to Egan and Latham.[8] This reactive response is that of a profession anxious to follow rather than determined to lead. The agenda and the response have been that of, and have been set by, the supply side – the construction industry – rather than the demand side – building promoters. While there are many merits in addressing these issues, to do so to the exclusion of promoting a debate about their impact on buildings and the environment is from the architect's position at the very least misguided.

Contractors as developers and clients

In what has since proven to be a remarkably prophetic piece, Gutman describes how contractors and construction managers as competitors to architects represent 'the principal source of competition'. He goes on to say that 'although they do not compete in the realm of design (they) pose a challenge in taking on functions of management before, during and following construction'.[9] Driven by low profit margins and the high risk inherent in traditional contracting together with the high transaction costs of competitive tendering, contractors have in increasing numbers sought to move up the food chain.

Most of the major, and some not so major British contractors have set up development arms or have sought, through injecting development finance, to take a stake in and negotiate contracts rather than compete in open tender. AMEC, one of the largest British contracting organisations, explains how 'in 1999 more than half of our United Kingdom workload was secured through negotiation with clients'. Also, how 'the overriding strategic focus in 1999 has been our continuing drive to maximise shareholder value through contractual relationships centred on an open book, partnering or alliance basis'. The language of the report is interesting – AMEC describes itself as competing on 'knowledge and value', not on cost and delivery as once would have been the case, and certainly not on bricks and mortar.[10]

Changes in building procurement

Davis Langdon and Everest's 1996 *Contracts in Use – A Survey of Building Contracts in Use* makes interesting reading.[11] The use of design and build contracts shows a sharp increase and represented 41.4 per cent of all contracts. Traditional contracts with a bill of quantities represented only 28 per cent of the total. Within these there is also a marked rise in the use of the contractor designed portion (CDP), which accounted for 28 per cent of the contract values. While much of the CDP is likely to be non-architectural design, such as building services and structural steelwork, it nevertheless shows an increased tendency on the part of clients to take the design work out of the consultant's hands, and to have large parts of the work designed later in the project process by the contractor.

It is of course a mistake to think that the increased popularity of design and build is driven by a view that the integration of the two will produce better buildings. All the evidence points to the shift being driven almost entirely by promoters' desire to unload (dump?) the commercial risk of the project. Indeed contractors, with a wry smile, frequently refer to 'design and build' as 'risk and build'.

Shifting professional boundaries

Quantity surveyors saw the writing on the wall, or more exactly on the PC monitor, some time ago. The move away from traditional competitive tendering together with the rise of accessible quantification computer hardware and software was in danger of seriously eroding their traditional pre-contract work. In the scramble for new markets, quantity surveyors were quick to establish themselves as project managers. With little hanging about, 'Chartered Quantity Surveyor' disappeared from the letterhead to be replaced by 'Construction Consultant'. With this new title came a raft of new consultancy services – risk management, value management, project management, and even should things go wrong (and it's hard to imagine how they would with all this managing going on) dispute management.

Quantity surveyors as construction management consultants sold themselves, and with some justification, as the people to advise and guide clients through the building development process. Seen from the client's position, at last there was someone who knew about value, cost and risk, and could advise on the things that mattered. They would even find a tame architect to look after the planning application and the look of the thing. Architects found themselves in the curious position of marketing their services to quantity surveyors, and slipped a little further downstream.

Property surveyors too saw the opportunity to cross-sell to their clients, and set up building consultancy groups staffed by building surveyors both to manage and even design buildings alongside their established marketing and valuation services.

Such shifting of traditional professional boundaries is not unique to architecture – lawyers and accountants for example are constantly redrawing boundaries. What has been remarkable is not that the boundaries shifted, but rather the ease with which architects have relinquished territory. As each of these areas have been lost, the skill and knowledge base that went with them has quickly atrophied and architects have almost willingly and with a sigh of relief unburdened themselves of yet another area of responsibility. That giving up the responsibility also meant giving up the influence either never occurred to architects or was not considered to be a problem.

The decline of professional status

We live in a society less accepting of professional status; clients are increasingly litigious and more readily inclined to sue professional advisers if things go wrong. For architects this was often the result of building failures but also increasingly failures to properly advise on planning and development matters or negligent contract administration. Architects were as a result seen as not best able to look after clients' commercial interests.

Driven by low profit margins and the high risk inherent in traditional contracting together with the high transaction costs of competitive tendering, contractors have in increasing numbers sought to move up the food chain.

...the increased popularity of design and build is...being driven almost entirely by promoters' desire to unload (dump?) the commercial risk of the project.

To add insult to injury, architects were forced to suffer the ultimate indignity for a profession that saw itself as financially impoverished, of being reviewed with solicitors, barristers and accountants by the Office of Fair Trading in their ongoing examination of overpaid professions of 2001. In as much as income is an indicator of status, the Construction Industry Council's *Survey of UK Construction Professional Services* provided a comparison of fee income with other construction and property professionals. It makes depressing reading for architects, where 'surveying firms have the highest per capita earnings (median £33,000) followed by engineers (£30,000) and architecture (£25,800)'.[12] This was in 1997, but matters have not improved dramatically. In the *RIBA Small Practice Survey*, of 1,112 practices employing less than 10 people that make up the bulk of the profession, 53 per cent of responding small practice principals earned less than £30,000, while only 11 per cent of principals in larger practices were in that position. Only 14 per cent of small practice principals earned more than £50,000, compared with 48 per cent of their peers in large practices.[13] What is noticeable here is that nearly half of principals in larger practices are earning less than £50,000, despite better economies of scale.

There is in any case from society at large very little residual sympathy for the architectural profession. Architects are often perceived as out of touch and arrogant, and seen by many as the creators of high-rise concrete buildings that blighted both the landscape and the lives of those who lived or worked in them. The little expert-authority architects have is often seen to be undermined by being subjective or just plain wrong, an occupational hazard for a profession concerned with that nebulous thing called design. So we see events that initiated change and gathered momentum over the last 20 years, all with the primary objective of improving the delivery of buildings and all with the side-effect, to varying degrees, of contributing to the reduction in influence of the architectural profession.

This constant theme of course suggests if not a causal link at least some association – that perhaps the pre-existing role of the architect was fundamentally a cause of the illness in the construction industry.

WHY DOES THIS DOWNSTREAM DRIFT MATTER?

Why does it matter? Is it not perhaps a more appropriate situation for architects to be in this downstream position or does something else suffer – something other than architects themselves?

The problem is not just a loss of influence per se but also a loss of effective and timely influence. By the time the architect is involved, a number of fundamental project decisions have been made – the site, operational brief, budget, allocation of funds between capital and running expenditure – all of which are difficult or impossible to undo, and all of which have a sustainable design implication. If architects were at the table earlier, their voice could be heard and the strategic direction of the project influenced. In some cases the strategic advice may even be to save resources by not building.

The problem is not just a loss of influence per se but also a loss of effective and timely influence.

As architects have moved downstream, the type of advice they give has changed. It has moved from being strategic advice to being detail advice. For most architects the design process would be seen to start from receipt of the brief. What goes before this – such as preparing the business case, finding the site and setting the budget – are the areas in which architects can add value. Architects will only be involved if promoters believe that they genuinely can add value, and architects will only be keen to be involved if it is commercially attractive.

Design is a push and pull process. As the physical form emerges it throws up new opportunities for a better design solution together with problems that call into question the brief or the budget. It is only when the architect is on board that these opportunities can be properly explored or the problems addressed. In short, the ability to add value by design diminishes as the architect moves downstream. The economic missed opportunities are manifest in less efficient operational design. The sustainable missed opportunities are revealed by the loss of balance between the capital and whole life 'costs'.

The cultural missed opportunities mean less uplifting cities and lost detail in buildings. This loss of influence also extends to a loss of the custodian of architecture role – the conscience of the building industry – that architects have always filled. The absence of anyone early on in the process with concerns beyond the immediate project – concerns relating to culture, the environment and history – inevitably runs the risk that the end result will be places that are not as inspiring to live and work in as they might have been.

The less architects are seen by promoters of buildings as strategic advisers, then the more vulnerable they will be to others further eroding their market base. At the level of architecture better building will happen where architects have influenced the direction of the development at the earliest stage. For this reason, to make a distinction between the well being of the architectural profession and the well being of architecture is of course completely artificial – the two are inextricably linked.

To sustain the profession of architecture and to ensure properly sustainable building solutions, it is essential that architects re-engage with and have a voice at the strategic stage of the building's genesis. This renaissance of influence with the upstream demand side could secure a role for architects that is both more appropriate and influential. For this to happen architects need to develop a sophisticated understanding of the construction industry and of property-based issues and their implications for design.

MOVING BACK UPSTREAM

The lie of the land upstream has changed considerably from the days when architects occupied this country. For architects to move back to this place will require a fundamental rethink of the skills architects need and the ways architecture is practised. Attempts to simply shoehorn the traditional architect into the new roles will not work. What is required is a 'new model architect', a paradigm shift for architects and architectural education. What is clear is that there is no longer one way to practise architecture but a number of models of architectural practice, each with their own characteristics and each requiring a new type of architect:

- The *partnering architect*, with an ability to understand the long-term business objectives of the partnering organisations, and able to develop and manage long-term relationships that will extend all the way up and down the supply chain.
- The *PFI architect*, able to understand the life-cycle cost implications of alternative designs and to translate abstract operational requirements into built solutions.
- The *design and build architect* able to incorporate true buildability without diminishing the architecture.
- Or even (for want of a better name) the *traditional architect*, leading the design team, administering the contract and advising the client.

This is not to suggest that architects align themselves to specific procurement systems but rather that they develop an ability to be at different times different architects to different clients.

Most of all, architectural practice needs to be responsive. There are two distinct aspects to responsiveness:

- responsiveness to market and consumer demand; and
- responsiveness to changes in the environment in which architecture is practised.

This requires architects to have appropriate transferable skills together with a high degree of enterprise. The architect–client interface is no longer a neat, well-understood relationship with clearly established roles. What is required is an ability to recognise the implications of the different organisational models that form the temporary project coalitions that pursue developments, and to adapt to fit within these models.

There was an established system for buying, designing and making buildings. It was far from perfect, indeed it contained many fundamental flaws. In this system the architect was a key, influential player (although arguably not a particularly well-qualified or capable player). A large part of that influence came from early involvement in the development process. This meant that architecture was kept on the agenda and that the architect fulfilled an important function as the creator of, and an advocate for, good architecture. But the system was fundamentally inefficient.

Changes that came about set out to improve efficiency in the building process; but they also pushed the architect (and therefore architecture) into a less influential position. For architects to survive either the world needs to move back to the way things were – unlikely and for many reasons undesirable – or architects need to find a new way of working within the new scheme of things. This will require of architects a new skill and knowledge base, which in turn requires rethinking both education and practice. Clients will as always vote with their chequebooks. When the new breed of architects can show an understanding of the market, profit- and risk-driven agenda of building promoters and demonstrably add value in the process, they will move to a more intimate upstream relationship with their clients.

The threat to our cities and to the environment is not that British architects are no good but more likely that they will have little influence. The battle is for the voice of architecture to be heard *at the right time* in the development process. As long as architects are excluded from the early strategic decision-making stage of a development, their ability to influence the quality of buildings – in particular the sustainability of buildings – will be significantly reduced.

Architects will only realise the full extent of their influence, and therefore be effective advocates for design and the environment, by acquiring the skill and knowledge base that allows them to articulately speak the language of the building promoter and of the property industry.

For architects to survive either the world needs to move back to the way things were – unlikely and for many reasons undesirable – or architects need to find a new way of working within the new scheme of things.

Notes

1. G. Winch and E. Schneider, 'The strategic management of architectural practice', in *Construction Management and Economics*, Vol. 11 (London: E&FN Spon, 1993), p. 469.
2. W. Reed and E. Gordon, 'Integrated design and building process – What research and methodologies are needed?', in *Building Research and Information*, Vol. 28, No. 5–6 (London: E&FN Spon, September to December 2000), p. 326.
3. S. Cox and A. Hamilton (eds), *The Architect's Job Book* (London: RIBA Publications, 1995), pp. 255–67.

4. Royal Institute of British Architects, *Standard Form of Agreement for the Appointment of an Architect* (London: RIBA Publications, updated April 2000).
5. S. Cox and A. Hamilton (eds), *The Architect's Job Book* (London: RIBA Publications, 1995), p. 267.
6. Sir Michael Latham, *Constructing the Team – Final Report of the Government and Industry Review of Procurement and Contractual Arrangements in the UK Construction Industry* (London: HMSO, 1994), p. 5.
7. Sir John Egan, *Rethinking Construction – The Report of the Construction Task Force* (London: HMSO, 1998).
8. RIBA, *Architects and the Changing Construction Industry* (London: RIBA Publications, 1999).
9. R. Gutman, *Architectural Practice – A Critical View* (New York: Princeton Architectural Press, 1988), p. 67.
10. AMEC Plc, *Annual Report and Accounts*, 1999.
11. Davis Langdon and Everest, *Contracts in Use – A Survey of Building Contracts in Use* (London: RICS, 1996).
12. Davis Langdon Consultancy for the Construction Industry Council and the Department of the Environment, Transport and the Regions, *Survey of UK Construction Professional Services – Survey Results, Part 1* (London: CIC, 1997), p. 37.
13. David Littlefield, 'Small firms face squeeze on work', *Architects' Journal*, 24 May 2001, p. 4.

The British Airways London Eye
London Eye in silhouette.

THE BRITISH AIRWAYS LONDON EYE

Construction managed by Mace, conceived and designed by Marks Barfield Architects, capsule design by Nic Bailey Design

ABOVE:
Exciting engineering for Alexander Abley.
LEFT TO RIGHT:
London Eye down onto pod roof.
Banner.
Structure lying horizontally.
At top with Houses of Parliament.
Down onto motor gantry.
Across to pod.
Pin joint.

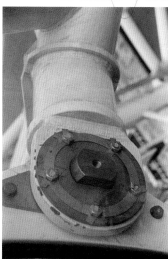

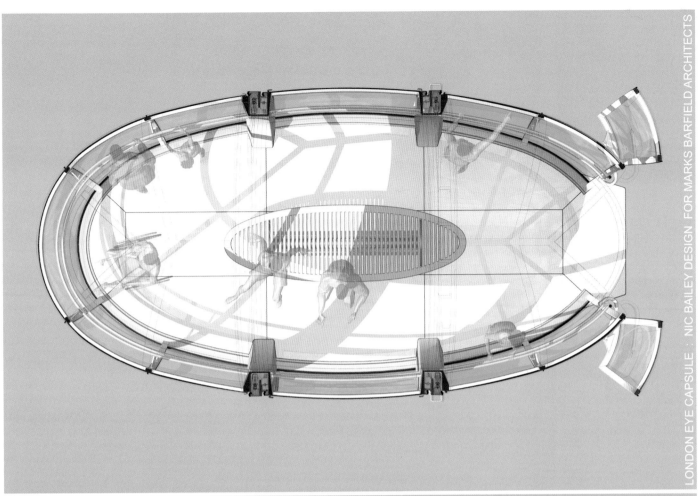

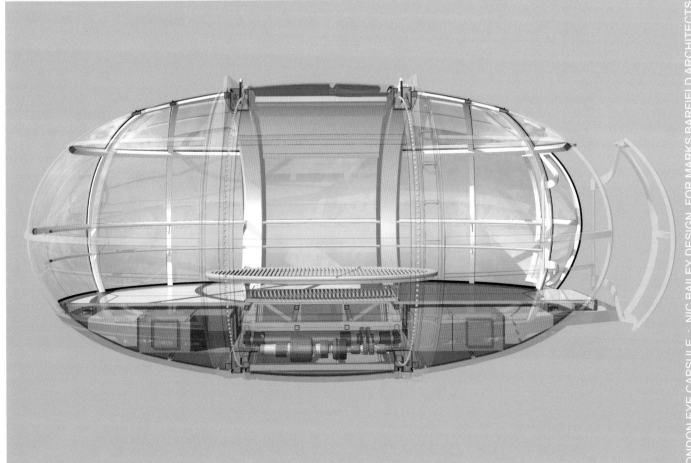

BEYOND CONVENTIONAL CONSTRUCTION

NatWest Media Centre
Lord's Cricket Ground
Future Systems

'This building abounds in firsts. It decisively parts company with conventional construction by being the first fully recyclable, all-aluminium, semi-monocoque building to be erected anywhere in the world...To say it is beyond the capabilities of the conventional construction industry to build such an object is to state the obvious. It is beyond conventional construction in the same way as advanced technology is beyond "High-Tech". This capsule building is an industrial product, a modular, computer dimensioned and cut aluminium hull, fabricated in sections in a Cornish shipyard, its segments trucked to London and welded together on site. Like cars, boats and aeroplanes it has few right angles and many compound curves. From its inclined optical glazing to its glistening white skin, every aspect of this revolutionary building has been honed by 20 years of single minded monocoque design development, so that its originals can be traced back to Jan Kaplicky's earliest capsule projects of the 1970s.'

Martin Pawley
1000 Words
Catalogue to the 'Future Systems' exhibition of April/May1998 at the ICA, London

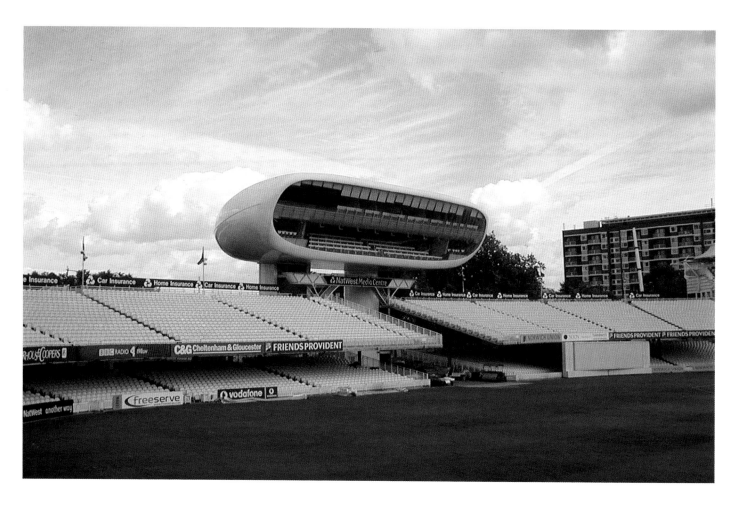

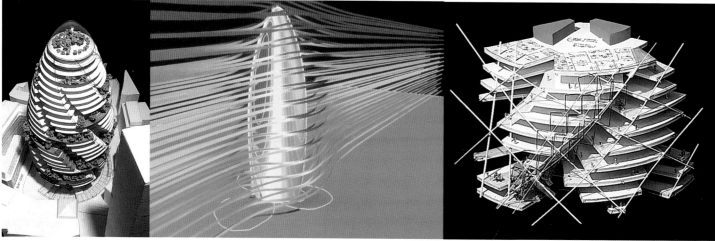

FROM TOP:

Swiss Re, London Headquarters,
photo-montage of the proposed building
on the skyline.

Working model.

Airflow diagram.

Detailed working model.

RIGHT:

Concept sketches by Norman Foster

OPPOSITE:

Photomontage view from street.
Diagrams showing the intersection of
the steel.

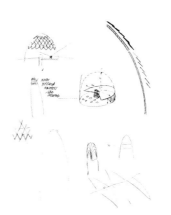

UNLIKE ANY OFFICE BUILDING SO FAR CONCEIVED

Swiss Re Headquarters, City of London
Foster and Partners

Swiss Re is one of the world's leading reinsurance companies. This new building will bring together all the company's London-based staff and will be the capital's first ecological tall building. Located on the site of the former Baltic Exchange in the City, the building will rise 40 storeys, about 180 metres above ground level. On a 0.57-hectare site the building will provide 41,810 square metres of office accommodation, together with a shopping arcade accessed from a new public plaza.

Conceptually, the project develops ideas first explored in the design of the Climatroffice (1971) with Buckminster Fuller. Climatroffice suggested a new rapport between nature and workspace; its garden setting created a microclimate within an energy-conscious enclosure, while its walls and roof were dissolved into a continuous triangulated skin.

Swiss Re is derived from a radial plan with a circular perimeter, which generates a profile that widens as it rises and then tapers towards its apex. It is fully glazed around a diagonally braced structure. Its double-curvature geometry was created using parametric modelling – a new digital technology originally developed by the aerospace industry. This form responds to the restraints of the site: the building appears more slender than a rectangular block of equivalent size; reflections are reduced and transparency is improved; the slimming of the profile towards the base maximises the public realm at ground level.

Atria are formed between the radiating fingers of each floor to combine in a series of sky gardens that spiral up the building. Socially these green spaces break down the scale of the building. Environmentally they help to regulate the internal climate, becoming the building's 'lungs'. Fresh air for mechanical ventilation is drawn in at each floor via slots lining the outer edges of each floor-plate, and is exhausted into the gardens where the plants have an oxygenating effect. The building's aerodynamic form generates pressure differentials that greatly assist this natural flow. The system is so effective that air-conditioning will not be required for the majority of the year. As a result, energy consumption is reduced dramatically in comparison with conventional office buildings.

The project is radical – technically, architecturally, socially, and spatially. Both from the outside and from within it is unlike any office building so far conceived.

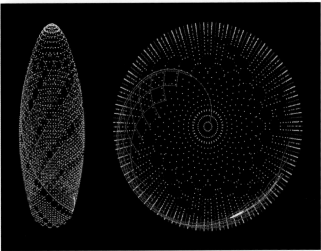

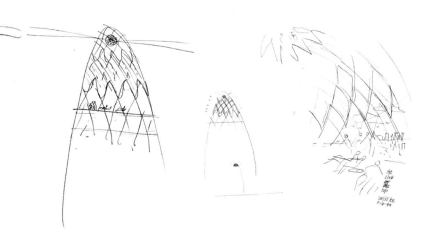

INDUSTRIAL PASTIMES

The Magna Project, Rotherham

Wilkinson Eyre Architects with Schal, Mott MacDonald, Deacon & Jones, Buro Happold, Spiers & Major and Event Communications Limited for The Magna Trust.

This is a Science Adventure Centre built inside the partially retained steel-works, exploring the elements of earth, air, fire and water. Funded by the Millennium Commission, English Partnerships and the European Regional Development Fund with land sales, sponsorship and private donations.

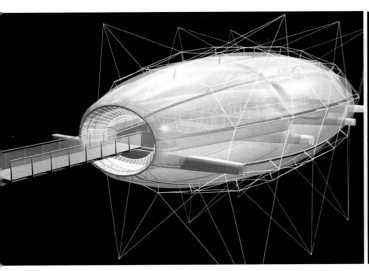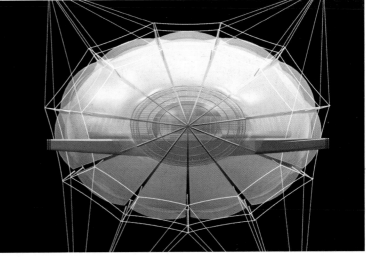

Chapter 18

Development Rights for the Hydrogen-Fuelled Future

Ian Abley, audacity.org

SUSTAINABILITY DOES NOT NECESSARILY MEAN LOW GROWTH

The World Commission on Environment and Development (WCED) published *Our Common Future* in 1987 as the Brundtland Report, calling for 'a new era of economic growth – growth that is forceful and at the same time socially and environmentally sustainable'.[1] In *Economic Growth and Environmental Sustainability*, Paul Ekins argues that environmentally sustainable economic growth is not necessarily the contradiction in terms it is often claimed to be. Yet he lacks confidence that the higher expectations of Brundtland can be realised:

> If a combination of technical change and efficient public policy begins to deliver both economic growth and improvements in environmental performance…then the faith of such documents as the Brundtland Report in the possibility of a synergy between growth and environment that goes beyond mere compatibility will have been vindicated. If not, then those who continue to insist that the environment will impose its own, perhaps catastrophic, limits to growth if humans do not learn to live without it first may well be proved right.[2]

There is no reason why sustainability should mean low economic growth. There is also no reason to suppose, as does the *Rough Guide to Sustainability*, that industry necessarily 'sows the seeds of its own destruction', or that 'consumption carries a corresponding burden of resource use, waste generation and, ultimately, CO_2 production'.[3] There seems to be a dislocation between recognising the potential of technology, such as the hydrogen fuel cell, and the means by which that potential is realised – sustained high economic growth. Rather than develop our way to a cleaner and more prosperous future the British preference is to talk about consuming less. Whether demand management is cynical, or advocated in the earnest belief that less consumption is better for our children's future, the attempt amounts to accommodating public expectations for living space to British construction output in long-term relative economic decline.

In Table 18.1, comparison of gross domestic product (GDP) and construction output figures, all at constant prices, shows that despite the speculative development boom from the mid-1980s to the early 1990s, the importance of construction in the British economy has steadily declined. Table 18.1 has been taken from the CITB *Construction Workforce Development Planning Brief – 2001 to 2005*, and also shows construction output and GDP for 1974–2001, with yearly growth rates in 1995 prices. This shows the declining amplitude of the 'boom and bust' of the construction industry exceeding the steadier fluctuations of the overall economy. Also in the latter half-decade the modest period of low but apparently sustained growth is evident.

In 2000, Davis Langdon and Everest produced *A Study of the UK Building Materials Sector* for the Department of the Environment, Transport and the Regions (DETR) and the Construction Products Association, giving the following overview:

> The UK economy has a long run growth rate in the region of 2.5% per annum. Over the period 1968 to 1997 contractors' output has barely grown by 1% per annum: the trend rate between the cyclical troughs of 1981 and 1993 was 2.25%.[5]

The British construction industry is simply not strong enough to support the level of environmental renewal needed. It may be true that there is a temporal mismatch between construction output and fluctuations in the growth of the economy if the detailed data is looked at in sectors. But over the long term the evidence is of a weak economy failing to stretch a construction industry that has been steadily in decline since the 1960s. The falling official construction statistics also do not show how people have managed to meet their own demands outside of the official economy to overcome supply-side inadequacies, as recognised by Martin Pawley:

> Britain's black economy has reached record levels. More than £124 billion of goods and services – about 13 per cent of the economy compared with 2 per cent in 1970 – will be bought this year without being declared to the tax man. The main component of our shadow economy is, guess what, the construction industry, which accounts for 35 per cent of the total and is expected *not* to account for £43.5 billion in 2001. All architects no doubt have their own anecdotal evidence one way or the other.[6]

Table 18.1: Comparison of construction output and GDP from 1963 to 2001, all at constant prices. Courtesy of EC Harris.[4]

Financial Year	GDP in real terms (£m)	Change on the previous year (%)	Construction output seasonally adjusted from a 1990 base (£m)	Construction output seasonally adjusted from a 1995 base (£m)	Change on the previous year (%)	GDP derived from 1995 based construction output (%)
1963 to 1964	389,476			52,700		13.53
1964 to 1965	406,332	4.3		49,118	-6.8	12.09
1965 to 1966	416,696	2.6		45,450	-7.5	10.91
1966 to 1967	427,034	2.5		41,904	-7.8	9.81
1967 to 1968	434,716	1.8		43,546	3.9	10.02
1968 to 1969	447,066	2.8		44,885	3.1	10.04
1969 to 1970	461,773	3.3		45,525	1.4	9.86
1970 to 1971	470,577	1.9		45,854	0.7	9.74
1971 to 1972	484,182	2.9		45,966	0.2	9.49
1972 to 1973	508,803	5.1		45,835	-0.3	9.01
1973 to 1974	530,935	4.3		46,080	0.5	8.68
1974 to 1975	525,034	-1.1		44,915	-2.5	8.55
1975 to 1976	527,438	0.5		43,194	-3.8	8.19
1976 to 1977	533,179	1.1		41,555	-3.8	7.79
1977 to 1978	552,566	3.6		39,940	-3.9	7.23
1978 to 1979	565,776	2.4		40,473	1.3	7.15
1979 to 1980	584,034	3.2		41,502	2.5	7.11
1980 to 1981	568,590	-2.6		41,190	-0.8	7.24
1981 to 1982	562,300	-1.1		40,140	-2.5	7.14
1982 to 1983	577,059	2.6		39,529	-1.5	6.85
1983 to 1984	599,012	3.8		39,332	-0.5	6.57
1984 to 1985	612,432	2.2		40,509	3.0	6.61
1985 to 1986	635,964	3.8	41,130	44,098	8.9	6.93
1986 to 1987	661,934	4.1	42,554	45,625	3.5	6.89
1987 to 1988	696,746	5.3	47,409	50,830	11.4	7.30
1988 to 1989	726,301	4.2	51,998	55,750	9.7	7.68
1989 to 1990	740,106	1.9	54,781	58,734	5.4	7.94
1990 to 1991	737,407	-0.4	55,307	59,298	1.0	8.04
1991 to 1992	731,356	-0.8	51,561	55,281	-6.8	7.56
1992 to 1993	735,363	0.5	49,522	53,095	-4.0	7.22
1993 to 1994	755,152	2.7	48,554	52,057	-2.0	6.89
1994 to 1995	790,204	4.6	50,124	53,741	3.2	6.80
1995 to 1996	806,423	2.1	49,696	53,282	-0.9	6.61
1996 to 1997	831,042	3.1	50,238	53,863	1.1	6.48
1997 to 1998	858,353	3.3		55,468	3.0	6.46
1998 to 1999	878,279	2.3		56,370	1.6	6.41
1999 to 2000	908,132	3.4		57,190	1.5	6.29
2000 to 2001				58,050	1.5	

If the £124 billion is added to the official GDP of £908 billion, and the £43.5 billion is added to the official construction output of £58 billion, then £101.5 billion of construction activity represents 9.84 per cent of the £1.032 trillion of British economic activity. This undeclared construction activity overlaps with the perfectly legitimate home-improvement sector, where construction has been reduced to a domestic chore largely due to the inability of householders to be able to afford to pay someone else to do the work. The real percentage of construction in the economy is nevertheless roughly equivalent to the percentage it was in 1970, if the black economy is considered. This shift obviously follows the rise of home ownership.

For a reversal of the trend, a high-growth economy is needed – the very thing the demand managers consider 'unsustainable'. It would be possible to draw a horizontal line at any height up the Construction

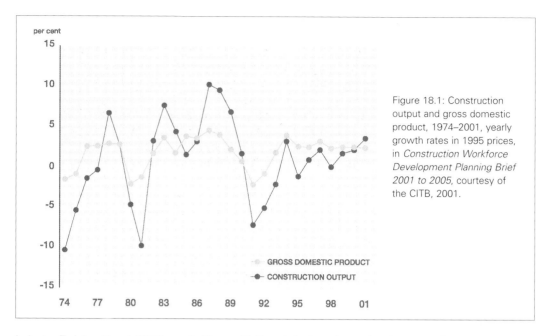

Figure 18.1: Construction output and gross domestic product, 1974–2001, yearly growth rates in 1995 prices, in *Construction Workforce Development Planning Brief 2001 to 2005*, courtesy of the CITB, 2001.

Industry Training Board (CITB) graph (Figure 18.1) and declare that to be the target for sustainability in either GDP or construction output. The problem is that such a high-growth target would not be a credible British policy option. Similarly, in the *Blueprint* edition, *Running on Empty – The End of the Mechanical Age*, Robert Webb, in a discussion of what he calls 'xCO$_2$' solutions, criticises the low expectations of the British government in its targets for modernisation:

> What's driving the xCO2 solutions revolution is a combination of new legislation on forthcoming carbon emissions trading, and consumer pressure. Bush's rejection is a blow to the diplomatic process, but Kyoto would have achieved only five per cent cuts in CO$_2$. While the diplomats talk, business is beginning to get on with it, led by multinational companies.[7]

Webb understands that 'mass production will remain central to the revolution, by its nature achieving astonishing efficiencies'. He wants improved supply backed up with demand management, while the tendency in Britain is for a general lowering of expectations to accept poorer supply. A *Study of the UK Building Materials Sector* shows that relative to the All Share Index the listed construction sector (of which materials companies represent about 80 per cent) values have declined to 40 per cent of their peak at the end of the 1980s. Perceptions of construction in the City are very poor:[8]

- The sector comprises companies that are perceived as relatively small, in a fragmented market.
- British domestic construction demand is relatively low and has little prospect of sufficient future growth.
- Britain is perceived as relatively backward in standardisation, prefabrication and off-site assembly – while mass customisation is seen as becoming increasingly important.
- The sector is also perceived as falling short in sound technical advice and aftersales service.

Obviously the City is choosing to ignore its part in perpetuating this sad state of affairs, and seems unable to risk even a modicum of the capital searching for lucrative investment.

Obviously the City is choosing to ignore its part in perpetuating this sad state of affairs, and seems unable to risk even a modicum of the capital searching for lucrative investment. Major investors, wanting readily tradeable stock, look for companies with capital valuations of £3–5 billion and 'the capacity to be world class', but there are only a handful of British construction companies in this league due to inadequate growth in the past. Rather than take risks, investors encourage the impulse to regulate the economy, as Daniel Ben Ami explored in *Cowardly Capitalism*:

> A pervasive fear of risk taking, which began to emerge in the USA and Britain in the 1980s, has…led to a shift in emphasis in the financial sector from raising capital to risk management. It has also created an environment in which extensive regulation is often welcomed by companies, as a protection against instability, rather than regarded as an imposition.[9]

For Ben Ami, the danger of financial instability is exaggerated while the problem of economic atrophy is understated. The forceful economic growth recommended by the Brundtland Report has been redefined as potentially destabilising and unsustainable. A backward construction industry is reposed as a prudent economic policy.

EMBODIED LABOUR TIME

The consequence that up to 30 per cent of construction is rework to correct poor workmanship or design, and labour is being managed at between 40 and 60 per cent of potential productivity given the level of technology employed, has been noted by the Construction Task Force. Accidents account for 3 to 6 per cent of total project costs and at least 10 per cent of materials are wasted.[10] There is little thought given to the waste of human time and effort by sustaining labour-intensive production to save energy and materials. For some products, of course, the amount of labour and the waste of materials are both immense. Slate roofing is the best example of a laborious construction technique that should involve selecting out most of the quarried material.

As Martin Pawley observed at the Building Audacity conference, environmentalists 'imagine that instead of using bulldozers and high energy consuming equipment, you should use men with shovels. The response to that idea of course is why not use ten times as many men with teaspoons?'[11]

In the foreword to the DETR report *Quality of Life Counts – Indicators for a Strategy for Sustainable Development for the United Kingdom*, Deputy Prime Minister John Prescott indicated that low growth and labour-intensive work was government environmental policy:

> In the past, focus has centred mainly on improving labour productivity. In the future, greater emphasis will be needed on resource efficiency. We need to break the link between continued economic growth and increasing use of resources and environmental impacts.[12]

The *Quality of Life Counts* report acknowledges the influence of *Factor Four*. Though *Factor Four* admitted technological change, the argument was still one of self-imposed limits in application:

> The economic boost from saving resources could thus erode the savings' benefits, if not channelled into a different pattern of development that encourages the substitution of people for physical resources.[13]

Capital-intensive, resource-efficient prefabricated construction appears optional to advocates of sustainability, and not the immediate priority. So regardless of the professional imagination, sustainable design defaults to marginally modernised site-based building methods, still reliant on laborious work to make material savings. Amory Lovins, an author of *Factor Four*, followed with *Natural Capitalism*, articulating the point in language that made the policy seem benign:

> Moving the economy toward resource productivity can increase overall levels and quality of employment, while drastically reducing the impact we have on the environment.[14]

The problem for Lovins is that capitalism is not natural but social. Capitalism progresses by producing more products with less labour in cost-cutting competition. This undermines the value of each product that can be compensated for by increased volume of sales, and hence cheapens the cost of living to

FROM TOP LEFT TO RIGHT:
Selecting the slate
Quarrying the slate
Transporting the slate
Handling and sawing the slate
Splitting, sizing and sorting the slate
Crating and marketing the slate
Roofing the slate

raise the quality of life for larger populations. As Alan Ashworth and Keith Hogg show, construction has fallen behind manufacturing:

> A family house at the beginning of the twentieth century cost approximately the same as a family car. By the beginning of the twenty-first century the ratio between the two was approximately 5:1.[15]

The 1998 Egan Report promoted productivity gains as the measure of improvement needed in construction, but by the publication of *Quality of Life Counts* the DETR had abandoned the Egan emphasis on productivity.[16] Environmentalists fail to recognise the need to reduce labour time embodied in ordinary products. Works of architectural art can have time lavished on them once sufficient mundane architectural accommodation is realised productively through the social division of labour. Sustainability has become an exercise in reducing the embodied energy in making buildings out of volumes of material regardless of the hours of labour required to build the construction. The aim should be to reduce the labour time required to produce products across society to minimal levels, and in the process realise resource efficiencies through the scale and technical sophistication of production. In failing to learn the lesson of the Egan Report, to make the most of the workforce by turning to capital-intensive manufacturing, the tendency has been to say that Egan was wrong. Construction and project management has simply learnt manufacturing phraseology while trying to keep control of site labour costs:

> To summarise, the Task Force wishes to emphasise that we are not inviting UK construction to look at what it does already and do it better: we are asking the industry and Government to join with major clients to do it entirely differently. What we are proposing is a radical change in the way we build. We wish to see, within five years, the construction industry deliver its products to its customers in the same way as the best consumer-led manufacturing and service industries. To achieve the dramatic increases in efficiency and quality that are both possible and necessary we must all rethink construction.[17]

The Egan Report was never about making contractors or construction managers behave like production engineers, because they cannot do it. This inability is not necessarily because they are personally incapable of achieving higher-quality buildings, but because contractors build on-site and products are made in a factory, whole or to be assembled by skilled people. Bad management compounds low productivity and poor quality, but it is hard for good managers to significantly improve productivity and quality. No car manufacturer would attempt to assemble a car on your drive, and no car salesperson would need to argue that the panels were aligned within tolerance because they would never have left the factory unless they were. Automotive industry products are 'better than any building ever built, and we know it'.[18] Michael Trudgeon explains why they are better designed:

> A totally new Japanese car requires 1.7 million hours of research and development time from blank sheet of paper to the first customer delivery. With an average run of one million cars, the design cost amortized across the production run comes in at only $425 per car, but each car has the benefit of 1.7 million hours of design thought. By comparison a new office building, costing $50 million with design consultancy fees running at 5 per cent of cost, has the benefit of only 10,000 hours of design thought. The worst case of all is a three-bedroomed architect-designed family home, with fees running at 11 per cent of cost. This will have only 1,750 hours of design thought. Under these conditions it is ridiculous to talk about 'smart buildings'.[19]

Unfortunately, British product designers are now advocating low productivity because former employers are unable to keep up. This anti-machine design reaction is happening at the very moment that the construction industry remembers it might manufacture architecture:

> Britain is well-placed to exploit growing demand for luxury cars. Because our native mass-production motor industry died, we were happily left with eccentric small manufacturers which provided a fertile breeding ground for idiosyncratic talent. No real dollar costs here, just the essence and thrill of thinking about exciting cars.[20]

For Stephen Bayley: 'function can look after itself', and we 'are left just with dreams and the irresponsibilities that begin there'. British designers seem to be retreating from the machine age imperative to cram more functionality into repetitive products containing fewer materials in less production time. This anti-machine delusion may seem to be the appropriate response in a country that has lost a leading role. We have to recognise that the stagnant British economy could waste the potential for manufactured, hydrogen-fuelled architecture. A recent editorial in *Detail* was less sceptical about wider European prospects:

> Now...the ecological and economic challenges facing the construction sector and the new manufacturing processes that are available would seem to have given system building a new impetus.[21]

Outside of Britain, the industrial or industrialising nations are likely to manufacture their architecture more successfully, and are developing cleaner energy generation or motive power technologies. The

Sustainability has become an exercise in reducing the embodied energy in making buildings out of volumes of material regardless of the hours of labour required to build the construction. The aim should be to reduce the labour time required to produce products across society to minimal levels, and in the process realise resource efficiencies through the scale and technical sophistication of production.

future for Britain might be direct foreign investment in production facilities or imports of products we cannot produce ourselves. What is certain is that we cannot continue as we are with the evident productive shortfall to meet the growth in societal demand for accommodation. Demand management will not work either.

HOUSEHOLD GROWTH SHOULD BE ENCOURAGED

Unless we are to extend the life of buildings we have to increase new construction volume so that manufactured buildings are replaced quicker. The only other way out of the accommodation shortage is to multiply the size of the labour force across construction. This might suggest scrapping immigration controls to allow free migration of labour, combined with a redoubling of the efforts to address the problems identified by the CITB:

> Price competition in the construction industry is very acute and, in the past, construction companies have often been obliged to ignore problems with workers' skills, and allow projects to come in late and over budget. However, demands from customers for improved quality, service and time-keeping means that the industry increasingly needs to compete on more than just price. This has serious implications for skill requirements and the industry will no longer be able to rely on poorly skilled workers in times of shortage.[22]

The worst development scenario now is that neither capital nor labour intensive construction output will be increased fast enough. Somewhere between 2016 and 2021 there will be between 22.5 and 25 million households in England.[23] In *Estimates of Future Housing Needs and Demand in Restructuring Housing Systems – from social to affordable housing*, Alan Holman suggests the revised projections would add 500,000 households to the currently projected increase between 1996 and 2021. This gives a 2021 total of 24.5 million households instead of 24 million under the 1996-based projections.[24] To achieve housing renewal on a 100-year cycle we need to be building at least 240,000 homes annually even before the estimated household growth after the first decades of the twentieth century is considered. It is unlikely that a 100-year life can be realised from most existing stock. Even a 50-year replacement cycle would require 480,000 units a year. That would mean variously sized and regionally based production facilities turning out a total of 1850 homes a day on a five-day week. Each of 50 of these facilities would have to produce an average of 37 homes per day on a production line, or the equivalent daily output of a conventional housing estate, to be distributed throughout the towns and countryside. More production facilities would be needed for Scotland, Wales and Northern Ireland.

Is it simply beyond Britain to be able to achieve this increase in output, to gain the resource efficiency savings and labour productivity gains at the point of new production? If it is, then what hope have we of achieving a sustainable urban renaissance built on site? At their all-time peak in 1968, housing completions had reached 413,700 a year. We should go a lot further, and actively encourage household growth.

By way of comparison the Volkswagon Wolfsburg headquarters near Hanover in Germany occupies 8 square kilometres with 1.5 million square metres of production halls, in which every day a mere 50,000 employees collaborate to produce 3,000 cars. Every day 200 customers personally collect their personalised vehicles from the Autostadt with its fully automated circular storage towers, and 3,000 spectators come to enjoy the entire process.[25] Until we achieve economies of scale in architectural design we will repeat and perpetuate the inadequacies of site-built construction:

> You can probably reduce a building's carbon dioxide emissions by half if you design it thoughtfully. We renew our stock by 1% per annum, so for all new buildings, over 10 years, we only get a 5% improvement…The other 15% of UK construction's contribution has to come from insulating and reducing energy consumption in existing buildings.[26]

The figures presented by Rab Bennetts assume it will take 100 years to fully replace building stocks. In *Building a Crisis – Long-term housing under-supply in England*,[27] John Stewart has observed that: 'in the three years to 1999, losses to the housing stock through slum clearance and other demolitions averaged 15,600 dwellings per year. At this rate, homes constructed today will have to last 1,350 years on average'.[28] Completions add only 1 per cent to the housing stock each year, and new homes represent between 10 and 12 per cent of the housing market. There is a predominant trade in existing property in need of further energy to be embodied through refurbishment to approach operating efficiencies available in new construction. As with investment in infrastructure, housing provision must be viewed from a long-term perspective. The consequences of a shortfall over five, or even ten years may not be immediately apparent, but the cumulative impact of long-term housing under-provision will become increasingly difficult to reverse. With the existing but insufficient housing stock worth a total of £1.4 trillion, averaging at £80,000 per household,[29] the last thing any politician will question is the restrictive development policy in respect of the countryside and the level of under-supply upon which current borrowing and lending rests.

Economist 31 March to 6 April 2001

We should go a lot further, and actively encourage household growth.

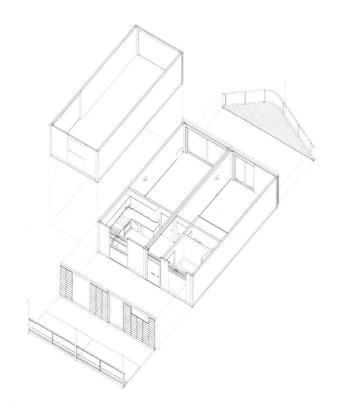

ECONOMY OF SCALE REQUIRED

Murray Grove and Shepherdess Walk, London
Cartwright Pickard Architects, Yorkon and The Peabody Trust

The prefabrication experiment by Cartwright Pickard Architects and Yorkon for The Peabody Trust at Murray Grove and Shepherdess Walk in Hackney, London, shows what is possible and required for a repetitive programme. A range of urban densities can be achieved by repetitively stacking fully fitted volumetric units, and finishing them with site-fixed cladding systems and smaller prefabricated components.[30] The fact that Peabody chose to rent rather than sell the properties means it is not proven but only likely that there is a market for such prefabricated home ownership in Britain today.

As a prototype scheme the budget had to be generous, and to go further the architects and manufacturers need to secure a high volume of orders to bring the unit cost down. Peabody has announced further commissions for Cartwright Pickard and other architects but until we start thinking on the scale of the daily output of regionally based production facilities these tentative adventures will have little impact outside of the trade press. The economies of scale are the key to prefabrication, as was recognised by C. Gray in *Value for Money – Helping the UK Afford the Buildings it Likes*.[31] An ambitious programme of prefabricated urban projects could meet the scale of the current under-supply of housing, but the critical factor is land availability. The difficulty in identifying brownfield land for projects is undoubted, but with planning reform the market for repetitive infill projects may be opened up.

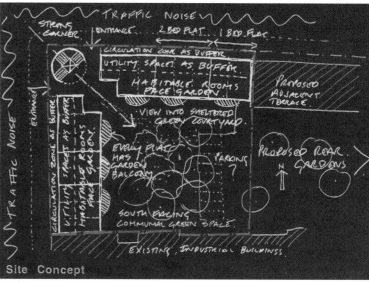

Site Concept

TOP: Exploded view of 1 bed unit.
CLOCKWISE FROM ABOVE: Craneage view from neighbouring building, © Yorkon

Sketch of site layout.

Yorkon factory facility, © Yorkon

Demonstration unit, © Yorkon

Craneage view from site, © Yorkon

THE MOUNTING HOUSING CRISIS

The previous government target was to achieve only 40 per cent of the 4.4 million new homes envisaged in the 1996 *Household Growth* on greenfield land. This translated into less than a 1.3 per cent loss of farmland to development, or about 170,000 hectares, resulting in a total of only 12 per cent of all land being developed by 2016 at an average density of over 25 homes per hectare.[32] These are projections of new households, which have often been underestimated. Household projections for Scotland extend only as far as 2010, whereas those for England and Wales extend to 2021. Housing under-supply is an English problem, partly due to patterns of economic migration across the country. Regional variations showing surpluses imply the housing situation is far from satisfactory. The calculations take no account of stock age, condition and vacancy rate, nor the geographical distribution of the stock in relation to need. The 1998 stock surpluses in Wales and Scotland were 5.6 per cent and 5.3 per cent respectively, compared with 1.1 per cent on average in England. For the DETR:

Housing under-supply is an English problem, partly due to patterns of economic migration across the country.

The challenges we face include:

- social changes with people living longer, having fewer children and many more living alone. As a result we may need to accommodate up to 3.8 million extra households by 2021;
- encouraging people to remain in, and move back into, our major towns and cities, both for the benefit of our urban areas and to relieve the pressure for development in the countryside;
- tackling the poor quality of life and lack of opportunity in certain urban areas;
- addressing the weak economic performance of some parts of our towns and cities and enabling all areas to compete successfully for jobs and investment in the global marketplace; and
- reducing the impact which urban living has on the environment, making sustainable choices practical and attractive.[33]

Immigration is not a challenge government is prepared to countenance, failing as it is in sustaining sufficient housing to cope with internal migration. This reduced New Labour figure of 3.8 million is for England alone, but it is arguable from the 1998-based population projections that it should be increased by a further 500,000 to 4.3 million.[34] The earlier 3.8 million comes from the 1996-based population and household projections that are believed to seriously underestimate gains from migration. It should not be forgotten that the economy depends on migration and mobility. There is generally a grudging recognition of the need for greenfield development, with an annoyance that households are migrating to find better living environments, larger homes and work. Most short-distance migration is for housing and personal reasons, while a high proportion of longer distance migration is job-related, all pushing up demand for suburban development, particularly in the southeast. Southern regional planning bodies have argued that future housing need is going to be less than implied by the 1996 projections. Yet the actual household growth in these regions since 1996 has been 15 per cent ahead of the rate of growth predicted in *Household Growth*. In other words, the southern regions are planning to undershoot projections that are themselves inadequate. This will cause a gross inflation of the housing market that will be unpopular to correct, as John Stewart appreciates:

In short, housing under-supply is not a cost-free option. Severely restricting housing supply, and then simply allowing the market to bring supply and demand back into balance through higher house prices and rents, will do enormous long-term social and economic damage.

...house building completions in 2000 fell to their lowest level since 1946. Excluding the wartime period 1940–1946, completions were at their lowest since 1924'.

Housing under-supply is evident. As John Stewart has observed, 'one momentous record you are not likely to hear is that house building completions in 2000 fell to their lowest level since 1946. Excluding the wartime period 1940–1946, completions were at their lowest since 1924'.[35] Production inertia set in during the late 1970s and 1980s. Last year, only 166,400 new homes were completed in Britain. For John Stewart:

- It is generally accepted that each household should have a separate home.
- Household formation at the national level is only very weakly responsive to changes in housing supply and housing costs. People form new and independent relationships regardless of whether affordable housing is available in their area.
- Long-term real income growth tends to increase household formation.

Examining data from 1939 up to the early 1990s for the Joseph Rowntree Foundation, Alan Holmans concluded that household growth at the national level was largely independent of the rate of expansion of the housing stock.[36] Restricting housing supply in the hope that this will deter household formation through higher house prices and rents will prove largely ineffective. Only house-price rises, negative economic effects and upward pressure on social welfare costs are achieved through inadequate supply. House-price rises give the appearance of prosperity, and if you can ever cash domestic property in at the right time the housing market has proven far more lucrative than the labour market. However, housing is financed from wages, and when the period of low interest rates comes to an end the price hike partially caused by an inadequate supply of housing will strain incomes hardly keeping pace with inflation. The cost of under-development is set to become immediate, and will be passed back to employers sooner or later, depending on how self-sacrificing their employees remain.

The public sector only completed an estimated 400 homes in 2000, and that figure has never exceeded 1,000 homes per year since 1996. In 1967, by contrast, public-sector house-building peaked at 198,900. A collapsed public-sector provision does not explain why the private sector has failed to make up the shortfall, and as Stewart argues, any resurgence in public housing will only discourage private housing if total supply is not increased:

> Government efforts to boost social housing provision through planning gain agreements will prove ineffective under conditions of aggregate housing under-supply. Such agreements reduce the already inadequate supply of private housing, thereby pushing up housing costs and further increasing the need for social housing in a vicious circle.[37]

Unfortunately it has been the public sector itself through the plan-led system of the early 1990s that has worsened the level of private-sector under-provision. Intended to remove uncertainty, it in fact removed flexibility in land supply. Theoretically, if the market were left alone house builders would increase the supply of new homes in response to rising demand and higher house prices. However, new housing supply is unlike the supply of most other products because a raw material, developable land, is heavily regulated. The need for every dwelling to be granted planning permission means that the planning system controls the location, scale, type and even tenure of new housing development. In other words, house builders are only able to produce the new homes allowed by the planning system. With supply determined largely by regulation, not by market forces, it is entirely possible the planning system might allow too few dwellings of the right type and in the right locations to be built.

In a futile effort to direct the market, planners have been given major new responsibilities to compile brownfield capacity studies for public scrutiny. An inflexibility in decision-making has been institutionalised since the late 1990s when it became common to fixate on technical distinctions in brownfield and greenfield sites, which explain little about economic, social and environmental relationships of town and country. The electoral meltdown the Conservatives faced in 1997 did not damage the policy presumption in favour of brownfield redevelopment. It suggested the DETR separate from the Ministry of Agriculture Fisheries and Food, briefed the Urban Task Force, and is the basis of *Housing*, Planning Policy Guidance (PPG) note 3. Like all such government planning-policy guidance notes, PPG3 should be taken into account by regional and local planning authorities in preparing their plans, and may also be material to decisions on planning applications and appeals. Compliance with PPG3 is not a statutory requirement, but is considered to be contemporary good practice:

> Urban land and buildings can often be significantly underused. In order to establish how much additional housing can be accommodated within urban areas and therefore how much greenfield land may be needed for development, all local planning authorities should undertake urban housing capacity studies.[38]

The capacity of existing urban areas to absorb the anticipated scale of development was for a while a hotly debated subject. The facts are hard to come by. The National Land Use Database of Previously Developed Land, the NLUD-PDL survey of brownfield sites, was the only capacity information available. This was supposed to distinguish brownfield sites that were vacant, derelict or in use with planning approvals or development potential. This data has since proved to be sparse, imprecise or out of date. In *Tapping the Potential – Assessing Urban Housing Capacity: Towards Better Practice* the DETR proposed to comprehensively update the NLUD-PDL survey with greater detail, relying on the overstretched resources of planning departments expected to implement PPG3:

> It is important that appraisals should consider as many sources of capacity as possible, no matter how unlikely some sources and locations may initially appear in terms of the current housing market.[39]

Planners were not only being asked to replicate and centralise the sorts of studies that developers and landowners variously undertake in the course of operating in the property market, they were being asked to think ahead of the market, a trick that is euphemistically called 'Plan, Monitor and Manage'. The previous approach was supposed to be 'Predict and Provide', or the achievable goal of recognising demand for land in the aggregate over a period of time, and allocating space for development in broad principle. Unfortunately the default condition was 'Predict and Under-provide':

> The essential difference between Plan, Monitor and Manage and the old predict-and-provide approach is that clear objectives – rather than trends – guide planning decisions, and the rate of land release for housebuilding is kept under constant review, rather than allowing land to be released to provide projected demands up to 20 years ahead.[40]

In a futile effort to direct the market, planners have been given major new responsibilities to compile brownfield capacity studies for public scrutiny.

This has pleased the Council for the Protection of Rural England (CPRE). The CPRE wants to further recommend that greenfield land should be released to meet development demand only if it can be shown that there are insufficient brownfield sites for more than five years ahead, and subject to annual review at public hearings. Collating and maintaining this detailed data on space in urban areas is an impossible task and a colossal waste of resources. Studies such as *The National Survey of Vacant Land in the Urban Areas of England*,[41] published in 1990, can no longer be relied upon but have not been updated. While planners in the capital have the benefit of the Greater London Authority producing *London's Housing Capacity*,[42] most regional planners are finding they have to start from scratch where any existing analysis is suspected of being out of date. To make the job more difficult, and before any new land can be outlined for future urban growth, planning authorities have been asked to categorise their constantly outdating capacity data under the headings elaborated in the DETR's *Tapping the Potential*.[43] David Rudlin rehearses most of the supposed capacity categories for Friends of the Earth in *Tomorrow, A Peaceful Path to Urban Reform*:[44]

Collating and maintaining this detailed data on space in urban areas is an impossible task and a colossal waste of resources.

- Subdivision of existing housing.
- Flats over shops.
- Empty homes.
- Previously developed vacant and derelict non-housing land and buildings.
- Intensification of existing areas.
- Redevelopment of existing housing.
- Redevelopment of car parks.
- Conversion of commercial buildings.
- Review of existing housing allocations in plans.
- Review of other existing allocations in plans.
- Vacant land not previously developed.

After the Urban Task Force report *Towards an Urban Renaissance*, and in response to his proposals being met with widespread but muted scepticism, Richard Rogers redoubled his efforts and wrote *Cities for a Small Country* with Anne Power, Professor of Social Policy at the London School of Economics. Believing that proximity equates to community, Rogers and Power insist that all housing must be to London densities. Not just greenfield sites in the process of development, but suburbs of 20 to 25 dwellings per hectare and rural housing at lower figures should be routinely intensified. Rogers and Power want to protect the

Table 18.2: Changing the capacity of brownfield and greenfield land through development density.[45]

Changing the supply of housing from brownfield development (%)	Capacity of brownfield land	Capacity of greenfield land
Based on 25 houses per hectare as typical in 1999	55	45
Increasing density by ⅕ to 30 houses per hectare	65	35
Increasing density by ½ to 37.5 houses per hectare	82	18
Doubling densities to 50 dwellings per hectare is equivalent to generalising 1999 London densities	100	0

countryside regardless of the quality of greenfield land available in the regions. In *Cities for a Small Country* the proposed policy is a doubling of density to reduce greenfield requirements to zero.

> We must apply brownfield targets to rural areas too, so that using small spaces, adding extra storeys, changing uses and densification can make these outlying settlements more compact and more viable. And we can certainly apply urban design principles to suburbs.
> Suburbs offer many of the spare corners, underused buildings and patches of land that cry out for small additions. Renovating, managing, diversifying and densifying suburbs so that they become neighbourhood centres in their own right and more integrated into urban patterns should be part of the renewal strategy of towns and cities.[46]

Intensification happens in suburbia anyway, as extensions into the loft or over the garage to provide additional space for the family. It does nothing to create accommodation for new households, and it was the increase in household numbers that prompted the equation of urban compaction with sustainability in the first place. Creating new dwellings above shops makes sense to anyone who has ever looked at the vacant property over Britain's high streets, but the loss of lucrative frontage is an obstacle.[47] The scope for creating new homes through subdivision is also limited. Previously, the DETR had suggested housing conversions might average 12,000 per year over the period 1996–2016, with another 3,000 per year from residential conversions of other buildings.[48] Annual gains since 1971 only ever reached these levels in the housing boom of the 1980s, when an affordability crisis altered the profile of effective demand towards smaller homes, including flats, and in the last three years. A more recent study for the DETR concluded that non-residential building conversions could contribute between 5,600 and 9,500 homes per year, with another 6,600 to 9,500 per year from residential conversion, giving a total range of approximately 12,000 to 19,000.[49] Clearly not spectacular numbers, and of diminishing scope.

Promoting a policy against the supposed profligacy of suburbia does not get a single urban home built affordably, and no amount of urban capacity studies will guarantee that house builders can profitably regenerate dilapidated property or brownfield sites in need of remediation to meet household demand. Planning consultant Llewelyn-Davies has perhaps done most to grapple with the problem of identifying

Table 18.3: Regional and national average densities of housing development.[52]

Average densities of housing development (units/hectare)	Average brown-field density	Average green-field density	Average over-all density
North East	27	21	24
North West and Merseyside	28	22	25
Yorkshire and Humber	26	21	24
East Midlands	24	22	24
West Midlands	31	23	27
Eastern	25	22	24
London	49	38	47
South East	23	22	23
South West	29	23	25
National	28	22	25

urban capacity, including the epic *Sustainable Residential Quality – New Approaches to Urban Living*.[50] The problem is daunting, as the DETR acknowledges in *The Use of Density in Urban Planning*.[51] Being a planner is now far removed from planning, and has become an exercise in surveying and statistical reporting. There is a tendency among professionals to obsess about achieving statistical policy targets of 60 per cent brownfield recycling, forgetting the caution from the House Builders Federation about urban regeneration:

Where they are attractive, our existing inner urban areas must not be made less so by over-development. The development of every available site in the inner urban areas would be inappropriate.[53]

To cram the population into what government recognises to be insufficient urban space is to sacrifice human interests for the sake of nature. The Urban Task Force is sensitive to the criticism of over-development:

Increasing the intensity of activities and people within an area is central to the idea of creating sustainable neighbourhoods. 'Intensity' and 'density' carry connotations of urban cramming: too many buildings and cramped living conditions.[54]

It remains to be seen how long the government can sustain PPG3, whether planners will openly criticise it, or whether the public will put up with spiralling house prices and a lack of housing choice. A single density and a crude distinction between brownfield and greenfield is far from having a subtle and responsive planning policy. In any event, as Stewart knows, the problem is one of finding land for housing production, not cramming land with housing density:

Whether house prices rise by 6% or 10%, and whether total housing market volumes expand or contract, is largely irrelevant to the outlook for house building. As house builders work through their current stocks of greenfield land with planning permission, the new restrictions introduced by PPG3 will not provide sufficient land to replenish these stocks.

The question is not whether a stronger-than-predicted housing market in 2001 will bring a recovery in private house building, but how long house builders will be able to maintain current production, and whether the PPG3-induced decline will cut completions from today's 145,000 to 130,000, 120,000, or perhaps even 100,000.[55]

Production is simply being frustrated by a restrictive planning process, policed by various groups of self-appointed environmentalists encouraged by government to be involved in development decision-making. Protecting land has become more important than making housing fit for habitation. The 1996 *English House Condition Survey* found 7.5 per cent of the housing stock was defined as 'unfit', with the most common reasons being unsatisfactory facilities for preparation and cooking of food, disrepair and dampness.[56] A dwelling is unfit for human habitation, as defined in the 1989 Government and Housing Act, if it fails to meet one or more of nine requirements and, by reason of that failure, is not reasonably suitable

Promoting a policy against the supposed profligacy of suburbia does not get a single urban home built affordably, and no amount of urban capacity studies will guarantee that house builders can profitably regenerate dilapidated property or brownfield sites in need of remediation to meet household demand.

Table 18.4: Change in regional housing surpluses.[57]

Housing surpluses, showing housing stock as a percentage of households	1971	1981	1991	1996	1998
North East	-	4.3	2.6	2.4	3.2
North West	-	4.3	2.8	2.8	3.2
Yorkshire & the Humber	-	4.1	1.6	0.9	1.4
East Midlands	-	5.2	2.6	1.8	2.0
West Midlands	-	4.4	2.0	1.4	1.4
East	-	5.4	3.2	1.9	1.0
Greater London	-	1.8	2.7	0.0	-2.4
South East	-	4.0	2.4	0.4	-0.9
South West	-	5.5	3.7	2.5	1.9
Average for England	0.9	3.7	2.6	1.4	1.1
Average for Scotland	-	6.5	5.3	5.2	5.3
Average for Wales	4.3	8.1	5.6	6.1	5.6

for occupation. On a wider definition of poor housing conditions, including unfit dwellings, those in substantial disrepair or requiring essential modernisation, the figure rises to 14.2 per cent of stock.

The quantity and broad distribution of housing supply in Britain is determined largely by the planning system, with a restricted role for market forces. Long-term under-investment in housing contributes towards economic and social inertia. The sustained under-provision over the last two decades has already left a shortfall of some 900,000 homes. It may take many years, if not decades to remedy the cumulative inactivity of sustained under-development. The social immobility that is created increases longer-distance commuting and requires many people to move further from work in search of more affordable housing. The lack of new housing in communication with economically dynamic locations is burdening the transport infrastructure that may already be insufficient to take an increase in forced commuting. As John Stewart says: 'it is not a question of whether England faces a housing crisis, but at what stage it will become undeniable'.[58] However, it need not be like this.

The quantity and broad distribution of housing supply in Britain is determined largely by the planning system, with a restricted role for market forces.

THE DENIAL OF DEVELOPMENT RIGHTS

Since 1 July 1948, the Town and Country Planning Act 1947 has established the planning system by denying the owners of all buildings and land the democratic freedom to develop their property without obtaining planning approval. The denial of development rights united Labour ministers with the landed aristocracy. The policy found support from those arguing for state intervention in the property market to protect British agricultural capacity in case of another war, professionals hoping for the authority to modernise society by modernist design, and architects who had despised 'bungaloid growth' since the 1920s. This was a reaction to increasing numbers of middle and later working-class car owners being able to buy and build on cheap farmland outside of the industrial towns and cities where they worked, as noted by David Jeremiah:

Bungalows at Pitsea

New arterial roads, road widening, ribbon development and building threatened the picturesque village and created a climate in which, after twelve months of planning, led to the inaugural meeting of the Council for the Protection of Rural England, at the RIBA, on 7 December 1926. 'Ugliness' and 'Disfigurement' became the slogans, the architects became the missionaries, and the suburbs the darklands of cultural savages.[59]

Two years later Clough Williams-Ellis, then hardly known as an architect, published the polemic *England and the Octopus*. The Octopus was London, but could have been any city stretching out into the countryside along the road network increasingly accessible to car owners. The Housing and Town Planning Act of 1909 had initially given local authorities limited powers to oversee development of buildings and land, but for Williams-Ellis this was insufficient. When Jonathan Dimbleby was president of the CPRE in 1996, a facsimile edition of *England and the Octopus* was printed. For Dimbleby: 'it is impossible to read this book without recognising that in the generations since it was published, we have done far more damage – with the car, our appetite for material goods and the great urban exodus – than Clough Williams-Ellis had imagined'.[60]

> The conditions favouring the changes that have come upon us are scarcely new, either in kind or degree, nor unforeseen – or at any rate not unforeseeable. What are they?
> *A monstrously swollen population.* Our steeply ascending birth-rate graph has been the pride and joy of our Jingo politicians for at least a century, and its trajectory could be calculated ahead with very tolerable accuracy.
>
> *The drift from agriculture to industry* – from the rural to the urban areas. That, too, is generations old and by no means incalculable.
>
> *Improved means of locomotion.* Surely the shock of finding the flying coaches on Macadam's wonderful new roads quickly and suddenly superseded by the railways should have prepared us, or at any rate our rulers, for the possibility of revenge and a reversal, when concrete, rubber and petrol might turn the tables on steam and steel?[61]

When Williams-Ellis wrote this in 1928 he was not anticipating sustainability, but to some extent sustainability has come to hold a 1920s prejudice about the technological culture of mass communication and mobility. There are apparently too many of us taking too much space and traversing it too quickly. Before 1947 it was the case that property ownership was coincident with development rights, as Clough Williams-Ellis bemoaned:

> Freehold property is at present almost as unreservedly yours to do as you please with as is your waistcoat or your watch. There is no legal compulsion on you to use it in a way that will be acceptable and inoffensive to your neighbours and the general public. If what you propose to do outrages them, their only remedy is to bribe you from your purpose by purchase or cajolery, or scare you from it by public protests – which is an extremely unsatisfactory state of things.[62]

Would this really be worse than the current situation, where decision-making powers rest with the planning committees of local government and their officers? There is a difference between power and authority. Is it better for councillors and professionals to determine planning applications for everyone, with the power of an Act of Parliament to justify the institutionalised distrust of the majority? Or would it be better to leave people free to decide exactly what the parameters of social responsibility in local development should be? People are capable of electing someone to a position of authority to deal with disputes when required. Would this really be chaos, or a democratisation of development activity that confronts the rise of consultation and third-party objection head on? Would this restore the meaning of freehold? It is not a new idea. Writing for *New Society* in 1969 Reyner Banham, Paul Barker, Peter Hall and Cedric Price argued that development could not be worse if planners were relieved of their powers and we had 'Non-Plan':

> as people become richer they demand more space; and because they become at the same time more mobile, they will be more able to command it. They will want this extra space in and around their houses, around their shops, around their offices and factories, and in the places where they go for recreation. To impose rigid controls, in order to frustrate people in achieving the space standards they require, represents simply the received personal or class judgements of the people who are making the decision.[63]

It would be interesting, as Martin Pawley argues in Chapter 13, to work through a policy to return development rights to land owners, a policy that was framed to encourage a commitment to development using hydrogen fuel-cell technologies. Obviously the development right will be undermined if qualified with conditions, but the debate would be fascinating in trying to work through such a policy. Planning could be democratised at little cost and almost immediately.

SOLVE THE AGRICULTURAL CRISIS

The policy of returning development rights would associate agricultural diversification with prefabricated, hydrogen-serviced housing, perhaps made conditional on densities of between one and ten houses per hectare for framed structures standing above the ground. This would enable the government to cancel all agricultural subsidies, and farmers would either consolidate further into agribusinesses, or sell up for development. As Andrew O'Hagan points out, a fundamental rethink is required:

> The bucking of market forces…was one of the founding principles of the [Common Agricultural Policy], and even today, when we finally see the bottom falling out of the system of rewards and grants for overproduction, the tendency is towards 'relief' packages, which New labour support through gritted teeth. It would appear that for a long time now British farming has been faced with two choices: a slow death or a quick one. And not even Thatcher could tolerate a quick one.[64]

Government is trying to get out of paying for rural maintenance without the countryside becoming wilderness and to make farming economically sustainable.[65] Since the Farming Summit held at Downing Street on 29 March 2000, the government advice is that farmers must diversify to manage without subsidy:

> At the summit the Prime Minister set out his vision for the agricultural sector: one that moves away from subsidy dependence; one that produces high quality, healthy and traceable produce; one that is environmentally responsible and one that diversifies intelligently and realistically.[66]

The schemes that try to deal with production surpluses by paying farmers to set land aside are being compounded with various environmental incentives. Sean Rickard appreciates that farmers need to prepare for competition from food produced cheaply around the world, and that means further consolidation into agribusiness. Put simply, 'other farmers must exit the industry in order to provide the scope for expansion'.[67] The only way government could cut the subsidy is to allow marginal farmers to sell their unproductive land for development, to consolidate agriculture around those farmers with the capital to run a profitable agribusiness.

This would have the advantage of freeing land for low-density housing, attractive to people who may want to cultivate their land intensively, keep exotic livestock, or get involved in the time-consuming work of landscape management. Not as subsistence farming, because household resettlement schemes have failed before (the most notable being the Land Settlement Association scheme in the 1930s and early 1940s). Smallholdings were uneconomic then.[68] Diversified landscape on the fringe between agribusiness and urban centres will work if done for pleasure. This would leave agribusiness to crop more produce of increasing quality and variety from less space and labour time for the benefit of all. Martin Pawley understands this perfectly well. Land without beneficial use is not scarce today. If it cannot be used to build on, what can it be used for?[69]

The Countryside Agency recognises that people vote with their feet where they can afford to, and 'there is a net movement of people from towns and cities to suburbs and rural areas:

> Those moving into the countryside tend to be relatively affluent families and their children, in pursuit of a better 'quality of life'.[70] Some areas are also receiving significant numbers of retired people. Those moving out of rural areas tend to be the less well-off and young adults in search of jobs and affordable housing. As a result, rural England has a higher proportion of older people than has the country as a whole.[71]

Unsurprisingly, one in three people living in British cities wants to live in the countryside, while fewer than 5 per cent of those already living in the countryside would move to a city.[72] The urban renaissance appears contrary to the prevailing aspiration for life in the country, in communication with the town.[73]

TRUST

The return of development rights to property owners would allow the government to remove agricultural subsidies and spur British construction to become the sort of industry that the Egan Report suggested it should be.

The return of development rights to property owners would allow the government to remove agricultural subsidies and spur British construction to become the sort of industry that the Egan Report suggested it should be. It would ease the difficulties the government has in funding the Urban Task Force agenda, and carried out the right way would have the added advantage of inaugurating the hydrogen-fuelled future. The government will not be able to avoid a housing policy review indefinitely, and the Town and Country Planning Act 1947 is long overdue for a serious rethink. However, the countryside has been neglected as part of housing policy ever since demand for 4.4 million new homes was anticipated in the 1996 report *Household Growth – Where Shall We Live?*:

> Only one thing has to be taken as read. That is that we should seek to provide as many as possible of these new units on land which has already been used, particularly that land which is found within our towns and cities. The principle of sustainable development, which lies behind all that the Government seeks to do, demands that we use every opportunity to protect green field sites. The wholesale destruction of the countryside is not an option.[74]

House building has been disconnected from any context. Neither economic growth nor household growth means higher levels of house building. The wholesale destruction of the countryside is not the intention. Nor is it the intention to blight urban areas or cities. At the other end of the density scale there would be exciting opportunities for high-rise projects, unless property owners locally brokered arrangements to impose height restrictions on themselves. As Kenneth Powell cautioned: 'recession may yet see the vision of a city of towers fade. Yet the urge to build high is unlikely to diminish. London has the talent to address it memorably,' and the City 'cannot simply turn its back on tall buildings'.[75] This remains to be seen.

Will the government trust landowners to use their development rights wisely, responsibly and democratically, initiate the hydrogen-fuelled future, and end the anti-machine age? Trust, both at home and towards immigrants, seems in very short supply.

Notes

1. World Commission on Environment and Development, *Our Common Future*, commonly known as the Brundtland Report (WCED, Oxford: Oxford University Press, 1987), p. xii.
2. Paul Ekins, *Economic Growth and Environmental Sustainability – the Prospects for Green Growth* (London: Routledge, 2000), p. 326.
3. Brian Edwards and Paul Hyett, *Rough Guide to Sustainability* (London: RIBA Publications, 2001), p. 4.
4. Data kindly supplied by Paul Moore, Head of the Cost Research Department at EC Harris. GDP figures have been taken from the Treasury web site. The construction output figures have been taken mainly from the HMSO publication *Housing and Construction Statistics*; the older figures were taken from the BCIS Online service where they are available on a quarterly basis only. Adding these quarterly figures together, to come up with yearly figures, there were slightly different totals for those years with two sets of figures, although the reason for these slight differences is unknown. Since the purpose of the statistics is to show the broad sweep of the relation between GDP and construction, these anomalies have been ignored.
5. Davis Langdon and Everest, *A Study of the UK Building Materials Sector* (London: DETR and the Construction Products Association, September 2000), p. 17.
6. Martin Pawley, 'There's no turning back the tide of technological "advancement"', *Architects' Journal*, 5 July 2001, p. 22.
7. Robert Webb, 'Sustained release', in 'Running on Empty – the End of the Mechanical Age', *Blueprint*, No. 184, June 2001, pp. 73–4.
8. Davis Langdon and Everest, *A Study of the UK Building Materials Sector* (London: DETR and the Construction Products Association, September 2000), pp. 74–5.
9. Daniel Ben Ami, *Cowardly Capitalism – the Myth of the Global Financial Casino* (Chichester: John Wiley & Sons, 2001), p. 154.
10. Sir John Egan, *Rethinking Construction – the Report of the Construction Task Force* (DETR, London: HMSO, 1998), p. 18.
11. Martin Pawley, speaking at the Building Audacity conference.
12. Deputy Prime Minister and Secretary of State for the Environment, Transport and the Regions, John Prescott MP, foreword to *Quality of Life Counts – Indicators for a Strategy for Sustainable Development for the United Kingdom: A Baseline Assessment* (London: DETR, 1999), p. 4.
13. Ernst von Weizsäcker, Amory B. Lovins and L. Hunter Lovins, *Factor Four – Doubling Wealth, Halving Resource Use* (London: Earthscan Publications, 1997), introduction, p. xxviii.
14. Paul Hawken, Amory B. Lovins and Hunter L. Lovins, *Natural Capitalism – the Next Industrial Revolution* (London: Earthscan Publications, 1999), p. 56.
15. Allan Ashworth and Keith Hogg, *Added Value in Design and Construction* (Harlow: Pearson Education, 2000), preface, page xi.
16. Sir John Egan, *Rethinking Construction – the Report of the Construction Task Force* (DETR, London: HMSO, 1998), p. 14.
17. Ibid., p. 40.
18. Martin Pawley, 'Lavish, visionary architecture puts the user in the driving seat', *Architects' Journal*, 1 March 2001, p. 26.
19. Michael Trudgeon, 'Architecture as an anti-technological virus: the work of Michael Trudgeon', *World Architecture*, Issue 23, May 1993, quoted by Martin Pawley, *Terminal Architecture* (London: Reaktion Books, 1998), p. 196.
20. Stephen Bayley, 'End to end', in 'Running on Empty – The End of the Mechanical Age', *Blueprint*, No. 184, June 2001, p. 55.
21. Editorial, *Detail 41*, series 2001, no. 4, p. 606.
22. Construction Industry Training Board, *Construction Workforce Development Planning Brief – 2001 to 2005* (London: CITB, 2001), p. 33.
23. Department of the Environment, *Household Growth – Where Shall We Live?* (London: DOE, November 1996), p. 5.
24. Alan Holmans, 'Estimates of future housing needs and demand', in Sarah Monk and Christine Whitehead

Will the government trust landowners to use their development rights wisely, responsibly and democratically, initiate the hydrogen-fuelled future, and end the anti-machine age?

(eds), *Restructuring Housing Systems: From Social to Affordable Housing* (York: York Publishing Services, 2000).

25. Layla Dawson, 'Motor City', *World Architecture*, issue 91, November to December 2000, p. 81.

26. Rab Bennetts, interviewed by Elaine Knutt, 'Wessex man', in 'The Green Century', *Building*, 5 January 2001, p. 21.

27. John Stewart, *Building a Crisis – Long-term Housing Under-supply in England*, draft of an unpublished report researched for the House Builders Federation, kindly provided to Ian Abley 25 April 2001.

28. Ibid.

29. Jane Padgham, 'House prices bouncing up', *Evening Standard*, 31 May 2001, p. 1.

30. Richard Partington, 'Urban Pioneer', *Architects' Journal*, 25 November 1999, p. 25.

31. C. Gray, *Value for Money – Helping the UK Afford the Buildings it Likes* (Reading: Reading Construction Forum, 1996).

32. Annex B, The Urbanization Projections and other Land Use Data, Department of the Environment, *Household Growth – Where Shall We Live?* (London: DOE, November 1996), p. 49.

33. Department of the Environment, Transport and the Regions, *Our Towns and Cities – the Future, Delivering an Urban Renaissance* (London: HMSO, November 2000), p. 7.

34. Alan Holmans, 'Estimates of Future Housing Needs and Demand', in Sarah Monk and Christine Whitehead (eds), *Restructuring Housing Systems: From Social to Affordable Housing* (York: York Publishing Services, 2000).

35. John Stewart in correspondence with Ian Abley, 25 April 2001.

36. Alan Holmans, *Housing Demand and Need in England 1991–2011* (York: Joseph Rowntree Foundation, 1995).

37. John Stewart, *Building a Crisis – Long-term Housing Under-supply in England*, draft of an unpublished report researched for the House Builders Federation, kindly provided to Ian Abley 25 April 2001.

38. DETR, *Housing*, Planning Policy Guidance note 3 (London: The Stationery Office, 2000), para. 24.

39. DETR, *Tapping the Potential – Assessing Urban Housing Capacity: Towards Better Practice* (London: DETR, 2000), p. 10.

40. Council for the Protection of Rural England, *Plan, Monitor and Manage* (London: CPRE, December 2000), p. 1.

41. J. Shepherd and A. Abakuks, *The National Survey of Vacant Land in the Urban Areas of England* (London: HMSO, 1990).

42. *London's Housing Capacity*, London Planning Advisory Committee and the Greater London Authority, 2000.

43. DETR, *Tapping the Potential – Assessing Urban Housing Capacity: Towards Better Practice* (London: DETR, 2000).

44. David Rudlin, *Tomorrow, a Peaceful Path to Urban Reform* (London: Friends of the Earth, 1998).

45. Richard Rogers and Anne Power, *Cities for a Small Country* (London: Faber and Faber, 2000), chart 6.3a, p. 189.

46. Ibid., pp. 213 and 249.

47. Anne Petherick, *Living Over the Shop* (London: Urban and Economic Development Group (URBED), 1997); *Dwellings Over and in Shops in London* (London: Civic Trust and London Planning Advisory Committee, 1998).

48. Department of the Environment, *Household Growth – Where Shall We Live?* (London: DOE, November 1996).

49. DETR, *Conversions and Redevelopment: Processes and Potential* (London: DETR, 2000).

50. Llewelyn-Davies, *Sustainable Residential Quality – New Approaches to Urban Living* (London: London Planning Advisory Committee, 1998).

51. DETR, *The Use of Density in Urban Planning* (London: DETR, 1998).

52. Urban Task Force, *Towards an Urban Renaissance – Final Report of the Urban Task Force* (London: E&FN Spon, 1999), figure 7.11, p. 187.

53. *Urban Life – Breaking Down the Barriers to Brownfield Development* (The House Builders Federation, 1998), p. 8.

54. Urban Task Force, *Towards an Urban Renaissance – Final Report of the Urban Task Force* (London: E&FN Spon, 1999), p. 60.

55. John Stewart in correspondence with Ian Abley, 25 April 2001.

56. DETR, *English House Condition Survey 1996* (London: The Stationery Office, 1998).

57. DETR, *Projections of Households in England to 2021; 1996-based estimates of the numbers of households for regions* (London: DETR, 1999), with DETR, *Housing Statistics 2000* (London: The Stationery Office, 2000), and various issues of *Housing & Construction Statistics*. Data compiled by John Stewart, *Building a Crisis – Long-term Housing Under-supply in England*, draft of an unpublished report researched for the House Builders Federation, kindly provided to Ian Abley 25 April 2001.

58. John Stewart, *Building a Crisis – Long-term Housing Under-supply in England*, draft of an unpublished report researched for the House Builders Federation, kindly provided to Ian Abley 25 April 2001.

59. David Jeremiah, *Architecture and Design for the Family in Britain – 1900–1970* (Manchester: Manchester University Press, 2000), p. 61.

60. Jonathan Dimbleby in a foreword to Clough Williams-Ellis, *England and the Octopus* (London: Geoffrey Bles, 1928), facsimile edition (London: Council for the Protection of Rural England, 1996).

61. Clough Williams-Ellis, *England and the Octopus* (London: Geoffrey Bles, 1928), facsimile edition (London: Council for the Protection of Rural England, 1996), p. 28.

62. Ibid., p. 107.

63. Reyner Banham, Paul Barker, Peter Hall and Cedric Price, 'Non-Plan – an experiment in freedom', *New Society*, 13, no. 338 (20 March 1969), pp. 435–43.

64. Andrew O'Hagan, *The End of British Farming* (London: Profile Books and the London Review of Books, 2001), p. 48.

65. Ministry of Agriculture Fisheries and Food, *England's Rural Development Plan 2000–2006* (London: MAFF, 2000).

66. Andrew Clark, 'Challenging the farming paradigm', *Landscape Design*, July–August 2000, p. 18.

67. Sean Rickard, 'Abandoning farm support', *Landscape Design*, July–August 2000, p. 22.

68. T. Alwyn Lloyd, 'Land settlement schemes in Wales', *Journal of the RIBA*, 22 May 1939, p. 719, quoted in David Jeremiah, *Architecture and Design for the Family in Britain – 1900–1970* (Manchester: Manchester University Press, 2000) p. 92.

69. Martin Pawley, 'So, Lord Rogers, why shouldn't we build on surplus rural land?', *Architects' Journal*, 24 February 2000, p. 20.

70. N. Stratford, *Rural and Urban Views on the Countryside – Findings from the British Social Attitudes Survey 1999*, Report for the Countryside Agency by National Centre for Social Research, 2000.

71. The Countryside Agency, *The State of the Countryside 2001* (Cheltenham: Countryside Agency Publications, 2001), p. 25.

72. Vital Statistics, *Architects' Journal*, 7 December 2000, p. 8.

73. J. Murdoch, *Why do People Move to the Countryside?*, report for the Countryside Commission, Department of City and Regional Planning, University of Wales, Cardiff; Mulholland Research Associates Ltd, *Towns or Leafier Environments? – A Survey of Family Home Buying Choices* (London: MRAL, 1995).

74. John Gummer, Secretary of State for the Environment, foreword to the Department of the Environment, *Household Growth – Where Shall We Live?* (London: DOE, November 1996), p. ii.

75. Kenneth Powell, 'High principles', *Architects' Journal*, 24 May 2001, p. 22.

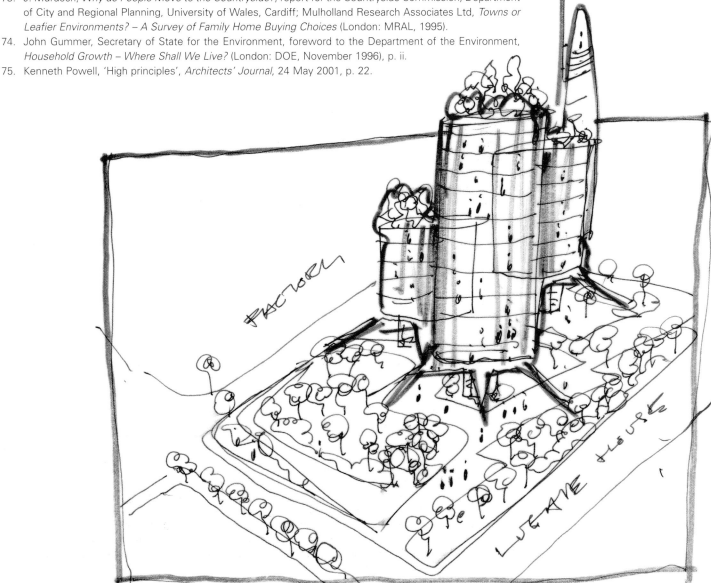

'Coca-Cola' can housing option for the Assemble Group.

Supporting audacity.org

WHAT IS AUDACITY.ORG?

audacity.org is a research company of industry professionals determined to question assumptions and limitations in British construction. Its aim is to advance development practice to make our working lives both easier and intellectually challenging. By confronting what we believe to be the platitudinous morality of sustainability we have sought to develop themes for further investigation. We hope that this book will encourage a wider range of specialists to join with us in these enquiries, and that readers will raise their own concerns and insights.

WHAT ARE WE INTERESTED IN?

- We believe there is considerable need to research the ways in which new contracting arrangements and methods of dispute resolution serve to undermine the teamworking that they rhetorically seek to encourage. We are grateful to Daniel Lloyd and Deborah Brown for this insight, and hope to broaden this discussion with other lawyers and project managers. Contracting fashions come and go, but the trend away from a reliance on clear commercial contracts in a fragmented construction industry is far from ideal for any party in the development process. We should not delude ourselves that the arrangements that succeed at the manufacturing economy of scale of capital investment will be directly transferable to site-based construction. Peter Walker and Paul Hyett both understand the need for a reassertion of professional expertise in the development process, but do not foresee a return to the discredited practices of the past. Yet without an immediate prospect of the construction industry entering the machine age through forms of mass-production architecture, are architects condemned to a sub-consultant role and the frustration of artistic pretension?

- We wish to investigate the potential for, and consequences of returning development rights to property owners in an age when almost anyone is considered a stakeholder in the planning process. Consultation has become habitual, as Miffa Salter considers, and objectors are being legally encouraged, as Margaret Casely-Hayford observes – all with no clear democratic benefit. The result is the inertia of state intrusion in the most mundane of development issues in a social system that promotes property ownership, but refuses to trust the populace to develop land. Paul Hyett has raised the prospect of the protection of function for architects, and not merely title. Alan Hudson has argued that there are better concepts of what planning might be. We are not against planners, but we reject the idea that people cannot be trusted to own living space without professional supervision. Indeed, as Sean Stanwick shows, expert planning seems either to promote a facile illusion of community or encourages a stifling social conformity. The question Sean raises is to what extent do people want such real or imagined social convention in the machine age of mobility and communication?

- We are also interested in the social opportunities and technical possibilities at the extremes of development density that, as Miles Glendinning and Stefan Muthesius remind us, are tending to be ignored. Martin Pawley and James Heartfield have argued for a historic reappraisal of land use. Is there the prospect for low-density architecture, a highly diversified agriculture and inhabited landscape to deliver the sense of dwelling that Phil Macnaghten hopes for? Austin Williams, Shane Slater, Ben Madden and Duncan Price ask how highly serviced the cities of the twenty-first century could be. It should be easy to find manufacturing, engineering and construction solutions to environmental challenges if Helene Guldberg and Peter Sammonds are correct, the doomsday scenario of global warming is not going to happen. Is the idea of the hydrogen-fuelled future a fantasy and should we be concentrating on demand management rather than the problems of under-supply? Or is it true, as Pamela Charlick, Natasha Nicholson and Paul Hyett maintain, that scientific advance fails to offer a technical fix to environmental problems through machine-age production?

ARE THERE SPECIFIC PROJECTS TO GET INVOLVED WITH?

- Ian Abley is researching the uneasy relationship of the Futurists and the subsequent twentieth-century avant-garde to machine production. This will provide the background to a contemporary argument that manufactured architecture will free up time and provide the resources required socially for architectural research, product design development, and any wider artistic endeavour. He would welcome any advice and assistance in this book proposal.

- Daniel Lloyd has argued that an environmental duty of care could become a popular legal fiction. We want to monitor the seemingly relentless formulation of a legal convention out of the moral imperative of sustainability. Such a fictional duty should be opposed on the basis that it would be undemocratic and antisocial, but it is unclear to us where a robust argument for the maintenance of precise legal principle might come from. We would be very pleased to be contacted on this subject.

- As both static- and motive-power fuel cell technologies develop in the next few years we want to help promote their early application, in particular through the association of 'electrofarming' or biomass reformation with architectural development. A discussion group of interested specialists is something we would like to establish.

We are always keen to consider commercial research projects, and would be very pleased to hear of construction-related initiatives to which we may be able to contribute.

On 10 July, 2000, audacity.org organized a one-day conference at the Building Centre, Store Street, London, entitled 'Building Audacity'. This was illustrated with an exhibition of the same name that ran in the foyer from 5 July to the end of the month. That event was our first attempt to interrogate the aspects of sustainability that we found contradictory, debilitating, or just plain wrong. This book came from that event. The transcript can be accessed on our website at www.audacity.org.

HOW TO CONTACT AUDACITY.ORG?

You may write to us at the following address:
Ian Abley
audacity.org
8 College Close
Hackney, London
E9 6ER
Email: abley@audacity.org
Web site: www.audacity.org

Building Audacity
Programme for the conference held on 10 July 2000

RESOURCING THE FUTURE
Will our children thank us for sustainable development?

Sustainability is a duty owed to future generations, but the resources we currently enjoy came from the unsustainable growth our parents realised. Returning to inefficient or polluting practices of the past is not, where avoidable, a sensible option. However, slowing the pace and scale of development is the big idea to survive from the latter years of the twentieth century. Technological modernisation can hardly be stopped, and is not inherently problematic, provided new methods and materials are environmentally assessed. Only by advancing with some social purpose are previously unimportant or inaccessible materials turned into a stock of resources, which means changing how we work and not merely modernising familiar work patterns.

We specifically question why construction professionals choose between resource efficiencies and labour productivity, rather than aspire to achieve both.

This approach considers human labour as a renewable resource. Such a polarisation tends to favour making savings in resource use, including land use, to the point that increasing urban density is now an obsession, while construction remains a site based chore. So will sustainability turn construction into an aspect of manufacturing industry, or just modernise the site?

Speakers:

Martin Pawley, Columnist for the *Architects' Journal* and Author of *Theory and Design in the Second Machine Age* and *Terminal Architecture*

Graeme Jennings, Architect and Director of b Consultants

Lucy Pedler, Product Specialist at Construction Resources, the first ecological building merchant in Britain

Ian Abley, Site Architect and Director of audacity.org

BEING INSPIRED
Is everything worth building naturally precedented?

You do not need to be an environmentalist to appreciate the elegance of sophisticated natural systems, structures, textures or colours. Nor is it new to be in awe of ecologies that have evolved to avoid waste. It is true that ecologically aware designers rely on natural metaphors as precedent for architectural experimentation.

Yet it seems paradoxical that environmentalists who advocate a deference to ecosystems are creating unprecedented buildings, demonstrating human ingenuity. Nature may inspire, but environmentalists further argue that we can do no better than imitate. It is the human ability to abstract scientific insights from nature that allow us to go beyond reproduction and transform both our surroundings and ourselves.

We use nature dynamically as a source of inspiration, whilst recognising that man has transformed nature.

The most imaginative of contemporary architectural and engineering practices are ecologically minded, but could they do better? Does it help to think sustainably when building human environments, or does a deference to nature limit creativity?

Speakers:

Brian Edwards, Head of Huddersfield School of Architecture and Author of *Sustainable Architecture*

Duncan Price, Building Physicist and Associate at Engineers Whitby Bird and Partners

Alex Cutler, Sustainable Development Consultant at SustainAbility Limited

Austin Williams, Technical and Practice Editor for the *Architects' Journal*

STANDING UP FOR OURSELVES
Does environmentalism turn humanism on its head?

It is considered a virtue to accept with humility that humans are just one of many species inhabiting supposedly incomprehensible ecosystems. Yet while rejecting ideas of a privileged position in nature, sustainability appeals to the humanitarian aspiration for a more equitable world. Advocates use these environmental and social justifications for introducing constraints on development practice. Yet while the Royal Institue of British Architects promotes sustainability as a duty for architects, we may face onerous extensions to the legal scope of our professional duty of care. This presumes a degree of foresight and planning.

Meanwhile experts have evidently lost professional self-confidence, by relying on interminable and inconclusive public consultation exercises. Environmentally sensitive designers are conscious to avoid a charge of arrogance.

We want to challenge the myths that to be daring is reckless and that artistic expression is incompatible with industry, but is a materialist and confident vision of society in any way compatible with an ecological sensibility?

Speakers:

Paul Hyett, Vice-president for Education at the Royal Institute of British Architects and Vice-president of the Architectural Association

Phil Macnaghten, Fellow of the Centre for the Study of Environmental Change and Co-author of *Contested Natures*

Miffa Salter, Head of Regeneration at the Office for Public Management

James Heartfield, Author of *Need and Desire in the Post-Material Economy*

Contributor Biographies

Ian Abley is the director of audacity.org, a research company determined to question the assumptions and limitations in British construction with the aim of advancing development practice. He works as a site architect in London for major commercial practices. The experiment of the Building Audacity conference and exhibition led to the commission for *Sustaining Architecture in the Anti-machine Age* and the opportunity to engage with more contributors to further assess where the architectural profession and construction industry are going with sustainability. The book will hopefully generate debate and lead to a more coherent criticism of the contemporary anti-humanism that is expressed through the anti-machine reaction of the age.
abley@audacity.org
www.audacity.org

Ian Abley

Deborah Brown is a lawyer in the real estate and construction group at CMS Cameron McKenna and the winner of the 1999 Society of Construction Law Hudson Prize. Currently working for employers and developers on non-contentious projects, she has also been involved in disputes on civil engineering and process plant contracts. CMS is a major transnational legal services organisation with 1,700 lawyers and offices in most of the principal European business centres. The real estate and construction group at CMS Cameron McKenna comprises over 60 partners and has extensive experience of property and construction transactions across Europe.
deborah.brown@cmck.com
www.cmck.com

Margaret Casely-Hayford is a Partner at Denton Wilde Sapte. She practises in planning, public law, private finance initiative and development matters. Her areas of expertise include retail, leisure, historic buildings, compulsory purchase, statutory appeals and judicial review. She provides strategic advice on major projects. These include town-centre regeneration, stadia redevelopment, energy installation and development schemes. Margaret also advises on hospitals, housing, large offices and major retail developments. In the strategic preparation of applications for planning, conservation areas and all relevant consents, she has extensive experience. In addition she co-ordinates and manages projects to public inquiry. This involves arranging for environmental assessments, ensuring presentation of relevant evidence, negotiation and advocacy.
mch@dentonwildesapte.com
www.planningadvice.co.uk
www.dentonwildesapte.com

Margaret Casely-Hayford

Pamela Charlick and **Natasha Nicholson** studied architecture in London and Edinburgh and are partners in the design practice charlick + nicholson. Their research and practice interests are in understanding urban dynamics and developing ecological strategies for architectural intervention. In 2000 they initiated and curated the 'London Living City' exhibition at the RIBA, exploring urban sustainability issues. They are continuing this investigation through the Internet project living-city.net, which is combined with a touring exhibition. They have taught at the University of North London.
mail@charlicknicholson.co.uk
www.charlicknicholson.co.uk
www.living-city.net

Pamela Charlick and Natasha Nicholson

Miles Glendinning works at the Royal Commission on the Ancient and Historical Monuments of Scotland. He has co-authored and edited various books on modern architecture and housing, and on

Miles Glendinning and his daughters Amy-Felicity and Sally

Helene Guldberg

James Heartfield and Holly in Fiji

Alan Hudson

Paul Hyett

Scottish architecture in particular. His most recent book, written with architect David Page, is *Clone City*, a polemical analysis of the effects of globalisation on the Scottish City.
milesg@rcahms.gov.uk
www.rcahms.gov.uk

Helene Guldberg is Managing Editor of the online publication *spiked*. She was co-publisher of *LM* magazine from its launch in 1997 to its closure in 2000. She has programmed and organised high-profile events on science and society, most recently co-directing 'Interrogating the Precautionary Principle' at the Royal Institution, London, in summer 2000. She has a PhD in developmental psychology and is an associate lecturer with the Open University. She has written for publications from *spiked* and *New Scientist* to the *Architects' Journal*, *The Independent* and the *Index on Censorship*.
info@spiked-online.com
www.spiked-online.com

James Heartfield writes and lectures on the creative industries and the new economy. He is teaching at Sussex University and the University of Delaware. He co-edited *Sustaining Architecture in the Anti-machine Age* for audacity.org, and has written for *The Times*, *The Guardian*, *Blueprint*, *Architects' Journal* and the *Fiji Times*. In 1998 James published *Need and Desire in the Post-Material Economy*, and in 2000 was commissioned by the think-tank Design Agenda to publish *Great Expectations – The Creative Industries in the New Economy*.
james@heartfield.demon.co.uk
www.heartfield.demon.co.uk/james1.htm
www.design-agenda.org.uk

Alan Hudson is the Director of Studies in Social and Political Science, University of Oxford Department for Continuing Education. He is the co-author of *Basildon – the Mood of the Nation*, as part of an ongoing longitudinal study of the attitudes of skilled workers in Basildon new town. Alan is now researching the new role of the front-line retail worker with particular reference to the Bluewater shopping centre.
alan.hudson@conted.ox.ac.uk
www.conted.ox.ac.uk

Paul Hyett had an unorthodox route into architecture. After a spell in the merchant navy and aviation insurance, he trained at the Architectural Association and worked for Cedric Price and then Alan Baxter before setting up his own practice. While in practice he gained an MPhil in town planning at the Bartlett, and has since taught architecture, planning and urban design in Germany and Britain. He has lectured widely and written extensively, most notably for six years as a columnist for the *Architects' Journal*. Currently President of the RIBA, Hyett is also a representative for Europe at the International Union of Architects on education. He is a past Vice-President for education at the RIBA, and a past Vice-President of the Architectural Association. His practice has carried out extensive work in the areas of social infrastructure, including the London Ambulance Service Control Centre, the Fire Research Testing Station for the Building Research Establishment, schools, college work, and a series of leisure buildings. The firm has also carried out projects for a variety of charities, of which the most interesting has been a treatment centre for Victims of Torture. His practice merged in 2000 with a long-established firm in Newcastle upon Tyne, Ryder Company, and he is now the London-based chairman of the new organisation Ryder, a successful practice committed to incorporating sustainable principles throughout its work.
phyett@ryders.com
www.ryders.com
president@inst.riba.org
www.architecture.com

Daniel Lloyd qualified as a barrister in 1996. After completing pupillage at Cloisters he worked for Freshfields. Daniel also taught public law at University College London for two years. He is a co-founder of the civil liberties group Freedom and Law. He has written widely on the legalisation of everyday life and

has organised many conferences on topical legal issues. He now works as an in-house lawyer for a large communications company.
dlloyd75@hotmail.com
www.flawsite.demon.co.uk/flawsite/more

Daniel Lloyd

Phil Macnaghten is a lecturer at the Centre for the Study of Environmental Change, Institute for Environment, Philosophy and Public Policy, Lancaster University. He studied psychology at Southampton and was awarded his PhD in Psychology from Exeter in 1991. Phil has worked on a wide range of projects broadly focusing on cultural dimensions of environmental policies. He was British Academy postdoctoral fellow at CSEC from 1995 to 1998, researching the cultural significance of British environmentalism. He has co-ordinated and been involved in a number of projects, both in Britain and Latin America, including those on sustainability, environmental rhetorics, forestry, GM foods, new technologies, environmental politics, the millennium and risk. His interests include social theory, culture and nature, sustainability and the sociology of everyday life. Publications include *Contested Natures* (with John Urry), and 'Bodies of Nature' as guest editor of a special issue of *Body and Society*.
P.Macnaghten@lancaster.ac.uk
www.lancs.ac.uk/users/csec

Phil Macnaghten

Ben Madden BSc(Hons) MSc specialises in integrated renewable energy systems, site-wide energy analysis and the development of renewable energy systems based on hydrogen. He is currently working on a number of projects including building-integrated wind and CHP systems, development of a site-wide energy strategy for a UK Universities new campus, and a number of projects involving the integration of hydrogen with other renewable energies.
bmadd@whitby-bird.co.uk
www.whitbybird.com

Stefan Muthesius teaches at the University of East Anglia, Norwich. His research interests include the history of housing and interior design in England and in Central and East Central Europe. His most recent book is *The Postwar University – Utopianist Campus and College*.
s.muthesius@uea.ac.uk
www.uea.ac.uk

Stefan Muthesius

Martin Pawley is a writer and critic best known for his weekly column in the *Architects' Journal*. He studied architecture at the École Nationale Supérieure des Beaux-Arts, Paris, and the Architectural Association, London. A former editor of the weekly newspaper *Building Design* he was later architecture critic for *The Guardian* and *The Observer,* and most recently editor of the international magazine *World Architecture*. His most recent books include *Theory and Design in the Second Machine Age, Buckminster Fuller: a Critical Biography, Future Systems: the Story of Tomorrow, Norman Foster: a global architecture, Terminal Architecture* and *20th Century Architecture: a Readers' Guide*.

Duncan Price BSc(Hons) MSc joined Whitby Bird and Partners in 1995 after completing a masters degree in renewable energy systems, and established the Building Physics Group, which develops the company's expertise in low-energy design, building environmental modelling, renewable energy and sustainable construction. Recent activities include a number of government-industry consultations and lobbying actions to bring about a sustained programme of support for solar-electric systems in Britain.
dpric@whitby-bird.co.uk
www.whitbybird.com

Martin Pawley with his son Bartholomew

Miffa Salter has spent more than 13 years working across the public, private and voluntary sectors to develop both thinking and practice around stakeholder engagement. Her work has predominantly focused on the construction and development industries, where she has been closely involved both in high-profile regeneration schemes as well as national policy development. After graduating with first-class honours

Miffa Salter (by J. Batty of OPM)

from the London School of Economics Miffa went on to work with the Civic Trust, Colin Buchanan and Partners, and, most recently as Senior Fellow at the Office for Public Management. She spent a year seconded to the DETR as part of the Urban Task Force team and then went on to a three-month placement with the South East England Development Agency (SEEDA). She also acts as an advisor on public participation in relation to major development projects in London – including most recently Swiss Cottage in Camden and Elephant and Castle in Southwark. Miffa is a regular contributor to a range of professional journals and has recently produced a booklet for the Commission for Architecture and the Built Environment (CABE) exploring the meaning of public participation in the context of the built environment. The views expressed in her chapter are those of Miffa Salter and not the Office for Public Management.
Miffa1@globalnet.co.uk
MSalter@opm.co.uk
www.opm.co.uk

Peter Sammonds

Peter Sammonds studied chemical physics at Bristol University. After working in industry he undertook postgraduate research at University College London on sea ice mechanics and was awarded his PhD (geophysics) in 1988. His research subsequently has been in ice dynamics in relation to climate change and crustal dynamics in relation to natural hazards. He won a Royal Society University Research Fellowship, which he held from 1992 to 2001, working at the Mineral Ice & Rock Physics Laboratory of the Department of Geological Sciences at UCL. He worked at the Earthquake Research Institute of Tokyo University as a JSPS Research Fellow between 1991 and 1992, and was Visiting Professor in 1999. In 2001 he was appointed Professor of Geophysics at UCL, and directs the MSci and BSci Geophysics degree courses.
p.sammonds@ucl.ac.uk
www.ucl.ac.uk/GeolSci/people/sammonds

Jonathan Schwinge (by Jenny Bäck)

Jonathan Schwinge was a scholarship student at the Architectural Association. His fourth-year diploma project 'Airlander' was exhibited at Imagination's Ford Journey Zone in the Greenwich Millennium Dome. His final-year project 'Lost-Exchange' won the Grand Prize and Category Prize for the Bentley Systems Student Design Competition, USA 2000. For their particular support and encouragement, Jonathan would like to thank Jenny Bäck, Nic Bailey, Tim Catton, Nikolei Dimmlich, Imagination, Martha La Gess, Stuart Lowther, Karen Mier at Bentley Systems, Mohsen Mostafavi as chairman at the AA, Thomas Muirhead, Hans-Joachim Schwinge, Armin Slijepcevic, Gotz Stockmann, Jane Wernick and Mary White. He currently works for a commercial architectural practice.
jonathan@schwinge.co.uk

Shane Slater, Ben Madden and Duncan Price

Shane Slater BEng PhD has a background in the analysis of complex systems, fluid dynamics and energy, and applies this to the design of low-energy buildings and naturally ventilated spaces. He is actively involved in renewable power generation and site strategies for the integration of renewable power, in particular wind power, solar and fuel-cell or other hydrogen systems.
sslat@whitby-bird.co.uk
www.whitbybird.com

Sean Stanwick

M. Sean Stanwick recently branched out from traditional architectural practice to write about architecture and design. He holds a Bachelor of Architecture and a Masters of Environmental Design with Doctoral aspirations. A Canadian freelance architectural writer, he has focused his attentions primarily on matters of the city with particular interest in the themed spectacular. A regular contributor to several international architectural journals, including *Architectural Design,* Sean was recently retained as the Canadian news and features correspondent for *World Architecture* magazine. He has taught at the University of Toronto and is currently working at Julian Jacobs Architects in Toronto.
msean@interlog.com

John Stewart is an independent housing market consultant. In the 1980s John was housing economist for the House Builders Federation and later the sales and marketing director of a regional house-builder. He remains economic adviser to the HBF. He is editor of the respected monthly *Housing Market Report,*

has been responsible for the HBF monthly industry survey since 1992, and maintains the quarterly *Construction Trends Survey* for the Construction Confederation. He was a founder member of the DETR Consultative Committee on Construction Industry Statistics. John is currently a member of the DETR and industry joint working group which prepares a twice-yearly *State of Industry Report* tabled at meetings with the construction minister. He writes an award-winning monthly 'Viewpoint' column in *HouseBuilder* magazine and is a frequent speaker at housing conferences, often giving presentations to company boards and staff conferences on housing-market trends, future prospects and key issues facing the market and the house-building industry.
jcmstewart@btinternet.com

Peter Walker is a partner with DEWJOC Architects, a practice with offices in the Northeast and London, specialising in the design of highly serviced laboratories and clean rooms in Britain and abroad. Prior to this he was a director of the Conran Design Group, a multidisciplinary design consultancy. Peter teaches part-time in the School of Architecture Planning and Landscape of Newcastle University and is variously an external examiner, on the Advisory Board, and a visiting lecturer at Northumbria, Huddersfield and Queen's University, Belfast. He has a particular interest in the way architects manage cost and value in the design process, and the education of architects in this area. He has advised on and acted as consultee on the establishment of a new architectural management degree. Peter has taught on in-house courses for a national contractor; on courses for senior managers in both the private and public sectors, and has researched the development of an 'Egan Module'.
pwalker@dewjoc-newcastle.com
www.dewjoc.com

Peter Walker (by Jim MacAdam Photography)

Austin Williams is the Technical Editor of the *Architects' Journal*, columnist with the *Saturday Telegraph*, and Director of the Transport Research Group. An architect and journalist, his primary interests are the politics and implications of sustainability on the built environment. He has written on subjects such as 'Architectural exorcism', 'The Dangers of Safety' and 'Brownfield Myths'. His current work includes *Carchitecture* and *The Consequences of Interchanges*. Austin supports a thoroughgoing critique of the precautionary principle and is currently compiling a 'no-blame index' of transport casualty statistics.
austin.williams@construct.emap.com
www.ajplus.co.uk

Austin Williams

BIBLIOGRAPHY

Ackrill, Robert, *The Common Agricultural Policy* (Sheffield: Sheffield Academic Press, 2000).

Ashworth, Allan and Keith Hogg, *Added Value in Design and Construction* (Harlow: Pearson Education, 2000).

Alan, William, *Studies in African Land Usage in Northern Rhodesia* (Manchester: Manchester University Press, 1949).

Allied Business Intelligence, *Automotive Fuel Cell Markets – The Future is Here*, Report code: AFC00 (Oyster Bay, New York: ABI, May 2000).

Allmendinger, Philip, *Planning in Postmodern Times* (London: RTPI Library Press and Routledge, 2000).

AMEC Plc, *Annual Report and Accounts*, 1999.

Anderson, R., M. Bulos and S. Walker, *Tower Blocks* (London: Polytechnic of the South Bank, 1985).

Anderson, Victor, *Redefining Wealth and Progress – New Ways to Measure Economic, Social and Environmental Change*, the Caracas report on Alternative Development Indicators (TOES Books, The Bootstrap Press, 1989.)

Annan, Noel, *Our Age* (London: Fontana, 1990).

Architects Registration Board, *Architects Registration Board Annual Report – 1999–2000* (London: ARB, 2000).

Architects Registration Board, *Architects Registration Board Annual Report – 2000–2001* (London: ARB, 2001).

Audit Commission, *Listen Up! – Effective Community Consultation* (London: Audit Commission, 1999).

BP, *Business and Operating Review*, 2000.

Baldwin, J., *Bucky Works – Buckminster Fuller's Ideas for Today* (Chichester: John Wiley & Sons, 1996).

Barnett, Anthony and Roger Scruton (eds), *Town and Country* (London: Jonathan Cape, 1998).

Beck, Ulrich, *Risk Society – Towards a New Modernity* (London: Sage, 1992).

Beck, Ulrich, *The Brave New World of Work* (Cambridge: Polity, 2000).

Ben Ami, Daniel, *Cowardly Capitalism – The Myth of the Global Financial Casino* (London John Wiley & Sons, 2001).

Benyus, Janine M., *Biomimicry – Innovation Inspired by Nature* (New York: Quill, William Morrow, 1997).

Bergdoll, B., *European Architecture 1750–1890* (Oxford: Oxford University Press, 2000).

Berman, Marshall, *All That Is Solid Melts Into Air* (London: Verso, 1995).

Bernstein, James, *Einstein* (New York: Fontana, 1973).

Booker, Christopher and Richard North, *The Mad Officials – How the Bureaucrats are Strangling Britain* (London: Constable, 1994).

Boorstin, D., *The Image – A Guide to Pseudo Events in America* (New York: Vintage Books, 1992).

Brown, Gordon (ed.), *The Red Paper on Scotland* (Edinburgh: EUSPB, 1975).

Brown, Lester, *Building a Sustainable Society* (New York: Worldwatch, 1981).

Brown, Lester and Christopher Flavin, World Watch Institute, *State of the World 1999* (London: Earthscan, 2000).

Buckminster Fuller, Richard, *Nine Chains to the Moon*, first published 1938, first reprint 1963, (London: Feffer and Simons Inc.), fifth reprint June 1970.

Bullock, N., *Building the Postwar World* (London: E&FN Spon, 2001).

Campbell, J., *Edward Heath* (London: Pimlico, 1994).

Carey, John, *The Intellectuals and the Masses* (London: Faber, 1992).

Carey, J. (ed.), *The Faber Book of Utopias* (London: Faber, 1999).

Carter, E. J. and E. Goldfinger, *The County of London Plan Explained* (London: Penguin, 1945).

Chapman, Douglas G., *Utilization of Pacific Halibut Stocks – Estimation of Maximum Sustainable Yield 1960*, Report of the International Pacific Halibut Commission (Seattle: United Nations Press, 1962).

Charter of the New Urbanism, Third Congress for the New Urbanism, San Francisco, 1997.

Chartered Institute of Housing and Tenant Participation Advisory Service, *Tenant Participation in Housing Management* (London: CIH & TPAS, 1989).

Civic Trust and London Planning Advisory Committee,

Dwellings Over and in Shops in London (London: Civic Trust & LPAC, 1998).

Cole, H. S. D., Christopher Freeman, Marie Jahoda and K. L. R. Pavitt, *Thinking About the Future* (London: Chatto and Windus for Sussex University, 1973).

Coleman, A., *Utopia on Trial* (London: Shipman, 1985).

Construction Industry Training Board, *Construction Workforce Development Planning Brief – 2001–2005* (London: CITB, 2001).

Le Corbusier, *The City of Tomorrow and its Planning* (London: Architectural Press, 1971), third edition.

Council for the Protection of Rural England, *Plan, Monitor and Manage* (London: CPRE, December 2000).

The Countryside Agency, *State of the Countryside – 2001* (Wetherby: The Countryside Agency, 3 April 2001).

Cox, S. and A. Hamilton (eds), *The Architect's Job Book* (London: RIBA Publications, 1995).

Crary, Jonathon and Sanford Kwinter (eds), *Incorporations* (New York: Zone, 1992).

Curtis, Mark, *The Ambiguities of Power – British Foreign Policy Since 1945* (London: Zed Books, 1995).

Davis, Mike, *Ecology of Fear – Los Angeles and the Imagination of Disaster* (Canada: Fitzhenry & Whiteside Ltd, 1998) and (New York: Metropolitan Books, 1998).

Davis Langdon Consultancy for the Construction Industry Council and the Department of the Environment, Transport and the Regions, *Survey of UK Construction Professional Services – Survey Results*, Part 1 (London: CIC, 1997).

Davis Langdon and Everest, *Contracts in Use – a Survey of Building Contracts in Use* (London: RICS, 1996).

Davis Langdon and Everest, *A Study of the UK Building Materials Sector* (London: DETR and the Construction Products Association, September 2000).

Dearstyne-Fowlow, L., *Nostalgia as Marketing Tool* (Calgary: Faculty of Environmental Design, University of Calgary, 1997).

Department of the Environment, *Rural England – A Nation Committed to a Living Countryside* (London: HMSO, 1995).

Department of the Environment, *Household Growth – Where Shall We Live?* (London: DOE, November 1996).

Department of the Environment, *What Did You Throw Out this Week? Going for Green* (London: DOE, 1996).

Department of the Environment, Transport and the Regions, *The Countryside – Environmental Quality and Economic and Social Development*, Planning Policy Guidance 7 (London: The Stationery Office, February 1997).

Department of the Environment, Transport and the Regions, *The Use of Density in Urban Planning* (London: DETR, 1998).

Department of the Environment, Transport and the Regions, *Analysis of the Responses to the UK Government's Consultation Paper on Sustainable Construction: Executive Summary* (London: DETR, December 1998).

Department of the Environment, Transport and the Regions, *English House Condition Survey 1996* (London: The Stationery Office, 1998).

Department of Environment, Transport and the Regions, *Every little bit helps – are you doing your bit?* London, DETR, 1999.

Department of the Environment, Transport and the Regions, *Quality of Life Counts – Indicators for a Strategy for Sustainable Development for the United Kingdom: A Baseline Assessment* (London: DETR, 1999).

Department of the Environment, Transport and the Regions, *Housing*, Planning Policy Guidance note 3 (London: The Stationery Office, 2000).

Department of the Environment, Transport and the Regions and the Ministry of Agriculture, Fisheries and Food, *Our Countryside – The Future, A Fair Deal for Rural England* (London: HMSO, November 2000).

Department of the Environment, Transport and the Regions, *Our Towns and Cities – The Future, Delivering an Urban Renaissance* (London: HMSO, November 2000).

Department of the Environment, Transport and the Regions, *Tapping the Potential – Assessing Urban Housing Capacity: Towards Better Practice* (London: DETR, 2000).

Department of the Environment, Transport and the Regions, *Conversions and Redevelopment: Processes and Potential* (London: DETR, 2000).

Department of the Environment, Transport and the Regions, *Building Regulations Approved Document Part L – Conservation of Fuel and Power*, Interim Draft (London: DETR, March 2001).

Department of Trade and Industry, *UK Energy in Brief – Digest of United Kingdom Energy Statistics* (London: Energy Policy and Analysis Unit, Dti, 2000).

Dickens, Charles, *David Copperfield* (London: Penguin Classics, 1997).

Dunleavy, P., *The Politics of Mass Housing in Britain* (Oxford: Clarendon, 1981).

Edwards, Brian and Paul Hyett, *Rough Guide to Sustainability* (London: RIBA Publications, 2001).

Edwards, Brian, *Green Architecture – An International Comparison* (Chichester: John Wiley & Sons, 2001).

Egan, Sir John, *Rethinking Construction – The Report of the Construction Task Force* (DETR, London: HMSO, 1998).

Ehrlich, Paul, *The Population Bomb* (London: Pan Books, 1971).

Ekins, Paul, *Economic Growth and Environmental Sustainability – The Prospects for Green Growth* (London: Routledge, 2000).

Emmanuel, Arghiri, *Appropriate or Underdeveloped Technology* (Chichester, John Wiley & Sons, 1982).

Engels, F., *Socialism – Utopian and Scientific*, foreword Alan Hudson (London: Junius, 1995).

Esher, L., *A Broken Wave* (London: Alan Lane, 1981).

European Commission, *Commission Communication to the Council and European Parliament on Remedying Environmental Damage*, COM(93)47fin (Brussels: EC, 1993).

European Commission, University College Dublin Energy Research Group and Suomen Arkkitehtiliito, *A Green Vitruvius – Principles and Practice of Sustainable Architectural Design* (London: James & James, 1999).

European Community, *Community Eco-Management and Audit Scheme*, Council Regulation 1836/93, 29 June 1993, in *Official Journal of the European Communities*, OJ 10.7.93 L 168, 10 July 1993.

Fairlie, S., *Low Impact Development – Planning and People in a Sustainable Countryside* (Charlbury: Jon Carpenter, 1996).

Foley, Julie, for the Institute of Public Policy Research, *H2 – Driving the Future* (London: IPPR, July 2001).

Forshaw, J. and P. Abercrombie, *The County of London Plan* (London: Macmillan, 1943).

Fox, Warwick (ed.), *Ethics and the Built Environment* (London: Routledge, 2000).

Garlake, M., *New Art, New World* (London: Yale University Press, 1998).

Garreau, J., *Edge City – Life on the New Frontier* (New York: Doubleday, 1991).

Giddens, Anthony, *Modernity and Self Identity – Self and Society in the Late Modern Age* (Cambridge: Polity, 1991).

Giddens, Anthony, *Beyond Left and Right – The Future of Radical Politics* (Cambridge, Polity, 1994).

Giedion, Sigfried, *Walter Gropius* (Dover Publications Inc., 1992).

Gillott, John and Manjit Kumar, *Science and the Retreat from Reason* (London: Merlin Press, 1995).

Girardet, Herbert, *Earth Rise – Halting the Destruction. Healing the World* (London: Paladin, 1992).

Girardet, Herbert, *The Gaia Atlas of Cities – New Directions for Sustainable Urban Living* (London: Gaia Books Ltd, 1996).

Glendinning, Miles and Stefan Muthesius, *Tower Block – Modern Public Housing in England, Scotland, Wales and Northern Ireland* (New Haven: Yale University Press, 1994).

Global Action Plan, *Action at Home: A Catalyst for Change* (London: GAP, 1998).

Gore, Al, *Earth in the Balance – Ecology and the Human Spirit* (Washington, DC: Plume, 1993). British title *Earth in the Balance – Forging a New Common Purpose* (London: Earthscan, 1992).

Gottdiener, M., *The Theming of America – Dreams Visions and Commercial Spaces* (Boulder, CO: Westview Press, 1997).

Graves, Hilary M. and Mark C. Phillipson, *Potential Implications of Climate Change in the Built Environment* (Watford: Building Research Establishment, 2000).

Gray, C., *Value for Money – Helping the UK Afford the Buildings it Likes* (Reading: Reading Construction Forum, 1996).

Green Balance, *Valuing the Land – Planning for the Best and Most Versatile Agricultural Land* (London: Campaign for the Protection of Rural England, September 2000).

Grove-White, R., P. Macnaghten and B. Wynne, *Wising Up – The Public and New Technologies* (Lancaster: Centre for the Study of Environmental Change, Lancaster University, 2001).

Gutman, R., *Architectural Practice – A Critical View* (New York: Princeton Architectural Press, 1988).

Hawken, Paul, Amory B. Lovins and L. Hunter Lovins, *Natural Capitalism – The Next Industrial Revolution* (London: Earthscan, 1999).

Hayes, D. and A. Hudson, *Basildon – The Mood of the Nation* (London: Demos, 2001).

Hayes, D. and A. Hudson, *Who are the C2s? Basildon Revisited – Change and Continuity* (Whitstable, Kent: E&WRG, 2001).

Heidegger, M., *Poetry, Language, Thought*, trans. A. Hofstadter (New York: Harper and Row, 1971).

Hennessy, Peter, *Never Again Britain 1945–1951* (London: Vintage, 1993).

Hewison, R., *Culture and Consensus* (London: Methuen, 1995).

Hewitt, Mark and Susannah Hagan, *City Fights – Debates on Urban Sustainability* (London: James & James (Science Publishers) Ltd, 2001).

Hobson, Dominic, *The National Wealth – Who Gets What in Britain* (London: HarperCollins, 1999).

Hodge, Sue, *Tort Law*, first edition (London: Willan Publishing, 2001).

Holmans, Alan, *Housing Demand and Need in England 1991–2011* (York: Joseph Rowntree Foundation, 1995).

Holyoak, Jon, *Negligence in Building Law – Cases and Commentary* (Oxford: Blackwell Scientific Publications, 1992).

The House Builders Federation, *Urban Life – Breaking Down the Barriers to Brownfield Development* (London: HBF, 1998).

Howard, E., *To-morrow! A Peaceful Path to Real Reform* (London: Swan Sonnenschein, 1898).

Howard, E., *Garden Cities of To-Morrow* (London: Swan Sonnenschein, 1902).

Hulme, M. and G. J. Jenkins, *Climate Change Scenarios for the United Kingdom – Scientific Report*, UK Climate Impacts Programme, Technical Report No. 1 (Norwich: Climatic Research Unit, University of East Anglia, 1998).

Huxley, A., *Brave New World* (New York: Harper and Row, 1932).

Huxtable, A., *The Unreal America – Architecture and Illusion* (New York: The New Press, 1998).

Hyett, Paul, *In Practice* (London: Emap Construct, 2000).

Independent Commission on International Development Issues, *North-South – A Programme for Survival*, commonly known as the Brandt Report (London: Foreign and Commonwealth Office, 1980).

Intergovernmental Panel on Climate Change, *The Science of Climate Change – Contribution of Working Group I to the Second Assessment Report of the Intergovernmental Panel on Climate Change* (Cambridge: Cambridge University Press, 1995).

Intergovernmental Panel on Climate Change, *Climate Change 2001 – The Scientific Basis*, draft report by the IPCC, 9 February 2001.

Intergovernmental Panel on Climate Change, *Summary for Policymakers of Working Group I of the Third Assessment Report of the Intergovernmental Panel on Climate Change* (Cambridge: Cambridge University Press, 2001).

International Scientific Council for Island Development, *Island 2010 – Towards 100% Renewable Energy Sources Supply for Island Sustainable Development* (INSULA, UNESCO, 1 Rue Miollis, 75015, Paris).

Jackson, Kenneth T., *Crabgrass Frontier – The Suburbanization of the United States* (Oxford: Oxford University Press, 1985).

Jacobs, Jane, *The Economy of Cities* (New York: Random House, 1969).

Jacobs, M., *Environmental Modernisation – The New Labour Agenda* (London: The Fabian Society, 1999).

Jacoby, M., *The Longing For Paradise* (Boston: Sigo Press, 1980).

Jencks, C., *The Prince, the Architects and New Wave Monarchy* (London: Academy Editions, 1988).

Jensen, R., *High Density Living* (London: L. Hill, 1966).

Jeremiah, David, *Architecture and Design for the Family in Britain – 1900–1970* (Manchester: Manchester University Press, 2000).

Korten, David C., *The Post-Corporate World – Life After Capitalism* (San Francisco: Kumarian Press & Berrett-Koehler Publishers Inc., 1999).

Landecker, H., 'Is New Urbanism Good for America', *Architecture*, New York, April 1996.

Langdon, P., *A Better Place to Live – Reshaping the American Suburb* (Amherst: The University of Massachusetts Press, 1994).

Larminie, J. and A. Dicks, *Fuel Cell Systems Explained* (Chichester: John Wiley & Sons, April 2000).

Latham, Sir Michael, *Constructing the Team – Final Report of the Government and Industry Review of Procurement and Contractual Arrangements in the UK Construction Industry* (London: HMSO, 1994).

Laws Smith, Margaret, *Towards the Creation of a Sustainable Economy* (London: Conservation Society, 1975).

Lerup, L., *After the City* (Cambridge, Mass.: MIT Press, 2000).

Lewis, J. and P. Walker (eds), *Participation Works!* New Economics Foundation in association with the UK Community Participation Network, 1998).

Lewis, Penny, Vicky Richardson and James Woudhuysen, *In Defence of the Dome – The Case for Human Agency in the New Millennium* (London: ASI (Research) Ltd, 1998).

Lichtenstein, Claude and Joachim Krausse, 'How to make the world work', *Your Private Sky – R. Buckminster Fuller – The Art of Design Science* (Baden: Lars Muller Publishers, 1999).

Llewelyn-Davies, *Sustainable Residential Quality – New Approaches to Urban Living* (London Planning Advisory Committee, 1998).

Lomborg Bjørn, *The Skeptical Environmentalist – Measuring the Real State of the World* (Cambridge: Cambridge University Press, 2001).

London Planning Advisory Committee and the Greater London Authority, *London's Housing Capacity* (London: LPAC and GLA, 2000).

Louv, R. (ed.), *America II* (Los Angeles: Jeremy P. Tarcher Inc., 1983).

Lowndes, V., G. Stoker, L. Pratchett, D. Wilson, S. Leach and M. Wingfield, *Enhancing Public Participation in Local Government* (London: DETR, September 1998).

Lowry, John and Rod Edmunds (eds), *Environmental Protection and the Common Law* (Oxford: Hart Publishing, 2000).

Lynch, F., *France and the International Economy – From Vichy to the Treaty of Rome* (London: Routledge 1997).

Maas, Winy, *Metacity/Datatown* (Rotterdam: 010 Publishers, 1999).

Macnaghten, P. and J. Urry, *Contested Natures* (London: Sage, 1998).

Macnaghten, P. and M. Yar, *Languages of the Environment* (Lancaster: Centre for the Study of Environmental Change, Lancaster University, 2000).

Macnaghten, P., R. Grove-White, M. Jacobs and B. Wynne, *Public Perceptions and Sustainability: Indicators, Institutions, Participation* (Preston: Lancashire County Council, 1995).

Maren, Michael, *The Road to Hell – The Ravaging Effects of Foreign Aid and International Charity* (New York: The Free Press, 1997).

Markus, T. A., *Buildings and Power* (London: Routledge, 1993).

Markus, T. A., *Order in Space and Society* (Edinburgh: Mainstream, 1982).

Marx, Karl, *Capital – A Critique of Political Economy* (Moscow: Progress Publishers, 1974).

William McDonough Architects, *The Hanover Principles* (Washington, DC: AIA Publications, 1992).

Meadows, Dennis L. (ed.), *Alternatives to Growth – a Search for Sustainable Futures* (Cambridge, Mass.: Ballinger, 1977).

Meadows, Donella H., Dennis L. Meadows and Jorgen Randers, *Beyond the Limits – Confronting Global Collapse, Envisioning a Sustainable Future* (New York: Universe Books, 1992) and (London: Earthscan, 1992).

Meadows, Donella H., Dennis L. Meadows, Jorgen Randers and William H. Behrens, *Limits to Growth – A Report for the Club of Rome's Project on the Predicament of Mankind*, commonly known as the 'Limits to Growth' (New York: Universe Books, 1974). Republished as The Dynamics of Growth in a Finite World (Cambridge, Mass.: Wright-Allen Press, 1974).

Merrett, S., *State Housing in Britain* (London: Routledge & Kegan Paul, 1979).

Meszaros, Istvan, *The Necessity of Social Control* (London: Merlin Press, 1971).

Michaels, P. J. and R.C. Balling Jr, *The Satanic Gases – Clearing the Air about Global Warming* (Washington, DC: Cato, 2000).

Ministry of Agriculture, Fisheries and Food, *A New Direction for Agriculture* (London MAFF, December 1999).

Ministry of Agriculture, Fisheries and Food, *Agriculture in the United Kingdom – 1999* (London: The Stationery Office, 2000).

Ministry of Agriculture Fisheries and Food, *England's Rural Development Plan 2000–2006* (London: MAFF, 2000).

Monk, Sarah and Christine Whitehead (eds), *Restructuring Housing Systems; from Social to Affordable Housing* (York: York Publishing Services, 2000).

Mulgan, Geoff, *Connexity – How to Live in a Connected World* (London: Chatto and Windus), or *Connexity – Responsibility, Freedom, Business and Power in the New Century* (London: Vintage, 1997).

Mumford, Lewis, *The City in History* (London: Harcourt, Brace and World, 1961).

Mulholland Research Associates Ltd, *Towns or Leafier Environments? – A Survey of Family Home Buying Choices* (London: MRAL, 1995).

Murdoch, J., *Why Do People Move to the Countryside?*, report for the Countryside Commission, Department of City and Regional Planning, University of Wales, Cardiff.

Muthesius, Stefan, *The High Victorian Movement in Architecture* (London: Routledge & Kegan Paul, 1972).

National Housing and Town Planning Council, *Yearbook 1955 of the National Housing and Town Planning Council* (London: NHTPC, 1956).

O'Hagan, Andrew, *The End of British Farming* (London: Profile Books and the London Review of Books, 2001).

Odum, Howard, 'Power for order and evolution', in Howard Odum, *Environment, Power and Society* (New York: Wiley-Interscience, 1971).

Offe, Claus and John Keane, *Contradictions of the Welfare State* (London: Hutchinson, 1984).

Office of National Statistics, *Britain 2000 – The Official Yearbook of the United Kingdom* (London: HMSO, 2001).

Ormerod, Paul, *The Death of Economics* (London: Faber and Faber, 1994).

Papadakis, A. (ed.), *Prince Charles and the Architectural Debate* (London: Architectural Design, 1989).

Paterson, W. S. B., *The Physics of Glaciers*, third edition (Oxford: Pergamon, 1994).

Pawley, Martin, *Buckminster Fuller – How Much Does the Building Weigh?*, 'Design Heroes' series (London: Grafton, Trefoil Publications, 1990).

Pawley, Martin, *Theory and Design in the Second Machine Age* (Oxford: Basil Blackwell, 1990).

Pawley, Martin, *Terminal Architecture* (London: Reaktion Books, 1998).

Pearce, David, *Sustainable Development, Economics and Environment in the Third World* (London: Earthscan 1990).

Pearce, David, Anil Markandya and Edward Barbier, *Blueprint for a Green Economy* (London: Earthscan, 1989).

Peccei, Aurelio and Alexander King, 'Commentary', in Mihaljo Mesarovic and Edward Pestel, *Mankind at the Turning Point* (London: Hutchinson, 1975).

Petherick, Anne, *Living Over the Shop* (London: Urban and Economic Development Group, URBED, 1997).

Pevsner, Nikolaus, *The Englishness of English Art* (London: Architectural Press, 1956).

Pirsig, Robert M., *Zen and the Art of Motorcycle Maintenance – An Enquiry into Values* (London: Vintage, 1974).

Poore, Duncan (ed.), *Where Next?* (London: The Board of Trustees, Royal Botanic Gardens, 2000).

Postman, N., *Amusing Ourselves to Death – Public Discourse in the Age of Show Business* (New York: Alfred A. Knopf, 1984).

Pratchett, Lawrence (ed.), *Renewing Local Democracy – The Modernisation Agenda in British Local Government* (London: Frank Cass, 2000).

Preston, Reverend Canon R. H., *The Question of a Just, Participatory and Sustainable Society* (Manchester: John Rylands University, 1980).

Pugin, A. W. N., *Contrasts* (London: Polman, 1836).

Pugin, A. W. N., *The True Principles of Pointed or Christian Architecture* (London: John Weale, 1853).

Puthod, Catherine, Paul Grover, Judy Hallgarten and Eleanor Jupp, *Creative Spaces – A Toolkit for Participatory Urban Design* (London: The Architecture Foundation, October 2000).

Rao, Susheel, Alan Yates, Deborah Brownhill and Nigel Howard, *EcoHomes – The Environmental Rating for Homes* (Watford: Building Research Establishment, 2000).

Ravetz, A., *Remaking Cities* (London: Routledge, 1980).

Ravetz, A., *Council Housing and Culture* (London: Routledge, 2001).

The Real World Coalition, *Politics of the Real World – Meeting the New Century* (London: Earthscan, 1996).

Reed, W. and E. Gordon, *Building Research and Information*, Vol. 28, No. 5–6 (London: E&FN Spon, September to December 2000).

Rethel, Alfred Sohn, *The Economy and Class Structure of German Fascism* (London: Free Association Books, 1987).

Reyner Banham, Peter, *Theory and Design in the First Machine Age* (Reed Educational and Professional Publishing, 1960), ninth reprint of paperback edition (Oxford: Architectural Press, 1997).

Ricardo, David, *Principles of Political Economy* (London: Everyman, 1984).

Ridley, Matt, *The Melbourne Age*, 22 September 2000.

Roberts, Hewitt and Gary Robinson, *ISO 14001 – Implementation Handbook* (Oxford: Butterworth Heinemann, 1998).

Roberts, N., *The Holocene – An Environmental History* (Oxford: Blackwell, 1998).

Robertson, G., M. Mash, L. Tickner, J. Bird, B. Curtis and T. Putnam (eds), *Future Natural – Nature, Science and Culture* (London: Routledge, 1996).

Robertson Scott, J. W., *England's Green and Pleasant Land* (Harmondsworth, Middlesex: Penguin, 1947).

Rodney, Walter, *How Europe Underdeveloped Africa* (Nairobi and London: East African Educational Publishers, 1995).

Rogers, Richard and Anne Power, *Cities for a Small Country* (London: Faber and Faber, 2000).

Rogers, Richard in Philip Gumuchdjian (ed.), *Cities for a Small Planet* (London: Faber and Faber, 1997).

Rogers, W. V. H., *Winfield and Jolowicz On Tort*, fifteenth edition (London: Sweet and Maxwell, 1998), first published 1937.

Roisin, Jacob and Max Eastman, *The Road to Abundance* (London: Rider and Company, 1955).

Rose, Chris, *The Dirty Man of Europe – The Great British Pollution Scandal* (London: Simon and Schuster Ltd, 1990).

Ross, A., *The Celebration Chronicles – Life Liberty and Pursuit of Property Values in Disney's New Town* (New York: Ballantine Books, 2000).

Nuclear Energy – the Future Climate (London: The Royal Academy of Engineering and The Royal Society, 1999).

Royal Institute of British Architects and Architects Registration Board Joint Validation Panel, *Criteria for Validation* (London: RIBA Publications, 1997).

Royal Institute of British Architects, *Architects and the Changing Construction Industry* (London: RIBA Publications, 1999).

Royal Institute of British Architects, *Meeting the Challenge – RIBA Strategy for Architecture and Architects 1999–2003* (London: RIBA Publications, April 1999).

Royal Institute of British Architects, *Standard Form of Agreement for the Appointment of an Architect* (London: RIBA Publications, 2000).

Rudlin, David, *Tomorrow, a Peaceful Path to Urban Reform* (London: Friends of the Earth, 1998).

Ruskin, John, *The Seven Lamps of Architecture* (London: Smith, Elder and Co., 1849).

Rybczynski, W., *Home – A Short History of an Idea* (New York: Viking, 1984).

Saint, A., *The Image of the Architect* (London: Yale University Press, 1983).

Schleimer, J., *Neo-Traditional Buyers Preference Survey*, based on Sample Survey of owners in Kentlands, Harbourtown, Seaside and Laguna West (Sacramento: Market Perspectives, 1996).

Schumacher, E. F., *Small is Beautiful – A Study of Economics as if People Matter* (London: Sphere Books, 1974).

Scruton, R., *The Aesthetics of Architecture* (London: Methuen, 1979).

Sennett, Richard, *The Fall of Public Man* (London: Faber, 1986).

Shelley, Percy Bysshe (1792–1822), *Peter Bell the Third*, part 3, 'Hell', 1819, quoted in *The Oxford Dictionary of Quotations*, third edition (Oxford: Book Club Associates for the Oxford University Press, 1979).

Shepherd, J. and A. Abakuks, *The National Survey of Vacant Land in the Urban Areas of England* (London: HMSO, 1990).

Shonfield, Katherine, *Walls Have Feelings – Architecture, Film and the City* (London: Routledge, 2000).

Sinclair, Geoffrey, Environment Information Services, *The Lost Land – Land Use Change in England 1945–1990* (London: Council for the Protection of Rural England, 1992).

Skeffington Report, *Report of the Committee on Public Participation in Planning – People and Planning* (London: HMSO, 1969).

Smith, Peter F., *Options for a Flexible Planet* (Sheffield: Sustainable Building Network, Sheffield University Press, 1996).

Smith, Peter F., *Architecture in a Climate of Change – A Guide to Sustainable Design* (Oxford: Architectural Press, 2001).

Smith, Peter F. and the Sustainable Futures Committee, *Design within a Climate of Change* (London: RIBA Publications, 2000).

Social Exclusion Unit, *Bringing Britain Together – A National Strategy for Neighbourhood Renewal*, Command Paper (London: TSO, September 1998).

Soper, Kate, *What is Nature? – Culture, Politics and the Non-Human* (Oxford: Blackwell, 1995).

Sorkin, M. (ed.), *Variations on a Theme Park – The New American City and the End of Public Space* (New York: Hill and Wang, 1992).

Speaight, Anthony and Gregory Stone, *Architect's Legal Handbook*, sixth edition (London: Butterworths Architecture, 1996), first published 1973.

Steele, J. and J. Sergeant, *Consulting the Public – Guidelines and Good Practice* (London: Policy Studies Institute, 1998).

Stein, M., *The Eclipse of Community* (Princeton: Princeton University Press, 1960).

Sterling, R., *The Weather of Britain* (London: Giles de la Mare, 1997).

Stratford, N., *Rural and Urban Views on the Countryside – Findings from the British Social Attitudes Survey 1999*, report for the Countryside Agency (London: National Centre for Social Research, 2000).

Taylor, L. (ed.), *Housing – Symbol, Structure, Site* (New York: Viking, 1995).

Taylor, N., *The Village in the City* (London: Temple Smith, 1973).

Toyne, P., *Environmental Responsibility – An Agenda for Further and Higher Education* (Department of Education, London: HMSO, 1993).

Trainer, Ted, *Towards a Sustainable Economy – The Need for Fundamental Change* (Oxford: Jon Carpenter, 1996).

Toennies, F., *Gemeinschaft und Gesellschaft*, 1889, W. J. Cahnman (ed.), *In Memoriam F. Toennies* (Cambridge: Leiden, 1973).

Toynbee, Arnold, 'England in 1760 – The Decay of the Yeomanry', in *The Industrial Revolution*, a reprint of lectures on the Industrial Revolution in England, popular addresses, notes and other fragments (Newton Abbot: David and Charles reprints, 1969).

United Nations Environment Programme, *Global Environmental Outlook 2000* (Nairobi: UNEP, 1999).

United Nations Framework Convention on Climate Change, *United Nations Framework Convention on Climate Change*, Article 3.3 (New York: UNFCCC, 1992).

Urban Task Force, *Towards an Urban Renaissance – Final Report of the Urban Task Force* (London: E&FN Spon, 1999).

Vale, Brenda and Robert, *Green Architecture – Design for a Sustainable Future* (London: Thames & Hudson, 1996).

Van Buiten, Paul, *Blowing the Whistle* (London: Politicos, 2000).

Venturi, R., *Learning from Las Vegas – The Forgotten Symbols of Architectural Form* (Cambridge, Mass.: MIT Press, 1972).

Von Weizsäcker, Ernst, Amory B. Lovins and L. Hunter Lovins, *Factor Four – Doubling Wealth, Halving Resource Use* (London: Earthscan, 1997).

Wan Ho, Mae, 'Human genome – the biggest sellout in human history', *ISIS-TWN Report* (Milton Keynes: Institute of Science in Society and Department of Biological Sciences, Open University, 2000).

Ward, Peter M. (ed.), *Self-Help Housing – A Critique* (London: H. M. Wilson, 1982).

Wells, N., *The Atmosphere and Ocean* (London: Taylor & Francis, 1986).

Williams-Ellis, Clough, *England and the Octopus* (London: Geoffrey Bles, 1928), facsimile edition London: Council for the Protection of Rural England, 1996).

Winch, G. and E. Schneider, *Construction Management and Economics*, Vol. 11 (London: E&FN Spon, 1993).

Wooley, Tom and Sam Kimmins, *Green Building Handbook*, Vol. 2 (London: E&FN Spon, 2000).

World Commission on Environment and Development, *Our Common Future*, commonly known as the Brundtland Report (WCED, Oxford: Oxford University Press, 1987).

The World Health Report, *Conquering Suffering, Enriching Humanity* (Geneva: WHO, 1997).

Worpole, Ken and Liz Greenhalgh, *Freedom of the City* (London: Demos, 1996).

Yeang, Ken, *The Skyscraper Bioclimatically Reconsidered – Design Primer* (London: Academy Editions, 1996).

Yeang, Ken, *The Green Skyscraper: The Basis for Designing Sustainable Intensive Buildings* (London: Prestel, 1999).

Yorke, F. R. S. and F. Gibberd, *The Modern Flat* (London: Architectural Press, 1937).